The Southern African Development Community (SADC) and the European Union (EU)

Johannes Muntschick

The Southern African Development Community (SADC) and the European Union (EU)

Regionalism and External Influence

Johannes Muntschick
Department of Political Sciences
Johannes Gutenberg
University of Mainz
Mainz, Germany

ISBN 978-3-319-45329-3   ISBN 978-3-319-45330-9 (eBook)
https://doi.org/10.1007/978-3-319-45330-9

Library of Congress Control Number: 2017940381

© The Editor(s) (if applicable) and The Author(s) 2018
This book was advertised with a copyright holder in the name of the publisher in error, whereas the author holds the copyright.
This work is subject to copyright. All rights are solely and exclusively licensed by the Publisher, whether the whole or part of the material is concerned, specifically the rights of translation, reprinting, reuse of illustrations, recitation, broadcasting, reproduction on microfilms or in any other physical way, and transmission or information storage and retrieval, electronic adaptation, computer software, or by similar or dissimilar methodology now known or hereafter developed.
The use of general descriptive names, registered names, trademarks, service marks, etc. in this publication does not imply, even in the absence of a specific statement, that such names are exempt from the relevant protective laws and regulations and therefore free for general use.
The publisher, the authors and the editors are safe to assume that the advice and information in this book are believed to be true and accurate at the date of publication. Neither the publisher nor the authors or the editors give a warranty, express or implied, with respect to the material contained herein or for any errors or omissions that may have been made. The publisher remains neutral with regard to jurisdictional claims in published maps and institutional affiliations.

Cover image: © miniature/Getty Images
Cover designer: Tom Howey

Printed on acid-free paper

This Palgrave Macmillan imprint is published by Springer Nature
The registered company is Springer International Publishing AG
The registered company address is: Gewerbestrasse 11, 6330 Cham, Switzerland

Preface

To a great extent, this study has its roots in Southern Africa. It was during a semester abroad at the University of Namibia when my interest in African politics, the state in Africa and regionalism in sub-Saharan Africa began to take shape. In the course of my studies, I understood that there certainly existed several deep-rooted social and political characteristics on national and regional levels that distinguished the state and political context in Africa from other regions such as Europe. The legacy of colonialism and post-colonial patterns of interdependence to powerful actors overseas—and to South Africa as the dominant regional power—appeared in many respects to have an effect on countries, governments and peoples in Southern Africa. But there was also enthusiasm about African renaissance and a spirit of optimism towards regional integration within the framework of the Southern African Development Community (SADC) which seemed to be a genuine regional solution to regional challenges and a beacon of hope for socio-economic development. Interestingly, I first came across the organisation when I registered as a student at the University of Namibia and was surprised by the fact that a substantial discount on study fees applied for students from SADC countries. Since then, the SADC became my constant companion and I became increasingly aware of the organisation's high political relevance, media presence, activities and dynamics.

For decades, the major part of political science research on regionalism has focussed on the integration process in Europe. This has led to an implicit Euro-centrism in most regional integration theories which weakened their explanatory power with regard to regionalisms outside Europe. It is therefore not surprising that there exists only very little academic literature on the SADC—at least in bookshelves in the Northern Hemisphere—which goes beyond describing the characteristics of the organisation. As a result, prejudged and rather hasty estimates concluded in most cases and with reference to the shining "European example" that regionalism in the SADC has failed or is little more than a paper tiger. This not only confused but challenged me and ultimately sparked the research project.

Being aware of the research gap, I realised that there was a need to analyse and explain regionalism in the SADC from a non-Euro-centric perspective but with a focus on the countries and political situation within the region. Adopting cooperation theory became a viable solution. Besides that, a comprehensive analysis of regionalism had to include additional policy areas besides the economy in order to capture empirical evidence about the organisation's wide range of activities. Finally, I deemed it necessary to provide an assessment of the performance of regionalism in the SADC in order to come increasingly on par with the literature and state of research on Europe. Once the project was under way, I realised that strong patterns of interdependence existed between regional and extra-regional actors in many policy areas. This implied external influence. As a consequence, this work adopts a modified situation-structural approach as a guiding theory for the study of regionalism which takes this particular structural aspect explicitly into account. This allowed me to highlight the role of the European Union and its ambivalent influence on regional integration in the SADC.

Before delving into the analysis and findings on regionalism in the SADC, I would like to thank the people who have made this research a pleasant and fruitful endeavour. The completion of this book could not have been accomplished without the support I received from many colleagues and experts from academia, friends and family. While being very grateful to everyone who has been involved in this process, I would like to express my special thanks to the following individuals.

First of all, I would like to sincerely thank Thomas Gehring for providing me with every guidance and expertise that I needed during the past years. His constant support helped me a lot during the time of research and writing of this book. I am very grateful that I had the opportunity to develop and discuss this research project as a fellow of the DFG-funded Graduate School "Markets and Social Systems" at the Otto-Friedrich-Universität Bamberg. My research has greatly benefited from its interdisciplinary and inspiring academic environment and the feedback of many colleagues. I am especially thankful to Reimut Zohlnhöfer and Richard Münch, who encouraged and supported me throughout these years.

A range of scholars contributed to this book by giving inspiring comments on this and earlier works on various occasions throughout the past years. Among others, Tanja Börzel, Fredrik Söderbaum and Michael Zürn offered fruitful suggestions and constructive criticism, particularly on the theoretical approach and argument of this work. My appreciation applies as well to several colleagues from the Chair for International Relations at the Otto-Friedrich-Universität Bamberg, especially those who have been involved in research on global regionalism. Their comments became very fruitful for deciding where to position myself and the book's argument in the academic debate on theorising and analysing regionalism. I am especially grateful to Benjamin Faude, whose sound comments I always appreciate, for providing valuable feedback and input.

This research project would not have been possible without field research in Southern Africa and the generous support of the German Academic Exchange Service (DAAD) as funding institution. I especially thank Peter Draper and the South African Institute of International Affairs (SAIIA) as well as Jonathan M. Kaunda and the Botswana Institute for Development Policy Analysis (BIDPA) for welcoming me to their organisations and for giving me the chance to combine my research with active participation in everyday business. I also would like to thank the friendly staff at the SADC Headquarters, who supported my research by giving me access to official documents and recommending interview partners. Moreover, I would like to express my gratitude to Dennis T. Othapile and his family for their hospitality and much practical advice throughout my research stays in Botswana.

I owe many thanks to Lukas Prinz and Valentin Bösing, who proofread several chapters, cross-checked most of the literature and helped me to compile the bibliography and index. I am also grateful to Anca Pusca and Anne Schult from Palgrave for their advice, support and patience.

Lastly, I wish to thank my family, especially my parents Armin and Ina, and all of my friends who encouraged and supported me in many different ways during the work on this book and beyond.

Mainz, Germany							Johannes Muntschick

GLOSSARY

ACP	African, Caribbean and Pacific
AEF	ACP-EU Energy Facility
APF	African Peace Facility
APSA	African Peace and Security Architecture
ASEAN	Association of Southeast Asian Nations
ASF	African Standby Force
AU	African Union
BLNS	Botswana, Lesotho, Namibia and Swaziland
CAN	Andean Community
CEMAC	Economic and Monetary Community of Central Africa
CEN-SAD	Community of Sahel-Saharan States
CET	Common External Tariff
CMA	Common Monetary Area
COM	SADC Council of Ministers
COMESA	Common Market for Eastern and Southern Africa
CONSAS	Constellation of Southern African States
DAM	Day Ahead Market
DBSA	Development Bank of Southern Africa
DRC	Democratic Republic of the Congo
EAC	East African Community
EBA	Everything-But-Arms
ECOWAS	Economic Community of West African States
EDF	European Development Fund
EPA	Economic Partnership Agreement
ESA	Eastern and Southern Africa
ESDP	European Security and Defence Policy

EU	European Union
FANR	Food, Agriculture and Natural Resources
FDI	Foreign Direct Investments
FLS	Front Line States
FOPRISA	Formative Process Research on Regional Integration in Southern Africa
FTA	Free Trade Area
GATT	General Agreement on Tariffs and Trade
GDP	Gross Domestic Product
GIZ	Gesellschaft für Internationale Zusammenarbeit
GWh	Gigawatt Hour
HDI	Human Development Index
IGAD	Intergovernmental Authority on Development
IMoU	Intergovernmental Memorandum of Understanding
IOC	Indian Ocean Community
IS	Infrastructure and Services
ISDSC	Inter-State Defence and Security Committee
ISPDC	Inter-State Politics and Diplomacy Committee
kV	Kilovolt
LDC	Least Developed Country
Mercosur	Common Market of the South
MMA	Multilateral Monetary Agreement
MMTZ	Malawi, Mozambique, Tanzania and Zambia
MoU	Memorandum of Understanding
MW	Megawatt
NAFTA	North American Free Trade Agreement
NATO	North Atlantic Treaty Organisation
NTB	Non-Tariff Barriers to trade
ODA	Official Development Assistance
OECD	Organisation for Economic Co-operation and Development
OPDS	Organ on Politics, Defence and Security Cooperation
PLANELM	Planning Element (of the SADC Standby Force)
PPRM	Policy, Planning and Resource Mobilisation
RIKS	Regional Integration Knowledge System
RISDP	Regional Indicative Strategic Development Plan
RoO	Rules of Origin
RPTC	Regional Peacekeeping Training Centre
RSA	Republic of South Africa
SACU	Southern African Customs Union
SADC	Southern African Development Community
SADCC	Southern African Development Co-ordination Conference
SADC-CD	Single Customs Administrative Document

SADC-CU	SADC Customs Union
SADC-FTA	SADC Free Trade Area
SAIIA	South African Institute for International Affairs
SANDF	South African National Defence Force
SAPP	Southern African Power Pool
SAPP-IMoU	Southern African Power Pool Inter-Utility Memorandum of Understanding
SCMC	Standing Committee of Senior Officials, the Sectoral and Cluster Ministerial Committees
SHDSP	Social and Human Development and Special Programmes
SIPO	Strategic Indicative Plan for the Organ
SIPRI	Stockholm International Peace Research Institute
SNC	SADC National Committees
SSF	SADC Standby Force
STEM	Short-Term Energy Market
TAU	Technical and Administrative Unit
TDCA	Trade, Development and Cooperation Agreement
TIFI	Trade, Industry, Finance and Investment
TIPS	Trade & Industrial Policy Strategies
TNF	Trade Negotiation Forum
Tralac	Trade Law Centre for Southern Africa
UMA	Arab Maghreb Union
UN	United Nations
USA	United States of America
USAID	United States Agency for International Development
WITS	World Integrated Trade Solutions
WTO	World Trade Organisation

Contents

1 Introduction: Research Interest and Research Questions   1

2 Theoretical Approach: The Situation-Structural Model as an Analytical Tool to Explain Regionalism   25

3 The Southern African Development Community (SADC): An Analytical Overview of Its History, Policies and Institutional Framework   83

4 The Protocol on Trade and the Creation of the Southern African Development Community Free Trade Area   105

5 Exogenous Interference: The European Union's Economic Partnership Agreements and the Stalled SADC Customs Union   153

6 Regional Security Cooperation and the SADC's Organ for Politics, Defence and Security: A Picture of Mixed Performance   187

7 The SADC Standby Force and Its Regional Peacekeeping Training Centre: Uncertain Operational Readiness and Future of an Externally Fuelled Brigade   229

8	The Southern African Power Pool: An Electrifying Project with Untapped Potential	267
9	Conclusion	307
	References	323
	Index	363

LIST OF FIGURES

Fig. 4.1	Problematic situation in view of the SADC-FTA	114
Fig. 4.2	Intra-regional trade in the SADC (as percentage of total trade)	131
Fig. 4.3	Intra-regional trade intensity in the SADC (in Index Points)	132
Fig. 4.4	SADC countries' intra-regional exports (as percentage of total exports)	133
Fig. 4.5	SADC countries' intra-regional imports (as percentage of total imports)	134
Fig. 4.6	Inward FDI flows to selected SADC countries (in millions USD at current prices and current exchange rates)	136
Fig. 4.7	Inward FDI flows to the SADC (in millions USD at current prices and current exchange rates)	137
Fig. 5.1	Genuine regional problematic situation in view of the SADC-CU	160
Fig. 5.2	Externally distorted problematic situation in view of the SADC-CU	172
Fig. 6.1	Problematic situation in view of a SADC Security Regime	196
Fig. 7.1	Genuine regional problematic situation in view of an envisaged SADC Standby Force	234
Fig. 7.2	Externally fuelled problematic situation in view of the planned SADC Standby Force	242
Fig. 8.1	Forecast of the SADC's internal electricity generation capacity (in MW) for 1996–2010	273
Fig. 8.2	Problematic situation in view of the SAPP	276
Fig. 8.3	Inflow of external funding to the SAPP (in USD)	280

Fig. 8.4 Contribution of external funding to the SAPP's total assets 281
Fig. 8.5 SAPP electricity trade through the STEM in GWh (2002–2006) 291
Fig. 8.6 SAPP electricity trade through the DAM in GWh (2010–2014) 293

List of Tables

Table 3.1	The SADC member states (in 2016)	90
Table 4.1	Share of intra-regional trade of SADC countries in 1995	109
Table 4.2	South African investment in SADC by country (1994–2003)	116
Table 4.3	Share of extra-regional trade of SADC countries with the EU in 1995	118
Table 4.4	Doing business indicator "Trading Across Borders" in the SADC	139
Table 5.1	Share of intra-regional trade of SADC countries in 2007	155
Table 5.2	Pattern of trade flows of SADC members with the SADC and the EU in 2007	162
Table 6.1	Strength of regular armed forces of SADC members (1994)	198
Table 6.2	Military expenditure of SADC members (1995)	200
Table 7.1	Strength of regular armed forces of SADC members (2007)	236
Table 7.2	Military expenditure of SADC members (2007)	236
Table 8.1	The SAPP members (1996)	285
Table 8.2	The SAPP members (2016)	289
Table 8.3	The SAPP's available installed electricity generation capacity (in MW)	296

CHAPTER 1

Introduction: Research Interest and Research Questions

The collapse of the bipolar world order after the end of the Cold War in combination with increasing international interdependence and inter-state interaction in the course of globalisation seems to have prepared the ground for the latest wave of new regionalism (Hettne 1999; Hettne and Söderbaum 1998; Robson 1993; Söderbaum and Shaw 2003). The latter manifested in a large number of new and renewed regional integration organisations in virtually every corner of the world. These include the Association of Southeast Asian Nations (ASEAN), the Economic Community of West African States, the Common Market of the South (Mercosur), the North American Free Trade Agreement (NAFTA) or the Southern African Development Community (SADC).

However, it is quite surprising that most of these so-called new regionalisms emerged outside the sphere of the Organisation for Economic Co-operation and Development and are composed, for the most part, of developing countries in the world's peripheral regions, in particular in the Global South[1]. This evidence is astonishing because conventional wisdom and classic regional integration theories assume that the preconditions for successful regionalism in the Southern Hemisphere are—for a variety of reasons (particularly economic ones)— less advantageous and promising compared with those in the developed and economically more interdependent Global North (e.g. Europe).

Nonetheless, these new regionalisms came into existence and showed (often considerable) institutional dynamics and performance with regard to their policy agendas. There is empirical evidence, however, that sometimes the development and performance of at least some of these new regionalisms are unstable and do not always seem to be entirely under the control of the regional actors only. Instead, powerful extra-regional actors seem to get involved and influence regional integration processes and projects on several occasions (Axline 1977; Doidge 2011; Muntschick 2013).

It is probably no coincidence that the phenomenon of new regionalism occurred during a time of important integration steps in the European Union (EU) which culminated in the implementation of the Single European Act and the creation of the Common Market in the early 1990s. The example of successful European integration had certainly been perceived with anxiety and admiration by many countries in the international arena, not least because this dawning "Leviathan" likewise stood for an intimidating economic superpower and for an inspiring model of sustainable cooperation.

If one takes a look over the rim of the European teacup towards the Southern Hemisphere, there is no clear evidence that the integration efforts and institutional strengthening of the EU had a direct impact on the formation and expansion of new regionalisms in less developed regions. Because systematic and theory-driven analyses of these interesting cases are still missing, one can only speculate about the motives of countries to become members in these regional integration schemes and about the major factors and mechanisms that exerted an influence on their dynamics, institutional design and performance. Against this background, and with regard to the increasing academic interest and discussion on the whole issue of new and comparative regionalism (Börzel and Risse 2016a; Jetschke and Lenz 2011; Rosamond and Warleigh-Lack 2011; Warleigh-Lack and Van Langenhove 2010), the African continent offers an excellent and comparably untouched field of research. This is because a significant number of more and less promising regional integration organisations have emerged and developed there during the last few decades (Grant and Söderbaum 2003b; Söderbaum 2007).

In regard to Africa, the SADC is recognised as one of the most realistic and promising regional integration organisations on the continent. It ranks as an outstanding example of the new regionalism in the Global South. Since its foundation in 1992, the SADC has changed its development strategy from sector-specific cooperation towards a more comprehensive approach of broader vertical and deeper horizontal integration. The organisation's common agenda is highly ambitious. However, the

SADC's institutional dynamics and progress towards deeper integration are proven by a growing number of protocols, agreements and regional cooperation projects. In the issue area of the economy, SADC member states adopted a Protocol on Trade in 1999 and successfully created a Free Trade Area (FTA) in 2008. Regarding peace and security, SADC countries established confidence-building mechanisms and set up a SADC Standby Force in August 2007. In regard to infrastructure, the SADC established, among other things, the Southern African Power Pool (SAPP) in August 1995 (Adelmann 2012; Oosthuizen 2006).

In addition, the SADC has shown remarkable intra-organisational dynamics. An institutional reform process starting in 2001 led to a centralisation of several competences at the organisation's secretariat and strengthened its capacity to guide and support member states' decision- and policy-making in matters of regional integration. Moreover, the SADC's organ for security and defence cooperation was restructured and formally became part of the organisation's institutional framework. In the same year, SADC leaders amended the founding SADC Treaty of 1992. The growth of the organisation in member countries corroborates the impression that regional integration under the SADC's umbrella is attractive and promising for in- and outsiders. This first evidence indicates that today the SADC is one of the (few) successful examples of regionalism among developing countries (Adelmann 2012; Jaspert 2010; Oosthuizen 2006).

Aside from success stories, however, empirical observation also indicates that regionalism in the SADC is not entirely immune to stagnation and setbacks. It seems, for example, that the establishment of the scheduled SADC Customs Union is not on track and the effects of the SADC-FTA are in question. The status and operational readiness of the SADC Standby Force remain fairly unclear, and its Regional Peacekeeping Training Centre seems not be on track either. Regional infrastructure projects like the SAPP are institutions—according to some—mere façades and not able to meet the expectations. Nonetheless, these regional institutions do exist and operate in certain ways. But there remains uncertainty whether they have actually been fully implemented and prove effective. This tentative evidence implies that regional integration is not a one-directional process towards goal attainment per se but can also go back and forth or even stagnate. Regionalism in the SADC is obviously not just "sunshine and roses" but also is prone to challenges and difficulties which lead to an overall picture of ambivalence. These perceptions and qualities are what add to the SADC's attractiveness as an interesting and very promising research case on regionalism.

In summary, the main reasons to identify the SADC as a promising example of the new regionalism in the South and to select it as an object of research for this study are as follows: Firstly, the SADC not only is a very typical and representative model of the latest wave of regionalism but also ranks among the most recognised, realistic and promising regional integration organisations in the South. Secondly, compared with other new regionalisms on global and continental levels, the SADC has reached deep and broad levels of vertical and horizontal integration respectively. The significant gap in systematic research on the SADC from a political science perspective counts as a third reason that motivates the selection of the SADC as a research object for this book.

Empirical Puzzles

Irrespectively of the allegedly less advantageous preconditions in the region, countries in Southern Africa have pursued a strategy of institutionalised regional cooperation and, in 1992, successfully established the SADC as a regional integration organisation in accordance to international law. The SADC's achievements, together with the pronounced activities of its member countries in promoting regional integration and modernising their common institutions, have given valid grounds for believing that today the SADC represents a very vibrant and promising example of the new regionalism in the Global South. The observed "ups and downs" of regionalism in the SADC, however, give evidence that the process of regional integration is not necessarily linear and produces institutions that are not always effective at all times. Based on this observation, the following major empirical puzzles unfold:

Against the background of allegedly disadvantageous structural preconditions and, in many respects, a great heterogeneity among countries in the region, it is in the first instance puzzling why regionalism in Southern Africa actually materialised—apparently even quite successfully—within the framework of the SADC. This is even more surprising because the establishment and maintenance of regional institutions are invariably costly and it is a matter of fact that most SADC members are developing countries with very limited financial capacities and relatively strong (economic) dependence on external actors beyond "their" region.

Secondly, it remains a puzzle why, at certain times, regional integration in the SADC shows distinct development and alternating dynamics with regard to the creation and modification of common regional institutions. Little is known about decisive factors or mechanisms that influence these dynamics and there are no systematic studies on which of these are possibly responsible for promoting, complicating or impairing institutionalised regional cooperation in the SADC. Examples of successful, delayed or paralysed regional integration projects give empirical evidence that fuel the idea that extra-regional actors and external influence may have played a role in this respect.

Thirdly, it remains puzzling whether regionalism in the SADC is actually successful and provides a mutually beneficial common club good for its member countries, or whether the SADC is functionally ineffective and only an institutional façade. Questioning this issue is motivated against the background of occasional claims that regional organisations in Africa have a record of failed cooperation and are merely symbolic in nature (Asche 2009; Herbst 2007: 138–141).

Research Questions

Taking the abovementioned empirical observations and puzzles into account, the book aims to give comprehensive and substantiated answers to more fundamental research questions in order to explain regionalism in the SADC. The following questions are of central importance as they represent the guiding research questions of this study:

- Why do countries in Southern Africa engage in regionalism within the organisational framework of the SADC? Why does regional integration take place, and what explains the emergence of regional institutions in the SADC?
- What explains the institutional design and dynamics of regionalism in the SADC? Which factors and mechanisms are responsible for and contribute to this process?
- How successful is regionalism in the SADC in terms of institutional performance and effectiveness? Is regionalism in the SADC perhaps only an expression of symbolism with façade institutions?

In a nutshell, the main task of this book is to explain the emergence, institutional design, and performance of regionalism in the SADC. This includes taking the potential impact of external actors explicitly into account.

Besides focussing on the research questions only, this book aims to fill the existing research gaps on theorising (new) regionalism in the Global South. For this purpose, the author conceptualises an innovative theoretical approach in order to conduct a profound and theory-driven case analysis from a political science perspective. Such an in-depth study of the SADC not only can generate case-specific knowledge but also can provide empirical evidence and insights for comparative research on global regionalism.

1.1 Relevance of the Topic and State of Research

A qualified and well-founded research topic needs to fulfil at least two central criteria: Firstly, it has to address a phenomenon that is important to the real world. This implies social relevance. Secondly, it should contribute to the academic debate about the phenomenon under observation and thus help to provide more general explanations beyond the observed case. This denotes scholarly relevance (King et al. 1994: 15–16).

With regard to social relevance, a systematic analysis on the emergence, institutional design, and performance of regionalism in the SADC is of major importance first and foremost for the organisation itself, its member states and all policy entrepreneurs involved. All of these actors have a strong interest to gain substantiated knowledge about how and why "their" regional organisation operates and develops in certain policy areas, about its strengths and weaknesses as well as about its performance. Profound empirical information on these issues—as well as on involved causal mechanisms and effects—is very important for the regional actors because it provides a basis for benchmarking and adjustments that may lead to improvements. Owing to financial or political constraints, regional integration organisations in the Global South, such as the SADC, often lack the capacity to conduct comprehensive scientific research on their own.

Moreover, this book's research questions are relevant for the real world because a number of important international actors (such as the EU, the World Bank, or individual countries) are (in)directly involved in the development of regionalism in the Global South and in the SADC by providing financial and political support. These extra-regional actors, including their stake-holders or peoples (e.g. the citizens of the EU), have a strong interest to be informed on how the addressees of their support actually develop and perform, not least in order to tailor specific partnership programmes or adjust funding policies (e.g. of the European Development Fund or national development agencies) vis-à-vis their cooperating partners.

With regard to scholarly relevance, a theory-driven and systematic in-depth analysis of an example of regionalism in the Global South, such as the SADC, helps to generate case-specific knowledge on a single organisation's emergence, institutional design, modus operandi and performance. In addition, the work contributes to the academic debate on theorising regionalism and systematic research on regionalism in comparison, particularly with regard to external influence.

In the SADC's case, there is evidence that regionalism is prone to external influence for structural reasons since the organisation and its member states seem to be dependent on extra-regional actors in a number of policy areas. Against this background, new empirical evidence, causal relations and theory-generating insights could help enhance, improve or qualify the explanatory power and generalisability of existing integration theories in view of regionalism in the Global South. Possibly, this could even culminate in the development of a new middle-range theory on regional integration.

Altogether, this study provides explanations and empirical evidence on how regionalism in the SADC does actually work. This implies focussing on the policies and actions of countries and regional powers at the regional level but also includes—explicitly—taking important extra-regional actors and their influence into account. Thereby it addresses a major research gap in research on (comparative) regionalism in general and the SADC in particular (Börzel and Risse 2016b; Warleigh-Lack 2008; Warleigh-Lack and Rosamond 2011). Finally, it seeks to provide an evaluation of regionalism in the SADC by analysing the organisation's performance and institutional effectiveness. So far, there has been a lack of comprehensive and valid information on the success of regionalism in the SADC, which is of direct concern given that the organisation occasionally faces allegations of being dysfunctional or little more than symbolic in nature.

1.1.1   *Theorising Regionalism: Classic Integration Theories*

Regionalism is not an entirely new phenomenon since states and non-state actors have been cooperating on a regional level in varying constellations for centuries. The term "old regionalism" refers to the first wave of regionalism that emerged after the end of the Second World War. A number of well-established regional integration organisations, particularly in the Western Hemisphere (with the EU as the example par excellence) but also among developing countries in the South (e.g. the Arab League or ASEAN), represent the old regionalism until today. One of its main characteristics is that the old regionalism is in general strongly inward-oriented in terms of pursuing policies of import substitution and economic discrimination against the rest of the world. Moreover, old regionalisms in general comprise members from either the Global South or the Global North only. Therefore, they are strictly south-south or north-north regional cooperation arrangements whose member states rarely hold multiple memberships in more than one regional integration organisation (Börzel 2011: 10–12; Ravenhill 2008).

Against this background the phenomenon of regionalism became an intriguing and challenging topic for researchers in the field of international relations and for theory development. The research topic has attracted growing attention of scholars and became increasingly important in the academic research community in parallel to Europe's process of deepening regional cooperation and successful integration. Since the European integration process is unparalleled and the EU is certainly a political entity sui generis, most classic integration theories use this $n = 1$ sample as a point of departure for generating generalisable assumptions on regional integration or as an empirical reference point to test and validate their hypotheses and theoretical approaches or as both. This of course bears the risk of circular reasoning.

Moreover, they generally claim universal validity of their assumptions and hypotheses in terms of having found a comprehensive explanation of the logic of regional integration and the phenomenon of regionalism. Most of these theories, however, refer in their central assumptions, argument and empirical analysis to only a single case of a—so far—successful story of regionalism: the one among developed countries in Europe.

(Neo)Realism

The main argument of (neo)realism is that states strive permanently to secure their survival. An international division of labour is not likely, because this could imply dependence on third actors and consequently endanger individual autarky and thus eventually survival. Lasting international or regional cooperation and integration are not feasible options for the states. This is because they calculate relative gains. Any cooperative agreement that gives a relative advantage to other participants implies a self-weakening (Grieco 1993, 1997; Waltz 1979). Hegemonic Stability Theory, however, argues that international cooperation can be possible, lasting and stable as long as a hegemonic power decides to provide the collective good—and reaps most of its relative gains (Gilpin 1987; Kindleberger 1981).

Neo-Functionalism

Neo-Functionalism argues that the interaction between strong subnational actors and supranational institutions is of crucial importance for achieving regional cooperation in international relations. Regional integration is thereby understood as a determined process that begins in technical and economic areas where countries assume cooperation to be functionally most efficient (Mitrany 1943). Common institutions are established and designed according to the regulatory requirements in the respective issue area ("form follows function"). The process of international as well as regional cooperation is driven by transnational and regional non-state actors, policy entrepreneurism, and supranational institutions and has self-enforcing tendencies. Functional spill-over effects occur when regional cooperation in one issue area entails problems in a related policy area which creates demand for further cooperation (Haas 1958, 1964; Lindberg and Scheingold 1971).

Liberal Intergovernmentalism

Liberal intergovernmentalism emphasises the role of sub-national societal and especially economic actors with regard to national preference formation and state policy. A country's preferences ultimately reflect the interests of the society's influential domestic actors and most assertive interest groups. Against the background of strong economic interdependence, which liberal intergovernmentalism assumes to exist among developed countries in the Western Hemisphere, states engage in international as well as regional cooperation in order to gain (economic) advantages for their national interest groups. Inter-state interaction and an exchange of interests lead to a process of intergovernmental bargaining and eventually to international compromise (Hoffmann 1966). This reflects the lowest common denominator and is "locked-in" by an institutional framework in order to credibly commit the involved participants (Moravcsik 1997, 1998).

Constructivism

Constructivists assume that actors' interests, motives, ideas and identities are socially constructed by reflective actors who are capable of adapting to challenges imposed by the action of others or a changing context or both. Norms, ideas, beliefs and other institutional or cultural factors have an important impact on countries' interests, choices and behavioural practices. They are determinants for action but not stable and may change over time. This is because they are constructed by histories and cultures, domestic factors, and—most importantly—interactions with other countries. Hence, most important is how countries interpret their social context because their perceptions influence their behaviour (Ruggie 1998; Söderbaum 2002: 41–42; Spindler 2005; Wendt 1992). Accordingly, regionalism is driven by ideational and inter-subjective factors rather than by a purely rationalist logic of cooperation (Acharya 2016: 120).

Political Economy
Neoclassical economists and theories of the political economy school of thought regard economic profit as the main driving force for international cooperation. Patterns of strong economic interdependence between countries increase individual prospects for absolute gains. This precondition is the sine qua non for successful international and regional (economic) integration (Ravenhill 2008). In line with the ideas of Balassa and others (Balassa 1961; Ricardo 1977; Viner 1950), countries are expected to benefit from rising economies of scale or exploiting comparative cost advantages in a larger, integrated market. Accordingly, regional integration is often simply understood as economic/market integration on a regional level that follows a predetermined linear process: FTA, customs union, common market, economic and monetary union, and complete economic and political union.

Conclusion on Classic Integration Theories
It is no surprise that a good deal of truth is found within each of these mainstream theories and approaches that have been introduced so far. All of them have strong explanatory power with respect to regionalism in Europe from their specific point of view. It is almost impossible to falsify them because they have been modelled on the subject they aim to explain and because Europe itself is a very exceptional case. This is because a comparably wide range of advantageous preconditions to regional integration can be found in Europe, such as influential political elites, strong and transnational civil society actors, high levels of socioeconomic development, strong intra-regional (economic) interdependence and shared values, beliefs and culture.

While the overall conditions for regionalism were very favourable in Europe, this does not mean that mainstream integration theories apply all over the world where the local political and economic setting could be significantly different than the European case. Particularly in the

Southern Hemisphere, where developing and non-industrialised countries prevail, such advantageous preconditions for successful regional integration—that do exist in Europe and the North—are often less distinctive or even missing entirely. This leads to the conclusion that the quality and explanatory power of the mainstream integration theories probably fall short in analysing and explaining regionalism in the Global South.

1.1.2 Theorising the New Regionalism: Recent State of Research

The scientific debate on global regionalism uses the term "new regionalism" in the context of the latest wave of regionalism which emerged after the end of the Cold War in parallel to the growing globalisation. In contrast to old regionalisms, the new regionalisms are more outward-oriented and put a greater focus on economic integration. Markets and global competition are major driving forces for these new regionalisms that pursue explicit strategies of regional trade liberalisation, export promotion and non-discrimination against the rest of the world. They often comprise members from the Global South and North. It is not uncommon for members to hold membership in more than one new regionalism which leads to the phenomenon of overlapping (new) regionalisms (Börzel 2011: 10–12; Laursen 2010).

A review of the recent academic literature and research on the new regionalism reveals that there is only a small number of comprehensive theoretical approaches and few theory-driven analyses that deal with this challenging new topic. The majority of the studies on the new regionalism from a political science perspective can be roughly divided into two categories as they apply two different strands of theories: One line of reasoning is dominated by the international political economy school of thought, whereas the second is explicitly critical to the first and takes concepts of constructivism into account. Because they represent the state of the art in recent research, both strands of theory on the new regionalism will be introduced in more detail and compared with classic mainstream integration theories.

International Political Economy Perspective
Mattli argues that a combination of specified demand and supply factors is crucial for successful regional integration. In line with the political economy school of thought, he emphasises the prospect of achieving economic gains as a major incentive for states to engage in regional

cooperation. Demand originates generally from private economic actors who follow gain- and profit-seeking interests and lobby for economy-related regional rules and regulations. Favourable supply conditions imply the willingness of political leaders to accommodate the upcoming demand for regional (economic) integration by appropriate measures such as adequate formal commitment institutions. Mattli concludes that regional integration is likely to happen only when economically motivated demand is met by favourable supply conditions. He argues that his theory is universally valid and bears explanatory power for regionalism all over the world (Mattli 1999). It comes as surprise, however, that Mattli disregards regional integration projects on the African continent in his landmark work.

Globalisation and the emergence and expanding of global markets are the starting points in Stefan Schirm's theoretical approach. He argues that globalisation and global markets have a strong impact on countries as both "imply a deterritorialisation and denationalisation of economic activity because their operational logic transcends the functional logic of the states" (Schirm 2002: 12). Against this background, governments regard regional integration as the best way to meet the global (economic) challenges for two reasons: Firstly, economic reforms, trade liberalisation and market creation on a regional level strengthen a region's economic efficiency and competitiveness. This implies positive effects and profits for all participant countries. Secondly, economic reforms are often politically and socially more acceptable on the national level if a government is "forced" to implement them by regional commitments instead of national agendas (Schirm 2002: 10–23).

One has to welcome Schirm's theoretical global markets approach because he does not confine his empirical study on regional integration to Europe or the North. With the case study on NAFTA, Schirm already touches the sphere of new regionalism but it is only his analysis of Mercosur where he tests his hypotheses on a hard case of the South (Schirm 2002: 102–135). Similar to other authors, Schirm academically ignores the regional integration organisations in Africa.

New Regionalism Approaches

The so-called New Regionalism Approach was developed during the mid-1990s and is rather a conglomerate of literature than a single consistent theory. It includes a variety of critical, mostly social-constructivist-orientated theoretical approaches that relate and correspond to certain degrees with each other (Bøås et al. 2005; Grant and Söderbaum 2003b;

Hettne and Söderbaum 1998; Söderbaum and Shaw 2003; Telò 2007). Authors from this school of thought do not adhere to a plain rationalist concept of agency but rather amalgamate the central ideas of critical international political economy and reflective constructivism. All new regionalism approaches tend to go beyond "conventional state-centric and formalistic notions of regionalism" (Grant and Söderbaum 2003a: 2) and emphasise the complex, multidimensional and sometimes contradictive concepts, causes and processes concerning regions, regionalisation and (micro-)regionalism. In view of an increasingly globalising world, they argue that the international system experiences a phase of restructuring with states increasingly losing influence to non-state, transnational actors and networks.

Most new regionalism approaches have been designed to explain regionalism outside Europe. Few case analyses have been conducted that explicitly apply the new regionalism approach. But the existing ones deal mainly with regionalism in Africa. However, these works do not seem to intend to conduct comprehensive analyses of entire regional integration organisations but rather focus on selected (transnational) micro-level cooperation projects—thereby sometimes neglecting the role of the state (Grant and Söderbaum 2003a; Söderbaum and Shaw 2003).

Area Studies Research and Empirical Works

Whereas there are only a few theory-driven works, there exists a comparably large number of empirical works on new and old regionalisms. It is mostly regional experts from the field of area studies who have contributed many in-depth studies on regionalism in the Global South, Africa and even the SADC. For this reason, there exists a small array of detailed and useful empirical works that constitute a treasure of high-quality secondary sources (Adelmann 2003, 2012; Lee 2003; Mair and Peters-Berries 2001; Oosthuizen 2007; Vogt 2007). However, this strand of empirical literature on the SADC is generally rather descriptive and does not attempt theory-driven analyses. Therefore, with the exception of the selection of the aforementioned books, the majority of empirical studies on the SADC are often illustrative and anecdotal in character.

Moreover, the existing literature on the SADC does not attempt an analysis and assessment of the performance and institutional effectiveness of the regional organisation in general or its cooperation projects in particular. At best, there exist studies on single integration projects, the majority thereof focussing on the state of market integration and free trade, but other important policy areas where regional cooperation does actually take place are generally neglected (Chipeta 1997; Iwanow 2011; Sandrey 2013). Hence, there is a large research gap in terms of a systematic and comprehensive evaluation of the performance and institutional effectiveness of regionalism in the SADC. This is quite surprising because the SADC receives significant amounts of external funding, and donors would be expected to monitor and assess how their money is used. On the other hand, it is perhaps not surprising, because there has been no confirmation of the existence of a comprehensive evaluation of the performance of the EU either.

Conclusion on New Regionalism Theories and the State of the Research
The majority of recent research and theories on (new) regionalism either belong to the international political economy school of thought or form part of the new regionalism approaches that make reference to constructivism in a sense. They address the latest wave of regionalism and partly aim to overcome Euro-centrism by explicitly including the analysis of regionalism in the Global South. While classic integration theories generally focus only on a vertical perspective on the study of regionalism, the recent theories take—or at least aim to take—possible horizontal effects into account as well (Börzel 2011; Jetschke and Lenz 2011; Warleigh-Lack 2008). Most of the latter explanatory models and theories, particularly those relating to diffusion theory, are still fairly Eurocentric in character because they conceptualise the EU as a model for global regionalism.

Hence, there is a lack of analytical and theory-driven studies on regionalism that take the potential impact of extra-regional relations and the influence of external actors systematically into account without tending to take a Euro-centric perspective. The very few existing works are either conceptual in character and without a comprehensive in-depth case study (Zimmerling 1991) or too narrow in scope in terms of focussing on the policy area of the economy only (Krapohl 2016). Other recent publications recognise the fact that regional integration organisations mutually influence each other by demanding and supplying governance transfer (Börzel and Van Hüllen 2015). This implies at least a logic of extra-regional influence. Börzel and Risse state, in one of the latest and most comprehensive publications on comparative regionalism, that there is empirical evidence of supportive and interfering external influence on regional integration processes in the Global South which deserves further attention by scholars but is still an under-researched topic (Börzel and Risse 2016b).

This study on regionalism addresses the existing academic void and research gaps. It provides a comprehensive and theory-driven analysis of regionalism in the SADC that takes extra-regional relations and the potential influence of external actors explicitly into account. The study addresses questions regarding the emergence, institutional design, and performance of institutionalised regional cooperation in the SADC and thereby aims to provide a profound evaluation of the entire regional integration organisation as a whole. Hence, this study is probably the first systematic and comprehensive analysis of regionalism in the SADC from a political science perspective.

1.2 Synopsis: Key Argument, Major Empirical Findings and Delimitations of This Study

The aim of this book is to explain the logic of regional integration and the emergence, institutional design, and performance of regionalism in the Global South on the example of the SADC. With concrete research questions guiding the theory-driven analysis, this study argues that regionalisms in the Southern Hemisphere can neither be regarded as isolated entities in the international arena nor be explained and understood by looking at them from a confined regional perspective only. In fact, these regionalisms are part of a globalising and increasingly interdependent international system which makes them subject to the influence of extra-regional actors. This happens for plain structural reasons and affects primarily those regionalisms that consist of developing countries that show patterns of strong and asymmetric extra-regional relations to actors beyond the region.

Taking these important background conditions into consideration, the book develops a theoretical approach to the analysis of regionalism which makes reference to Zürn's situation-structural model but expands it by taking the impact of extra-regional actors additionally into account. The result is a pair of lines of argument on the emergence, institutional design, and performance of regionalism that can be described as an internal and an external logic. Deduced from assumptions inherent to these two logics are the work's central hypotheses on regionalism and extra-regional influence. The key argument, in a nutshell, is that the emergence, institutional design, and performance of regionalism depend in the first instance on the inherent structure of the underlying cooperation problem among countries on a regional level. In line with the first logic, powerful regional states are assumed to act as catalysts to regional integration while strong relations of regional actors to powerful extra-regional actors, in accordance with the external logic, implicate an ambivalent impact on regional integration efforts, institutions and their performance. In addition to this functional logic of regional integration, the study elaborates an alternative explanation for regionalism that makes reference to mechanisms of diffusion, isomorphism and symbolism. The purpose of this residual argument is to strengthen the explanatory power of this analysis by including the possible existence of non-functional and inoperative regional integration institutions.

The SADC represents one of the most recognised, dynamic and promising examples of the new regionalism in the Global South. This makes the SADC an ideal and representative case for analysis. In order to find answers to the research questions, achieve the research objective and produce a substantiated piece of work, the author has focussed on the SADC's most important policy areas of regional integration. These are the issue areas of the economy, security and infrastructure. Dividing the single case of the SADC into five sub-cases makes sense from a methodological point of view because the selected sub-cases count as hard cases and represent the organisation as a whole.

The major empirical findings from theory-driven case analysis, in a nutshell, are as follows: The SADC represents a typical example of the new regionalism of the Global South. The organisation, for the most part, is composed of developing countries. South Africa plays a key role in the SADC because of its status as a regional hegemon which is based on its advanced economy and superior military capabilities. Economically, several SADC countries are strongly dependent on South Africa, but more member states—including the SADC as a whole—are even more dependent on extra-regional actors, namely the EU, in terms of trade and exports, investments, or donor funding and (development) assistance. This structural pattern of asymmetric interdependence between the SADC and the EU provides the latter with leverage over the first and has proven to have an ambivalent impact on the emergence, institutional design, and performance of regional integration projects in the SADC. While the EU had virtually no influence on the formation of the SADC-FTA and the institutionalisation of the "Organ" for security cooperation, Brussels had a cooperation-conducive impact on the build-up of the SADC Standby Force and—to a lesser degree—on the establishment of the SAPP's integrated electricity market. An interfering external impact on regionalism in the SADC occurred in the case of the scheduled SADC customs union which had been undermined by the EU's EPA policies. Apart from this ambivalent external influence, it was in general South Africa that acted as the most dedicated proponent and assertive designer of regionalism in the SADC. This underpins the importance of regional key countries for successful regionalism.

Delimitations of this work relate to the theoretical approach and to the scope of the empirical research subject. The situation-structural approach implies a rational logic of thinking as it conceptualises the states as utility-maximising actors. Therefore, the theory to some extent neglects the potential meaning of ideas and norms for the actors' process of preference formation in the context of regionalism. Moreover, the situation-structural model concentrates on structural patterns and on states as central actors in international relations. Therefore, it neglects non-governmental organisations, individual policy entrepreneurs, political parties and lobby groups to some degree with regard to their actual influence on regional integration processes.

The selection of five sub-cases within the SADC as a single-case study could be subject to criticism as well. Although the analysis certainly deals with the crucial cases insofar as it focusses on the SADC's most important regional cooperation projects, there exist other issue areas beyond the economy, security and infrastructure where SADC countries initialised regional cooperation (e.g. tourism, health care, wildlife and anti-corruption). While these less important cases could certainly provide additional empirical insights and thus widen the scope of this work, it is still impossible to take all regional cooperation projects under the SADC's umbrella into consideration since this would go beyond the scope of this study.

1.3 Organisation and Structure of the Book

This book is divided into two major parts: The first part provides—besides an introduction to the research topic and state of the art—the theoretical framework, central assumptions and the research-guiding hypotheses. The second part is dedicated to theory-driven empirical analysis and case study research. The analysis of the five empirical case studies is guided by the central research questions and makes reference to the underlying theoretical framework. In regard to its structure, the book unfolds as follows:

This chapter explains the main research interest of this book and clarifies the social and scientific relevance of the topic. It outlines the underlying empirical puzzle and presents the guiding research questions. Moreover, the chapter provides a comprehensive introduction to the current state of research on regionalism and makes reference to classic integration theories and recent new regionalism approaches.

Chapter 2 puts a focus on theory and provides the analytical framework for this study. It gives definitions on regions and regionalism and elaborates on the link between regionalism and cooperation theory. It proceeds with developing a situation-structural model to the analysis of regionalism which seeks to explain the emergence, design and performance of regional cooperation projects and their inherent institutional frameworks. What is most innovative of this theoretical approach is that it takes the impact of extra-regional relations and external actors on regionalism explicitly into account. The chapter closes with a residual assumption on regional integration which refers to symbolism as an alternative explanation. Lastly, it informs the reader about the research design and methodology of the study.

Chapter 3 gives an introduction to the history of regionalism in Southern Africa and presents an overview of the SADC as an organisation. This includes information about its constituent members, central policy agenda as well as its institutional superstructure and main organs. With its focus on the institutional framework conditions, the chapter aims to provide important background information and analytical insights on the nature of regionalism in the SADC. This shall pave the way for a better understanding of the setting in which the five sub-case studies are embedded.

Chapter 4 analyses regional economic integration and explains the successful establishment of the SADC-FTA. It highlights the demand for regional market integration in SADC's member states from a structural perspective and explains the provisions of the SADC Protocol on Trade which determines the institutional design of the FTA. The role of South Africa as the regional economic hegemon together with other representative key countries will be the focus of analysis. Finally, the chapter determines the performance of the SADC-FTA and evaluates its prospects for the future.

Chapter 5 reveals that extra-regional actors can have a negative impact on regional economic integration in the SADC. The chapter refers to the organisation's agenda on market integration and, in a first step, elaborates the regional demand for the envisaged SADC customs union. In a second step, it highlights the SADC members' trade relations to the EU and in the light of this evidence explains the interfering impact of Brussel's European Partnership Agreements on deeper regional economic integration in the SADC.

Chapter 6 investigates regional security cooperation and pays special attention to the institutionalisation and performance of the SADC's Organ on Politics, Defence and Security. For this purpose, it firstly illustrates the regional security complex and clarifies the countries' demand for institutionalised security cooperation in the SADC. Secondly, the chapter explains the institutionalisation of the SADC's central security organ while making reference to conflicting inter-state interests and to South Africa. The chapter concludes with an assessment of the SADC's confidence-building and conflict management measures.

Chapter 7 explains why and how SADC countries pushed ahead with security cooperation in terms of regional military integration and put efforts in establishing a regional standby brigade together with a training centre. It pays special attention to the impact of extra-regional actors and donors' funding since the development of the SADC Standby Force occurred at a time when the region lacked an actual external threat. Finally, the chapter discusses the operational readiness of the brigade and its training centre in this context.

Chapter 8 turns to infrastructure and focusses on regional electricity cooperation in the SADC within the framework of the SAPP. It highlights the regional imbalances in electricity generation and consumption and explains the countries' demand for a regional electricity market and interconnected regional power grid. In the course of evaluating the performance of the regional electricity market, the chapter reveals the importance of extra-regional donors' funding for the operating capacity of the power pool.

Chapter 9 is the conclusion and synthesises the main theoretical and empirical insights of this work. It provides an interpretation of the findings in view of generalisations and theory-building and gives an outlook on the prospects and future development of regionalism in the SADC.

NOTE

1. The Global South is understood as a "meta- region" that covers areas with predominantly non-industrialised, developing countries in the Southern Hemisphere; in outdated terms, it is often referred to as the Third World (Söderbaum and Stålgren 2010: 2). The term South neither has a normative connotation nor refers to system or development theories.

REFERENCES

Acharya, A. 2016. Regionalism Beyond EU-Centrism. In *The Oxford Handbook of Comparative Regionalism*, ed. T.A. Börzel and T. Risse, 109–130. Oxford: Oxford University Press.
Adelmann, M. 2003. *Regionale Kooperation im südlichen Afrika*. Freiburg: Arnold-Bergstraesser-Institut.
Adelmann, M. 2012. *SADC—An Actor in International Relations? The External Relations of the Southern African Development Community*. Freiburg: Arnold-Bergstraesser-Institut.
Asche, H. 2009. Die SADC? Welche SADC? Afrikanische Regionalgemeinschaften im Übergang. In *Entwicklung als Beruf*, ed. T. Hanf, H.N. Weiler, and H. Dickow, 69–84. Baden-Baden: Nomos.
Axline, W.A. 1977. Underdevelopment, Dependence and Integration: The Politics of Regionalism in the Third World. *International Organization* 31 (1): 83–105.
Balassa, B. 1961. *The Theory of Economic Integration*. London: George Allen & Unwin.
Bøås, M., M.H. Marchand, and T.M. Shaw. 2005. Conclusion: Possible Projections for the Political Economy of Regions and Regionalisms. In *The Political Economy of Regions and Regionalisms*, ed. M. Bøås, M.H. Marchand, and T.M. Shaw, 167–174. Basingstoke: Palgrave.
Börzel, T.A. 2011. *Comparative Regionalism. A New Research Agenda*. KFG Working Paper 28. Berlin: Otto-Suhr-Institut für Politikwissenschaft.
Börzel, T.A., and T. Risse (eds.). 2016a. *The Oxford Handbook of Comparative Regionalism*. Oxford: Oxford University Press.
Börzel, T.A., and T. Risse. 2016b. Three Cheers for Comparative Regionalism. In *The Oxford Handbook of Comparative Regionalism*, ed. T.A. Börzel and T. Risse, 621–647. Oxford: Oxford University Press.
Börzel, T.A., and V. Van Hüllen (eds.). 2015. *Governance Transfer by Regional Organizations: Patching Together a Global Script*. Basingstoke: Palgrave Macmillan.

Chipeta, C. 1997. *Review and Rationalisation of the SADC Programme of Action. Volume 2: Main Report*. Cape Town: Council for Scientific and Industrial Research (CSIR) and Imani Development (Pvt) Ltd.
Doidge, M. 2011. *The European Union and Interregionalism*. Farnham: Ashgate.
Gilpin, R. 1987. *The Political Economy of International Relations*. Princeton: Princeton University Press.
Grant, J.A., and F. Söderbaum. 2003a. Introduction: The New Regionalism in Africa. In *The New Regionalism in Africa*, ed. F. Söderbaum and J.A. Grant, 1–20. Aldershot and Burlington: Ashgate.
Grant, J.A., and F. Söderbaum (eds.). 2003b. *The New Regionalism in Africa. The International Political Economy of New Regionalism Studies*. Aldershot and Burlington: Ashgate.
Grieco, J.M. 1993. Anarchy and the Limits of Cooperation: A Realist Critique of the Newest Liberal Institutionalism. In *Neorealism and Neoliberalism: The Contemporary Debate*, ed. D.A. Baldwin, 116–142. New York: Columbia University Press.
Grieco, J.M. 1997. Realist International Theory and the Study of World Politics. In *New Thinking in International Relations Theory*, ed. M. Doyle and J. Ikenberry, 163–201. Boulder: Westview Press.
Haas, E.B. 1958. *The Uniting of Europe: Political, Social, and Economic Forces 1950–1957*. Stanford: Stanford University Press.
Haas, E.B. 1964. *Beyond the Nation State: Functionalism and International Organization*. Stanford: Stanford University Press.
Herbst, J. 2007. Crafting Regional Cooperation in Africa. In *Crafting Cooperation. Regional International Institutions in Comparative Perspective*, ed. A. Acharya and A.I. Johnston, 129–144. Cambridge: Cambridge University Press.
Hettne, B. 1999. Globalisation and the New Regionalism: The Second Great Transformation. In *Globalism and the New Regionalism*, ed. B. Hettne, A. Inotai, and O. Sunkel, 1–24. London: Macmillan.
Hettne, B., and F. Söderbaum. 1998. The New Regionalism Approach. *Politeia: Journal for Political Science and Public Administration* 17 (3): 5–19.
Hoffmann, S. 1966. Obstinate or Obsolete? The Fate of the Nation-State and the Case of Western Europe. *Dædalus Journal of the American Academy of Arts and Sciences* 95 (2): 862–915.
Iwanow, T. 2011. *Impact of Derogations from Implementation of the SADC FTA Obligations on Intra-SADC Trade*. Gaborone: USAID, Southern Africa.
Jaspert, J. 2010. *Regionalismus im südlichen Afrika. Die Handels-und Sicherheitspolitik der SADC*. Wiesbaden: VS Verlag.
Jetschke, A., and T. Lenz. 2011. Vergleichende Regionalismusforschung und Diffusion: Eine neue Forschungsagenda. *Politische Vierteljahresschrift* 52 (3): 448–474.

Kindleberger, C. 1981. Dominance and Leadership in the International Economy. Exploitation, Public Goods, and Free Rides. *International Studies Quarterly* 25 (2): 242–254.
King, G., R.O. Keohane, and S. Verba. 1994. *Designing Social Inquirey: Scientific Inference in Qualitative Research*. Princeton: Princeton University Press.
Krapohl, S. (ed.). 2016. *Regional Integration in the Global South. External Influence on Economic Cooperation in ASEAN, MERCOSUR and SADC*. Cham: Palgrave Macmillan.
Laursen, F. 2010. Regional Integration: Some Introductory Reflections. In *Comparative Regional Integration. Europe and Beyond*, ed. F. Laursen, 3–20. Farnham: Ashgate.
Lee, M.C. 2003. *The Political Economy of Regionalism in Southern Africa*. Lansdowne and London: Lynne Rienner.
Lindberg, L.N., and S.A. Scheingold. 1971. *Regional Integration: Theory and Research*. Cambridge, MA: Harvard University Press.
Mair, S., and C. Peters-Berries. 2001. *Regionale Integration und Kooperation in Afrika südlich der Sahara. EAC, ECOWAS und SADC im Vergleich*. Forschungsbericht des Bundesministeriums für wirtschaftliche Zusammenarbeit und Entwicklung (BMZ), vol. 127. Bonn and München: Weltforum Verlag.
Mattli, W. 1999. *The Logic of Regional Integration: Europe and Beyond*. Cambridge: Cambridge University Press.
Mitrany, D. 1943. *A Working Peace System*. Chicago: Quadrangle Books.
Moravcsik, A. 1997. Taking Preferences Seriously: A Liberal Theory of International Politics. *International Organization* 51 (4): 513–553.
Moravcsik, A. 1998. *The Choice for Europe: Social Purpose and State Power from Messina to Maastricht*. Ithaca: Cornell University Press.
Muntschick, J. 2013. Explaining the influence of extra-regional actors on regional economic integration in Southern Africa: the EU's interfering impact on SADC and SACU. In *Mapping Agency: Comparing Regionalisms in Africa*, ed. U. Lorenz-Carl and M. Rempe, 77–95. Farnham: Ashgate.
Oosthuizen, G.H. 2006. *The Southern African Development Community: The Organisation, its Policies and Prospects*. Midrand: Institute for Global Dialogue.
Oosthuizen, G.H. 2007. The Future of the Southern African Development Community. In *South African Yearbook 2006/2007*, ed. E. Sidiropoulos, 87–98. Johannesburg: South African Institute of International Affairs.
Ravenhill, J. 2008. Regionalism. In *Global Political Economy*, 2nd ed, ed. J. Ravenhill, 172–210. Oxford and New York: Oxford University Press.
Ricardo, D. 1977. *On the Principles of Political Economy and Taxation*, Reprint ed. Hildesheim: Olms.
Robson, P. 1993. The New Regionalism and Developing Countries. *Journal of Common Market Studies* 31 (3): 329–348.

Rosamond, B., and A. Warleigh-Lack. 2011. Studying Regions Comparatively. In *New Regionalism and the European Union. Dialogues, Comparisons and New Research Agenda*, ed. A. Warleigh-Lack, N. Robinson, and B. Rosamond, 18–35. Abingdon: Routledge.
Ruggie, J.G. 1998. What Makes the World Hang Together? Neo-Utilitarianism and the Social Constructivist Challenge. *International Organization* 52 (4): 855–885.
Sandrey, R. 2013. *An Analysis of the SADC Free Trade Area*. Stellenbosch: Trade Law Centre for Southern Africa.
Schirm, S.A. 2002. *Globalization and the New Regionalism: Global Markets, Domestic Politics and Regional Cooperation*. Malden: Blackwell Publishers.
Söderbaum, F. 2002. *The Political Economy of Regionalism in Southern Africa*. Dissertation. Gothenburg: University of Gothenburg.
Söderbaum, F. 2007. African Regionalism and EU-African Interregionalism. In *European Union and New Regionalism. Regional Actors and Global Governance in a Post-hegemonic Era*, 2nd ed., ed. M. Telò, 185–202. Aldershot and Burlington: Ashgate.
Söderbaum, F., and T.M. Shaw (eds.). 2003. *Theories of New Regionalism. A Palgrave Reader*. Basingstoke: Palgrave Macmillan.
Spindler, M. 2005. *Regionalismus im Wandel. Die neue Logik der Region in einer globalen Ökonomie*. Wiesbaden: VS Verlag für Sozialwisenschaften.
Söderbaum, F., and P. Stålgren. 2010. The EU and the Global South. In *The European Union and the Global South*, ed. F. Söderbaum and P. Stålgren, 1-11. Boulder: Lynne Rienner.
Telò M. (ed.). 2007. *European Union and New Regionalism. Regional Actors and Global Governance in a Post-Hegemonic Era*. The International Political Economy of New Regionalism Series, 2nd ed. Burlington: Ashgate.
Viner, J. 1950. *The Customs Union Issue*. New York: The Carnegie Endowment for International Peace.
Vogt, J. 2007. *Die Regionale Integration des südlichen Afrikas. Unter besonderer Betrachtung der Southern African Development Community (SADC)*. Baden-Baden: Nomos.
Waltz, K. 1979. *Theory of International Politics*. Reading, MA.: Addison-Wesley.
Warleigh-Lack, A. 2008. Studying Regionalisation Comparatively. A Conceptual Framework. In *Regionalisation and Global Governance. The Taming of Globalisation?* ed. A.F. Cooper, C.W. Hughes, and P. de Lombaerde, 43–60. London and New York: Routledge.
Warleigh-Lack, A., and B. Rosamond. 2011. Introduction. In *New Regionalism and the European Union. Dialogues, comparisons and New Research Directions*, ed. A. Warleigh-Lack, N. Robinson, and B. Rosamond, 3–17. Abingdon: Routledge.

Warleigh-Lack, A., and L. Van Langenhove. 2010. Rethinking EU Studies: The Contribution of Comparative Regionalism. *Journal of European Integration* 32 (6): 541–562.

Wendt, A. 1992. Anarchy is what States Make of It: The Social Construction of Power Politics. *International Organization* 46 (2): 391–425.

Zimmerling, R. 1991. *Externe Einflüsse auf die Integration von Staaten. Zur politikwissenschaftlichen Theorie regionaler Zusammenschlüsse*. Freiburg: Verlag Karl Alber.

CHAPTER 2

Theoretical Approach: The Situation-Structural Model as an Analytical Tool to Explain Regionalism

The phenomenon of new regionalism in the South can be neither analysed nor sufficiently explained without looking beyond the selected region under observation. This is the logical implication of an increasingly interdependent and globalising world that feeds back to political thinking as well as theorising international relations. In view of the above, the author develops a theoretical approach to the analysis of regionalism that builds on the situation-structural model (Zürn 1992, 1993) to the study of international cooperation. The applied theoretical model is innovative insofar as it takes the external dimension and the impact of extra-regional actors on regionalism explicitly into account. In this respect, the term external, synonymous to extra-regional, shall refer to a relation to any actor (country or organisation) that is not part of a group that has been previously defined as a (geographically or politically) confined region (cf. Zimmerling 1991: 57).

2.1 INTRODUCTORY REMARKS

Any political science analysis that seeks to gain profound knowledge of regional cooperation, regionalism and the emergence, design and effectiveness of regional integration organisations demands an adequate theoretical approach and a clear definition of the underlying terms and concepts. However, the many years of studying global regionalism by a countless number of professionals have "blessed" the academic literature of this field of research with nearly as many concepts and an array of specialist terms. This chapter's primary purpose is to introduce central concepts and terms that are important for understanding this book's object of research. This includes a clarification of important notions by clear definitions as well as a delineation of conceptual ideas. Moreover, this chapter provides the theoretical framework for the analysis, which is of key importance in order to explain the logic of regional integration from a political science perspective as well as to better understand the empirical observation.

In a nutshell, this study adopts a constraint rationalist theory to explore the conditions under which regional cooperation takes place and becomes successful. It seeks to explain why and in which way international institutions—here, regional institutions—are established or, to put it differently, constructed by states. Cooperation problems in a regional setting of complex interdependence are assumed to be the decisive factors that lead to the emergence of institutionalised regional cooperation and global regionalism. This phenomenon will be analysed and explained by applying an extended situation-structural model that takes the possible impact of extra-regional actors on regional cooperation problems explicitly into account.

2.1.1 Conceptualisation of Regions and Regionalism

Generally speaking, a region is a spatial area that shares a certain set of common characteristics by which it can be distinguished from other areas. A glance at the scientific literature reveals that concepts of regions and regionalism are neither consistent nor fixed with regard to their meaning. This is because they are used in a different manner in different disciplines. In geography, for example, most definitions of a region generally accentuate geographical proximity but can also put a focus on common natural features such as climate, topography or vegetation (Cahnman 1944). In sociology, in contrast, a region is an area where a certain socio-cultural homogeneity exists that manifests, for example, in terms of a common social class, occupation, ethnicity, language, customs or religion (Cox 1969).

In political science in general and in the field of international relations in particular, regions are often understood as macro-regions, that is intergovernmental or supranational subsystems within the international system, whose constituents are states that are geographically close and share some degree of interdependence (Hettne 2005: 544; Nye 1968b:

VII). Thus, geographical proximity is still an important factor because without this limitation "the term "regionalism" becomes diffuse and unmanageable" (Hurrell 1995: 333). Following these views, regionalism shall be understood as planned, multilateral, and state-led organisation of interdependence within a confined regional space that manifests in various, multidimensional or specific regional projects and accompanying formal institutions (Bach 2003: 22; Breslin and Higgot 2000: 344; Stein 1993: 316).

Although a number of theoretical approaches and scholars might possibly challenge this rather reductionist and allegedly abridged perception of regionalism for good reasons (Hettne and Söderbaum 1998; Söderbaum and Shaw 2003), a state-centric approach will be applied in this book because it favours the analysis of structural features and causal relations on the macro level. Furthermore, to presume that the states remain the central actors in international relations is not least a major guiding principle of virtually all mainstream theories in this field of research.

Some scholars have a dyadic understanding of regionalism (Bhalla and Bhalla 1997: 21; Ravenhill 2008; Warleigh-Lack 2008). They subdivide the phenomenon according to empirical observations as well as theoretical explanatory models into the two categories of so-called "old" and "new" regionalism.

Old regionalism is a phenomenon of the Cold War period. It is strongly institution- or government-driven and puts an emphasis on issues related to planned development, security and intra-regional trade. This is sometimes referred to as inward-oriented regionalism (Hettne 1999: 7–8). Regional integration organisations that belong to the so-called old regionalism aim particularly for import substitution and trade discrimination against the rest of the world. They generally do not overlap and their members are part of either the Global South or North (Bhalla and Bhalla 1997: 21).

New regionalism, in contrast, is a phenomenon of the post–Cold War world and the age of globalisation. It is strongly market-driven and puts an emphasis on regional trade liberalisation, export promotion, investment and non-discrimination against the rest of the world. That is why it is sometimes referred to as outward-oriented or open regionalism (Hettne 1999: 7–8). Regional integration organisations of this type do sometimes comprise members from the Global South and North and their constituents do often belong to more than one regional integration organisation. This is said to lead to the frequent overlapping of two or more organisations that count as new regionalisms (Bhalla and Bhalla 1997: 21).

This book recognises some differences between both categories but does not adopt the idea of a clear-cut distinction or antagonism (Hettne and Söderbaum 2008: 62) between the old and new regionalism. Instead, it suggests a rather universal and timeless theoretical approach towards explaining regional cooperation and the emergence of regionalism. This shall become clear in the following sections of this chapter.

The term "regionalism" should not be confused with the terms "regional cooperation" or "regional integration". Regional cooperation may occur in all fields of politics when countries' actions "are brought in conformity with one another through a process of policy coordination" (Keohane 1984: 51) in order to achieve a common goal for mutual benefits. Regional cooperation is often issue-centred and does not necessarily have to be accompanied by the creation of common formal institutions.[1] Therefore, joining and leaving such loose cooperation arrangements do not involve high costs, which means that loyalty to the cooperating partners can be rather limited.

Regional integration is generally considered to have a more binding character compared with regional cooperation because it implies the establishment of formal institutions and demands a (partial) surrender of states' sovereignty rights. This is highlighted by Haas's definition of "political integration" which he understands as a "process whereby political actors in several distinct national setting are persuaded to shift their loyalties, expectations and political activities toward a new centre, whose institutions possess or demand jurisdiction over the pre-existing national states" (Haas 1958: 16). Such a new centre—for example, a regional integration organisation—goes beyond more or less committing regional cooperation initiatives (such as a common Declaration of Intention or Memorandum of Understanding) because it always gains a certain legitimate capacity to act on its own. Defective action and exit from (or entry into) such institutional arrangements become comparably difficult and costly for any member involved.

For practical reasons, however, the terms "regional integration" and "regionalism" shall be applied rather synonymously in the course of this book although the notion "regional integration" can *strictu sensu* refer to a static as well as a dynamic state of affairs—depending on the context (Bach 2003: 22; Hurrell 1995: 334).

2.1.2 The Nexus of Regionalism and Cooperation Theory

Regionalism shall be understood as a cluster of various, multidimensional regional cooperation projects bounded by a territorial dimension confined by its member states. This lean conception has the advantage of making the phenomenon of regionalism tangible for basic theories of rational action and (international) cooperation. With respect to international relations theories, this understanding of regionalism fairs well with the theory-driven debate on the emergence and functioning of nonhierarchic international/regional regimes (Gehring 1996: 232; Gehring and Oberthür 1997: 17). The conceptual characteristics of regionalism—according to this book's definition—and international regimes match very closely and have a common theoretical background. This is most obvious if one takes the central meaning of institutions into account: Regionalism can be subdivided into a multitude of issue-specific institutionalised regional cooperation projects, whereas international regimes can be understood as issue-specific cooperative agreements among a specific number of countries within a region (Gehring and Oberthür 1997: 15; Hasenclever et al. 1997: 57; Stein 1982: 317).

Following this understanding, a regional integration organisation represents not only the individual member states as a group but also the embracing superstructure of all issue-specific institutionalised regional cooperation projects that are part of the organisation. The strongly integrated and highly differentiated EU serves as a good example for this understanding of regionalism because it can be interpreted as a multi-layered system of nested international cooperation projects with respective institutions under the umbrella of a common organisational superstructure (Gehring 1994: 216; 2002; Hoffmann 1982: 33–35; Moravcsik 1998: 15).

Deepening regional integration is a continual process whereby the member countries of a regional integration project/organisation increasingly create, enhance and modify common regional institutions in order to better realise absolute cooperative gains. The dynamics of regional integration are reflected accordingly in the number, array and sequence of consecutive regional cooperation projects and their related institutional manifestation (e.g. common regulations, protocols and institutional bodies or physical achievements). Therefore, positive dynamics imply a growing horizontal and vertical expansion and consolidation of regional institutions whereas negative dynamics imply a standstill and tendencies of institutional disintegration. Critics may argue that this conceptualisation of dynamics is too static. However, this idea follows Andrew Moravcsik, who understood the dynamics of regional integration as a series of interlinked "grand" bargains; and he demonstrated the appropriateness of his concept in the case of the European integration (Moravcsik 1998). The logic behind this conceptualisation of dynamics does make sense because the impact of an existing institution may lead to a new situation in international relations and trigger states' demand to engage in further cooperation and establish related follow-up institutions.

Since regionalism is conceptualised as a cluster of various issue-specific or multidimensional institutionalised regional cooperation projects, it must be emphasised that regionalism should not be confined to a single, isolated issue area.[2] In this current era of neoliberalism and economisation, however, this statement is often challenged: With the economistic paradigm dominating global practice and thought at the present time, it is particularly the followers of economic and politico-economic approaches to the study of international relations who often misleadingly equate regionalism with plain regional market integration (Mansfield and Milner 1999: 592; Winters 1999: 8). However, this view on regionalism, with its focus on the economic sphere and a narrowly defined economic logic of international and regional interaction, is too simplistic (Hurrell 1995: 337). In fact, it does not provide satisfactory explanatory power for other important issue areas beyond the realm of the economy and thus falls short to explain why regional security cooperation has often been the nucleus of many regionalisms (e.g. ASEAN, AU, EU or SADC).

From an epistemological point of view, inherent to this work's understanding of regionalism is a constraint rational-choice approach to international relations. This perception allows an application of game and cooperation theory as a starting point for the analysis of the emergence, design and effectiveness of institutionalised regional cooperation and therefore follows the neo-institutionalist school of thought in a broader sense. Although this procedure is surely not the most comprehensive way to interpret and explain reality in every detail, the proposed theoretical approach is best suited for this book's analysis because it allows an illustration and modelling of (problem) structures, causalities and development trends on an abstract macro level by means of reduction in complexity (Keohane 1982: 329–331).

2.1.3 Complex Interdependence and the Demand for Institutionalised Regional Cooperation

According to the (neo)realist school of thought, the international system is structured by anarchy and characterised by the absence of any hierarchic order or global coercive mechanism. A norm-setting and rule-enforcing institutional arrangement—for example, a *Weltstaat* (world state) does not exist. Against this background of insecurity, states are basically well advised to pursue their interests without consideration for third parties in order to maximise their individual welfare, accumulate gains and thus ultimately safeguard their survival. In view of these underlying assumptions, egoistic action becomes rational action and it is the relative gains that finally count for every actor and make a difference to its competitors (Grieco 1997; Waltz 1979). However, anarchy in the international system does not necessarily imply the threatening, cooperation-averse and eventually war-torn scenario that has been bluntly exemplified by Thomas Hobbes in his opus *Leviathan*. In contrast to (neo) realism, cooperation theory and rational institutionalism argue that egoistic, utility-maximising actors are principally enticed to cooperate under conditions of anarchy if they face specific situations where a strategy of cooperation is mutually beneficial and leads to absolute gains (Axelrod and Keohane 1993; Keohane 1982; Oye 1985; Taylor 1987).

The incentive for international cooperation emanates first and foremost from the structure of the international system and its inherent collective action (or cooperation) problems. The latter refer to recurrent constellations of interests where actors' individual rationality entails strategies and actions that may "lead to a strictly Pareto-inferior outcome, that is, an outcome which is strictly less preferred by every individual than at least one other outcome" (Taylor 1987: 19). In international relations, cooperation problems are principally based on a structural phenomenon called international interdependence—which can be described as "mutual dependence" (Keohane and Nye 1977: 7).

Cooperation problems in international relations are based on patterns of complex interdependence between various actors in various specific issue areas of international politics.[3] Generally speaking, "interdependence in world politics refers to situations characterized by reciprocal effects among countries or among actors in different countries" (Keohane and Nye 1977: 7). This understanding implies that policies, actions, and policy outcomes of one individual state are not isolated events in international relations but rather are interlinked and, to a certain extent, a function of the strategies and actions of its counterparts (Keohane and Nye 1987: 730–731, 737–740; Stein 1982: 301). In fact, one actor's egoistic and unilateral policies and actions in a certain issue area almost inevitably produce externalities for all other actors involved. Therefore, an interdependent relationship can bear costly effects insofar as it principally restricts the respective actors' autonomy—at least as long as joint gains are not generated from a state of interdependence by means of policy coordination and collective action (Keohane and Nye 1977: 8).

The concept of complex interdependence extends the notion of interdependence for three reasons: It emphasises the plurality of (possibly interdependent) issues and the absence of hierarchies among issues in international politics. In contrast to (neo)realist thinking, a primacy of power, security or force is not presupposed. Furthermore, the concept assumes that states will refrain from the use of military force towards each other for asserting their interests under such conditions of complex interdependence because they are easily vulnerable due to the circumstance of a multifaceted mutual dependency (Keohane and Nye 1977: 21). Therefore, complex interdependence implies, in particular, that interdependence is multi-layered and occurs in virtually every policy field of international politics such as trade, infrastructure, climate, environment or security. For this reason, security-related cooperation problems[4] in international relations, for example, are based primarily on security interdependence while economic cooperation problems are based on economic interdependence (Wallander and Keohane 1999; Zürn 1992).

Against a background of complex interdependence, actors' demand for coordination or cooperation accrues not only from the actors' perception of an existent and recurrent cooperation problem but particularly from their cost-benefit calculations concerning possible solutions thereof. Any rational-egoist actor's preference[5] will be in favour of a cooperative strategy if the (expected) absolute gains of such action surpass the related costs and pay-offs of unilateral strategies and an uncoordinated status quo. In this respect, cooperation may not only create a collective good but help actors to achieve individually Pareto-superior outcomes while any unconstrained individual strategy of action would lead instead to Pareto-suboptimal results (Zürn 1987: 9–10). Stein systematised this logic and highlights two general situations under which rational-egoistic actors have strong incentives to cooperate: firstly, "dilemmas of common interest" where any resolution requires the involved actors' active engagement and the commitment for collaboration and collective action; secondly, "dilemmas of common aversion" where actors seek to avoid an undesired outcome by means of coordination (Stein 1982: 316).

Once a dilemma of common aversion is resolved through coordination, the solution is expected to be rather stable and even self-enforcing as long as rules are specified and all actors act accordingly. However, once a collective good has been created by a sufficient number of actors following a cooperative strategy of action, the actors' demand to sustain the cooperative arrangement by sticking to the same collective strategy of action could always be challenged by the incentive of "free-riding". The latter implies following a unilateral, non-cooperative strategy of action in order to maximise individual benefits to the disadvantage of the collective. Rational-egoistic actors' enticement to become free-riders is based on simple cost-benefit calculations because the most attractive option is always to consume the benefits of a collective good without bearing the costs for it (Gehring 1994: 214–215; Krasner 1982: 194–196). Therefore, an initial demand for cooperation does not necessarily guarantee a lasting collective solution. It is the actors' mixed motives and their latent tendency to free-ride that ultimately are responsible for the "dilemmas of cooperation" which occur in many situations where social interaction takes place—for example, in international relations and world politics (Axelrod and Keohane 1993; Taylor 1987).

Therefore, the nature of complex interdependence among actors does ultimately produce every cooperation problem and specifies its structural characteristics. With regard to the latter, this has a decisive effect on the actors' actual predisposition in terms of demand for a particular institutional solution. The nature of the pattern of interdependence among actors significantly shapes an actor's strength of demand to cooperate and brings the necessary institutions into being. Hence, any actor's demand for an institutional solution to an existing cooperation problem depends on two central factors:

Firstly, the demand for institutions depends to a varying extent on the structural character of the underlying cooperation problem (Young 1982: 288). With reference to the terminology and taxonomy of game theory, it will be zero in situations of harmony and increasingly strong in situations resembling mixed-motive games such as coordination games (with distributive conflict) or dilemmas of common interests (Rittberger 1990: 360–361; Zürn 1987: 6, 36, 44–45). According to Keohane and others, the most common cooperation problems in international relations resemble mixed-motive games (i.e. a situation in which actors' interests are to some extent in conflict and at the same time partly converging) such as prisoner's dilemmas (Hasenclever et al. 1997: 46; Stein 1982: 308).

Examples include issues of climate and marine protection, trade liberalisation, and nuclear arms control. The issue area of security is no exception since security-related collective action problems are called security dilemmas (Herz 1950; Jervis 1978; Wagner 1983: 337). The latter are reminiscent of a classic prisoner's dilemma where states face a constant military threat—or at least security risks—due to mutual uncertainty and lack of information about the military capabilities and intentions of their counterparts (Wallander and Keohane 1999: 25–29). Despite these, other types of cooperation problems in international relations do exist and may correspond to coordination situations or assurance games such as problems of international standardisation or problems involving coordinated action against an external threat or attack (Oye 1985; Stein 1982).

Secondly, increasing levels of interdependence among actors generate increasing demand for cooperation and institution-building for plain structural reasons (Hurrell 1995: 350; Keohane and Nye 1977; Young 1982: 287). This is because the cooperation problems increasingly emerge in parallel to a growing number of connecting factors among actors. Likewise, the degree of intensity of an interdependent relation affects the demand for cooperation insofar as a strong level of mutual interdependence generally implies—ceteris paribus—the prospect of higher cooperation gains compared with what can be expected under similar conditions with a low level of mutual interdependence (Young 1969: 741–743). With a view to international relations, these theoretical assumptions are easy to understand with regard to infrastructure connections and trade relations. For example, in regions with predominantly developing countries and therefore a rather low level of intra-regional economic interdependence, demand for regional economic cooperation will be generally weaker than in regions characterised by a strong level of intra-regional economic interdependence. For structural reasons, one can therefore expect to see more institutions emerging under conditions similar to the first scenario than under conditions similar to the second. However, the strength of interdependence among actors—this must be pointed out—may principally vary not only from region to region in geographic terms but also from one policy area to another—even within the same region (Young 1969: 727).

Different structures of cooperation problems imply demand for different institutional solutions. Correspondingly, there will be a variance in the institutional design and the degree of formality of the regulative institutions coming into being. The reason for this is that the nature of a cooperation problem specifies appropriate demands towards an adequate institutional solution that best meets the involved actors' requirements in assuring mutual cooperation and facilitating the generation of cooperation gains.

Informal or rather weakly formalised institutions are expected to materialise in situations reminiscent of (recurrent) coordination games with distributive effects. This is because institutionalised cooperation may develop quite "automatically" after a short period of time through repeated interaction on the condition that actors apply reciprocal strategies of tit-for-tat (Axelrod 1987). A cooperative solution, once it is found, will be self-enforcing under these conditions and the problem of cheating hardly exists. For these reasons, institutions in the form of coordination regimes are generally less formalised since the need for strong compliance mechanisms that ensure cooperative behaviour is low. Instead they provide an arena that facilitates the resolving of conflicts of interests (e.g. concerning the distribution of cooperative gains) and finding of a corresponding solution (Hasenclever et al. 1997: 48–49).

Comparably stronger and more formalised institutions are likely to emerge in situations resembling (recurrent) dilemmas of common interest. Rational actors facing a prisoner's dilemma situation, for example, have the dominant strategy to defect, even though this would lead to Pareto-inefficient outcomes. Even under iterated conditions, strategies of reciprocity, and constant pay-off structures, the chance for a spontaneous cooperative solution is rather low because cheating and unilateral free-riding remain tempting options for all actors at any time (Oye 1985: 12–13). In order to achieve a Pareto-superior solution and put absolute cooperative gains for all actors into effect, dilemma-type situations require concrete and formalised ex-ante institutions in the form of collaborative regimes. Rational actors anticipate this necessity and frame their demands in this respect according to their cost-benefit calculations (Gehring 1994: 214–215; Hasenclever et al. 1997: 48–49).

In summary, demand for institutionalised cooperation depends, in principle, on two factors: firstly, on the degree of interdependence among actors; secondly—and more decisively—on the specific structure of the underlying cooperation problem. For this reason, the degree of formalisation and the specific functions of different cooperative institutions are manifold.

2.1.4 The Added Value of Institutions as Catalysts for Cooperation

International and regional cooperation does not come about by itself. It has become clear that it is in particular dilemmas of common interest where cooperation is difficult to achieve because actors have incentives to free-ride. Here, institutions come into play because they can make a difference:

According to rational institutionalism and regime theory, international institutions may act as catalysts of international cooperation—provided a recurrence of the respective cooperation problem (Keohane 1984; Krasner 1982; Scharpf 2000; Stein 1982). This is because they reduce the incentives for free-riding and instead make a different strategy of action (here, a cooperative strategy) more rational for the actors involved. In a nutshell, institutions facilitate, consolidate, ensure and—at best—advance and deepen cooperation among rational-egoistic actors under circumstances where unilateral, unconstrained action otherwise would not provide for individually and collectively improved pay-offs (i.e. mutually beneficial outcomes) (Hasenclever et al. 1997: 32–36).

The added value of institutions seems clear in regard to this enumeration above, but how do they achieve this difficult task? Generally speaking, institutions provide a variety of different mechanisms that nevertheless have a similar effect: facilitate and stabilise cooperation by creating circumstances that make actors more secure and comfortable to respond to each other in a cooperative manner for the sake of reaping mutual benefits. In the context of our international system that is characterised by the absence of a global hierarchical authority and the periodical occurrence of (potential) interstate conflict, institutions help to remove mutual mistrust and uncertainty among states, stabilise mutual expectations and reduce transaction costs (Keohane 1988: 386).

According to Keohane (1984: 85–109, 1988, 1998), Zürn (1992: 140–150) and others (Hurrell 1995: 350; Oye 1985: 11, 20–22), these objectives can be achieved because international institutions:

- Generate and enhance a "shadow of the future" (i.e. enhance the actors' willingness to follow strategies of reciprocity, perpetuate the political relationship between them over time and stabilise their mutual expectations with regard to future behaviour)
- Promote transparency and systematic monitoring
- Reduce information costs or provide information (e.g. through monitoring)
- Promote cooperative behaviour and reputation (e.g. by institutionalising interaction, providing an arena for exchange and discussion, and by defining standards that allow the measurement and review of compliance and performance)
- Identify or discourage (or both) defection and free-riding (e.g. with the help of monitoring or sanctioning mechanisms or both)
- Encourage actors' commitment to cooperation and "lock-in" cooperation agreements (with monitoring mechanisms and by, for example, increasing costs of non-compliance, defection and free-riding)
- Foster cross-linking various political issues (this implies that actors' positive experiences of cooperating in one policy area may lead to cooperation in another, somehow related issue area; additionally, issue linkage implies that failing to comply in one issue could have negative/costly effects with regard to cooperation in a related policy area).

International institutions make lasting international cooperation possible because they lead to a change in actors' behaviour and provide—once established—concrete instructions on behaviour/action by means of regulative mechanisms (codified in their inherent norms, principles and rules) that consolidate and foster cooperation (Krasner 1976; Stein 1982: 317). This understanding corresponds to the book's earlier conceptualisation of regionalism where similarities to international regimes (on a regional level) have been outlined.

However, one could ask whether these general assumptions also count for the policy field of "security". Do international institutions make any sense or difference in this issue area of so-called "high politics"? The answer is yes they do! All of the abovementioned assumptions and functions concerning international institutions remain valid with respect to the policy area of security. This fact needs an emphasis because mainstream integration theories (in particular, those related to the political economy school of thought) often seem to neglect this "inconvenient" issue area. Followers of (neo)realism even hold the view that lasting international cooperation is rather improbable in this issue area of security since conditions of an international self-help system prevail. They assume that cooperation among states may occur only in form of short-term ad hoc alliances or as a result of hegemonic coercion (Gilpin 1987; Kindleberger 1981).

In contrast to the latter, followers of cooperation theory and rational institutionalism postulate that security problems based on mutual threat or external risk likewise can be interpreted as collective action or coordination problems that generate common interests, demand collective action or coordination efforts and can be solved with the help of institutions (Buzan and Wæver 2003; Morgan 1997). In the language of game theory, situations like the first are reminiscent of a classic security dilemma. The latter is a dilemma of common interest where all actors prefer a peaceful coexistence but have the dominant strategy to follow at least a policy of deterrence. The second situation resembles a dilemma of common aversion where all actors seek to avoid to be left alone acting against a common threat since they derive the greatest benefit from the mutual assurance to take joint action (Wallander et al. 1999: 6–8; Zürn 1992: 174–184).

Analogous to the added value of international institutions, security arrangements and security management institutions can reduce uncertainty and mutual threat by providing transparency, information or monitoring mechanisms (Jervis 1982; Rittberger and Zürn 1990: 52). They help to extend the "shadow of the future", control risk, offer an arena for communication and consultations, facilitate policy coordination (e.g. against an external threat), and ideally promote and reward cooperative behaviour among its members. Thus, security institutions operate principally in the same way as any other institutions and likewise can help to achieve Pareto-superior outcomes for all actors involved (Rittberger and Zürn 1991; Wallander and Keohane 1999: 21–23). Needless to say, these general assumptions on the added value of international security institutions apply to the regional level as well.

In sum and with reference to all issue areas of international politics, institutions—and in particular their inherent codified norms, principles and rules—alleviate more Pareto-efficient cooperation and help participating states to achieve gains from collective action. They facilitate integration because they can act as a "tracking system" for further and deeper steps of cooperation and "lock-in" cooperation arrangements over time by assuring the participants' credible commitment (Keohane 1984; Moravcsik 1998). In their capacity as catalysts of interaction and mutually beneficial regional cooperation, the regulative and "civilising" elements of international institutions increase collective and country-specific absolute welfare and foster a stable and peaceful international environment. Thus, on condition of their effectiveness, international and regional institutions ideally contribute to sustainable development in a broader sense (Rittberger 1990: 360–361; Zürn 1987: 6, 36, 44–45).

2.2 THE SITUATION-STRUCTURAL MODEL

The theoretical approach of this book builds on rational institutionalism and cooperation and game theory. Its main purpose is to scientifically analyse and elaborate the emergence, design and effectiveness of regionalism by taking potential external influence explicitly into account. However, Keohane argues that "rationalistic theories of institutions need to be historically contextualized" (Keohane 1988: 393) because plain rationalist analyses fall short in clarifying and explaining the (concomitants of) occurrence, appearance, configuration and functioning of non-hierarchic international and regional institutions thoroughly.

Against this background, Zürn's situation-structural model (Zürn 1987, 1992, 1993) shall serve as the guiding theoretical framework for this work's analysis of regionalism. An important reason to select Zürn's approach relates to the fact that situation-structuralists address the issue of cooperation problems and institutionalised international cooperation regardless (!) of certain predefined policy areas or an exclusive geographical setting. Accordingly, situation structuralists assume that whether actors create international institutions and what the nature of the respective institutional solutions will be depend only on the specific situational structure and situational context of an international cooperation problem (Hasenclever et al. 1997: 53). Since the situation-structural model does not have narrow self-imposed restrictions, notably with regard to geographical settings and policy areas, it best serves to analyse global regionalism because the scope conditions and explanatory power of this theoretical approach are comprehensive and universal.

In order to gain valid research findings, it is important to accurately model the situation structure of the real-world cooperation problem under investigation according to game theory terminology—and this is best done in the form of a matrix. With regard to the field of international relations, this can be challenging because one has to strictly avoid ex-post modelling on the grounds of the observed outcomes. According to Zürn, the procedure on how to properly model a real-world situation structure is as follows:

In a first step, a clear-cut issue area for analysis (e.g. a particular cooperation problem with distinct "boundaries") has to be selected. Secondly, the most important actors involved (e.g. a certain group of states) have to be identified. Thirdly, the central behavioural options perceived by these actors (for themselves) have to be worked out and the actors' ordinal preferences have to be determined. This shall be done with the help of recognised qualitative and quantitative research methods and this includes gathering empirical evidence and also explicitly reflecting on the historical background of the specific conflicting situation and the participating actors (Rittberger 1993: 12; Zürn 1992: 151). With respect to determining the structure of a real-world situation on the basis of exogenous information, it is important to deduce the actors' preferences independently of their actual behaviour. In order to avoid ex-post modelling and circular reasoning, preferences must never be traced back to the actors' observed action (Rittberger and Zürn 1990: 38–39; Zürn 1993: 65–66).

With this technical procedure on how to abstract a complex pattern of interaction and how to model the situation structure of a real-world cooperation problem in the field of international relations in mind, the next steps are to explain the emergence, institutional design and effectiveness of institutionalised regional cooperation and provide details on the logic of regional integration.

2.2.1 Regionalism Under Primarily Regional Conditions: Internal Line of the Argument

This subchapter focuses on the analysis and explanation of regionalism under primarily regional conditions. This specification on "regional conditions" actually shall not be understood as a restriction, because it is entirely in accordance with the standards of situation structuralism where a chosen issue area shall be constrained by "clear enough boundaries so that it can be modelled being distinct form other interaction patterns" (Zürn 1993: 65). For this reason, this chapter explains the common logic of "classic" situation structuralism on how to analyse and explain institutionalised regional cooperation which I call the "internal line of the argument" because of its focus on the regional setting.

2.2.1.1 Problematic Situations and the Demand for Institutionalised Regional Cooperation

In order to explain the demand for institutionalised regional cooperation, it is first necessary to identify the underlying cause of this demand. According to situation-structuralists, demand for institutionalised regional cooperation can be traced back to patterns of interaction and the inherent structure of a situation. A (recurrent) cooperation problem or, to be more precise, problematic situation[6] on the ground of complex interdependence in international relations provides the basic incentives for states to engage in mutual cooperation and establish regulative institutions (Taylor 1987: 19; Zürn 1987, 1992, 1993). This is the fundamental prerequisite and sine qua non for any demand and subsequent emergence of institutionalised regional cooperation. A problematic situation in regional relations is therefore the <u>independent variable</u> with regard to the rise of regionalism.

Against the background of the aforementioned basic assumptions of game and cooperation theory (Axelrod 1987; Oye 1985; Stein 1982), problematic situations can be modelled and illustrated by means of different types of games (Zürn 1993: 69–70). The situation-structural approach distinguishes four ideal types of problematic situations on the basis of their situation structure:

- Coordination situations without distributional conflict ("assurance" game)
- Coordination situations with distributional conflict ("battle of the sexes" game)
- Collaboration situations (dilemma situations; "prisoner's dilemma game")
- Suasion situations ("Rambo" game).[7]

The classification above has a meaning for theorising the formation and development of regionalism. This is because different types of situation structures imply different degrees of propensity to the emergence of international cooperation and the formation of common regulative institutions (Rittberger and Zürn 1990; Zürn 1992, 1993).

In accordance with the ordinal order of the list, cooperation is comparably easy to achieve in problematic situations corresponding to coordination games without distributional conflict (assurance games) and slightly more difficult to accomplish in those reminiscent of coordination games with distributional conflict (battle of the sexes games). This is because rational utility-maximising actors in such problematic situations tend to identify a mutually beneficial cooperative solution rather quickly and have thereafter no incentives to unilaterally defect from cooperation once a tangible solution has been recognised and consolidated.

In contrast, cooperation is more difficult to achieve in situation structures resembling the dilemma type and is most difficult to accomplish in so-called "Rambo" games. This is because these latter types of collective action problems have no salient solutions, and rational utility-maximising actors are unlikely to follow a cooperative strategy ab initio. Moreover, they always have strong incentives to free-ride. In the case of Rambo-type situations, one actor reaches the individually optimal outcome only by following a strategy of defection (Rittberger 1993: 15).

Hence, it depends in principle on the character and structure of an underlying problematic situation—i.e. the type of game—as to what degree a realisation of international cooperation is likely and how strong the need and demand for regulative institutions will be (Zürn 1993: 69–70). Institutionalised regional cooperation with its specific design and inherent set of rules at its core—i.e. regionalism in the sense of the states' codified response to a specific problematic situation in international relations—is therefore the *explanandum* and constitutes the dependent variable in the course of this analysis.

In addition, the situation-structural model assumes that intervening context variables can affect situation structures and have an influence on the solvability of a cooperation problem. Recurring to the ordinal list above (this time in reversed order), each of these four different types of problematic situations is, to a different degree, prone to intervening context variables regarding the formation of an institutionalised solution. Context variables are assumed to be most relevant and influential in problematic situations corresponding to Rambo games and (to a lesser degree) dilemma games. In contrast, they have principally less relevance in problematic situations corresponding to coordination problems with distributional conflict (battle of the sexes games) and only rather little relevance in the case of coordination problems without distributional conflict (assurance games). The reason for the different situations' different degrees of conduciveness to the influence of intervening context variables resides basically in their inherent structural pattern and thus in their different degrees of propensity to international cooperation (as explained before). Therefore, the relevance of intervening context variables for achieving cooperation and an institutionalised solution increases in parallel with a problematic situation's "level of difficulty" in terms of solvability (Zürn 1992: 168–220, 1993: 69–70).

According to Zürn and the game theory literature, a number of potential context variables may become relevant and exert influence on the formation of institutionalised cooperation (Zürn 1993: 70). However, the factor "power" is generally seen as the most pivotal context variable—not least since power is a recognised key aspect in the international relations field of research (Keohane and Nye 1977; Martin 1992: 783–786; Stein 1993: 319; Zürn 1993: 70). For this reason, the factor "power" shall gain focal attention in this book and serve as the decisive context variable with regard to the theoretical framework and empirical analysis. Therefore, aspects of power distribution between states are carefully scrutinised in the course of the analysis.

2.2.1.2 Regional Power Distribution and Its Impact on the Establishment and Design of Regional Institutions

Keeping its meaning as the most important context variable in mind, the factor power not only has strong influence on the occurrence of international cooperation but has a significant impact on the nature of an institutional solution—in other words, its institutional design. However, what exactly is "power" and how can it be conceptualised for this theoretical framework? Freely adapted from Max Weber, power can be defined as "the ability of an actor to get others to do something they otherwise would not do (and at an acceptable cost to the actor)" (Keohane and Nye 2001: 10). Other scholars determine power as "go-it-alone power" in the sense of freedom to act without constrains (Gruber 2000). Classic international relations theories determine a state's power position in the international arena by the strength of its capabilities in relation to other countries (i.e. by the nature of the relative power distribution among all actors) (Grieco 1988; Morgenthau 1948; Waltz 1979).

This book conceptualises power in a slightly different way and supplements the assumptions of (neo)realist thinking. Owing to the theoretical framework's orientation on structure and interdependence, this work follows Keohane and Nye's argument and idea of power. Both do not say that "classic" power resources are totally obsolete, but emphasise the close relation of patterns of interdependence and potential power resources in a given issue area. They argue that "it is *asymmetries* in interdependence [...] that are most likely to provide sources of influence for actors in their dealings with one another" (Keohane and Nye 2001: 268). According to this understanding, power implies not only control over (power) resources and actors but control over events and outcomes (Keohane and Nye 1977; Young 1969: 747).

This line of argument points out that a state's relative power does not primarily rest on its absolute power in classic terms of military or economic capacity. Instead, a country's power is situationally determined by its overall and particularly issue-specific power position on the basis of asymmetric interdependence. This aspect must be kept in mind with regard to modelling situation structures and the operationalisation of power as a (potentially) intervening context variable.

Now that we have clarified the nature and origin of power, the question remains how the factor "power" can actually exert an impact on the design of regional institutions. In contrast to spontaneous orders, regionalism belongs to the class of negotiated orders which are "characterized by conscious efforts to agree on their major provisions, explicit consent on the part of individual participants, and formal expression of the results" (Young 1982: 283). In order to understand their process of formation, it is necessary to have a closer look at the preceding interaction—and possibly bargaining—of the involved actors (Young 1982: 282–284).

Assuming that all rational utility-maximising actors have the common interest of obtaining absolute gains from mutually beneficial collective action and cooperation in problematic situations, they nevertheless have divergent and egoistic preferences with regard to the distribution of the contingent costs and assets as well as in respect to the particulars of relevant control and sanctioning mechanisms. These subordinate conflicts on relative gains have been described as "second-order problems" and resemble coordination games with distributional conflict according to game theory modelling (Krasner 1991; Zangl 1994: 284–287). In any case, the involved actors will have to address and solve the issue of second-order problems before any effective international or regional cooperation will take place (Snidal 1985: 934–935).

In order to achieve the individually best outcome, actors engage consequently in negotiations over the institutional embedding and design of a common cooperation project. This is an important as well as conflict-ridden endeavour because the cooperation project's regulative institutions with their inherent principles, norms and rules set the actors' rights and responsibilities. This includes to determine the involved actors' cost-benefit ratio (i.e. their relative gains and individual pay-offs). Hence, every individual actor has strong incentives to pass the costs of an institutionalised solution as much as possible to the others (Zangl 1994: 285).

Although sophisticated arguments may also play a non-negligible role (Gehring 1994: 216), international negotiations on such second-order problems among egoistic, utility-maximising actors are characterised in the first place by bargaining. According to intergovernmental bargaining theory, a country's bargaining power position can be similarly deduced as state power (i.e. from the character of overall—and particularly issue area specific—interdependence between the actors involved). A structure of asymmetric interdependence determines the relative bargaining power of the negotiators because it implies an actor's dependency on a certain outcome and indicates its plausibility of a "threat of non-agreement" based on the availability of attractive unilateral policy alternatives and exit options (Gehring 1995: 207–211; Hirschmann 1945: 16; Keohane and Nye 2001: 9–10, 268–270).

An actor's weak issue-specific bargaining position is rooted in its limited exit options and strong dependence on the cooperative agreement in negotiation. This implies a strong need for a cooperative solution, high cooperative benefits, and lack of attractive unilateral policy alternatives. On the contrary, a strong or superior bargaining position derives from an actor's independence (or at least indifference) to the negotiated cooperative agreement. This implies less need for the cooperative solution, less meaning of the enclosed benefits, or an existence of attractive unilateral policy alternatives—including alternative coalitions—and therefore an availability of plausible exit options (Keohane and Nye 2001: 9–11; Moravcsik 1998: 60–67).

In inter-state bargaining on the regional level, those states that are dependent on their counterparts in a certain issue area and do not have credible exit options at their disposal are likely to find themselves in a comparably weak position during negotiations, particularly if they are not able to plausibly post a threat with an alternative coalition formation.

In contrast, states in a central position—that is, those on which others are dependent—occupy a stronger power position and thus represent essential cornerstones for the occurrence and success of a cooperative arrangement and its institutional framing. On the regional level, such key countries are in a position to foster or inhibit the process of regional integration and may predicate their engagement and participation in regional cooperation projects on their weaker regional partners' willingness to compromise and make concessions (Gehring 1994: 216; 1995: 207–211; Moravcsik 1998: 64–65).

If inter-state negotiations on regional cooperation problems are successful and result in a mutually acceptable agreement, the negotiation outcomes need to be institutionalised in order to obtain a binding character and ensure credible commitment of the involved participants (Gehring and Oberthür 1997: 16). The nature of the institutional enshrinement—that is, the institutionalised regional cooperation project—then will reflect not only the constellation of the participating states' underlying preferences but most prominently the relative power positions of the involved negotiators. This logic has been proven correct with regard to the process of European integration in general and specific regional cooperation projects in Europe, for example the Treaty of Amsterdam, in particular (Moravcsik 1998; Moravcsik and Nicolaïdis 1999: 73–75).

With the factor "power" being the most meaningful context variable, hegemonic actors such as regional great powers play, for plain structural reasons, a pivotal role with regard to the emergence, design and effectiveness of regionalism (Keohane 1988: 387; Zürn 1993: 70). This central assumption is in line with a great deal of scientific literature that offers alternative explanations for regionalism but likewise highlights the crucial meaning of regional powers for successful regional integration (Buzan and Wæver 2003; Mattli 1999; Schirm 2002).

2.2.1.3 Performance and Effectiveness of Regional Institutions

Regional institutions facilitate and stabilise cooperation by various means. In particular, this includes reducing mutual uncertainty (e.g. through the provision of information or reduction of information costs), enhancing the "shadow of the future" (i.e. perpetuating the political relationship), avoiding defection of participating actors (e.g. through monitoring and sanctioning mechanisms), and fostering their commitment and reputation (Oye 1985: 11, 20–22). By these means, institutions facilitate more Pareto-efficient cooperation, avoid collectively suboptimal outcomes, and allow participating actors to siphon off cooperation gains (Rittberger 1990: 360–361; Zürn 1987: 6, 36, 44–45).

However, these aspects are rather general and vague in character. In order to evaluate the performance and effectiveness of regional institutions, which in other words means the impact or success of regionalism (Underdal 1992: 227–229), a clear framework is necessary. The academic literature dealing with "regime effectiveness" and the fundamental question of whether regimes matter at all provides a good starting point for this task (Krasner 1982: 189–194; Mayer et al. 1993: 421; Raustiala 2000; Young 1992). Reference to these approaches is reasonable since the conceptual similarities of international regimes and this work's understanding of regionalism are indeed distinctive.

In order for a regime (or, in this case, an institutionalised regional cooperation project) to become effective, at least two conditions must be fulfilled in advance: implementation and compliance. This is because simply signing and ratifying an international agreement concerning regional cooperation does not mean that it will become effective (Müller 1993: 44–46; Underdal 1998: 6).

Implementation, defined as "measures that governments take to translate international accords into domestic law and policy" (Underdal 1998: 26), is the first and most necessary step for such cooperative arrangements to become functional and take any effect. However, appropriate implementation does not guarantee effectiveness, because paper doesn't blush and norms or rules may not be enforced in some cases for a variety of reasons (Zürn 1997: 54–56).

Compliance is the second necessary condition and shall be understood as "matter of whether and to what degree countries do in fact adhere to the provision of the accord" (Underdal 1992: 26). Compliance, however, should not be seen in binary terms as either "compliant" or "non-compliant," because it can be a complex matter if an accord's obligations are comprehensive, manifold and complex as well. For these reasons, compliance shall instead be understood in terms of a relative degree. This has the conceptual advantages insofar as an actor can be regarded as "compliant" even if 100% fulfilment of obligations cannot be ascertained (yet) (Chayes and Handler Cayes 1993; Young 1992: 162).

Provided that satisfactory (degrees of) implementation and compliance are present, a regional cooperation project's provisions may eventually show performance and effectiveness. While the academic literature distinguishes a variety of possible regime consequences and types of effectiveness (Kohler-Koch 1989: 44–49; Mayer et al. 1993: 424), this book adapts a simplified and very feasible approach to the so-called "problem of effectiveness". Following Oran Young, an institution—or a regime—is first and foremost regarded as effective "to the extent that its operation impels actors to behave differently than they would if the institution did not exist or if some other institutional arrangements were put in its place" (Young 1992: 161). However, this notion emphasises only the aspect of actors' change in behaviour. Effectiveness therefore shall be understood as "problem solving effectiveness" (Downs 2000: 34) with the degree of goal attainment determining the performance and success of an institution (Downs et al. 1996). According to Young, goal-oriented effectiveness is "a measure of the extent to which a regime's (stated or unstated) goals are attained over time" (Young 1994: 144). These views imply a non-dichotomous and rather elastic concept of institutional effectiveness—corresponding to the understanding of compliance—which is understood in terms of relative improvement with respect to a certain reference point (Underdal 1992: 231; Young 1992: 162). Thus, institutional performance and effectiveness do not imply that a cooperation problem is totally solved by the involved institutions, but rather that actors change their behaviour according to the institutional provisions as well as that a certain degree of goal attainment can be observed (Kohler-Koch 1989: 46–47).

Measuring the concrete performance and effectiveness of an institution is a difficult task (Underdal 1992: 229–230). However, it is possible to evaluate the impact and effectiveness of institutionalised cooperation by measuring the difference between the actual outcomes with reference to the situation that would prevail in the absence of the relevant institutional solution to the problematic situation (Keohane 1988: 380). This contra-factual method sets the non-existence of the institutional arrangement as a reference point against which the actual achievements and relative improvements are compared. Hence, measuring effectiveness shall happen on a strictly ordinal level even if numerical values contribute to the evaluation (Underdal 1992: 230, 235–237).

Coming back to regionalism, the measurable effects of regional institutions are likely to correspond to the strength of interdependence between the participating states in a confined issue area. If a low level of mutual interdependence precedes the establishment of a regulative regional institution in a certain problematic situation, the institutional effects and gains from regional cooperation are likewise assumed to be relatively low—at least in comparison with a similar regional institution that has been established on the basis of the same problematic situation but, in contrast, against a background of a pattern of comparably stronger intra-regional interdependence.

2.2.1.4 Assumptions and Hypotheses According to the Internal Line of the Argument

According to the situation-structural model, the likelihood for institutionalised regional cooperation (and accordingly the chance for successful regionalism) depends first and foremost on the structure of the underlying problematic situation and, to a lesser degree, on patterns of intra-regional interdependence and the presence of a regional power. Irrespective of whether the geographic location is in the generally more developed Global North or in the comparably less developed South, the emergence of regionalism and the shape of its related institutional frameworks will ceteris paribus principally follow the same logic in both hemispheres (i.e. worldwide). Institutions are expected to provide cooperative solutions in the same way on all continents for prevailing collective action problems.

Therefore, in regard to the insights from the situation-structural model, the major assumptions on regionalism according to the internal line of the argument unfold as follows:

- Institutionalised regional cooperation is, on an ordinal scale, most likely to occur if the underlying structure of the genuine regional problematic situation corresponds to a coordination game without distributional conflict ("assurance" game) and likely to happen if it resembles a coordination game with distributional effects ("battle of the sexes" game). Institutionalised regional cooperation is more difficult to achieve in problematic situations corresponding to a dilemma game ("prisoner's dilemma") and least likely if the underlying situation structure resembles a suasion game ("Rambo" game).
- Strong degrees of intra-regional interdependence in the issue areas cause a strong demand for a cooperative solution as, in contrast, weak intra-regional interdependence implies less demand for institutionalised cooperation.
- Patterns of asymmetric interdependence among interacting states on a regional level entail an uneven relative power distribution.

Those countries in a superior power position—i.e. a regional power on which others are dependent—play a key role and are able to most significantly influence the emergence, institutional design and success (in terms of effectiveness) of regionalism.
- If a regional problematic situation and corresponding demand for mutually beneficial institutionalised regional cooperation on the basis of interdependence do exist, regionalism is likely to show good degrees of performance, effectiveness and success.

Against the background of the situation-structural model and the abovementioned assumptions, the following central hypotheses on regionalism under regional conditions according to the <u>internal line of the argument</u> can be deduced:

- The more the underlying structure of a regional problematic situation corresponds to a dilemma game or even coordination game, the more likely the emergence and success (in terms of effectiveness) of regionalism. The more it resembles a suasion game, the less likely the emergence and success of regionalism.
- The stronger the degree of intra-regional interdependence and the more pronounced the presence of a state in a regional power position, the greater the latter's influence on the institutional design and the more likely the emergence and success (in terms of effectiveness) of regionalism.

2.2.2 Regionalism Against the Background of Strong Extra-Regional Relations: External Line of the Argument

One could argue that, according to the aforementioned assumptions and hypotheses, the process of regional integration in the Global South follows basically the same logic as it does in the more developed Northern Hemisphere (e.g. in Europe or North America). While this is ceteris paribus principally true, such a presumption would neglect distinct structural conditions to which regions and many countries in the South—e.g. in Southern Africa—are exposed. It is a proven fact that—in many issue areas, particularly in the economy—states and regional organisations in the Southern Hemisphere show strong and asymmetric extra-regional[8] relations to third, external actors. This is the most obvious difference between developed and economically strongly interdependent countries in the North (whereupon most mainstream regional integration theories have been tailored and unfold good explanatory power) and between developing, economically less interdependent and comparably more "extra-dependent" countries in the South (Axline 1977: 101; Nye 1965: 883).

Regarding the important issue area of the economy, this asymmetry can be demonstrated not only by the direction and quantity of trade and investment flows but also with regard to foreign aid, structural adjustment and donors' funding. For plain structural reasons, this kind of economic disequilibrium distinguishes the (economic) situation in the Southern Hemisphere from the one in North—if one dares to generalise (Krapohl and Fink 2013; Krapohl and Muntschick 2009).

A similar pattern can be observed in the issue area of security with regard to military and security interdependence. All risks and threats to national security have the common feature that states are interdependent so that any unit can cause negative security externalities that affect others. Security interdependence—sometimes referred to as military interdependence (Nye 2008)—is based primarily on (reciprocal) perceptions of rivalry, threat and fear that are intensified by uncertainty (Buzan 1992: 170). Against this background, states and organisations in the Northern Hemisphere, particularly Western great powers, are far more powerful than their southern counterparts when it comes to military capabilities and defence spending. The relational aspect of this asymmetry becomes even clearer if one considers the unidirectional military aid flows, presence and strongholds of external forces in several southern regions (Crocker 1974; Gregory 2000; Keohane 1990: 38).

Be it a legacy of colonialism or not, this shadow structure of asymmetric extra-regional interdependence—in a way, a structural background variable—cannot be argued away. It has a significant impact on the emergence, dynamics, design and effectiveness of regionalism and regional integration organisations that for the most part are composed of developing countries (Young 1969; Zimmerling 1991: Chaps. 3–5). From a theoretical perspective, this is because such a pattern of asymmetric extra-regional interdependence between regional and extra-regional actors implies an unequal power relationship. This connection—according to the logic of power and interdependence (Keohane and Nye 1977)—has already been highlighted and explained earlier with reference to a confined regional level.

In order to take the factor of external influence to the analysis of regionalism theoretically into account, this important structural aspect shall be conceptualised as an additional intervening context variable. In doing so, the "classic" situation-structural approach is extended by an extra-regional dimension and thereby enriched by a second logic, which shall be called the "external line of the argument". Thus, any aspects of extra-regional interdependence and potential external influence shall be taken into account with regard to modelling the situation structure of a real-world problematic situation. If present, this factor is assumed to take significant effect on the structure of a problematic situation, the level of second-order problem negotiations, and the nature and effectiveness of an institutional solution. Hence, the following additional assumptions on regionalism unfold.

2.2.2.1 External Impact on the Structure of Regional Problematic Situations and the Demand for Institutionalised Regional Cooperation

A background pattern of strong and asymmetric extra-regional interdependence between regional and external actors may have an impact on the structure inherent to a genuine regional problematic situation. This is because it can affect the allocation of pay-offs related to the array of "choices" available to the actors (i.e. their policy options) in two directions: by raising the attractiveness and gains of a strategy of either defection or cooperation.

Firstly, patterns of strong and asymmetric extra-regional interdependence can cause a problematic situation's underlying structure to shift towards a more cooperation-aversive situation and consequently impede the solvability of a prima facie entirely regional collective action problem. A genuine dilemma-type situation, for example, can accordingly be transformed into a situation structure corresponding to a "Rambo" game in which those actors who have more attractive extra-regional alternatives at their disposal become the uncooperative "Rambos" on a regional level. In game theory terms, it is then an extra-regional option that provides (at least for one regional actor) the highest pay-offs but implies a strategy of defection with regard to the collective regional good (Axline 1994: 26; Hansen 1969: 269–270).

In practice, such a situation can arise if regional actors prefer to cooperate with comparably more promising external parties on the basis of strong relationships instead of engaging in (perhaps mutually exclusive) cooperation projects within their less promising region (Muntschick, 2012). The stumbling process of European security integration gives an example of this destructive logic: For plain structural reasons, the EU's efforts to form a deeper common European Security and Defence Policy will probably not become successful as long as selected EU member states, which are also members of NATO, regard defence cooperation with extra-regional partners (e.g. with the USA within the framework of NATO) as more beneficial compared with an intensified engagement in a (competing) regional institution on the EU level (Howorth 2007: Chap. 5).

Secondly, patterns of strong and asymmetric extra-regional interdependence can also become supportive to the formation of regional cooperation projects. This is if external parties assist regional actors to overcome collective action problems and provide incentives for an institutional solution on a regional level by, for example, providing side payments,[9] increasing absolute cooperative pay-offs, reducing costs of implementation, control and compliance and improving institutional functionality (Axline 1994: 24–25; Burns and Buckley 1974; Nye 1965: 883). By these means, a genuine dilemma-type or even "Rambo"-type situation can be alleviated into a situation that is more conducive to cooperation, e.g. a coordination game with distributive conflict, in which the external inflows constitute the essence of the collective good (common pool resource) that is subject to distribution by means of coordination (Martin 1992: 774–777; Rittberger 1990: 360).

In practice, such a situation can arise if external actors make a provision of financial or logistical resources conditional on regional cooperation efforts or the existence of regional institutions. With regard to the economic issue area, this could, for example, stimulate economic block-building among developing countries that aim to gain better inflows of foreign direct investments (FDI) or donor funding by means of regional integration (Kennes 1999: 38–39; Schirm 2002; Winters 1999). A similar logic exists with regard to the issue area of security since an extra-regional threat by a hostile external state can be conducive to the formation of a regional security institution—for example, a defence alliance—among a group of weaker countries. In extreme cases, it could even be that regional actors become enticed to cooperate only because the expected cooperation gains are largely fuelled from the outside (Muntschick 2012).

The successful process of early European integration gives a good example of this supportive logic: The United States fuelled regional cooperation among former enemies in Western Europe with significant amounts of money that they channelled through their European Recovery Program (Marshall Plan). This measure provided incentives for regional cooperation and paved the way for further European cooperation projects—and not the least for the EU as we know it today (Behrmann 2008; Hitchcock 2010).

In view of these two scenarios, it becomes clear that, in principle, external influence may unfold an ambivalent impact on any process of regional integration. Whether this more often has an interfering or supportive effect remains a question that demands further empirical research. One could possibly argue that for structural reasons external impact is more likely to unfold an interfering rather than a supportive effect on regional integration. This is because it is not obvious that rational extra-regional actors (who are perceived to be rational utility-maximising actors) bear the costs for the regional integration efforts of third countries or an organisation for simply altruistic reasons.

Be that as it may, a problematic situation that offers potentially fruitful chances for mutually beneficial cooperation needs to be pre-existing on the regional level in any case as a necessary condition in order for external impact to unfold its supportive or interfering impact.

2.2.2.2 External Influence on Regional Power Distribution and the Establishment and Design of Regional Institutions

External influence is not confined to affect only the structural level of genuine regional cooperation problems. Moreover, a pattern of strong and asymmetric extra-regional interdependence between external actors on the one hand and regional parties on the other hand has the potential to impact the latters' relative power positions with regard to inter-state bargaining on a regional level. Making reference to the aforementioned line of the argument concerning asymmetric interdependence and the distribution of relative (bargaining) power, a similar logic applies with respect to a relationship between regional and external actors. This can be transmitted to the distribution of (bargaining) power in a certain regional issue area. Hence, patterns of strong and asymmetric interdependence can principally alter the conditions of interaction for regional actors on the problem-solving level during inter-state negotiations.

Strong extra-regional relations can improve a state's bargaining power position on regional issues on a regional level because it may imply that additional alternative policy strategies, alternative coalitions and plausible exit options beyond the scope of the region could be available (Moravcsik 1993: 499–503). For states privileged by this kind of extra-regional relation, this external dimension extends the scope of action significantly. This is because states with a wide range of external connections are less dependent on issues related to their own region, that is region-specific cooperation problems and the negotiation and solution thereof (Moravcsik 1997: 523; Sebenius 1983: 301–314).

However, this kind of regional actors' externally boosted bargaining power is rather unstable since it is determined by the behaviour of their extra-regional counterparts which remains out of their own control. Therefore, this kind of enhanced bargaining power may fade as soon as external actors decide to make the relevant extra-regional policy alternatives, exit options or related incentives by unilateral means less promising, impracticable or unavailable for their dependent counterparts on a regional level.

Accordingly, a strong and asymmetric relationship to extra-regional actors does not only hold the abovementioned advantages for regional actors who engage in inter-state negotiations on a regional level. Moreover, a structural pattern of strong and unidirectional asymmetry puts extra-regional actors in a position to potentially exert measures of coercion or persuasion. The potential impact of external actors on genuine regional issues becomes even stronger if this influence directly permeates to the level of regional second-order problems. In practice, such external influence materialises if regional actors take positions in regional inter-state negotiations that are strongly motivated by external actors' input and their means of pressuring or enticing (Axline 1977: 90–91; 1994: 23–26).

Therefore, the external impact on a regional actor's bargaining power can be principally of an ambivalent character. Since strong and asymmetric relations to external actors in most cases imply an availability of additional, possibly attractive, options and policy alternatives for regional actors, it can be assumed that this feature has primarily a negative impact for the emergence, dynamics and success of regionalism in the South, not least because extra-regional actors can eventually be in a position to make regional actors design a regional cooperation project according to their own external intentions.

In sum, the creation of common regional institutions and the institutional choice in the South are, in principle, more likely to be (in)directly influenced by external actors compared with other regional integration projects where member states are less dependent on "outsiders" (Harbeson 1994: 292). Thus, institutions not only may function in an inward-oriented manner for "locking-in" agreements and committing their members to a certain policy but are more likely to have an additionally outward-oriented purpose with respect to fulfilling the expectations of external patrons (Mattli 1999: 58–59; Schirm 2002: 20–23).

As a consequence, the nature and design of these institutions are more likely to show an "external fingerprint" compared with similar institutions in the North. This is not surprising because if extra-regional actors pay the "regional piper" they can expect to call the tune. It may also imply that institutions in the South are more likely to be intergovernmental in character. This is because the involved regional actors are principally more prone to follow policies involving cooperation with extra-regional actors instead of focussing on their own region. Therefore, they may be less enthusiastic about "chaining" themselves with inflexible, strictly binding or even supranational institutions. Such a phenomenon of state behaviour was not uncommon during the early stages of European integration as well.

2.2.2.3 External Influence on the Performance and Effectiveness of Regional Institutions

Strong and asymmetric extra-regional interdependence between regional and external actors may have an impact on the operability and effectiveness of regional institutions. External impact not only can transform the inherent structure of problematic situations and thus influence the likelihood of an institutional solution a priori but also can undermine or support the performance and effectiveness of an already-existing institution at a later stage (Young 1992: 185–189).

Externally induced damage to an existing institution's performance and effectiveness happens if regional actors defect from their commitment to implement or comply with the regulative framework of a regional cooperation because of extra-regional incentives. This can be the case if regional cooperative gains diminish or fail to materialise because of an availability of more attractive—or mutually incompatible—alternative options that are based on extra-regional relations. While members of regional institutions who let their commitment slide or finally opt out for the sake of extra-regional cooperation are directly responsible for institutional malfunction and ineffectiveness, it is nevertheless the structural pattern of strong relations to external actors that causes this effect and therefore indirectly exerts influence.

On the other hand, external support to existing regional institutions may enhance the institutions' functionality and have a catalytic impact on their performance and effectiveness. This is the case if dedicated external actors foster regional cooperation by raising incentives or lowering the costs of establishing and maintaining the necessary institutional framework of the regional cooperation projects. Possible measures include the external provision of additional information, logistical support to enhance institutional capacity and other forms of side payments directly affecting the operability of the institutions (Young 1992: 189; Zimmerling 1991: 212–240). Be it for altruism or *realpolitik*, external actors' support to the institutional framework of regional cooperation projects will not only enhance the overall effectiveness but most likely also increase the regional actors' commitment as well (Kennes 1999: 37–39; Sebenius 1983: 308–313). This is because the resulting pay-offs strengthen the participants' preferences for regional cooperation and the beneficiaries are more likely to obey the institutions' provisions in order to keep the external source of support bubbling. Under such circumstances, regionalism is likely to flourish.

However, for those regional institutions that are primarily fuelled externally, an end of this external support may cause institutional breakdown if benefits are not yet self-generated effectively and independently. Thus, external influence on the performance and effectiveness of regionalism is not always a stabilising factor since the supportive impact cannot be taken for granted and might be unstable over time.

2.2.2.4 Assumptions and Hypotheses According to the External Line of the Argument

It is a given fact that numerous states in the South—particularly developing countries—exhibit patterns of strong and asymmetric extra-regional interdependence to external actors in a variety of important policy areas (particularly in the field of the economy). Provided that such an asymmetric relationship exists, external actors are for plain structural reasons in a position to (in)directly exert influence on regional matters concerning the establishment, institutional design and effectiveness of such regionalisms. Hence, even the "success" of regionalism in the South could strongly depend on external actors' policies and actions that are beyond the region's own scope.

If these structural patterns of strong and asymmetric extra-regional interdependence and the related impact of external actors as intervening variables are taken explicitly into account, the following major assumptions on regionalism according to the <u>external line of the argument</u> unfold:

- Patterns of strong and asymmetric extra-regional interdependence between states on a regional level and extra-regional actors entail an uneven relative power distribution. If external actors are in the superior power position vis-à-vis regional actors, they are able to exert influence on the emergence, institutional design and success (in terms of effectiveness) of regionalism.
- This kind of external influence may:
- <u>Disturb and interfere</u> with regionalism if it transforms the inherent structure of a genuine regional problematic situation towards a more cooperation-averse situation, provides regional actors in negotiations on regional second-order problems with attractive alternative exit options, or undermines the capacity of regional institutions to achieve effectiveness.
- <u>Facilitate</u> regionalism if it alters the inherent structure of a genuine regional problematic situation towards a more cooperation-conducive situation, constrains the availability or practicability of potentially attractive alternative exit options for regional actors in negotiations on regional second-order problems, or supports the capacity of regional institutions to achieve effectiveness.
- If a pattern of strong and asymmetric interdependence prevails on a regional level in parallel to one between regional and external actors, the influence on regionalism is contested between the involved regional and external powers.

In theory, external influence on regionalism can be principally ambivalent in character: it can have interfering and supportive effects on regional cooperation efforts on a regional level. However, for plain structural reasons, a negative impact of external actors on regionalism is probably more likely to occur. This is because an altruistic, cooperation-supportive behaviour cannot be assumed to be the dominant strategy of action for those external actors who become involved in third actors' regional issues

(Muntschick 2013c). Hence, extra-regional support to regionalisms may materialise under certain conditions—somewhat like "manna from the sky"—but may likewise unexpectedly cease for reasons beyond the region's own control.

In accordance with the extended situation-structural model and the additional assumptions, the following central hypotheses on regionalism and external impact, according to the <u>external line of the argument</u>, can be deduced:

- The stronger the degree of asymmetric extra-regional interdependence between states on a regional level and extra-regional actors, the more likely that the underlying pattern of a genuine regional problematic situation will be prone to external influence and will transform into a more cooperation-averse situation structure.
- The stronger the degree of asymmetric extra-regional interdependence and the more distinct the presence of an extra-regional actor in a power position vis-à-vis the region, the greater the possibility of external influence on the design of regional institutions and therefore the less likely—and also less stable—the emergence and success (in terms of effectiveness) of regionalism.

2.3 Alternative Assumption: Regionalism as a Result of Isomorphism and Symbolism

The aforementioned theoretical framework basically attributes institutionalised regional cooperation and the emergence of new regionalisms to functional pressures and specific problematic situations in international relations (Keohane 1984; Zürn 1992, 1993). However, some constructivist strands of the academic literature challenge this rationalist line of argument quite fundamentally. Some scholars argue that institutions are not necessarily a result of cost-benefit calculations and strategic choices made by rational actors. Instead, institution-building could be rooted in a "non-functional" *rationale* with states constructing and configuring institutions seemingly not for the purpose of solving collective action problems (e.g. DiMaggio and Powell 1983; Martin and Simmons 1998; Meyer and Rowan 1977).

Making reference to regionalism, some doubts may arise with regard to the applicability and explanatory power of plainly rationalist arguments (Robson 1993). According to some scholars (e.g. Börzel and

Risse 2009a, b; Farell 2007; Jetschke and Lenz 2011), cooperation theory, mainstream institutionalism and plain functionalist forms of reasoning fall too short in explaining the puzzle why regional integration organisations have been mushrooming in the aforementioned developing regions despite disadvantageous preconditions. Fuelled by prima facie empirical evidence, some existing regional integration organisations of the new regionalism—particularly in the Southern Hemisphere—seem to show insufficient degrees of operability, functionality and effectiveness (cf. Gray 2012; Söderbaum 2007). Critics argue that such apparently dysfunctional and inefficient examples of regionalism are not likely to be based on actual underlying regional cooperation problems. As parts of the relevant literature reveals, this (first) impression sometimes culminates in the assumption that the new regionalisms in the South— especially the ones in sub-Saharan Africa (cf. Asche 2009; Proff 2000)— are no more than delusions and *Scheinriesen*[10] with façade institutions (Hansen 1969: 262; Mattli 1999: 66; Yang and Gupta 2005).

According to this line of the argument, the emergence, dynamics and design of at least some of the recent regionalisms are therefore possibly the result of a non-functional logic and different kinds of causal mechanisms. In the research field on regionalism, the most elaborated alternative explanatory approaches make reference to the rich body of literature on diffusion.[11]

Theoretical models based on international policy diffusion have become central research topics in political science in general and more particularly for the study of regionalism (e.g. Börzel 2011; Börzel and Risse 2009b; Farell 2007; Jetschke and Lenz 2011). Therefore, it is necessary to take these alternative explanations to the analysis of regionalism into consideration. Within the framework of this study, this shall materialise by formulating a rival assumption that is based on the core arguments proposed by the relevant literature on diffusion, institutional isomorphism and symbolism. The theoretical foundations for the argument above are as follows:

According to early sociological literature on diffusion, it is principally possible to adopt all kinds of (social) practices and (cognitive) institutions independently from functional pressure. Instead, the plain desire to gain legitimacy can be a major driving force for any form of institutionalisation or, more precisely, institution-building. This can culminate in actors taking practices and institutions for granted as appropriate without critically questioning their purpose and without further searching for or testing alternatives (Scott 1995: 108–109). A similar logic can apply with respect to the creation of formal structures and institutions. Under these circumstances, formal institutions could have priority objectives that aim not on satisfying concrete functional demands but instead on proving the involved actors' adequate handling of an issue and appropriateness of action, in particular for the purpose of gaining legitimacy (Meyer and Rowan 1977). Hence, social practices and institutions as well as even formal structures and institutions may simply diffuse because of their symbolic properties and the related surplus value (Gilardi 2008: 82–87).

Transferring this line of thought to the field of international relations, world polity theorists assume that a sort of global culture has devolved in an increasingly interdependent international system in recent decades. Inherent to this global culture, which had diffused transnationally from the West to the rest of the world after the end of the Second World War, is a growing global consensus on what is appropriate with respect to international actors, goals and policy means (Meyer et al. 1997; Simmons et al. 2006: 787–789). With nation-states and their societies apparently more and more integrating into a global system and a world society, established and "appropriate" worldwide models—such as regional organisations along with their institutional frameworks—represent benchmarks for other countries that are prone to take these as examples and align their practices, policies and actions accordingly (Boli and Thomas 1997: 172–173; Meyer et al. 1997: 157–162; Münch 2008).

Institutional isomorphism produces a similar argument. Stemming from observations that organisations in a given field often become increasingly similar over time, DiMaggio and Powell argue that under conditions of general uncertainty, insufficient organisational legitimacy and resource dependency, organisations generally tend to model and adapt to their allegedly more legitimate or successful counterparts in the same respective field. Isomorphic change in the first place affects the organisations' (formal) structures with the similarity becoming the more pronounced the greater the (financial) dependence of an organisation on another (DiMaggio and Powell 1983: 150–156; Meyer et al. 1997: 152–154).

The mechanisms of international policy diffusion, which provide plausible accounts of how an international actor's policies and practices are affected by another international actor, can be subdivided into a plethora of categories. According to the literature on diffusion, the central mechanisms are coercion, competition, learning and emulation (Gilardi 2008:

79, 90; Simmons et al. 2006: 789–801). Institutional isomorphism occurs through similar mechanisms which can be of a coercive, normative or mimetic nature (DiMaggio and Powell 1983: 150–154). The diffusion mechanisms of emulation and mimicry shall be the focus of attention in this book, not least since part of the literature on regionalism more or less openly suspects that several of the recent regionalisms are rather dysfunctional, ineffective and little more than institutional paper tigers. Moreover, a delimitation to emulation is justified because some observers report that many of these regional integration organisations apparently show a strong degree of institutional homology with similar formal structures—but allegedly for non-functional purposes (e.g. Börzel and Risse 2009b; Jetschke and Lenz 2011; Meyer et al. 1997: 152). Therefore, emulation and mimicry mechanisms are best suited to corroborate the book's theoretical approach and key arguments for an alternative, non-rationalist explanation of regionalism on the ground of international diffusion.

The diffusion mechanism "emulation" functions by logic of appropriateness where actors in a given context adopt strategies and behaviours of their peers which they have regarded as adequate and best practices, notwithstanding their actual practicability or effectiveness. In a political context, this implies that governments may adopt policies or create institutions that are not intended to solve actual cooperation problems but rather established by plain activism and for purely symbolic reasons (Gilardi 2008: 98–99; Simmons et al. 2006: 799–801). This latter form of emulation is called symbolic imitation. It is a strategy whereby governments adopt policies or practices primarily in order to gain recognition and legitimacy by the added ceremonial value. In this context, an institution's symbolic pay-offs are much more important than its actual outputs (Braun and Gilardi 2006: 311–313; Meyer and Rowan 1977: 349). Correspondingly, mimetic isomorphism describes a process in which organisations are simply modelled on supposedly more legitimate and successful organisations. This behaviour of institutional "copy-and-paste" is rather a reaction to uncertainty with symbolic properties than a true response to concrete functional pressure (DiMaggio and Powell 1983: 151–152; Meyer et al. 1997: 158).

Against this background, symbols can be of crucial importance for political institutions because they contribute to the construction of their (social) reality and visualise their existence and relevance. This is because symbols epitomise fundamental ideas and guiding principles and therefore convey an institution's coherence, integrated profile and corresponding capacity for action. An immaculate symbolic representation may help to disguise a lack in concreteness, rationality, functionality and efficiency of an organisation's structures and practices (Göhler 1997: 24, 31, 48–52; Jetschke and Liese 1999: 295). Therefore, the additional value of symbols not only compensates for a potential deficit of institutions but also may contribute to enhance its stability, power, legitimacy and (international) recognition. Moreover, a shiny reputation adds to an institution's attractiveness regarding, for example, the inflow of financial resources from third actors. For aid-dependent developing countries, this could be an incentive to create symbolic or façade institutions which "operate" on only a surface level to the outside world (Blatter 2001: 32–34; Simmons et al. 2006: 800).

Altogether, this line of argument provides a potential alternative explanation to the emergence, design and effectiveness of (international) institutions in general and regional integration organisations in particular. The central ideas of isomorphism and symbolism constitute this work's alternative assumption for explaining the recent new regionalisms as they represent a substantiated theoretical approach that to some degree competes with rationalist cooperation theory. Accordingly, the alternative assumption shall read as follows:

- If an institutionalised regional cooperation project does not show any intended, evaluable institutional effects, it is likely that the observed manifestation of regionalism is not based on a concrete problematic situation but is merely the result of isomorphism and symbolic imitation with (façade) institutions that have been created to serve non-functional purposes.

In the recent examples of the new regionalisms in the international arena, this alternative assumption implies that regional integration organisations with apparently dysfunctional institutions are likely to be the result of diffusion mechanisms, such as emulation and especially mimicry, or plain symbolism. According to some authors, these rather symbolic regionalisms prevail most notably in the South (cf. Gray 2012; Herbst 2007: 137–141; Terlinden 2004).

The EU seems to play an outstanding and important role in this context. According to a rich body of literature, the EU is the most important and influential agent of international and inter-regional diffusion.

This relates not only to certain ideas, norms and policies but also to the diffusion of global regionalism. In this respect, Europe has always been a promoter of regional integration in other parts of the globe because the EU is seen as the world's exemplary, most elaborated and most successful regional integration organisation (Börzel and Risse 2009a, b; de Lombaerde and Schulz 2009). Nonetheless, a more recent work of this strand of research has also pointed to the limits of external Europeanisation (Börzel 2010).

Against the background of the aforementioned central assumptions on theories of international diffusion, institutional isomorphism and symbolism, the alternative hypothesis of this work is as follows:

- The lesser the degree of observable and measurable institutional effectiveness of a specific regional cooperation project or a regional integration organisation, the more likely that it represents a dysfunctional façade institution and is an example of institutional isomorphism, emulation and symbolic imitation.

2.4 Research Design and Methodology

The book's analysis of the SADC, guided by the research questions, represents a theory-driven case study that uses a variety of profound research methods and techniques based on empirical social science. Together with its underlying research design, this guarantees a solid analysis, valid results and sound explanations.

The selection of the SADC as the case of analysis has been motivated by the fact that it represents one of the most prominent and simply best examples of the new regionalism in the Global South. This is because the organisation (i) is well recognised on an international level, (ii) is generally considered to be functioning, stable and even dynamic, (ii) has reached a considerable breadth and depth of regional integration in terms of scope, but (iii) received little academic attention from political science so far and therefore is still under-researched.

Strictly speaking, this book comprises a single-case study in which the SADC is "the case" and unit of observation. According to Yin, single-case studies are in general "the preferred strategy when 'how' or 'why' questions are being posed [...] and when the focus is on a contemporary phenomenon within some real-life context" (Yin 2003: 1). This is because single-case studies offer sufficient space for documenting processes and investigating complex (social) situations and units that may consist of multiple variables of potential importance for understanding empirical observations and causal relations. Therefore, case studies prove highly valuable if an in-depth scientific examination, rich description and comprehensive analysis of a complex yet unexplored phenomenon are the tasks to do (de Lombaerde et al. 2010: 30–31; Odell 2001: 169–171).

Simply analysing the SADC as a single case, however, could raise a few problems from a methodological point of view: this relates, for example, to an insufficient number of observations on the dependent variable, random case selection, the risk of case selection bias, a questionable validity and generalisability of research results, or the infeasibility of hypothesis generation (George and Bennett 2005: 22–34; Keman 2008: 68–71).

A viable solution to avoid this $n = 1$ problem is to generate more observations on the dependent variable. On that account, this study increases the number of cases insofar as the analysis of regionalism in the SADC is divided into five sub-cases according to the method of the most crucial/critical case design (Levy 2008: 12–13; Przeworski and Teune 1982; Yin 2003). Crucial/critical cases represent exemplarily a larger whole and have in this regard "strategic importance in relation to the general problem" (Flyvbjerg 2006: 229) and research object under observation. Applying the method of crucial/critical case design avoids not only random case selection but also selection bias (King et al. 1994: 128–138).

Subdividing research on a single case of regionalism by means of probing hypotheses on a number of sub-cases of different issue areas not only leads to more reliable analytical results but also has already proven successful in terms of theory-building. Moravcsik's book on European integration is an outstanding example in this respect. He avoided the obvious $n = 1$ problem by disaggregating his analysis of regionalism in Europe into different issue areas at different points in time. Accordingly, he selected five "grand bargains" that became subjects for testing his hypotheses on (European) regional integration, which finally led to generalisations, theory-building and the birth of liberal intergovernmentalism (Moravcsik 1998).

Following this method of crucial/critical case design (Levy 2008: 12–13; Przeworski and Teune 1982; Yin 2003), this work employs an analytical segregation of the SADC into crucial sub-cases in order to generate general conclusions on regionalism in the SADC as a whole. This procedure is conclusive because it corresponds to the book's understanding of regionalism as a cluster of various, multidimensional regional cooperation projects bounded by a territorial dimension confined by its member states. Accordingly, it is the different issue areas and various regional cooperation projects under the umbrella of the SADC as an organisation that represent the universe of (sub-)cases.

In line with the above understanding, the universe of (sub-)cases within the SADC in terms of policy areas comprises politics, defence and security, economic development, disaster risk management, infrastructure, agriculture and food security, natural ressources, meteorology and climate, health social and human development as well as poverty eradication and policy dialogue—according to the organisation's statement on regional intergation themes. Additional, cross-cutting areas of cooperation include also gender, science and technology, information and communication, environment and sustainable development, private sector, statistics and diseases.[12]

Above all, the SADC Protocols represent the "core areas" where substantial and institutionalised regional integration actually should take place in the SADC. This is because they are legally binding documents that commit member states to specific cooperation objectives and concrete procedures codified in all its particularities. Examples include the Protocol on Trade, the Protocol on Mining, the Protocol on Health, the Protocol against Corruption and the Protocol on Politics, Defence and Security Cooperation.[13] It is therefore the array of protocols and the policy areas they address which constitute the universe of (sub-)cases where institutionalised regional cooperation in the SADC may actually take place.

Taking this into consideration and employing an analytical seggregation of the SADC in accordance with the method of the most crucial/critical case design (Przeworski and Teune 1982; Yin 2003), this work's analysis is based on the following sub-case selection: Firstly, there is no doubt that the economy, security and infrastructure account for the most important and crucial policy areas of regional integration in the SADC. Secondly, the most important and critical regional cooperation projects in these three issue areas are (i) the SADC Free Trade Area and the scheduled SADC Customs Union (issue area of the economy), (ii) the Organ on Politics, Defence and Security as well as the SADC Standby Force (issue area of security) and (iii) the Southern African Power Pool (issue area of infrastructure). With these five sub-cases standing for the SADC's most important policy areas of regional cooperation and therefore representing regionalism in the SADC as a whole, the $n = 1$ problem of a single-case study is solved.

What justifies this selection? The *rationale* for these choices stems from research conducted by area studies experts, assessments of political scientists from Southern African institutes, statements of SADC officials and not least the organisation's self-perception according to agendas and official documents. The variance of the selected cases appears to be even greater with regard to the independent and context variables because one can expect different degrees of issue-specific extra-regional interdependence in the selected policy areas. This approximates the applied research design to a most different case design and therefore contributes to the validity and generalisability of the analysis's empirical results and theoretical implications (Przeworski and Teune 1982). Following the idea that the general often lies in the particular, one can expect that regional integration in the SADC's other, non-crucial policy areas follows a similar pattern and (functional) logic as explained in view of the organisation's three central issue areas (economy, security and infrastructure).

In order to avoid the drawing of hasty generalisations from a small number of cases by simply demonstrating supporting evidence for a theoretical argument, this book has proposed a set of testable hypotheses derived from two competing schools of thought (rational institutionalism and the situation-structural model versus isomorphism and symbolism). Using alternative theories and competing explanations prevents circular reasoning on the case and will enhance the objectivity and reliability of the whole case study analysis (King et al. 1994: 35–38). Probing competing hypotheses obliges the analyst to carefully weigh up the evidence in order to be in the position to make an informed decision in favour of a certain explanation.

The exploration of this book's research questions and the analysis of regionalism in the SADC adhere to the research principles mentioned above and follow the concept of a plausability probe (Eckstein 1975: 108–113; George and Bennett 2005: 75). A plausability probe of an innovative "candidate-theory" (Eckstein 1975: 108) helps to figure out its validity and "service potential" without having to undertake a large-scale analysis with a great number of multifaceted cases. For these reasons, this book's analysis refrains from explicit and strict hypothesis-testing in the narrow sense.

However, this case study analysis not only is theory-driven but also seeks to elaborate a (middle-range) theory on regionalism and extra-regional influence. For this purpose, this work's overall positivist research is also inspired by the concept of "analytic narratives". This concept "combines analytic tools that are commonly employed in economics and political science with the narrative form, which is more commonly employed in history" (Bates et al. 1998: 10). Analytic narratives aim to go to the bottom of things by paying careful attention to descriptive and qualitative materials, grasping the complexity of situations, context and other empirical evidence that narratives in a broader sense may offer. Besides the empirical in-depth exploration of cases, analytic narratives are at the same time parsimonious and analytic insofar as they "extract explicit and formal lines of reasoning" (Bates et al. 1998: 10) and apply rational choice and game theory to model the puzzle, situation or process under observation. This method of theory-guided modelling facilitates the explanation of outcomes (e.g. the establishment of a regional institution) very well because it captures the "essence of a story", focusses on central actors and helps to identify the relevant causal mechanisms (Bates et al. 1998: 8–13). Conducting case study research according to this concept probably best corresponds to the theoretical approach applied in this book. This is because Zürn had emphasised that a situation-structural analysis of international cooperation requires prior modelling and reconstruction of the relevant problematic situation in international relations with reference to context and the historical setting (Zürn 1992: 115).

Careful process tracing is the guiding principle for the empirical part of this research. Making use of this method generates detailed knowledge on the relations between the independent variable and the observable implications. This helps to reveal fundamental causal meachanisms and rule out potentially intervening but ultimately meaningless factors (George and Bennett 2005: Chap. 10; Levy 2008). Where process tracing seems difficult or unsatisfactory because of, for example, a lack of available information, empirical key results will be controlled for contrafactuality in order to strengthen their validity (George and Bennett 2005: 117–120). Such a method is partcularly useful to determine institutional outcomes, performance and effectiveness in terms of pre-post comparison (i.e. before the establishment of an institution and thereafter).

The empirical analysis and knowledge collection are conducted mainly with the help of qualitative research methods. Content analysis of primary sources and (official) documents gets first priority. As they provide the most reliable evidence, such "hard" sources are best suited to support any empirical findings and the arguments based upon them. Field research at the SADC Headquarters, particularly in the organisation's library and archive, was very fruitful for this purpose.

Numerous semi-structured, explorative and systematising expert interviews have been conducted for gathering additional information and eventually complement the content anylysis of documents (Bogner and Menz 2005: 36–38). Besides interviewing officials from the SADC and the EU, the author has chosen to interview foreign consultants to the SADC Secretariat; experts of relevant research institutes in Belgium (e.g. European Centre for Development Policy Management), Botswana (e.g. Botswana Institute for Development Policy Analysis), Namibia (e.g. Namibian Economic Policy Research Unit) and South Africa (e.g. South African Institute for International Affairs, Institute for Global Dialogue and Institute for Security Studies); experts of development agencies (e.g. Deutsche Gesellschaft für Technische Zusammenarbeit) and well-reputed experts from Southern Africa's academia for this purpose.

Apart from evaluating the content analysis of primary sources, the author evaluated newspaper articles and consulted numerous secondary sources for the empirical research. During the research process, the author considered more than 600 secondary sources, of which a quintessence of almost 500 secondary sources became useful to complement and cross-check the information collected from primary sources or expert interviews. For their exceptional and exclusive informational content as well as their topicality, the most valuable books and articles on the SADC were generally found and published in the Southern African region.

Where applicable and availabale, quantitative data is used to complement empirical information gathered by qualitative methods. A technique of triangulation (Flick 2007: 44–54; Yin 2003: 14) provides an opportunity to make use of relevant indicators and is very suitable to strengthen depictions of structural characteristics, patterns of interdependence and measurement of effectiveness (de Lombaerde and van Langenhove 2006; Tavares and Schulz 2006). For the purpose of collecting adaequate and up-to-date quantitative data, the author consulted, among other things, the World Integrated Trade Solutions (WITS) database, the Trade & Policy Strategies (TIPS) SADC Trade Database, the Regional Integration Knowledge System (RIKS), the Stockholm International Peace Research Institute (SIPRI), and other country-specific or institutional databases. However, research has proven that quantitative data in the SADC context is often less reliable, fragmentary or even simply unavailable compared with data from regions in the North, such as Europe and the EU.

Procedural Steps of Analysis and Operationalisation
The procedural steps of analysing regionalism in the SADC follow a similar pattern and can be divided into the three analytical stages detailed below:

Firstly, the regional cooperation problem in a given policy area is identified and modelled to its specific situational structure at the time the involved actors intended to initialise cooperative action. In this context, the actors' preferences and potential demand for institutionalised regional cooperation are determined. Furthermore, patterns of intra- and extra-regional interdependence as well as the involved actors' power positions are worked out in detail in order to model the underlying problematic situation. In this regard, the potential influence of extra-regional actors on the genuine structure of regional cooperation problems is explicitly taken into consideration.

Secondly, the analysis addresses inter-state negotiations leading to the particular institutional outcomes (i.e. the cooperative arrangement with its specific institutional design) in order to identify and explain the involved actors' degrees of assertiveness and influence. Moreover, the inter-state negotiations and the character of the resulting institutional arrangements will be critically scrutinised in order to determine potential influence by extra-regional actors.

Thirdly, the performance and effectiveness of the observed institutionalised regional cooperation projects will be evaluated. These assessments of institutional goal attainment not only allow substantiated issue-specific and general statements on the functionality, capacity and cooperation gains of regionalism in the SADC but also elaborate on reproaches of institutional isomorphism and symbolism. This allows one to determine the veracity and success of regionalism.

In summary, arguing in an explanatory manner by probing the plausibility of hypotheses is a good method to answer the research questions of this study in a scientific and convincing way. It is no coincidence that the proposed mode of analysis is reminiscent of international regime analysis. Given the book's understanding of regionalism, this approach adapts best to the theoretical framework and is the optimal strategy to analyse the emergence, institutional design and effectiveness of regional integration in the SADC.

NOTES

1. There is no uniform definition of the term institution. In this book, institutions shall be understood as "related complexes of rules and norms, identifiable in space and time" (Keohane 1988: 383).
2. An issue area can be defined as "sets of issues that are in fact dealt with in common negotiations and by the same, or closely coordinated, bureaucracies, as opposed to issues that are dealt with separately and in uncoordinated fashion" (Keohane 1984: 61).
3. This argument implies that strong or rising levels of interdependence, notably economic interdependence, do not per se lead to increasing cooperation or lasting peace in international relations. Such assumptions of some economists not only are too simplistic but also have been proven wrong by history: Germany and Britain were best trading partners before World War I, just as the US and Japan were before World War II (Jervis 1978: 177; Keohane 1990: 38).
4. Security cooperation problems in international relations relate to "security complexes". The latter is "a group of states whose primary security concerns are sufficiently closely linked that their national securities cannot realistically considered apart from one another" (Buzan 1992: 169).
5. Preferences shall be understood as individual and self-centred policy options that reflect the actors' utility-maximising calculations on absolute pay-offs against the background of "issue-specific patterns of substantive interdependence" (Moravcsik 1998: 61). In principle, preferences for (alternative) policy options can be ranked on an ordinal scale according to their pay-offs (Schimmelfennig 2001: 53).
6. A problematic situation shall be defined as a "collective action problem [...] where rational individual action can lead to strictly Pareto-inferior outcome, that is, an outcome which is strictly less preferred by every individual than at least on other outcome" (Taylor 1987: 19). To put it more simply, a problematic situation constitutes an issue area, may trigger demand for processing a cooperative solution and implies a significant position difference among the involved actors. Sometimes, a problematic situation is also referred to as a conflict situation (Rittberger and Zürn 1990: 38).
7. In a suasion situation (or "Rambo" game), either one actor has a dominant strategy to cooperate, which the other can exploit, or one actor has a dominant strategy to defect while the other must cooperate in order to avoid an even worse outcome (Hasenclever et al. 1997: 51).
8. Extra-regional shall refer to a relation with any actor (country or organisation) that is not part of a group that has been previously defined as a region.

9. So-called "external seed money" from external sources (mostly donors) has been identified as an important catalyst for regional institution-building in a number of observed cases (Berg and Horall 2008: 183–184).
10. Means "illusory giant"; Michael Ende explained this phenomenon very well and in the most fanciful manner (cf. Ende 2004: Chap. 17).
11. Generally speaking, diffusion can be conceived as a consequence of interdependence and a process through which ideas are spread across dimensions of time and space (Gilardi 2013). International policy diffusion occurs "when government policy decisions in a given country are systematically conditioned by prior policies made in other countries" (Simmons et al. 2006: 787).
12. Reference made to the SADC's web pages: http://www.sadc.int/themes and http://www.sadc.int/issues (05/05/2017).
13. Reference made to the SADC's web pages: http://www.sadc.int/documents-publications/protocols/ (05/05/2017).

REFERENCES

Asche, H. 2009. Die SADC? Welche SADC? Afrikanische Regionalgemeinschaften im Übergang. In *Entwicklung als Beruf*, ed. T. Hanf, H.N. Weiler, and H. Dickow, 69–84. Baden-Baden: Nomos.

Axelrod, R. 1987. *Die Evolution der Kooperation*. München: R. Oldenbourg Verlag.

Axelrod, R., and R.O. Keohane. 1993. Achieving Cooperation Under Anarchy: Strategies and Institutions. In *Neorealism and Neoliberalism: The Contemporary Debate*, ed. D.A. Baldwin, 85–115. New York: Columbia University Press.

Axline, W.A. 1977. Underdevelopment, Dependence and Integration: The Politics of Regionalism in the Third World. *International Organization* 31 (1): 83–105.

Axline, W.A. 1994. Comparative Case Studies of Regional Cooperation Among Developing Countries. In *The Political Economy of Regional Cooperation. Comparative Case Studies*, ed. W.A. Axeline, 7–33. London: Pinter Publishers and Associated University Press.

Bach, D. 2003. New Regionalism as an Alias: Regionalisation Through Trans-State Networks. In *New Regionalism in Africa*, ed. J.A. Grant, F. Söderbaum, 21–30. Burlington: Ashgate.

Bates, R.H., A. Greif, M. Levi, and J.-L. Rosenthal. 1998. Introduction. In *Analytic Narratives*, ed. R.H. Bates, A. Greif, M. Levi, and J.-L. Rosenthal, 3–22. Princeton: Princeton University Press.

Behrmann, G. 2008. *The Most Noble Adventure: The Marshall Plan and How America Helped Rebuild Europe*. London: Aurum Press.

Berg, S.V., and J. Horall. 2008. Networks of Regulatory Agencies as Regional Public Goods: Improving Infrastructure Performance. *Review of International Organizations* 3 (2): 179–200.
Bhalla, A.S., and P. Bhalla. 1997. *Regional Blocs: Building Blocks or Stumbling Blocks?*. Houndmills, NY: Macmillan.
Blatter, J. 2001. Integrative Symbolik und regulative Normen bei der Institutionenbildung. Erkenntnisse vom Gewässerschutz am Bodensee. *Zeitschrift für Internationale Beziehungen* 8 (1): 5–40.
Bogner, A., and W. Menz. 2005. Das theoriegenerierende Experteninterview. Erkenntnisinteresse, Wissensformen, Interaktion. In *Das Experteninterview: Theorie, Methode, Anwendung*, ed. A. Bogner, B. Littig, and W. Menz, 33–70. Wiesbaden: VS Verlag.
Boli, J., and G.M. Thomas. 1997. World Culture in the World Polity: A Century of International Non-Governmental Organization. *American Sociological Review* 62 (2): 171–190.
Börzel, T.A. 2010. *The Transformative Power of Europe Reloaded. The Limits of External Europeanization*. KFG Working Paper 11. Berlin: Otto-Suhr-Institut für Politikwissenschaft.
Börzel, T.A. 2011. *Comparative Regionalism. A New Research Agenda*. KFG Working Paper 28. Berlin: Otto-Suhr-Institut für Politikwissenschaft.
Börzel, T.A., and T. Risse. 2009a. *Diffusing (Inter-)Regionalism. The EU as a Model of Regional Integration*. KFG Working Paper 7. Berlin: Otto-Suhr-Institut für Politikwissenschaft.
Börzel, T.A., and T. Risse. 2009b. *The Transformative Power of Europe. The European Union and the Diffusion of Ideas*. KFG Working Paper 1. Berlin: Otto-Suhr-Institut für Politikwissenschaft.
Braun, D., and F. Gilardi. 2006. Taking 'Galton's Problem' Seriously: Towards a Theory of Policy Diffusion. *Journal of Theoretical Politics* 18 (3): 298–322.
Breslin, S., and R. Higgot. 2000. Studying Regions: Learning from the Old, Constructing the New. *New Political Economy* 5 (3): 333–352.
Burns, T., and W. Buckley. 1974. The Prisoners' Dilemma Game as a System of Social Dimension. *Journal of Peace Research* 11 (3): 221–228.
Buzan, B. 1992. Third World Regional Security in Structural and Historical Perspective. In *The Insecurity Dilemma. National Security of Third World States*, ed. B.L. Job, 167–189. Boulder: Lienne Rienner.
Buzan, B., and O. Wæver. 2003. *Regions and Powers. The Structure of International Security*. Cambridge: Cambridge University Press.
Cahnman, W.J. 1944. The Concept of Raum and the Theory of Regionalism. *American Sociological Review* 9 (5): 455–462.
Chayes, A., and A. Handler Chayes. 1993. On Compliance. *International Organization* 47 (2): 175–205.

Cox, K.R. 1969. On the Utility and Definition of Regions in Comparative Political Sociology. *Comparative Political Studies* 2 (69): 68–98.

Crocker, C.A. 1974. Military Dependence: The Colonial Legacy in Africa. *Journal of Modern African Studies* 12 (2): 265–286.

de Lombaerde, P., and L. van Langenhove. 2006. Indicators of Regional Integration: Conceptual and Methodological Aspects. In *Assessment and Measurement of Regional Integration. Routledge/Warwick Studies in Globalisation*, vol. 13, ed. P. de Lombaerde, 9–41. London: Routledge.

de Lombaerde, P., and M. Schulz (eds.). 2009. *The EU and World Regionalism: The Makability of Regions in the 21st Century*. London: Ashgate.

de Lombaerde, P., F. Söderbaum, L. van Langenhove, and F. Baert. 2010. Problems and Divides in Comparative Regionalism. In *Comparative Regional Integration. Europe and Beyond. The International Political Economy of New Regionalisms Series*, ed. F. Laursen, 21–39. Farnham: Ashgate.

DiMaggio, P.J., and W.W. Powell. 1983. The Iron Cage Revisited: Institutional Isomorphism and Collective Rationality in Organizational Fields. *American Sociological Review* 48 (2): 147–160.

Downs, G.W. 2000. Constructing Effective Environmental Regimes. *Annual Review of Political Science* 3 (1): 25–42.

Downs, G.W., D.M. Rocke, and P.N. Barsoom. 1996. Is the Good News about Compliance Good News about Cooperation? *International Organization* 50 (3): 379–406.

Eckstein, H. 1975. Case Study and Theory in Political Science (Handbook of Political Science). In *Strategies of Inquiry*, vol. 7, ed. F.I. Greenstein and N.W. Polsby, 79–138. Reading: Addison-Wesley.

Ende, M. 2004. *Jim Knopf und Lukas der Lokomotivführer*. Stuttgart: Thienemann Verlag.

Farell, M. 2007. From EU Model to External Policy? Promoting Regional Integration in the Rest of the World. In *Making History: European Integration and Institutional Change at Fifty. The State of the European Union*, vol. 8, ed. S. Meunier and K.R. McNamara, 299–315. Oxford, Bloomington: Oxford University Press.

Flick, U. 2007. *Qualitative Sozialforschung. Eine Einführung*. Reinbeck: Rowohlt.

Flyvbjerg, B. 2006. Five Misunderstandings About Case-Study Research. *Qualitative Inquiry* 12 (2): 219–245.

Gehring, T. 1994. Der Beitrag von Institutionen zur Förderung der internationalen Zusammenarbeit. Lehren aus der institutionellen Struktur der Europäischen Gemeinschaft. *Zeitschrift für Internationale Beziehungen* 1 (2): 211–242.

Gehring, T. 1995. Regieren im internationalen System. Verhandlungen, Normen und Internationale Regime. *Politische Vierteljahresschrift* 36 (2): 197–219.

Gehring, T. 1996. Integrating Integration Theory: Neo-Functionalism and International Regimes. *Global Society* 10 (3): 225–253.
Gehring, T. 2002. *Die Europäische Union als komplexe internationale Organisation. Wie durch Kommunikation und Entscheidung soziale Ordnung entsteht*. Baden-Baden: Nomos.
Gehring, T., and S. Oberthür. 1997. Internationale Regime als Steuerungsinstrumente der Umweltpolitik. In *Internationale Umweltregime. Umweltschutz durch Verhandlungen und Verträge*, ed. T. Gehring and S. Oberthür, 9–26. Opladen: Leske + Budrich.
George, A.L., and A. Bennett. 2005. *Case Studies and Theory Development in the Social Sciences*. Cambridge: MIT Press.
Gilardi, F. 2008. *Delegation in the Regulatory State. Independent Regulatory Agencies in Western Europe*. Cheltenham: Edward Elgar Publishing.
Gilardi, F. 2013. Transnational Diffusion: Norms, Ideas, and Policies. In *Handbook of International Relations*, ed. W. Carlsnaes, T. Risse, and B.A. Simmons, 453–477. London: SAGE.
Gilpin, R. 1987. *The Political Economy of International Relations*. Princeton: Princeton University Press.
Göhler, G. 1997. Der Zusammenhang von Institution, Macht und Repräsentation. In *Institution—Macht—Repräsentation: Wofür politische Institutionen stehen und wie sie wirken*, ed. G. Göhler, 11–62. Baden-Baden: Nomos.
Gray, J. 2012. *Life, Death, or Zombies? The Endurance of Inefficient Regional Economic Organizations*. Unpublished Manuscript. Philadelphia: University of Pennsylvania.
Gregory, S. 2000. The French Military in Africa: Past and Present. *African Affairs* 99: 435–448.
Grieco, J.M. 1988. Anarchy and the Limits of Cooperation: A Realist Critique of the Newest Liberal Institutionalism. *International Organization* 42 (3): 485–507.
Grieco, J.M. 1997. Realist International Theory and the Study of World Politics. In *New Thinking in International Relations Theory*, ed. M. Doyle and J. Ikenberry: 163–201. Boulder: Westview Press.
Gruber, L. 2000. *Ruling the World: Power Politics and the Rise of Supranational Institutions*. Princeton: Princeton University Press.
Haas, E.B. 1958. *The Uniting of Europe: Political, Social, and Economic Forces 1950–1957*. Stanford: Stanford University Press.
Hansen, R.D. 1969. Regional Integration: Reflections on a Decade of Theoretical Efforts. *World Politics* 21 (2): 242–271.
Harbeson, J.W. 1994. Civil Society and the Study of African Politics: A Preliminary Assesment. In *Civil Society and the State in Africa*, ed. J.W. Harbeson, D. Rothchild, and N. Chazan, 285–300. Boulder: Lynne Rienner.

Hasenclever, A., P. Mayer, and V. Rittberger. 1997. *Theories of International Regimes*. Cambridge Studies in International Relations, vol. 55. Cambridge: Cambridge University Press.

Herbst, J. 2007. Crafting Regional Cooperation in Africa. In *Crafting Cooperation. Regional International Institutions in Comparative Perspective*, ed. A. Acharya and A.I. Johnston, 129–144. Cambridge: Cambridge University Press.

Herz, J.H. 1950. Idealist Internationalism and Security Dilemma. *World Politics* 2 (2): 157–180.

Hettne, B. 1999. Globalisation and the New Regionalism: The Second Great Transformation. In *Globalism and the New Regionalism*, ed. B. Hettne, A. Inotai, and O. Sunkel, 1–24. London: Macmillan.

Hettne, B. 2005. Beyond the 'New' Regionalism. *New Political Economy* 10 (4): 543–571.

Hettne, B., and F. Söderbaum. 1998. The New Regionalism Approach. *Politeia: Journal for Political Science and Public Administration* 17 (3): 5–19.

Hettne, B., and F. Söderbaum. 2008. The Future of Regionalism. Old Divides, New Frontiers. In *Regionalisation and Global Governance. The Taming of Globalisation?*, ed. A.F. Cooper, C.W. Hughes, and P. de Lombaerde, 61–79. London and New York: Routledge.

Hirschmann, A.O. 1945. *National Power and the Structure of Foreign Trade*. Berkeley, Los Angeles and New York: University of California Press.

Hitchcock, W.I. 2010. The Marshall Plan and the Creation of the West. In *The Cambridge History of the Cold War Volume 1: Origins*, ed. M.P. Leffler and O.A. Westad, 154–174. Cambridge: Cambridge University Press.

Hoffmann, S. 1982. Reflections on the Nation-State in Western Europe Today. *Journal of Common Market Studies* 21 (2): 21–77.

Howorth, J. 2007. *Security and Defence Policy in the European Union*. Houndmills: Palgrave Macmillan.

Hurrell, A. 1995. Explaining the Resurgence of Regionalism in World Politics. *Review of International Studies* 21 (4): 331–358.

Jervis, R. 1978. Cooperation Under the Security Dilemma. *World Politics* 30 (2): 167–214.

Jervis, R. 1982. Security Regimes. *International Organization* 36 (2): 357–378.

Jetschke, A., and T. Lenz. 2011. Vergleichende Regionalismusforschung und Diffusion: Eine neue Forschungsagenda. *Politische Vierteljahresschrift* 52 (3): 448–474.

Jetschke, A., and A. Liese. 1999. Die kulturelle Prägung staatlicher Interessen und Handlungen. Anmerkungen zur sozialkonstruktivistischen Analyse von "Kultur" in den Internationalen Beziehungen. *Österreichische Zeitschrift für Politikwissenschaft* 28 (3): 285–300.

Keman, H. 2008. Comparative Research Methods. In *Comparative Politics*, ed. D. Caramani, 63–82. Oxford: Oxford University Press.
Kennes, W. 1999. African Regional Economic Integration & the European Union. In *Regionalism in Africa. Integration & Disintegration*, ed. D.C. Bach, 27–40. Oxford and Bloomington: James Currey.
Keohane, R.O. 1982. The Demand for International Regimes. *International Organization* 36 (2): 325–355.
Keohane, R.O. 1984. *After Hegemony. Cooperation and Discord in the World Political Economy*. Princeton: Princeton University Press.
Keohane, R.O. 1988. International Institutions: Two Approaches. *International Studies Quarterly* 32 (4): 379–396.
Keohane, R.O. 1990. The Concept of Interdependence: Current American Thinking. In *Soviet-American Dialogue in the Social Sciences. Research Workshops on Interdependence Among Nations*, ed. Education CoBaSSa, 37–41. Washington: National Academy Press.
Keohane, R.O. 1998. International Institutions: Can Interdependence Work? *Foreign Policy* 10 (1): 82–96.
Keohane, R.O., and J.S. Nye. 1977. *Power and Interdependence. World Politics in Transition*. Boston and Toronto: Little, Brown.
Keohane, R.O., and J.S. Nye. 1987. Power and Interdependence revisited. *International Organization* 41 (4):725–753.
Keohane, R.O., and J.S. Nye. 2001. *Power and Interdependence*. New York, London, Boston: Longman.
Kindleberger, C. 1981. Dominance and Leadership in the International Economy. Exploitation, Public Goods, and Free Rides. *International Studies Quarterly* 25 (2): 242–254.
King, G., R.O. Keohane, and S. Verba. 1994. *Designing Social Inquirey: Scientific Inference in Qualitative Research*. Princeton: Princeton University Press.
Kohler-Koch, B. 1989. Regime in den Internationalen Beziehungen. In *Regime in den Internationalen Beziehungen*, ed. B. Kohler-Koch, 17–85. Baden-Baden: Nomos.
Krapohl, S., and J. Muntschick. 2009. Two Logics of Regionalism: The Importance of Interdependence and External Support for Regional Integration in Southern Africa. In *Proceedings of the 2008 FOPRISA Annual Conference*, vol. 7, ed. J.M. Kaunda and F. Zizhou, 3–17. Gaborone: Lightbooks.
Krapohl, S., and S. Fink. 2013. Different Paths of Regional Integration: Trade Networks and Regional Institution-Building in Europe, Southeast Asia and Southern Africa. *Journal of Common Market Studies* 51 (3): 472–488.
Krasner, S.D. 1976. World Politics and the Structure of International Trade. *World Politics* 28 (3): 317–347.

Krasner, S.D. 1982. Structural Causes and Regime Consequences: Regimes as Intervening Variables. *International Organization* 36 (2): 185–205.
Krasner, S.D. 1991. Global Communications and National Power: Life on the Pareto Frontier. *World Politics* 43 (3): 336–366.
Levy, J.S. 2008. Case Studies: Types, Designs, and Logics of Inference. *Conflict Management and Peace Science* 25 (1): 1–18.
Mansfield, E.D., and H.V. Milner. 1999. The New Wave of Regionalism. *International Organization* 53 (3): 589–627.
Martin, L.L. 1992. Interests, Power, and Multilateralism. *International Organization* 46 (4): 765–792.
Martin, L.L., and B.A. Simmons. 1998. Theories and Empirical Studies of International Institutions. *International Organization* 52 (4): 729–757.
Mattli, W. 1999. *The Logic of Regional Integration: Europe and Beyond*. Cambridge: Cambridge University Press.
Mayer, P., V. Rittberger, and M. Zürn. 1993. Regime Theory: State of the Art and Perspectives. In *Regime Theory and International Relations*, ed. V. Rittberger and P. Mayer, 391–430. Oxford: Clarendon Press.
Meyer, J.W., and B. Rowan. 1977. Institutionalized Organizations: Formal Structure as Myth and Ceremony. *The American Journal of Sociology* 83 (2): 340–363.
Meyer, J.W., J. Boli, G.M. Thomas, and F.O. Ramirez. 1997. World Society and Nation State. *The American Journal of Sociology* 103 (1): 144–181.
Moravcsik, A. 1993. Preferences and Power in the European Community: A Liberal Intergovernmentalist Approach. *Journal of Common Market Studies* 31 (4): 473–524.
Moravcsik, A. 1997. Taking Preferences Seriously: A Liberal Theory of International Politics. *International Organization* 51 (4): 513–553.
Moravcsik, A. 1998. *The Choice for Europe: Social Purpose and State Power from Messina to Maastricht*. Ithaca: Cornell University Press.
Moravcsik, A., and K. Nicolaïdis. 1999. Explaining the Treaty of Amsterdam: Interests, Influence, Institutions. *Journal of Common Market Studies* 37 (1): 59–85.
Morgan, P.M. 1997. Regional Security Complexes and Regional Orders. In *Regional Orders. Building Security in a New World*, ed. D.A. Lake and P.M. Morgan, 20–42. Pennsylvania: The Pennsylvania State University.
Morgenthau, H. 1948. *Politics Among Nations. The Struggle for Power and Peace*. New York: Alfred A. Knopf.
Müller, H. 1993. *Die Chance der Kooperation. Regime in den internationalen Beziehungen*. Darmstadt: Wissenschaftliche Buchgesellschaft.
Münch, R. 2008. *Die Konstruktion der europäischen Gesellschaft. Zur Dialektik von transnationaler Integration und nationaler Desintegration*. Frankfurt: Campus Verlag.

Muntschick, J. 2012. *Theorising Regionalism and External Influence: A Situation-Structural Approach.* Mainz Papers on International and European Politics 2012/2. Mainz: Chair of International Relations, Johannes Gutenberg University.

Muntschick, J. 2013c. Regionalismus und Externer Einfluss: Stört die Europäische Union die Regionale Marktintegration im südlichen Afrika? *Politische Vierteljahresschrift* 54 (4): 686–713.

Nye, J.S. 1965. Patterns and Catalysts in Regional Integration. *International Organization* 19 (4): 870–884.

Nye, J.S. 1968a. Central American Regional Integration. In *International Regionalism: Readings*, ed. J.S. Nye, 377–420. Boston: Little, Brown.

Nye, J.S. 1968b. Introduction. In *International Regionalism: Readings*, ed. J.S. Nye, V–XVI. Boston: Little, Brown and Company.

Nye, J.S. 2008. *Understanding International Conflicts: An Introduction to Theory and History*, 7th ed. London: Pearson.

Odell, J.S. 2001. Case Study Methods in International Political Economy. *International Studies Perspective* 2: 161–176.

Oye, K.A. 1985. Explaining Cooperation Under Anarchy: Hypotheses and Strategies. *World Politics* 38 (1): 1–24.

Proff, H.W. 2000. *SADC—Another Institutional Papertiger in Sub-Saharan Africa or a Chance for Joint Industrial Development?* Darmstadt Discussion Papers in Economics 101. Darmstadt: TU Darmstadt.

Przeworski, A., and H. Teune. 1982. *The Logic of Comparative Social Inquiry.* Malabar: Krieger.

Raustiala, K. 2000. Compliance & Effectiveness in International Regulatory Cooperation. *Case Western Reserve Journal of International Law* 32 (2): 387–440.

Ravenhill, J. 2008. Regionalism. In *Global Political Economy*, 2nd ed, ed. J. Ravenhill, 172–210. Oxford and New York: Oxford University Press.

Rittberger, V. 1990. International Regimes in the CSCE Region—From Anarchy to Governance and Stable Peace. *Österreichische Zeitschrift für Politikwissenschaft* 19 (4): 349–364.

Rittberger, V. 1993. Research on International Regimes in Germany: The Adaptive Internalization of an American Social Science Concept. In *Regime Theory and International Relations*, ed. V. Rittberger and P. Mayer, 3–22. Oxford: Clarendon Press.

Rittberger, V., and M. Zürn. 1990. Towards Regulated Anarchy in East-West Relations: Causes and Consequences of East-West Regimes. In *International Regimes in East-West Relations*, ed. V. Rittberger, 9–63. London: Pinter Publishers.

Rittberger, V., and M. Zürn. 1991. Regime Theory: Findings from the Study of "East-West Regimes". *Cooperation and Conflict* 26 (4): 165–183.

Robson, P. 1993. The New Regionalism and Developing Countries. *Journal of Common Market Studies* 31 (3): 329–348.
Scharpf, F.W. 2000. *Interaktionsformen. Akteurzentrierter Institutionalismus in der Politikforschung*. Opladen: Leske + Budrich.
Schimmelfennig, F. 2001. The Community Trap: Liberal Norms, Rhetorical Action, and the Eastern Enlargement of the European Union. *International Organization* 55 (1): 47–80.
Schirm, S.A. 2002. *Globalization and the New Regionalism: Global Markets, Domestic Politics and Regional Cooperation*. Malden: Blackwell.
Scott, R.W. 1995. *Institutions and Organizations*. Thousand Oaks: Sage.
Sebenius, J.K. 1983. Negotiation Arithmetic: Adding and Subtracting Issues and Parties. *International Organization* 37 (2): 281–316.
Simmons, B.A., F. Dobbin, and G. Garrett. 2006. Introduction: The International Diffusion of Liberalism. *International Organization* 60 (4): 781–810.
Snidal, D. 1985. Coordination Versus Prisoners' Dilemma: Implications for International Cooperation and Regimes. *The American Political Science Review* 79 (4): 923–942.
Söderbaum, F. 2007. African Regionalism and EU-African Interregionalism. In *European Union and New Regionalism. Regional Actors and Global Governance in a Post-Hegemonic Era*, ed. M. Telò, 185–202, 2nd ed. Aldershot and Burlington: Ashgate.
Söderbaum, F., and T.M. Shaw (eds.). 2003. *Theories of New Regionalism. A Palgrave Reader*, International Political Economy Series. Basingstoke: Palgrave Macmillan.
Stein, A.A. 1982. Coordination and Collaboration: Regimes in an Anarchic World. *International Organization* 36 (2): 300–324.
Stein, A. 1993. Coordination and Collaboration: Regimes in an Anarchic World. In *Neorealism and Neoliberalism: The Contemporary Debate*, ed. D.A. Baldwin, 29–59. New York: Columbia University Press.
Tavares, R., and M. Schulz. 2006. Measuring the Impact of Regional Organisations on Peace Building. In *Assessment and Measurement of Regional Integration*, ed. P. de Lombaerde, 232–251. London: Routledge.
Taylor, M. 1987. *The Possibility of Cooperation. Studies in Rationality and Social Change*. Cambridge: Cambridge University Press.
Terlinden, U. 2004. *IGAD—Papiertiger vor Mammutaufgaben*. Bonn: Friedrich-Ebert-Stiftung.
Underdal, A. 1992. The Concept of Regime 'Effectiveness'. *Cooperation and Conflict* 27 (3): 227–240.
Underdal, A. 1998. Explaining Compliance and Defection: Three Models. *European Journal of International Relations* 4 (5): 5–30.

Wagner, R.H. 1983. The Theory of Games and the Problem of International Cooperation. *The American Political Science Review* 77 (2): 330–346.
Wallander, C.A., and R.O. Keohane. 1999. Risk, Threat, and Security Institutions. In *Imperfect Unions. Security Institutions Over Time and Space*, ed. H. Haftendorn, R.O. Keohane, and C.A. Wallander, 21–47. Oxford: Oxford University Press.
Wallander, C.A., H. Haftendorn, and R.O. Keohane. 1999. Introduction. In *Imperfect Unions. Security Institutions Over Time and Space*, ed. H. Haftendorn, R.O. Keohane, and C.A. Wallander, 2–18. Oxford: Oxford University Press.
Waltz, K. 1979. *Theory of International Politics*. Reading, MA: Addison-Wesley.
Warleigh-Lack, A. 2008. Studying Regionalisation Comparatively. A Conceptual Framework. In *Regionalisation and Global Governance. The taming of Globalisation?* ed. A.F. Cooper, C.W. Hughes, and P. de Lombaerde, 43–60. London and New York: Routledge.
Winters, L.A. 1999. Regionalism vs. Multilateralism. In *Market Integration, Regionalism and the Global Economy*, ed. R. Baldwin, D. Cohen, A. Sapir, and A. Venables, 7–48. Cambridge: Cambridge University Press.
Yang, Y., and S. Gupta. 2005. *Regional Trade Arrangements in Africa: Past Performance and the Way Forward*. IMF Working Papers, vol WP/05/36. Washington: International Monetary Fund.
Yin, R.K. 2003. *Case Study Research. Design and Methods*, 3rd ed. Thousand Oaks: Sage.
Young, O.R. 1969. Interdependencies in World Politics. *International Journal* 24 (4): 726–750.
Young, O.R. 1982. Regime Dynamics: The Rise and Fall of International Regimes. *International Organization* 36 (2): 277–297.
Young, O.R. 1992. The Effectiveness of International Institutions: Hard Cases and Critical Variables. In *Governance Without Government: Order and Change in World Politics*, ed. J.N. Rosenau and E-O. Czempiel, 160–194. Cambridge: Cambridge University Press.
Young, C. 1994. In Search of Civil Society. In *Civil Society and the State in Africa*, ed. J.W. Harbeson, D. Rothchild, and N. Chazan, 33–50. Boulder: Lynne Rienner.
Zangl, B. 1994. Politik auf zwei Ebenen. Hypothesen zur Bildung internationaler Regime. *Zeitschrift für Internationale Beziehungen* 1 (2): 279–312.
Zimmerling, R. 1991. *Externe Einflüsse auf die Integration von Staaten. Zur politikwissenschaftlichen Theorie regionaler Zusammenschlüsse*. Freiburg: Verlag Karl Alber.
Zürn, M. 1987. *Gerechte internationale Regime. Bedingungen und Restriktionen der Entstehung nicht-hegemonialer internationaler Regime untersucht am Beispiel der Weltkommunikationsordnung*. Frankurt am Main: Haag Herchen.

Zürn, M. 1992. *Interessen und Institutionen in der Internationalen Politik: Grundlegung und Anwendung des situationsstrukturellen Ansatz.* Opladen: Leske + Budrich.

Zürn, M. 1993. Problematic Social Situations and International Institutions: On the Use of Game Theory in International Politics. In *International Relations and Pan-Europe: Theoretical Approaches and Empirical Findings*, ed. F. Pfetsch, 63–84. Münster: Lit-Verlag.

Zürn, M. 1997. 'Positives Regieren' jenseits des Nationalstaates. Zur Implementation internationaler Umweltregime. *Zeitschrift für Internationale Beziehungen* 4 (1): 41–68.

CHAPTER 3

The Southern African Development Community (SADC): An Analytical Overview of Its History, Policies and Institutional Framework

Regionalism is not an entirely new phenomenon in Southern Africa despite what some might think. Several countries—and even territories under colonial administration—have engaged in various cross-border regional cooperation projects for more than a century. Some regional institutions date back to the time of colonialism whereas others were established more recently during the time of the Cold War and Apartheid. Some have survived to the present day whereas others became obsolete and were dissolved. Nevertheless, they all belong to the category of the so-called old regionalism whereas the SADC is clearly an example of the new regionalism.

This chapter will firstly give a short overview of the history of regional integration in the SADC region and introduce the most important old regionalisms to this end. Secondly, it turns to the new regionalism and highlights central aspects of the SADC as an organisation with respect to its constituent member states, policy agenda and institutional character. The major purpose of this chapter is to provide the reader with encompassing, profound information on the general and regional framework conditions in which the SADC operates and in which the organisation's five most important regional cooperation projects (i.e. the selected sub-cases) are located in.

In the course of this, the analytical focus shall be on examining the underlying institutional framework conditions in the SADC. Knowledge of these allows one to draw conclusions on the organisational capacity as well as on the room for manoeuvre of the member states—including

© The Author(s) 2018
J. Muntschick, *The Southern African Development Community (SADC) and the European Union (EU)*,
https://doi.org/10.1007/978-3-319-45330-9_3

83

prospects for dynamics and performance of regional integration in the SADC. Therefore, elaborating on this historical and organisational overview not only provides important background information on regionalism in Southern Africa but also generates a good knowledge on the SADC case which shall enable the reader to better understand the empirical analyses of the organisation's five major regional cooperation projects.

3.1 Old Regionalisms: A Brief History of Regional Integration in the SADC Region

The following subchapters give a brief introduction on the history of regionalism in Southern Africa in terms of illustrating major regional integration projects of the past and providing an overview of the old regionalisms in the pre-SADC period of time.

The Southern African Customs Union

The region experienced a lasting first manifestation of formal regionalism in 1910 with the establishment of the Southern African Customs Union (SACU) between the Union of South Africa and the three bordering High Commission Territories of Basutoland, Bechuanaland Protectorate and Swaziland. Although this old "imperial" regional integration project was rather "pushed" into existence by the Union of South Africa as a quasi-colonial power in a political environment obviously lacking the freedom of decision, it nevertheless still exists and operates fairly well (McCarthy 2003). The SACU's approach to regional integration corresponds precisely to Viner's model of customs unions and represents a typical example of the old regionalism (cf. Viner 1950).

Today, the highly institutionalised but rather intergovernmental organisation is composed of the Republic of South Africa, Botswana, Lesotho, Namibia and Swaziland. South Africa has a hegemonic position in the SACU, although the decision-making authority rests de jure in all member states. Pretoria administers the organisation's common revenue pool upon whose annual revenue distribution the smaller member states are heavily dependent. With a revised SACU Agreement adopted in 1969 and an institutional reform process starting in 2002, the organisation has repeatedly shown institutional dynamics (Kirk and Stern 2005; McCarthy 2006: 136–138). Despite recent (controversial) speculations on a disintegration of the organisation in the course of free-trade negotiations with the European Union and interfering extra-regional influence by Brussels (Draper and Khumalo 2009), the SACU continues to be the oldest operating customs union in the world (Muntschick 2013).

The Multilateral Monetary Agreement and the Common Monetary Area
The Multilateral Monetary Agreement (MMA) is the legal base for the only monetary union in Southern Africa. With Namibia joining in 1992, the MMA replaced the preceding Common Monetary Area (CMA) and today comprises all SACU member states with the exception of Botswana. The CMA started in 1986 but has its roots in the Rand Monetary Area that was founded in 1974. According to the MMA's provisions, the South African Rand is legal tender in all countries belonging to the institution. However, the smaller members' currencies are no legal tender in South Africa. That is why Lesotho, Namibia and Swaziland continue to have their own distinct denominations which are strictly pegged to the Rand at par (Jefferis 2007: 93–94; McCarthy 1999). The fact that the South African Reserve Bank manages de facto the common monetary policies of all member states of the MMA until the present time gives the impression of a rather "hegemonically" induced institution (Tavlas 2009: 4). Like the SACU, the MMA is highly institutionalised and intergovernmental in character because the member states have the ultimate decision-making authority at their disposal.

The Front Line States
The origins of the SADC are rooted to some extent back to the Front Line States (FLS) alliance. It was formed in 1974 as a loose bond of the black majority-ruled countries Botswana, Mozambique, Tanzania and Zambia in reaction to growing regional threats in the course of the armed struggle in Rhodesia. In defence against the belligerent white minority-ruled governments, the FLS alliance facilitated regional political and security cooperation and the coordination of security policies and mutual (military) assistance among its members (Khadiagala 2007). Collective action became extremely important since the Apartheid government in South Africa conducted sabotage and armed raids on FLS countries in its fight against black liberation movements in the course of its destabilising "Total Strategy" (Evans 1984; Ngoma 2005: 96). In this way, the FLS were notably successful as an arena where members ensured themselves solidarity and acted as a single regional block. Although the alliance was weakly institutionalised and rather a sequence of summits of Heads of States (Adelmann 2012: 72), it is the nucleus for institutionalised regional security cooperation in the SADC. The FLS alliance was

dissolved only in 1994 when South Africa freed itself from the yoke of Apartheid.

The Constellation of Southern African States

With the fear of an impending "total onslaught" by communist-led African countries allegedly stimulated by the Soviet Union and additionally facing the newly formed FLS alliance, South Africa as a white minority-ruled country perceived itself increasingly isolated in the Cold War period. A way out of this dilemma was to enhance economic, political and security cooperation with friendly countries in the region that were not critical of its Apartheid policies. This culminated in the concept of a Constellation of Southern African States (CONSAS) proposed by South Africa's Prime Minister P.W. Botha in November 1979 (Tsie 1993). The intention of the CONSAS was not to achieve regional cooperation among equals but to cement political, economic and security collaboration with those countries already dependent on South Africa's economy. Pretoria anticipated that Botswana, Lesotho, Swaziland, Malawi and (Southern) Rhodesia together with the internationally not recognised "Bantustans" were to become members of CONSAS and help to improve the tattered legitimacy and global reputation of South Africa's ostracised government. Although, owing to suspicion and reluctance among the countries of the "target group", the CONSAS never came into existence, it demonstrates the strong South African demand to establish a regional organisation under its dominance (Christopher 1994; Meyns 2000: 62).

The Southern African Development Co-ordination Conference

It was not least the looming CONSAS concept that made nine black majority-ruled states in Southern Africa (Angola, Botswana, Lesotho, Malawi, Mozambique, Swaziland, Tanzania, Zambia, and Zimbabwe) decide to intensify regional cooperation beyond the scope of the FLS (Vogt 2007: 60–61). This intent manifested in the adoption of a common declaration entitled "Southern Africa: Towards Economic Liberation" (better known as the Lusaka Declaration) in April 1980.[1] It led to a common Memorandum of Understanding and the formal institutionalisation of the Southern African Development Co-ordination Conference (SADCC) in July 1981.

The central goals of the SADCC were to reduce economic dependence from South Africa and enhance regional cross-border development cooperation among its members as a countermeasure. Moreover, member states shared the common interest to coordinate security policies, infrastructure projects and the inflow of external donors' money in their struggle against the hostile Apartheid government (Amin et al. 1987; Mufune 1993). Zimbabwe, by then only recently independent, soon became the driver of the organisation because of its economic strength, industrial base and strong degree of intra-regional interdependence in terms of infrastructure and merchandise trade (Haarlov 1997: 28–29).

The SADCC chose a decentralised, issue- and project-oriented approach for the purpose of development cooperation. Instead of creating a large administrative body and supranational institutions, the organisation followed a strategy of sector coordination. Each member state was assigned one particularly policy field of responsibility. For example, Angola was allocated the energy sector; Malawi, wildlife, forestry and fisheries; Tanzania, industrial development; and Zambia, the minerals and mining sector (Anglin 1983; Meyns 1984). Decision-making in the SADCC was based on consensus—by an unwritten practice. The organisation's small secretariat was merely a service provider and liaison office with very limited capacity. The member states willingly accepted the fact that the SADCC's institutions were decentralised and weak in character because this was cost-efficient and implied that virtually no sovereign rights—which they had only recently obtained from their colonial masters—had to be ceded to the organisation (Hanlon 1989; Thompson 1992: 234–236).

In retrospect, the SADCC's pragmatic approach to institutionalised regional cooperation gained at large rather positive assessments (le Pere and Tjønneland 2005: 14; Mair and Peters-Berries 2001: 301–302; Oosthuizen 2006: 63, 67–68). The organisation proved effective in the issue areas of regional food security and infrastructure cooperation. In particular, the SADCC helped to link some of its members' major transport routes in order to give them safe access to seaports beyond South African territory. Despite this change of trade and transport routes, the organisation failed to reach its ultimate goal: its member states were only slightly less economically dependent on Pretoria by the early 1990s compared with a decade before. Critics often complain about the SADCC's lukewarm actions and argue that some of its regional development projects were guided by national interests and for the benefit of individual member states (Adelmann 2003: 25–26; Oosthuizen 2006: 68–69).

Altogether, the SADCC was probably most successful in mobilising foreign aid, donors' funding and official development assistance—originating particularly in Western countries and organisations. According to experts, more than 90% of total funding to the SADCC came from outside the region during the 1980s (Oosthuizen 2006: 64; Tsie 1993: 140). Although these external (financial) incentives fuelled regional cooperation efforts among SADCC members, they made the organisation heavily dependent on extra-regional actors.

With the crumbling of the Berlin Wall (1989), the independence of Namibia (1990) and the end of Apartheid in South Africa (1994), the geopolitical and regional environment experienced a massive shift. In the early 1990s, the SADCC stood at the crossroads because the organisation's founding purpose had vanished along with its former enemies (Meyns 1997). In the SADCC Heads of States, this started a process of rethinking and initialised work on a strategic policy paper entitled "SADCC: Towards Economic Integration".[2] This document became the blueprint for the new SADC declaration.

In sum, the abovementioned more or less institutionalised and sometimes quite "imperialistically" induced forms of state-driven institutionalised and formalised regional cooperation in Southern Africa all belong to the category of old regionalism. They shall not attract focal attention in the course of this book's analysis since they are not considered to be part of the recent new regionalism. However, in order to gain profound knowledge and understand the evolution and logic of regional integration in the present-day SADC, these earlier and preceding regional institutions deserve adequate attention as important reference points throughout the whole analysis.

3.2 New Regionalism: A Brief Overview of the SADC as an Organisation

After the end of Apartheid in South Africa, the political setting in Southern Africa changed and became less hostile and divided as well as more dynamic and prone to regional cooperation. Today, the region is almost an "island" of stability on a continent that is often said to be ridden by crises, conflict and chaos. However, the region and its countries share a number of trans-boundary challenges and, as a consequence, face various regional cooperation problems. Most of them are rooted in the specific structural conditions of the region and relate to the policy areas of the economy, security and infrastructure. It was these problems on regional level that fuelled demand in Southern African states to engage in institutionalised regional cooperation and led to the creation of the SADC as a regional integration organisation.

The overall aim of the SADC, which was founded on 17 August 1992 on the constituent states' own accord, is to generate socio-economic development and prosperity in the region and its member states in a broad range of policy areas through measures of regional coordination, cooperation and integration. At the time of its foundation, regional security and infrastructure cooperation were at the top of the organisation's agenda. Since the mid-1990s, however, SADC member states adjusted their development strategies step-by-step from an inward-oriented policy of import substitution towards a more outward-looking approach to the global markets. Their organisation increasingly put its focus on regional economic cooperation and market integration.[3] In fact, around the turn of the millennium, the SADC's basic idea of regionalism experienced a paradigm shift from closed to open regionalism.

3.2.1 The SADC's Member States

At present, the SADC comprises 15 member states and covers an area of almost 10 million km² with a population of more than 330 million inhabitants. Members of the SADC are Angola, Botswana, the Democratic Republic of the Congo (DRC), Lesotho, Madagascar, Malawi, Mauritius, Mozambique, Namibia, the Seychelles, South Africa, Swaziland, Tanzania, Zambia and Zimbabwe. Since its foundation in 1992, the organisation experienced considerable growth in membership with South Africa joining in 1994, Mauritius in 1995, the DRC in 1997, the Seychelles in 1997 (resigned membership between 2004 and 2008 for economic reasons) and Madagascar in 2005 (membership suspended between 2009 and 2014 due to a military coup).[4]

In general, SADC member states show a considerable degree of structural heterogeneity. Strong disparities exist with regard to the countries' size of territory and the number of inhabitants. Moreover, six members are land-locked countries (Botswana, Lesotho, Malawi, Swaziland, Zambia and Zimbabwe) whereas three are island states (Madagascar, Mauritius and the Seychelles). Besides this, the SADC reflects a strong geographical and cultural diversity because its member countries are located in different climate and vegetation zones and their peoples speak various (indigenous) languages or belong to different ethnic groups (Christopher 2001) (Table 3.1).

Table 3.1 The SADC member states (in 2016)

Country	Territory (km^2)	Population (million)	GDP (billion, current US-$)
Angola	1,247,000	28.8	89.6
Botswana	581,700	2.3	15.3
DR Congo	2,345,095	78.7	35.0
Lesotho	30,355	2.2	2.2
Madagascar	587,051	24.9	10.0
Malawi	118,484	18.1	5.4
Mauritius	2040	1.3	12.2
Mozambique	799,380	28.8	11.0
Namibia	825,615	2.5	10.3
Seychelles	455	0.1	1.4
South Africa	1,219,090	55.9	294.8
Swaziland	17,364	1.3	3.7
Tanzania	945,200	55.6	47.4
Zambia	752,612	16.6	19.6
Zimbabwe	390,757	16.2	16.3

Data taken from the World Bank Indicators (http://data.worldbank.org/indicator)

At the same time, however, SADC countries share common ground in many ways. In contrast to regional integration organisations in the Northern Hemisphere, such as the EU or NAFTA, the SADC consists of developing and mainly least developed countries.[5] Most SADC countries show low levels of socio-economic development, weak economies with negligible industrial sectors, low intra-regional economic interdependence, various degrees of political instability, lack of adequate and interlinked infrastructure, weak national institutions, and strong dependence on extra-regional actors—particularly trading partners and donors—to name just a few (Oosthuizen 2006).

Exceptions are South Africa, Botswana and Mauritius, which are classified as middle-income economies.[6] South Africa and Mauritius remain the only countries in the region with diversified economies and considerable industrial production capacities after Zimbabwe plunged into political crisis and economic depression after the turn of the millennium. South Africa takes a special position for its superior economic strength and advanced level of industrialisation. This gives the country the rank of a hegemonic power in the region and within the organisation. For this reason, the Republic of South Africa (RSA) is not only a regional key country in many ways but also in the position to act as "motor for integration" in the SADC (Amos 2010).

All countries in Southern Africa share a similar history of colonialism and experienced the influence by external actors during the period of imperialism—and thereafter. Colonial powers from Europe, in most cases the British, not only established arbitrary borders, colonial administrations and infrastructure projects for maximising control and exploitation of their subjects from the nineteenth century onwards but cemented in parallel an asymmetric inter-regional (economic) interdependence between the colonies and mother countries (Christopher 2001). Today this legacy of colonialism is reflected not only in many SADC countries' strong extra-regional trade relations to Europe, their dependence on external Official Development Assistance (ODA) and the weakness of their national state institutions but also in the fact that English, French and Portuguese have become national—and the SADC's—official languages.

Moreover, some states in Southern Africa—such as Malawi, Zambia and Zimbabwe (as part of the Federation of Rhodesia and Nyasaland between 1953 and 1963) or Namibia (as South-West Africa de facto part of South Africa between 1919 and 1990)—look back upon a common history because they had been merged together during the time of colonialism. Transnational liberation movements, wars of independence and subsequent political instability of governments and states are also to some extent part of the legacy of colonialism and have affected several countries in the SADC region, particularly Angola, the DRC, Mozambique, Namibia and Zimbabwe (Omari and Macaringue 2007: 45–47).

In sum, the region, the SADC as an organisation and its member states today share a number of trans-boundary challenges and related regional cooperation problems. Most of them in the first place are surely not a result of colonialism but rather a consequence of specific structural conditions in the region—often related to the economy, security and infrastructure. Against this background, the general preconditions for successful and sustainable regional integration in the SADC region seem to be comparably disadvantageous at first sight, at least in comparison with those in the Northern Hemisphere, such as Europe or North America, where countries show higher degrees of socio-economic development and stronger patterns of intra-regional economic relations.

3.2.2 The SADC's Agenda and Key Policy Areas

The SADC is first of all a regional organisation that aims for development cooperation. In this respect, it clearly follows in the footsteps of the SADCC, its predecessor organisation. The SADC's vision, major goals, and strategic objectives are written down in its founding document, the SADC Treaty.[7] Condensed into one sentence, the aims of the organisation are "to achieve development, peace and security, and economic growth, to alleviate poverty, enhance the standard and quality of life of the peoples of Southern Africa, and support the socially disadvantaged through regional integration."[8]

Moreover, these long-term goals found written expression in the SADC's main strategy documents and give an impression of the member states' idea of a developmental regionalism. In this respect, the SADC Programme of Action of the early 1990s is the organisation's first master plan for achieving these targeted objectives. The document contains about 500 specific cooperation projects, of which 30 were later identified as flagship projects with high priority (Oosthuizen 2006: 127). However, the SADC Programme of Action has always been in large part a rather utopian wish list addressed to external donors than a plan for solving concrete regional cooperation problems. Shortly after the millennium, it lost its meaning as member states agreed upon other, more realistic and more specific agendas.

A prioritisation of the long-term goals and a substantiation of the rather vague intentions of the SADC Treaty can be found in two documents that today are the key instruments for the SADC's common agenda on regional integration: The Regional Indicative Strategic Development Plan (RISDP) and the Strategic Indicative Plan for the Organ (SIPO). Both plans have practical relevance for SADC's regional integration process because they act as comprehensive guidelines, set specific objectives and include concrete projects. They were approved by the Summit in August 2003 and therefore express the common intention of all member states.[9]

The RISDP is a 15-year plan with a focus on regional socio-economic development and economic integration. Besides some cross-sectoral areas of cooperation like poverty eradication and the fight against communicable diseases, its essential part is on regional trade liberalisation, market integration and development of infrastructure. In this respect, the RISDP gives clear statements on regional cooperation priority areas, provides for strategic directions and formulates concrete objectives such as regional economic block-building by creating a SADC Customs Union. A major overall objective is to make the SADC more competitive and integrate the region into the global economy.[10] Thus, the RISDP clearly stands for a policy of open regionalism. A supplementary implementation framework with monitoring and evaluation mechanisms had been approved by the SADC Summit in 2004, and a first overall review of the RISDP took place in 2010.[11]

The SIPO is the SADC's key strategic plan for political, defence and security cooperation. Its overall objective is to foster political stability and security in the region and thus create conditions for lasting peace among the organisation's (formerly to some extent hostile) member states. Launched in 2004, the SIPO relates to the RISDP since it recognises a peaceful environment as a necessary precondition for socio-economic development and regional cooperation in other issue areas. Although its objectives are rather vague and less detailed compared with the RISDP, the SIPO contains guidelines on the implementation of the Protocol on Politics, Defence and Security Cooperation and provides, among other things, for the establishment of a regional peacekeeping force.[12] From 2009 onwards, the SIPO had been revised and consolidated in a lengthy process until the SADC Summit decided to approve the Harmonised Strategic Indicative Development Plan for the Organ[13] (often referred to as SIPO II) in August 2010 (van Nieuwkerk 2012: 11).

The two strategic plans on regional socio-economic and security cooperation give an outline of the SADC's idea of regionalism and long-term goals of regional integration (Oosthuizen 2006: 120). Since the RISDP and the SIPO are not legally binding and for the most part provide rather vague aims and objectives, they act more as declarations of intention than as obligatory policy directives. Besides adopting these two, SADC member states have adopted a multitude of other, legally non-binding documents such as Charters, Declarations and Memoranda of Understanding which give formal expression to common agendas.

Nonetheless, the most important and legally binding documents, besides the SADC Treaty, are the organisation's Protocols.[14] They reflect the main policy areas of regional cooperation in the SADC and provide for member states' credible commitment to regionalism. Protocols enter into force after they have been ratified by a two-thirds majority of SADC members. However, Protocols are legally binding only for those countries that have actually signed and ratified them. Therefore, the member countries are ultimately responsible for the implementation of a protocol's provisions. States that do not initially join an adopted protocol have, in principle, the right to accede to the agreement at a later stage.[15]

In sum, the overall aim of the SADC and its member states is to achieve socio-economic development and peace in the region by means of regional coordination, cooperation and integration in a broad range of policy fields. According to the SADC's common agenda and central agreements, the issue areas of economy, security and infrastructure are in this respect of outstanding importance for the SADC to achieve its main goals. In contrast to the old SADCC's idea of a primarily inward-oriented, "closed" regionalism and strategies of import substitution, today's SADC follows an inward- as well as outward-oriented approach to regionalism. This idea of an open, new regionalism becomes clear by the fact that the organisation has put its focus on regional block-building and market integration since the mid-1990s. Today both measures are decisive development strategies for coping with the challenges of an increasingly interdependent and globalising world. The SADC's strong interaction with external actors in terms of increasing and institutionalising inter-regional relations with partners in the North and South underpins the organisation's growing outward orientation.

3.2.3 The SADC's Main Organs

The organisational structure of the SADC seems rather complex and a bit confusing at first glance. Describing every single institutional body certainly goes beyond the scope of this book. Moreover, this has already been done in detail in other works (Oosthuizen 2006; Vogt 2007). For this reason and in order to focus on the essentials, the following outline of the SADC's organisational structure provides only an introduction of the organisation's main institutions that either hold major power or bear central functions. According to the SADC's own statement,[16] these are the Summit of Heads of State or Government (Summit), the Organ on Politics, Defence and Security Cooperation (OPDS), the SADC Tribunal, the SADC Council of Ministers (COM) and the Standing Committee of Senior Officials, the Sectoral and Cluster Ministerial Committees (SCMC), the Secretariat, the SADC National Committees (SNC) and the SADC Parliamentary Forum.[17]

3 THE SOUTHERN AFRICAN DEVELOPMENT COMMUNITY (SADC): AN ... 95

The Summit of Heads of State or Government
The Summit is the SADC's supreme policy-making institution, gives policy directions and exercises control over all functions of the organisation. The Summit consists of all member states' Heads of State or Government. Decisions are based on consensus, which classifies the Summit as a clearly intergovernmental institution to the core. A Troika system, consisting of the Summit's current Chairperson, the Deputy Chairperson and the previous Chairperson, holds responsibility for directing the Summit, making quick decisions outside regular meetings and guaranteeing smooth operation over time.

The Organ on Politics, Defence and Security Cooperation
The OPDS, also known simply as 'the Organ', is the SADC's second most important institution. Shrouded in some kind of mystery, it has a wide range of specific objectives but ultimately is responsible to promote peace, security and stability in the region by facilitating confidence-building and defence cooperation among the member states (Hammerstad 2003). In past years, regional military exercises and peacekeeping efforts have become increasingly important. Under the umbrella of the Organ, the SADC formed a Standby Force and established a Regional Peacekeeping Training Centre. In the course of the SADC's institutional overhaul in 2001, the OPDS finally became a formal body of the organisation after its status had been somehow detached and unclear for several years. Similar to the Summit, the Organ is managed by a Troika system whose representatives are elected by the SADC Summit. The operative structure of the OPDS consists of the Ministerial Committee and two sub-committees, the Inter-State Defence and Security Committee (ISDSC) and the Inter-State Politics and Diplomacy Committee (ISPDC).

The SADC Tribunal
The Tribunal is the SADC's supreme judicial and dispute settlement body. It was established by Article 16 of the organisation's founding treaty in 1992 but started operating only in 2005. The Tribunal has the power to ultimately interpret the SADC's treaties, protocols and so on in case of invocation and has exclusive jurisdiction over disputes between the SADC and member countries, disputes among member countries, disputes between the SADC and its employees, disputes between natural/legal persons and the SADC, and disputes between natural/legal persons and member states. Owing to a Summit decision in 2010, however, the Tribunal is at the moment effectively suspended. The reasons behind this

were several Tribunal rulings against Zimbabwe in favour of expropriated white farmers. With President Mugabe's pressuring the Summit to consider a curtailment of the Tribunal's mandate and negotiate a new jurisdiction (Ndlovu 2011), the future of this courageous institution remains still unclear.

The SADC Council of Ministers and the Standing Committee of Senior Officials

The Council of Ministers is a vital institution of the SADC. Responsible only to the Summit, it advises the latter on priority strategies and (development) policies with a particular focus on regional socio-economic and security cooperation. In addition, it monitors the correct functioning of the organisation and ensures the implementation of its policies. The COM usually consists of the member countries' ministers of foreign affairs as well as those responsible for finance or economic planning. The Standing Committee of Senior Officials is composed of one permanent/principal secretary from every member country. It operates as a technical advisory board to the COM.

The Sectoral and Cluster Ministerial Committees

The Sectoral and Cluster Ministerial Committees are relatively new institutions and took over the responsibilities of the former Integrated Committee of Ministers. The latter was abolished in November 2007 by Summit decision as it was considered to be malfunctioning and overstrained in its tasks (Kösler 2010: 168–169). The SCMC give policy advice to the COM and are responsible to monitor the activities and progress of regional cooperation in the SADC's central issue areas of integration. In addition, they promote synergetic effects across different policy sectors and oversee the implementation of the RISDP's provisions in their fields of competence. Altogether, six SCMCs currently exist. Each SCMC consists of the relevant ministers from every SADC member country.

The Secretariat

The Secretariat is the principal executive institution of the SADC where all administrative tasks are bundled. It is located in Gaborone (Botswana) and headed by the executive secretary, who is the highest representative of the organisation. The SADC Secretariat is responsible for strategic planning and the facilitation, coordination and management of the organisation's programmes and regional cooperation projects. It provides policy analysis, promotes and reviews the harmonisation of national policies and strategies, helps to implement the decisions of the

Summit and the COM, monitors the implementation of the organisation's policies and programmes, manages its finances, engages in fundraising, applies sanctions against a member state (if necessary) and represents the SADC to the outward world. The secretariat experienced a significant upgrade in the course of the SADC's institutional overhaul starting in 2001. Its position within the whole organisation has been strengthened by a delegation of responsibilities and a centralisation of tasks. The main policy areas of regional integration—despite the sensitive issue area of security—are today managed by five directorates, which are all under the umbrella of the secretariat and report to its executive secretary. These are the directorates for Trade, Industry, Finance and Investment (TIFI); Infrastructure and Services (IS); Food, Agriculture and Natural Resources (FANR); Social and Human Development and Special Programmes (SHDSP); and Policy, Planning and Resource Mobilisation (PPRM).

Against the background of all of these tasks and functions, the secretariat is sometimes referred to as the SADC's "motor for integration" and compared to the European Commission. However, its formal power remains very weak. Therefore, it fulfils mainly an advisory function—despite the institutional reform and centralisation process (Tjønneland 2005). Part of the secretariat's institutional weakness can be explained by the fact that is often the playground for national rivalries and that it is chronically underfinanced and lacks sufficient (qualified) staff.[18]

The SADC National Committees

The SADC National Committees were formally established in 2001 in the course of the organisation's institutional overhaul. They act as an institutional interface between the SADC and the corresponding, issue area–specific mirror departments at the member states' national level. Therefore, the SNC fulfil a dual function: A major objective is to ensure that member states and national stakeholders can provide input to the SADC and participate in the organisation's regional programme and policy-formulating process. On the other hand, the SNC's task is to assist in monitoring and coordinating the implementation of SADC policies and projects on a national level. In practice, however, owing to financial constraints and vague guidelines, the SNC have not played a major role yet.

The SADC Parliamentary Forum

The SADC Parliamentary Forum was formed in 1997 as an autonomous institution of the SADC. The forum represents all Members of Parliament of the SADC member states' national assemblies and consists of five representatives of each country's national parliament. Its major objectives are to foster regional inter-parliamentary cooperation and to provide a platform for elected representatives, people and NGOs to become more involved in the SADC's activities and regional integration process. However, the role and influence of the Parliamentary Forum are still very limited because it is only loosely attached to the SADC and lacks legally binding power and institutional capacity. Therefore, it currently resembles a bit of a toothless talking shop.

3.3 Résumé

The empirical information and analytical insights on the history of regionalism in Southern Africa and on the character of the SADC as an organisation lead to the following two major findings:

Firstly, the historical overview on the old regionalisms reveals that regional integration in the SADC region has always been a state-driven and state-centric endeavour with common institutional frameworks that are highly intergovernmental in character. This is because states were reluctant to cede part of their national sovereignty to regional institutions and designed the latter in a way that allows them to maintain their decision-making authority in all major affairs. It is for this reason that no supranational institutions had been established and that many of the abovementioned old regionalisms were only weakly institutionalised. The dissolved FLS and SADCC give good examples of this matter of fact. Only those old regionalisms that were driven by South Africa as regional hegemon (e.g. the SACU and the MMA) show higher degrees of institutionalisation—and have proven to be stable and operating for decades until today.

Secondly, it has become clear that the SADC comprises a heterogeneous group of mostly developing countries of which South Africa is in a key position as superior (economic) power. While the SADC inherited some visions and organisational characteristics from the SADCC, South Africa's accession to the SADC certainly made a difference to the old SADCC since the country is generally considered to be an important factor for the success of regionalism in Southern Africa as the SACU and the MMA show. Even though the SADC is an example of the inward- and outward-oriented new regionalism, the organisation still follows some traditions of the aforementioned old regionalisms, particularly in terms of being state-centric and strongly intergovernmental in character. This is proven by the fact that the SADC Summit of Heads of State or Government is the organisation's ultimate policy- and decision-making body whereas the Secretariat and the Tribunal—which can both soonest be described as supranational organs—remain weak and underfinanced.

It is for this reason that all major regional cooperation projects under the umbrella of the SADC are highly intergovernmental in character because they have been demanded, negotiated and adopted by the member states themselves (i.e. on the Summit level). These major regional cooperation projects have been institutionalised by framing them into SADC Protocols (or similar arrangements) that are legally binding for all participating member states. This indicates a comparably strong degree of institutionalisation in the SADC—at least on the level of specific cooperation projects. The organisation's overall agenda on regional integration, laid down in large part in the RISDP and the SIPO, is comparably less institutionalised since both framework documents are non-binding in character. However, they constitute the SADC's broader vision of regionalism in which every single Protocol is factored and embedded in. Therefore, the five selected sub-cases in the following chapters represent key components of regionalism in the SADC in the form of highly institutionalised cooperation projects in central policy areas.

Summarising these insights, one can conclude that the SADC is a state-driven and intergovernmental regional integration organisation with a comparably weak institutional framework on an organisational level wherein, however, several highly institutionalised regional cooperation projects are embedded.

Notes

1. SADCC (1980): Record of the Southern African Development Coordination Summit Conference. Held at Mulungushi Conference Centre, Lusaka, on 1 April 1980. Annex V. pp. 35–39.
2. SADCC (1992): Towards Economic Integration—Policy Document prepared for the 1992 Annual Conference. Belville: Centre for Southern African Studies.
3. Reference made to the SADC's web page: http://www.sadc.int/about-sadc/overview/history-and-treaty/ (12/03/2017).
4. SADC (2005): Record of the Summit. Held in Gaborone, Republic of Botswana, 17–18 August 2005. SADC/SM/1/2005/1-A. 27.
5. Categorisation according to the United Nations: http://unohrlls.org/about-ldcs/ (05/07/2017)

6. Categorisation according to the World Bank: http://siteresources.worldbank.org/DATASTATISTICS/Resources/CLASS.XLS (12/03/2017).
7. SADC (1992): Treaty of the Southern African Development Community. Article 5.
8. Reference made to the SADC's web page: http://www.sadc.int/about-sadc/overview/ (12/03/2017).
9. SADC (2003): Record of the Summit. Held in Dar Es Salaam, United Republic of Tanzania, 25–26 August 2003. p. 5.
10. SADC (2004a): Regional Indicative Strategic Development Plan. Gaborone: SADC Secretariat.
11. SADC (2012): Desk Assessment of the Regional Indicative Strategic Development Plan 2005–2010. Gaborone: SADC Secretariat.
12. SADC (2004b): Strategic Indicative Plan for the Organ on Politics, Defence and Security Cooperation. Gaborone: SADC Secretariat.
13. SADC (2010): Revised Edition. Harmonised Strategic Indicative Plan for the Organ on Politics, Defence and Security Cooperation. Maputo.
14. As of August 2012, the SADC has produced 27 Protocols, of which 19 have entered into force so far. Information according to the SADC Secretariat: http://www.sadc.int/files/2013/6249/1610/10.1.xls (14/12/2016).
15. Reference made to the SADC's web page: http://www.sadc.int/about-sadc/overview/sa-protocols/ (12/03/2017).
16. Reference made to the SADC's web page: http://www.sadc.int/about-sadc/sadc-institutions (12/03/2017).
17. Details on the SADC's most important institutions are based on the SADC's web page.
18. Interview with Mike Humphrey (EPA Support Facility Programme Manager) at the SADC (09/27/2010).

References

Adelmann, M. 2003. *Regionale Kooperation im südlichen Afrika*. Freiburg: Arnold-Bergstraesser-Institut.

Adelmann, M. 2012. *SADC—An Actor in International Relations? The External Relations of the Southern African Development Community*. Freiburg: Arnold-Bergstraesser-Institut.

Amin, S., D. Chitala, and I. Mandaza (eds.). 1987. *SADCC: Prospect for Disengagement and Development in Southern Africa*. London: Zed Books.

Amos, S. 2010. The Role of South Africa in SADC Regional Integration: The Making or Braking of the Organization. *Journal of International Commercial Law and Technology* 5 (3): 124–131.

Anglin, D.G. 1983. Economic Liberation and Regional Cooperation in Southern Africa: SADCC and PTA. *International Organization* 37 (4): 681–711.

Christopher, A.J. 1994. *The Atlas of Apartheid*. London and New York: Routledge.
Christopher, A.J. 2001. *The Atlas of Changing South Africa*, 2nd ed. London and New York: Routledge.
Draper, P., and N. Khumalo. 2009. The Future of the Southern African Customs Union. *Trade Negotiations Insights* 8 (6): 4–5.
Evans, M. 1984. The Front-Line States, South Africa and Southern African Security: Military Prospects and Perspectives. *Zambezia* XII (5): 1–19.
Haarlov, J. 1997. *Regional Cooperation and Integration Within Industry and Trade in Southern Africa. The Making of Modern Africa*. Aldershot, Brookfield, and Hong Kong: Ashgate.
Hammerstad, A. 2003. *Defending the State or Protecting the People? SADC Security Integration at a Crossroads*. Johannesburg: South African Institute of International Affairs.
Hanlon, J. 1989. *SADCC in the 1990s. Development on the Front Line*. London: Economist Intelligence Unit.
Jefferis, K.R. 2007. The Process of Monetary Integration in the SADC Region. *Journal of Southern African Studies* 33 (1): 83–106.
Khadiagala, G.M. 2007. *Allies in Adversity. The Frontline States in Southern African Security, 1975–1993*. Lanham: University Press of America.
Kirk, R., and M. Stern. 2005. The New Southern African Customs Union Agreement. *World Economy* 28 (2): 169–190.
Kösler, A. 2010. *Die Entwicklung der Southern African Development Community (SADC) als Building Block der panafrikanischen Einheit. Die Herausforderungen der doppelten Integration und wichtige Einflussfaktoren*. Hamburg: Verlag Dr. Kovač.
le Pere, G., and E.N. Tjønneland. 2005. *Which Way SADC? Advancing Co-Operation and Integration in Southern Africa*. Midrand: Institute for Global Dialogue.
Mair, S., and C. Peters-Berries. 2001. *Regionale Integration und Kooperation in Afrika südlich der Sahara. EAC, ECOWAS und SADC im Vergleich*. Forschungsbericht des Bundesministeriums für wirtschaftliche Zusammenarbeit und Entwicklung (BMZ), vol. 127. Bonn and München: Weltforum Verlag.
McCarthy, C. 1999. SACU & the Rand Zone. In *Regionalisation in Africa: Integration & Disintegration*, ed. D.C. Bach, 159–168. Oxford and Bloomington: James Currey.
McCarthy, C. 2003. The Southern African Customs Union in Transition. *African Affairs* 102 (409): 605–630.
McCarthy, D.M.P. 2006. *International Economic Integration in Historical Perspective*. London: Routledge.
Meyns, P. 1984. The Southern African Development Coordination Conference (SADCC) and Regional Cooperation in Southern Africa. In *African Regional*

Organizations, ed. D. Mazzeo, 198–224. Cambridge: Cambridge University Press.
Meyns, P. 1997. From Co-ordination to Integration. Institutional Aspects of the Development of SADC. In *The Regionalization of the World Economy and Consequences for Southern Africa*, ed. H. Dieter, 163–184. Marburg: Metropolis-Verlag.
Meyns, P. 2000. *Konflikt und Entwicklung im Südlichen Afrika*. Opladen: Leske + Budrich.
Mufune, P. 1993. The Future of Southern African Development Coordination Conference (SADCC). *Pula: Botswana Journal of African Studies* 7 (1): 14–34.
Muntschick, J. 2013. Explaining the Influence of Extra-Regional Actors on Regional Economic Integration in Southern Africa: The EU's Interfering Impact on SADC and SACU. In *Mapping Agency: Comparing Regionalisms in Africa*, ed. U. Lorenz-Carl and M. Rempe, 77–95. Farnham: Ashgate.
Ndlovu, P.N. 2011. Campbell v Republic of Zimbabwe: A Moment of Truth for the SADC Tribunal. *SADC Law Journal* 1: 63–79.
Ngoma, N. 2005. *Prospects for a Security Community in Southern Africa. An Analysis of Regional Security in the Southern African Development Community*. Pretoria: Institute for Security Studies.
Omari, A., and P. Macaringue. 2007. Southern African Security in Historical Perspective. In *Security and Democracy in Southern Africa*, ed. G. Cawthra, A. du Pisani, and A. Omari, 45–60. Johannesburg: Wits University Press.
Oosthuizen, G.H. 2006. *The Southern African Development Community: The Organisation, its Policies and Prospects*. Midrand: Institute for Global Dialogue.
Tavlas, G.S. 2009. The Benefits and Costs of Monetary Union in Southern Africa: A critical Survey of the Literature. *Journal of Economic Surveys* 23 (1): 1–43.
Thompson, L. 1992. Southern Africa. Regional Institutions and Dynamics. In *Southern Africa at the Crossroads? Prospects for Stability and Development in the 1990s*, ed. L. Benjamin and C. Gregory, 227–254. Rivonia: Justified Press.
Tjønneland, E.N. 2005. Making SADC Work? Revisiting Institutional Reform. In *Monitoring Regional Integration in Southern Africa Yearbook*, vol. 5, ed. D. Hansohm, W. Breytenbach, T. Hartzenberg, and C. McCarthy, 166–185. Windhoek: Namibian Economic Research Unit.
Tsie, B. 1993. The Place and Role of Imperialism in the Conflict between CONSAS and SADCC. *Pula: Botswana Journal of African Studies* 7 (1): 138–155.
van Nieuwkerk, A. 2012. *Towards Peace and Security in Southern Africa. A Critical Analysis of the Revised Strategic Indicative Plan for the Organ on Politics, Defence and Security Co-operation (SIPO) of the Southern African Development Community*. Maputo: Friedrich-Ebert-Stiftung.

Viner J. 1950. *The Customs Union Issue*. New York: Carnegie Endowment for International Peace.

Vogt, J. 2007. *Die Regionale Integration des südlichen Afrikas. Unter besonderer Betrachtung der Southern African Development Community (SADC)*. Baden-Baden: Nomos.

Primary Sources

SADC. 1992. Treaty of the Southern African Development Community. Gaborone: SADC Secretariat.

SADC. 2003. Record of the Summit. Held in Dar Es Salaam, United Republic of Tanzania, 25–26 August 2003.

SADC. 2003. Regional Indicative Strategic Development Plan. Gaborone: SADC Secretariat.

SADC. 2004b. Record of the Meeting of SADC Council of Ministers held in Arusha 12–13 March 2004.

SADC. 2005. Record of the Summit. Held in Gaborone, Republic of Botswana, 17–18 August 2005. SADC/SM/1/2005/1-A. 27.

SADC. 2010. Revised Edition. Harmonised Strategic Indicative Plan for the Organ on Politics, Defence and Security Cooperation. Maputo.

SADC. 2012. Desk Assessment of the Regional Indicative Strategic Development Plan 2005–2010. Gaborone: SADC Secretariat.

SADCC. 1980. Record of the Southern African Development Coordination Summit Conference. Held at Mulungushi Conference Centre, Lusaka, on the 1st April 1980.

SADCC. 1992. Towards Economic Integration—Policy Document Prepared for the 1992 Annual Conference. Belville: Centre for Southern African Studies.

Interviews

Mike Humphrey (EPA Support Facility Programme Manager) at SADC (09/27/2010).

CHAPTER 4

The Protocol on Trade and the Creation of the Southern African Development Community Free Trade Area

The adoption of the Protocol on Trade in August 2000 and the subsequent establishment of the Free Trade Area (FTA) in August 2008 are outstanding examples for regional integration projects within the framework of the Southern African Development Community (SADC). The SADC-FTA not only reflects the member states' interest and willingness to cooperate in an important issue area but also ranks among the major achievements of regionalism on the entire African continent. The following chapter analyses and explains why SADC member states pursued a strategy of institutionalised regional economic cooperation towards the successful creation of the SADC-FTA. Furthermore, it shall give answers on its institutional design and inherent rules as well as how the FTA actually operates and performs.

4.1 TRADE RESTRICTIONS AND TRADE POTENTIAL: THE DEMAND FOR REGIONAL MARKET INTEGRATION

In general, the SADC countries' demand for regional market integration is for structural reasons assumed to be motivated by two strands of regional problems—in terms of obstacles to trade—and two corresponding strands of expected positive effects. This is because regional market integration has an outward- and inward-oriented dimension:

In regard to outward orientation, the less developed SADC countries increasingly regarded regional market integration from the mid-1990s onwards as the optimal strategy to slowly integrate the region into the competitive world economy. The creation of an economically liberalised and integrated regional market ought to be the first "stepping-stone" on this way and prepare the member countries for the economic challenges of globalisation. A regional economic block with common institutions—such as a SADC-FTA would be—could help to strengthen the region's economic standing and bargaining power in a globalising world where individual countries become increasingly faced with powerful (economic) actors from the North and other regional blocks (Weeks 1996: 106–108). Furthermore, regional market integration and related credible commitment institutions would make the own area more attractive for foreign direct investment (FDI) inflows which are assumed to have a positive impact on the host countries' development. This is because regional economic integration provides potential investors a relatively larger, easier accessible and liberalised market with better chances for increasing economies of scale compared with a single state or an uncoordinated group of countries (Moran et al. 2005).

Besides having these rather outward-oriented aspects, regional economic integration in the SADC is an inward-oriented project that aims to address regional problems: Against a prevalent pattern of intra-regional economic interdependence within the region, countries demand regional trade liberalisation and expect prosperity from institutionalised economic cooperation because this allows them to better benefit from comparative cost advantages and economies of scale. Ideally, this would result in increasing intra-regional trade and investment flows and thus contribute to economic development (Ricardo 1977; Viner 1950). In this context, developing and economically less interdependent countries often pursue measures of regional integration in order to clear obstacles to an expected growth of intra-regional economic interdependence in the future and thus act preemptively to a prospective problematic situation rather than to an actually existing one (Weggoro 1995: 40–44). Such action involves for example addressing the problem of non-tariff barriers to trade (NTBs). The latter are serious obstacles to any trade liberalisation efforts, and countries seeking to increase intra-regional trade must take appropriate measures to remove NTBs parallel to tariff reduction in order to gain positive effects of free-trade arrangements (Ebrill and Stotsky 1998).

The SADC countries' economic preferences prior to the negotiations on the Protocol on Trade can be deduced from structural characteristics such as their pattern of economic interdependence and the corresponding benefits expected from regional trade liberalisation. One can deduce the character and degree of economic interdependence on the basis of trade data and investment flows. However, sole reliance and non-critical use of intra-regional trade shares as determinant factors for economic interdependence have been strongly criticised: They may lead to distorted results and misinterpretations because the indicator "intra-regional trade share" always correlates with the size and number of member countries of a region and therefore is biased by these two dimensions (de Lombaerde and van Langenhove 2006; Tavares and Schulz 2006: 241). Simply said, the more countries in the world join one specific regional organisation the relatively larger the intra-regional trade share of this very organisation (as well as of its member states) will be. This is because the number of possible extra-regional outsiders decreases under such conditions.

In order to encounter the geographical bias inherent to the intra-regional trade share measure, the intra-regional trade intensity index[1] shall be applied as an additional, complementary indicator in order to carefully determine the actual pattern of economic interdependence within the SADC and among its member states. The intra-regional trade intensity index works well for this purpose because it controls for the abovementioned problem of a region's geographical extent insofar as it introduces in this respect a neutrality criterion. It measures the ratio of a region's intra-regional trade share to the region's share in world trade, and index values above zero indicate that the region's intra-regional trade is relatively more important than trading with the rest of the world (Tavares and Schulz 2006: 241).

Formal intra-regional trade[2] in the SADC area has always been relatively low—at least in comparison with regional integration organisations in the Northern Hemisphere that consist of more industrialised and developed countries (e.g. the EU or NAFTA). During the period of 1992–1999 (i.e. a few years prior to the conclusion of the Protocol on Trade), formal intra-regional trade in the SADC oscillated between only 4.1 and 6.8% of total trade.[3] However, these figures neglect unrecorded and informal trade flows that amount up to more than an additional 30% of formal trade in Southern Africa—particularly trade in agricultural products (Foroutan and Pritchett 1993: 98; Kennes 1999: 29). Therefore, actual intra-regional trade flows and regional trade potential in the SADC prior to the negotiations of the Trade Protocol were considerably larger than recorded trade data would suggest (Lyakurwa 1999: 264).

The intra-regional trade intensity index adjusts this first impression and clearly highlights the importance of the SADC market for its member countries. During the same period of 1992–1999, this econometric index oscillated between 6.2 and 13.1 index points and therefore depicted figures well above zero.[4] These figures imply that the intra-regional trade flows in terms of volume, value and meaning were considerably greater than one would expect on the grounds of the SADC's significance in world trade. This structural background of comparably weak but nevertheless existing intra-regional economic interdependence in the SADC generated an initial demand for regional economic integration in the organisation and its member states. Several official documents,[5] studies and statements support this view and give good examples of the expected benefits and enthusiasm vis-à-vis market integration in the SADC (African Development Bank 1993; Jenkins et al. 2000; von Kirchbach and Roelofsen 1998).

A more differentiated look at the SADC's intra-regional trade relations a few years prior to the negotiations of the Protocol on Trade reveals the following pattern of modest intra-regional economic interdependence that was even rather extensive for a number of countries (Table 4.1):

In terms of total merchandise trade, the SADC market was a very important trading destination for Botswana, Lesotho, Malawi, Mozambique, Namibia, Swaziland, Zambia and Zimbabwe during the mid-1990s. Regarding exports only (percentage of total exports), the SADC was the top or a major export market for Swaziland (53.1%), Lesotho (45.3%), Zimbabwe (30.2%), Mozambique (29.9%), Namibia (29.7%) and to a lesser degree Botswana (24.6%). Both enumerations each account for a good half of the SADC's then–member states. For plain structural reasons, these figures support the assumption that the stronger the intra-regional economic interdependence of a SADC country—particularly in terms of exports—the greater its demand for regional economic integration because of the expected beneficial effects of trade expansion will be.

This demand for trade facilitation was intensified by the existence of various restrictive and costly NTBs to regional trade. In Southern Africa, with the exception of the SACU, borders were "thick" because NTBs were widespread and manifold and affected at least 25% of intra-regional trade flows. During the mid-1990s, the most significant NTB-related obstacles to regional trade were complex and cumbersome customs

Table 4.1 Share of intra-regional trade of SADC countries in 1995

Country	Exports to SADC (% of total exports)	Imports from SADC (% of total imports)
Angola	<1.0	8.6
Botswana[a]	24.6	79.5
DR Congo	7.0	18.9
Lesotho[b]	45.3	90.5
Madagascar	1.3	6.6
Malawi	16.9	44.5
Mauritius	1.0	11.8
Mozambique	29.9	33.7
Namibia[b]	29.7	89.2
Seychelles	0.8	12.6
South Africa	9.9	1.5
Swaziland[b]	53.1	94.0
Tanzania	3.1	8.6
Zambia	8.2	45.5
Zimbabwe	30.2	42.1

Trade data generated with the help of the World Integrated Trade Data Solution (WITS) database: http://wits.worldbank.org/witsweb/default.aspx (06/06/2016). The WITS uses combined data from the United Nations Statistical Division of the United Nations Conference on Trade and Development (UNCTAD) and the World Trade Organisation (WTO)
[a]Data from 1996 according to the Botswana Central Statistics Office: http://www.cso.gov.bw/templates/cso/file/File/total_tradeTable1.pdf (10/10/2016)
[b]Intra-SADC trade shares (average 1991–1993) according to the database of the Industrial Development Corporation of South Africa (Valentine 1998: 10)
Countries in italics were not yet an SADC member state in 1995

procedures, toll fees and expensive permits, import bans and quotas, export taxes and of course the overall weakness of the border posts and the region's infrastructure with numerous costly bottlenecks (Pierides 2008; Teravaninthorn and Raballand 2009).[6]

4.1.1 Comparative Cost Advantages

Trade data aside, it was also regional comparative cost advantages that fuelled demand for regional economic integration in the SADC. Part of the mainstream literature tends to downplay the potential for trade growth among SADC counties upon the generalisation that the economies in Southern Africa are too similar in terms of a strong specialisation in exports of virtually the same primary products such as minerals and raw materials. However, this scepticism is to some degree inappropriate because comparative advantages did exist in the region (Cleary 1999: 7–8; Weeks 1996: 107–108):

According to a study that analysed the comparative advantage for SADC countries in regional trade prior to negotiation of the Protocol on Trade (1991–1993), virtually all countries had a comparative advantage in the regional export of certain agricultural products and foodstuffs, such as beef and food products (for Botswana, Lesotho, Namibia and Mozambique), tobacco (for Angola, Malawi, Tanzania, Zambia and Zimbabwe), tea and coffee (for Malawi and Zimbabwe), beverages (for Swaziland), horticulture (for Malawi, Tanzania and Zambia), sugar (for Mauritius, South Africa and Zambia) and cotton (for Tanzania). Furthermore, Lesotho, Malawi, Mauritius, Mozambique and Zambia had comparative advantages in the export of light manufactures such as wood products, furniture, textiles and clothing. In South Africa, the most developed and diversified SADC economy, comparative advantages existed across a broad spectrum of sectors and involved, in particular, the heavy and light manufacturing industry. This made the Cape Republic a special case among all SADC countries, although Mauritius's and Zimbabwe's economies had a small industrial base at that time, too (Keet 1997: 290; Valentine 1998: 15–16).

The following examples provide detailed insights on country-specific demand for regional market integration in the SADC. South Africa, Zimbabwe and Mauritius represent typical SADC members because the first is the region's economic power house and the latter respectively stand for a core and peripheral SADC country.

4.1.2 South Africa

The era of Apartheid in South Africa entailed a partly dysfunctional economy that to a certain extent had been disconnected and isolated from regional as well as global markets because of export embargos and other (economic) sanctions (Becker 1988: 61–63; Bell 1993). With the end of Apartheid in 1994, the macro-economic policies of the new South Africa changed rapidly towards regional trade liberalisation and market integration in order to take advantage of the country's economic potential (Adelmann 2003: 63–70; Chipeta and Schade 2007: 66–67).

Its economy and array of exports were diversified and included basic manufactures, minerals, precious metals and metal products, transport equipment, chemical products, machinery, and processed food. Pretoria's exports to the SADC region consisted mainly of capital-intensive value-added manufactured goods whereas imports were for the most part labour-intensive, lower-value primary commodities such as raw materials and agricultural products (Valentine 1998: 15–18).

By the mid-1990s, South Africa had significant yet unexploited potential to substitute some of its imports from overseas with equivalents from the region. Given comparative cost advantages, a fruitful interaction between South Africa and the rest of the SADC was most likely to occur in sectors such as fossil energy sources, raw materials and minerals, agricultural products and certain (processed) foodstuffs (Bauer 2004: 30; Odén 2001: 90–91; Valentine 1998: 15). A "quick and dirty" study of the South African Industrial Development Corporation suggested that South Africa could gain a 4.6% increase in total exports and an 8.0% increase in manufactured exports from regional tariff removal (Davies 1996: 35). It was against this economically promising background that major political and economic actors in the country demanded increasingly regional trade liberalisation and market integration in the SADC.

However, this demand did not unconditionally favour an open regionalism. Pretoria also had selective preferences towards protectionism, especially with regard to its export-oriented sugar and automotive industry as well as its textile and clothing sector where neighbouring SADC countries often had a competitive advantage due to cheaper costs of labour. Moreover, about one third of South Africa's manufacturing sector's exports and more than one quarter of its automotive industry's exports went to SADC members back in 1994 (Davies 1996: 33). Pretoria had a strong interest in safeguarding this important regional export-destination—not least against cheap imports from Asia—by means of an adequately tailored trade regime as the country's manufacturing sector could not yet compete on global markets (Coussy 1996: 5; Jenkins and Thomas 2001: 167–170).

4.1.3 Zimbabwe

Landlocked Zimbabwe is a typical example of a core country of the SADC. Its regional trade pattern is closely linked with several Southern African states, particularly with the former British colonies South Africa, Zambia, Malawi and Botswana. In the early 1990s, the Zimbabwean economy was one of the few in the region that was fairly industrialised and had a diversified export base with a noteworthy manufacturing sector (Haarlov 1997: 90; Hanlon 1986: 90). Owing to its large agricultural sector, the country was often called the "Breadbasket of Southern Africa," and agricultural products, food and processed foodstuffs as well as tobacco, tea and coffee contributed a major share to the country's exports (Weeks and Mosley 1998).

By the mid-1990s, Zimbabwe began to advocate an open market economy and regional trade liberalisation in order to exploit the benefits of its (regional) comparative advantages. Policy papers and the frameworks of important national trade promotion agencies (e.g. Zimtrade) substantiated these objectives and demanded not only to explore new markets but also to increase trade with its regional market in order to realise the expected profits. This regional market became increasingly accessible after the end of Apartheid in South Africa because this implied an end of economic sanctions (Hess 2001; Zwizwai 2007).

Owing to Zimbabwe's strong intra-regional economic interdependence, any reduction of barriers to trade in Southern Africa was in Harare's strong interest. According to surveys taken from numerous Zimbabwean companies, the Zimbabwean business community perceived the regional tariff barriers—particularly customs tariffs, import duties and related taxes—as the major obstacles to intra-SADC trade (Zwizwai 2007: 88–90). Only few sectors of the Zimbabwean economy—namely its (uncompetitive) light manufacturing sector as well as the clothing and sugar industry—feared a negative impact from regional market integration because their most active competitors operated in neighbouring South Africa or in the SACU area (Hess 2001; Zwizwai 2007: 17–21, 41–46).

4.1.4 Mauritius

Being a small island state, Mauritius is a typical example of a peripheral SADC country with a comparably low level of economic interdependence with the region. Therefore, the country's economic preferences could be assumed to be rather indifferent towards regional economic integration in the SADC. However, this was not the case, because Mauritius's trade with the SADC outweighed its trade with other neighbouring regional organisations such as the Common Market for Eastern and Southern Africa (COMESA) or the Indian Ocean Community (IOC). Furthermore, Mauritius increasingly followed export-oriented as well as investment-friendly economic policies since the mid-1990s. The country was enthusiastic about the idea of open regionalism and regarded market integration as a key strategy to foster socio-economic development (Erasmus et al. 2004: 3–4; Sobhee and Bhowon 2007: 68–73).

The major driving force behind Mauritius's demand for regional trade liberalisation and economic integration in the SADC was an expectation to exploit its regional comparative advantages and stimulate untapped trade potential—particularly with South Africa—in the agricultural, food and manufacturing sectors. On the sub-national level, private economic stakeholders and societal actors were involved in the policy-making process through the "Mauritian Chamber of Commerce" or the "Joint Economic Council" where lobbying took effect. However, Mauritius's general demand for regional trade liberalisation in the SADC had limitations, particularly with respect to the country's light manufacturing industry (especially textiles) and its sugar industry where South Africa—the largest African supplier of goods to Mauritius—was seen as a growing competitor (Sobhee and Bhowon 2007: 68–73).

Altogether, regional comparative cost advantages existed for the most part between South Africa and the rest of the SADC; that is—briefly speaking—capital-intensive and manufactured products on the one hand and labour-intensive and agricultural products (and, to a lesser degree, natural resources) on the other. If regional trade barriers were removed, the overall intra-SADC trade was expected to increase significantly, particularly in the sectors of agricultural and unprocessed food products, (precious) minerals and metals, yarns, paper products and particularly fossil energy sources (Carrère 2004: 203; Chauvin and Gaulier 2002: 24–25). In addition, a part of the vast amount of informal trade—for the most part across the borders of Angola, the Democratic Republic of the Congo, Namibia, Zambia and Zimbabwe—could be directed into formal channels (Cleary 1999: 7; Holden 1996: 25). According to official statements and research studies, the successful implementation of the SADC-FTA was expected to cause an increase of intra-regional trade up to more than 20%, at best 35%, of the region's total trade (Adelmann 2003: 52; Chauvin and Gaulier 2002: 12–14).

4.1.5 Interim Summary and Situation Structure

In sum, virtually all SADC countries showed a strong demand and willingness to engage in regional market integration. Regional trade

Fig. 4.1 Problematic situation in view of the SADC-FTA

	SADC Country B	
	Free Trade	Protection
SADC Country A — Free Trade	3 / 3	1 / 4
SADC Country A — Protection	4 / 1	2 / 2

liberalisation made good economic sense for structural reasons—despite a comparably low level of intra-regional economic interdependence. With regard to the SADC's intra-regional trade pattern and according to general agreement in the academic literature (Adelmann 2003: 63–70; Chipeta and Schade 2007: 68–69; Draper et al. 2006: 31–35), South Africa was expected to gain most from regional economic integration in the SADC because the country could exploit most benefits from economies of scale and regional comparative advantages. A liberalised regional market would boost Pretoria's export-oriented economy which was expected to flood even the less developed neighbouring countries with (globally uncompetitive) products "Made in RSA". It was not least for this reason that South Africa was the strongest advocate for a SADC-FTA.

Against this structural background and with reference to the theoretical framework, the genuine underlying cooperation problem of regional trade liberalisation in the SADC was by the mid-1990s clearly reminiscent of a prisoner's dilemma (Fig. 4.1):

Mutual tariff reduction and the creation of a club good in the form of a liberalised regional market could provide better economic pay-offs for every participant SADC member state than a non-regulated status quo. At the same time, however, each country had, in principle, egoistic incentives to free-ride from the aspired club good; that is, take profits from the tariff removal of its regional neighbours while keeping its own tariffs unchanged. Referring to the theory-driven hypotheses, SADC countries are expected to solve this regional cooperation problem by establishing regional institutions—in this case, a regional trade regime in the form of an SADC-FTA. The latter is not expected to be of symbolic nature but instead demonstrate a clear degree of effectiveness because it is based on a genuine and real regional cooperation problem. However, its institutional effects could be only modest because the level of intra-regional economic interdependence in the region was rather low.

4.2 MONOCENTRIC INTRA-REGIONAL ECONOMIC INTERDEPENDENCE: SOUTH AFRICA AS REGIONAL ECONOMIC HEGEMON

In the issue area of the economy, comparably well developed and industrialised South Africa is not only the uncontested economic giant in regional terms but also the key trade hub in the whole SADC area. In 1995, South Africa contributed approximately 75% to the SADC's total GDP and Pretoria's national GDP per capita was more than 250% larger than the regional average. The country also represented the lion's share of SADC's international trade volume and accounted for more than 60% of the organisation's total exports and almost 50% of its imports. The trade balance between the RSA and the rest of the SADC had always been in favour of Pretoria—in fact, it had been for decades—because of the "unequal" trade pattern the Cape Republic inherited from its colonial past (Coussy 1996: 2–7; Valentine 1998: 9). In 1994, for example, South Africa's trade surplus with the rest of the region amounted to more than $4.2 billion USD (Gibb 1998: 290–291).

Given its absolute and relative economic strength, South Africa clearly dominated intra-regional trade in the SADC. By the first half of the 1990s, imports from the RSA were the single most important source for Botswana, Lesotho, Malawi, Namibia, Swaziland, Zambia and Zimbabwe. Furthermore, the economies of Lesotho, Malawi, Mozambique, Namibia, Swaziland, Zimbabwe and to a lesser degree Botswana depended strongly on South Africa as an (if not the most) important export destination (Gibb 1998: 290–291).[7]

This observation is corroborated by the fact that most SADC countries had their top regional comparative advantage with South Africa as a trading partner, a circumstance that multiplied their economic

Table 4.2 South African investment in SADC by country (1994–2003)

Country	Share of South African FDI of total FDI inflows (%)	South Africa's rank as foreign investor in the country
Angola	1	6
Botswana	58	1
DR Congo	71	1
Lesotho	86	1
Malawi	80	1
Mauritius	9	3
Mozambique	31	1
Namibia	21	3
Swaziland	71	1
Tanzania	35	2
Zambia	29	1
Zimbabwe	24	3

Data taken from Grobbelaar (2004: 93–95)

dependence on the Cape Republic (Valentine 1998: 17). In contrast, less than 10% of the RSA's total exports went to the SADC in 1995 (Table 4.2). This puts the overall importance of the SADC market for Pretoria into perspective, but only at first glance because about 30% of exports from South Africa's capital-intensive manufacturing sector were shipped to SADC members, a fact that emphasises the sector-specific importance of this regional market for the RSA (Davies 1996: 33).

With regard to FDI flows, the picture of strong and asymmetric intra-regional interdependence is similar: For the period of 1994–2003, South African investment in the SADC area represented about 25% of total FDI inflows to the region. The Cape Republic not only provided the major share of incoming FDI to the SADC as a whole but was even the top foreign investor in seven member countries (Page and te Velde 2004: 22).

The share of South African FDI (as a percentage of total FDI inflows) was particularly important for the economies of Lesotho (86%), Malawi (80%), Swaziland (71%), the DRC (71%), Botswana (58%), Tanzania (35%), Mozambique (31%) and Zambia (29%) during this period. These countries depended strongly on South African investments, not least because South African companies were for the most part market-seeking, provided comparatively more new jobs and were well adjusted to the specific "African business environment" (Daniel et al. 2003; Hartzenberg and Mathe 2005: 11).

In a nutshell, South Africa was the economic hegemon and dominant country in the SADC region—not only because of its superior level of economic development or the size of its economy but particularly for structural reasons. The prevailing pattern of intra-regional economic interdependence was strongly asymmetric in character. Its structure resembled a "hub-and-spoke" (McCarthy 1998: 79) with South Africa in the centre position and the rest of the SADC members—as its economic "dependencies"—at the periphery (Makgetlaneng 2005). For this reason, the RSA was expected to become not only the driver for regional market integration as the "SADC's locomotive of growth" (Kibble et al. 1995: 48) but also the most influential designer in view of its institutional framework.

4.2.1 Asymmetric Extra-Regional Economic Interdependence

The SADC is not a regionally isolated entity but instead an organisation whose member states look back over a long history of political and economic dependence on extra-regional actors. In regard to the economic structure, the EU was the major extra-regional trading partner and export destination for the SADC region as a whole, for South Africa as its economic powerhouse, and for a number of the organisation's member states during the mid-1990s—and had been for decades before. This pattern of strong and asymmetric extra-regional economic interdependence is not surprising at all, because it reflects the traditional trade relationship between former colonial masters in Europe and their dependencies in Southern Africa[8] (Table 4.3).

In regard to total merchandise trade in 1995, Angola, the DRC, Madagascar, Malawi, Mauritius, the Seychelles, South Africa and Tanzania traded comparably more with the EU than with co-members of their own regional organisation. In regard to export shares only (as a percentage of total exports), the EU was the top destination for Botswana (34.0%), the DRC (61.4%), Madagascar (70.1%), Malawi (49.2%), Mauritius (74.4%), the Seychelles (50.1%), Tanzania (32.6%) and Zimbabwe (42.4%) in the year under observation. According to aggregated trade flows and relative trade shares, about 30% of the region's total exports went to the EU. Whereas Europe was of great importance as a trading partner and export destination for most SADC countries, Southern Africa was only a very marginal trading partner for the EU.

Table 4.3 Share of extra-regional trade of SADC countries with the EU in 1995

Country	Exports to the EU (% of total exports)	Imports from the EU (% of total imports)
Angola	21.2	62.5
Botswana	34.0	8.5
DR Congo	61.4	39.4
Lesotho	0.6	1.6
Madagascar	70.1	51.7
Malawi	49.2	26.5
Mauritius	74.4	34.0
Mozambique	40.5	23.2
Namibia	28.6	6.9
Seychelles	50.1	32.4
South Africa	17.6	32.9
Swaziland	6.3	2.5
Tanzania	32.6	32.2
Zambia	16.2	20.7
Zimbabwe	42.5	23.0

Trade data generated with the help of the WITS database: http://wits.worldbank.org/witsweb/default.aspx (06/06/2016). WITS uses combined data from the UNCTAD and the WTO
Countries in italics were not yet an SADC member state in 1995

This asymmetric economic relationship between Europe and the SADC becomes even more pronounced if one takes the pattern of unidirectional North-South inflows of FDI and development aid, structural adjustment funding and so on into account (Oosthuizen 2006: 155–159; Sidiropoulos 2002: 23). With regard to extra-regional investment inflows, South Africa sourced virtually all of its FDI from overseas—particularly from the EU. Therefore, the SADC as a whole was in absolute terms in the first instance heavily reliant on extra-regional FDI from Europe, although a significant number of SADC member countries depended basically more on South African FDI (Goldstein 2004: 45–46).

Owing to this pattern of strong and asymmetric extra-regional economic interdependence between the EU on the one side and a significant number of SADC member states on the other side, Brussels was for plain structural reasons in a position to exert significant influence on the SADC as a whole—particularly in the issue area of the economy. This implies having the (potential) power to interfere with the organisation's plan to negotiate and implement a common Trade Protocol and institutionalise a SADC-FTA.

However, contrary to this rather gloomy picture, the SADC's relationship of dependence on an extra-regional actor—the EU—was not that alarming: By the mid-1990s, the organisation looked back over a long history of external donors' support or, put another way, to a considerable degree of external "donor dependency" (Oosthuizen 2006: 64, 181). This is not least because the late 1990s saw a widening of the geographical scope of the EU's external involvement in general (Pietrangeli 2009: 10–11) and of its support of regional economic integration processes among developing countries in particular.[9] During the years before the negotiation of the Trade Protocol, the European Community—in addition to bilateral support of mostly European countries—provided €129 million for the purpose of strengthening regional cooperation and development in the SADC through the 7th European Development Fund (EDF) during the period of 1990–1995. Ten percent of this amount had been dedicated for "Trade Promotion and Business" and 20% for capacity building. The following 8th EDF (1995–2000) became operative at the time of the SADC's trade negotiations. It budgeted €121 million for the SADC's programme of action and earmarked 20% of this amount for the focal area "Trade, Investment and Finance" and 10% for strengthening the capacity of the SADC's Secretariat.[10] In addition, the EU enhanced its efforts for inter-regional dialogue and multidimensional cooperation in the SADC region with the adoption of the Berlin Declaration in 1994, in which Europe committed itself to "promote the development of a long term closer economic cooperation in Southern Africa."[11]

Altogether, a major part of the SADC's overall regional integration efforts and programme of institutionalisation within the organisation's framework had been financially and logistically supported by extra-regional donors. In 1995–1996, more than 80% of the organisation's regional cooperation projects were externally funded by extra-regional donors, and the EU played the leading role in this respect.[12] Of course, not all of this external support focussed explicitly on promoting institutionalised regional economic cooperation in the SADC. However, it was in particular the economic sector and the issue of regional market integration that earned much of the donors' attention and donations (Lee 2003: 58). This implies that important extra-regional actors like the EU were in general positive and encouraging towards the idea of regional economic integration in the SADC because they earmarked significant financial means for its realisation.

Against the background of this specific pattern of extra-regional interdependence and external influence, the problematic situation prior to the negotiation of the SADC Protocol on Trade can be sketched as follows: It remained reminiscent of a prisoner's dilemma. This is because membership in a regional trade regime in the form of a Trade Protocol or SADC-FTA neither restricted a participant's room to manoeuvre (e.g. in terms of being part of a third organisation or trade regime) nor affected it existing or future (bilateral) trade relations with extra-regional actors. This is because, in principle, different FTAs can overlap without interfering with each other since an FTA does not demand its members to implement a common external tariff. Moreover, external influence was rather promoting than indifferent to the SADC's market integration project. This is because the individual SADC countries' costs for cooperation—that is, the implementation of the Protocol and establishment of the SADC-FTA—have been reduced by the EU's external funding offers. Thus, the genuine dilemma-type situation was possibly even externally cushioned to a certain degree.

In sum, and with reference to the theoretical framework, one can assume that the emergence, design and success of an FTA in the SADC depend first and foremost on South Africa since the pattern of intra-regional economic interdependence put Pretoria in the economic issue area in a regional power position. However, owing to the fact that a strong and asymmetric economic interdependence of a number of SADC member states with the EU exists, the SADC's approach towards regional market integration is expected to proceed and perform only as long as this important extra-regional actor does not explicitly play against it.

4.3 Driven and Formed by South Africa: The SADC's Protocol on Trade and the Establishment of the SADC-FTA

The SADC Protocol on Trade expresses the need for regional economic cooperation in order to enhance intra-regional trade-flows, increase investment, combat illicit trade, and adjust to international standards. It gives legal and practical effect to the member states' commitments to market integration under the provisions of the SADC Treaty. In a nutshell, the protocol calls for regional trade liberalisation and obliges its participants to reduce barriers to intra-regional trade, harmonise trade procedures and specify Rules of Origin (RoO), and it envisages the creation of an SADC-FTA within eight years after its ratification.[13] The actual version of the protocol entered into force in August 2000 and resulted in the launch of the SADC-FTA on 17 August 2008.[14]

4.3.1 Trade Negotiations and Design of the Protocol

The initial trade negotiations in the SADC started after an extra-ordinary council meeting of the Ministers responsible for Industry, Trade, Finance and Investment in December 1995.[15] Following this event, it took only four meetings in the newly created Trade Negotiation Forum (TNF), the central arena of inter-state bargaining on trade issues, before the member states agreed to sign a first version of the SADC Trade Protocol at the 1996 Summit in Maseru.[16] However, most member states were not ready to ratify this speedy draft version, because they felt uneasy about its contents and demanded various specifications. Therefore, SADC member states met again within the TNF and several other sub-committees and started to discuss a new design and new provisions of an amended version of the SADC Protocol on Trade. The toughest negotiations concerned the schedule of trade liberalisation and the composition of commodities that were to be liberalised. Furthermore, intense bargaining occurred with regard to special agreements on sensitive products and the complex issue of the RoO. Altogether, the negotiations on the amended SADC Protocol on Trade took about three years and 19 rounds of bargaining within the TNF before it became finalised and entered into force at the Windhoek Summit in August 2000 (Lee 2003: 112).[17]

All SADC countries shared the basic and rather outward-oriented demand for regional economic cooperation and regional block-building. This overall aim did not harbour any dissent. Furthermore, all member states had rather congruent preferences in terms of intra-regional trade liberalisation and of how to institutionalise regional market integration in general. Consequently, these overall objectives did not lead to any serious dispute. This regional consensus manifested in the Trade Protocol's general stipulations:

Its preamble refers explicitly to Article 22 of the SADC Treaty (1992), the Abuja Treaty (1991) and the General Agreement on Tariffs and Trade (GATT) Uruguay Round on global trade liberalisation and calls for regional market integration in the SADC region in order to foster national and regional socio-economic development.[18]

The protocol's first part is its most important because it contains the agreement's central objectives. In a nutshell, these are (a) to liberalise and increase intra-regional trade, (b) to ensure efficient production by allowing member states to exploit regional comparative advantages, (c) to improve the region's investment climate and increase intra-regional as well as foreign investments, (d) to enhance economic development and (e) to establish a SADC-FTA.[19]

The protocol's second part gives details on how to achieve these objectives and calls for the reduction of tariffs and non-tariff barriers to intra-SADC trade. Article 3, 1 (b) schedules the establishment of the SADC-FTA to a time frame of eight years after the protocol coming into force. Moreover, the article allows exceptional permissions for member states that are negatively affected by tariff reduction and permits varying time frames and tariff lines for different products within the whole process of tariff elimination.[20] Article 6 demands that states take adequate measurements to eliminate existing NTBs—and refrain from establishing new ones. Article 13 calls explicitly for cooperation in customs matters and exemplifies strategies on the simplification and harmonisation of national customs regulations, for example the standardisation of trade documents, with reference to Annex II.[21]

The third part of the protocol addresses the issue of the RoO. It states in a very general manner that RoO should be introduced in order to guarantee that only those products that have been mainly produced/processed within the SADC-FTA actually do benefit from regional trade liberalisation.[22]

Part four calls for member states to introduce common technical standards. Furthermore, it emphasises the participants' consensus to refrain from dumping measures and subsidies. However, Article 21 allows for exemptions insofar as members may, after authorisation by the Committee of Ministers responsible for trade matters, protect their national infant industries by "suspending certain aspects of this Protocol in respect of like goods imported from other Member States."[23]

Part eight refers to trade relations between member states and third countries. Article 27 allows member states to agree on preferential trade agreements among themselves and with third parties as long as they do not harm the intention of the protocol. Article 28, 2 stipulates that states extend the trade privileges inherent to such third-party agreements on all other member states (most-favoured nation treatment). However, these provisions are watered down by Article 28, 3, which states that member countries are not obliged to do so if they have been a member of another regional trading block prior to the signing of the protocol. With reference to the SADC Treaty,[24] member states are advised to cooperate with third countries or organisations in order to achieve the protocol's objectives.

The ninth part provides details on institutions related to the implementation of the protocol, notably dispute settlement procedures. Dispute settlement follows an escalating two-step procedure: firstly, at the panel of trade experts; secondly—and ultimately—at the SADC Tribunal as per Article 32 of the SADC Treaty.

In summary, the general content of the SADC Protocol on Trade consists of visionary aims as well as rather non-specific paragraphs, policy directives and obligations that reflect the member states' consensual need for regional market integration and their receptiveness to outward-oriented block-building.

4.3.2 Tariff Reduction Schedule and Rules of Origin

In fact, a closer look into the protocol reveals that it is not based entirely on regional consensus but instead a product of tough inter-state bargaining and compromise. The "non-general" particularities and supplements of the Trade Protocol concern basically the distribution of cooperative gains and costs (i.e. the relative benefits) of regional trade liberalisation. They deal with the second-order problems of the club good "SADC Free Trade Agreement". It is therefore not surprising that the specific design of the Protocol became subject to tough inter-state bargaining—obviously in areas with most conflicting preferences between SADC states: trade offers regarding the schedule and composition of the products/goods to be liberalised, the complex issue concerning the RoO, and special agreements on sensitive products (Flatters 2001).

The conduct and performance of South Africa during the TNF negotiations clearly reflected the country's regional economic supremacy, its relatively stronger political influence and advanced bargaining power (Vogt 2007: 199). The country's regional dominance appeared several times during the negotiations on the Trade Protocol's design as "nothing happened without the will or push of South Africa."[25] Accordingly, Pretoria attempted in the first instance to unilaterally present a "common" tariff phase-down offer on behalf of the whole SACU,[26] despite diverging national economic interests between the RSA and the economically weaker BLNS countries.[27] Moreover, South Africa proposed "its" tariff phase-down schedule during one of the first TNF meetings (in December 1999) towards the other SADC members as a given and non-discussable fact: a prelude to bargaining that contradicted the previously proclaimed intention to conduct open-ended negotiations and aspire to consensus-based decisions (Lee 2003: 116–119). Such a guiding principle of mutual consensus had been declared in advance because the negotiators feared "the legitimate interests of sovereign Governments to withdraw from the trade deal if the negotiations are threatening or perceived to threaten [...] vital interests"[28] of the involved actors.

However, in the course of the negotiations on the protocol's tariff reduction schedule, Pretoria finally recognised the imbalance between its own economy on the one hand and the economies of the comparably less developed SADC states on the other. In response to pressures from the latter group of states and the BLNS countries, it was agreed that not all members to the protocol were obliged to phase down national tariffs at the same pace. The reason behind this was to cushion potentially negative effects of trade liberalisation to the economies and industries of the least developed member states by giving them spare time to better prepare for entering a liberalised regional SADC market. This measure implied a South African concession to economically weaker SADC countries since the latter were allowed to prolong the tariff phase-down (i.e. protection) of their markets against the expected mass inflow of South African export commodities (Erasmus et al. 2004: 7; Flatters 2001: 8).

This compromise resulted in an agreement on a linear approach to tariff reduction and an asymmetrical strategy. Accordingly, merchandise goods were divided into three categories that implied different time slots for liberalisation:

- Category A: immediate liberalisation
- Category B: gradual liberalisation (within eight years after the protocol coming into force)
- Category C: Sensitive products (liberalisation not earlier than eight years after the protocol coming into force)
- Category E: Exclusion list (no liberalisation—products such as firearms and ammunition).

Furthermore, SADC member states agreed on an asymmetric strategy of phasing down tariffs with respect to the gradual liberalisation of Category B goods. They agreed to classify countries into three categories on the basis of their economic power and state of socio-economic development:

- Category I: Developed countries (SACU member states)
- Category II: Developing countries (Mauritius and Zimbabwe)
- Category III: Least developed countries (Malawi, Mozambique, Zambia, etc.).

Each category implied a different time frame with regard to the liberalisation process. Countries with comparably strong economies were obliged to start reducing tariffs from the first year onwards and complete the process within eight years after the protocol coming into force (front-loading). States belonging to Category II were allowed to start their gradual liberalisation process later—that is, within four to eight years (mid-loading)—and the countries of Category III six to eight years (back-loading) after the protocol coming into force.[29]

Apart from this, negotiations on regional market integration in the SADC led to very intense bargaining on the contentious issue of the RoO. The latter are interesting insofar as they reflect diverging economic preferences of the involved member states. The initially proposed RoO for SADC were comparably simple, non-restrictive and closely aligned to COMESA's RoO according to which goods would have qualified for preferential trade within the SADC if they contained at least 30% regional value added and not more than 60% of their total value of imported materials from non-SADC countries (Erasmus et al. 2004: 6). However, several countries had concerns. Their intention to protect their national industries caused them to advocate exemptions and more restrictive RoO in those sectors affected.

In most cases, it was South Africa (together with the other SACU members) that represented a position quite different to the other participants. This led to a lengthy bargaining process on sector- and product-specific RoO (Brenton et al. 2005: 13–17; Lee 2003: 130). The general motivation for South Africa to demand tougher and product-specific RoO was to protect its market—and industry—from the external inflow of competing products via non-SACU members, products that are made from imported, cheap materials originating in, for example, Asia

(Brenton et al. 2005: 27). Owing to South African pressure (Erasmus et al. 2004: 23–28), the SADC countries finally agreed that goods should enjoy preferential treatment only if they wholly originated in the SADC or were produced by using imported materials of undetermined origin whose value "does not exceed 60% of the total cost of the materials used in the production of the goods" or "the value added resulting from the process of production accounts for at least 35% of the ex-factory cost of the goods."[30]

However, the catalogue of RoO contains several exemptions to this general rule and moreover further restrictions with regard to specific sectors and products. They are listed in Appendix I of Annex I and reflect particularly those sectors and product groups where most competition between South Africa (!) and the rest of the SADC existed at the time of the regional negotiations (Erasmus et al. 2006):

In the agricultural sector, very restrictive RoO have been imposed on coffee, tea, spices, tobacco and certain products of the milling industry. Wheat flour and certain products made of wheat flour and cereals were even exempted from preferential trade. Furthermore, products and components of the vehicle and motor industry—such as (road) tractors and chassis—became subject to restrictive RoO.[31] Other complicated RoO can be found in the labour-intensive textile and garments sector where intra-regional competition is very high and conflicting preferences existed between several SADC countries—particularly South Africa, Zimbabwe, Mauritius and Malawi—because of their significant local industries (Brenton et al. 2005: 27; Flatters 2004: 55). The array of goods being subject to the very strict RoO reflects mainly rather labour-intensive industrial branches that exist to a significant degree in South Africa and (existed) to a lesser degree in Zimbabwe. According to several sources (COSATU 1999; Hentz 2005), it is particularly these exemplified restrictions and exemptions to the already strict RoO that best reflect South Africa's strong self-assertion in the SADC's trade negotiations.[32]

4.3.3 Sensitive Products and Special Agreements on Sugar and Textiles

Trade negotiations on the sensitive-product groups were also remarkably difficult. This was because several countries had conflicting interests on how to liberalise regional trade in those commodities where intra-SADC competition was comparably strong (i.e. product groups in which more than one member country specialised and on which the country heavily relied in terms of its merchandise exports) (Lee 2003: 112). The focus of inter-state bargaining was on the issue of how much time countries should be given to liberalise regional trade in sensitive products—notably sugar and textiles—in order to allow their industries to adequately adjust to increasing intra-regional competition. Because the industries of these sectors fed many employees in the respective countries and were backed by strong lobby groups, the negotiation process on the sensitive-product groups was tough and uncompromising (Draper et al. 2006: 78–82).

Two major supplement agreements to the SADC Protocol on Trade— one on sugar and one on textiles and garments—give a representative impression of the SADC countries' divide on sensitive products. In regard to these commodities, it was in general South Africa together with the institutionally affiliated SACU members that formed one negotiation group (i.e. the comparably developed SADC countries that were moreover protected by the SACU's common external tariff) versus the rest of the SADC states that were less developed and fairly dependent on the South African/SACU block in economic terms (Brenton et al. 2005: 16; Erasmus et al. 2004: 16). In fact, the "South African" group was in a better bargaining position but did not fully play its advantage. Otherwise, the negotiations would not have resulted in a compromise that is reflected in the following two supplements to the Protocol:

The SADC *Sugar Cooperation Agreement* comprises an agreement on the trade in sugar which was adopted and implemented by SADC countries in the year 2000 against the alleged background of a dumping of sugar prices on the world market. However, the real reasons for this agreement resided within the SADC and its highly competitive regional sugar market: In 1998, South Africa, Mauritius, Zimbabwe, Swaziland, Malawi, Zambia and Tanzania were the major sugar-producing countries in the SADC and several thousand people directly and indirectly were being employed in this labour-intensive sector (Lee 2003: 122–126; Lincoln 2006). The intention of the SADC *Sugar Cooperation Agreement* was to fully liberalise regional trade in sugar by 2012. At its core, however, the agreement remains an obstacle to free trade and only stipulates an asymmetric, non-reciprocal liberalisation of the sugar trade between South Africa/SACU and non-SACU member states of the SADC in an interim period on a complicated quota system until full liberalisation takes place. Only those countries that fall in the latter category and have a net surplus in sugar production (Mauritius, Malawi, Mozambique, Zambia and Zimbabwe) have been granted non-reciprocal duty-free access to the SACU market with quotas of about 40,000 tons per annum each.[33]

The SADC's second separate trade regime on sensitive goods, the *Regulation on the tariff Quotas, time periods, and arrangements for the administration and enforcement in respect of products of HS chapters 50 to 63 exported to SACU by MMTZ*[34] *member states*, was adopted in 2001 and is quite similar to the agreement on sugar in terms of its aims and institutionalisation. Dealing with textiles and garments, it provides for an asymmetric, non-reciprocal liberalisation of trade—namely a waiver of the general double transformation RoO—and a quota system between South Africa/SACU and the least developed SADC member states (i.e. the MMTZ) in the interim period (up to 2012) until full liberalisation of trade should come into force.[35] Similar to the sugar agreement, the SADC-MMTZ trade regime on textiles and garments reveals a distinct pro-South African design: On the one hand, it pursued trade facilitation between South Africa/SACU and the MMTZ states in this sensitive sector and obviously grants some of the poorest SADC benefits because of its asymmetric character. However, it is at the same time a mere alleviation of the restrictive parts and implications of the SADC Protocol on Trade (Brenton et al. 2005: 27; Lee 2003: 132–135).

Both special agreements contain some concessions from the more developed SADC (i.e. the SACU) countries towards the least developed SADC members. The specific and restrictive character of the RoO, taken as a whole, clearly bears a South African trademark and substantiates the impression that the SADC Protocol on Trade is primarily inward-oriented, with its participants trying to protect their vital industries and sensitive sectors as much as possible from regional—and even international—competitors.

4.4 Evaluation of the SADC-FTA

Evaluating the functionality of the SADC-FTA and measuring its effectiveness are challenging tasks. In order to achieve a reliable assessment, the analysis proceeds to firstly examine whether the organisation's member states implemented the Protocol on Trade and complied with its provisions. The effectiveness of regional economic integration in the SADC (i.e. goal attainment of the SADC-FTA) shall be assessed by adequate quantitative indicators, trade analysis and statements of experts.

4 THE PROTOCOL ON TRADE AND THE CREATION OF THE SOUTHERN ... 129

4.4.1 Implementation and Compliance

The SADC Protocol on Trade, with amendments adopted in August 2000, paved the way for the institutionalisation of the SADC-FTA in August 2008. In accordance with the WTO's formal requirements on defining FTAs, the SADC's participant member states acknowledged that a minimum of 85% of intra-regional trade in goods had to be liberalised and free from customs duties in order to qualify for an FTA and constitute the desired SADC-FTA. The remaining 15%, mostly sensitive products, were decided to be phased down at a later stage.[36] The SADC Protocol on Trade entered into force in August 2000 after the document had been signed and ratified by the grand majority of SADC member countries. Beside Angola, the DRC and the Seychelles, all member countries ratified the Protocol in the year 2000. Only Zambia ratified it one year later, in 2001.

In the years after the Protocol on Trade came into force, the member states initiated its implementation process on national levels and phased down tariffs in order to comply with the protocol's provisions. Referring to tariffs as "regular" barriers to regional trade, the more developed member countries—South Africa and the BLNS states (i.e. the SACU countries)—phased down most tariffs to 0% by the year 2000. These countries provided for immediate liberalisation and implementation of the protocol and even outperformed the Protocol's provisions by lowering some of their tariffs ahead of the time schedule and thus beyond their obligations (Maiketso and Sekolokwane 2007). The developing, mid-loading countries like Mauritius and Zimbabwe gradually phased down their tariffs during the years of 2000–2008. They also complied in general with the protocol's demands on trade liberalisation and corresponding time frame. The remaining least developed countries, such as Malawi, Mozambique and Zambia, started to reduce their tariffs only from the years of 2007/2008 onwards. This process is ongoing and some countries (besides Zimbabwe, mostly least developed countries of the back-loading group such as Malawi, Mozambique and Tanzania) are still lagging behind schedule. Angola, the DRC and the Seychelles have not begun to implement the Protocol and therefore have not initiated any tariff phase-down.[37]

Given the intended elimination of NTBs, the situation looks slightly different and slightly unsatisfying. Nevertheless, progress has occurred and some relevant steps have been taken. In regard to customs cooperation and simplification, a SADC Single Customs Administrative

Document (SADC-CD) was designed and has already replaced various national customs forms for different customs regimes. In addition, a single customs guarantee bond (i.e. customs seal) has been introduced. Furthermore, several important traffic routes "one-stop" border posts are upgraded to simplify customs clearance.[38] In regard to the issue area of standardisation, harmonisation and quality assurance, several institutions have been created to develop standards, formulate technical regulations and quality requirements, and assist regional and local producers. These include the "SADC Cooperation in Standardisation, Quality Assurance, Accreditation and Metrology" and various smaller institutions, predominantly dealing with the removal of technical barriers to trade like the "SADC Technical Regulations Liaison Committee" and the "SADC Technical Barriers to Trade Stakeholder Committee".[39]

To sum up, all participant SADC countries that have signed and ratified the Protocol on Trade have implemented the essential provisions and seem to be compliant with its central directives on the whole. Certainly, minor exceptions confirm the rule: Zimbabwe, for instance, occasionally violated the Protocol on Trade in the course of the country's economic and political crisis by randomly taking action contradictory to its central provisions. Such illicit measures included raising of tariffs between May and June 2001 on selected goods or imposing certain fees on road-freight transports (Lee 2003: 140). These irregularities aside, the participating SADC states implemented the directives of the Protocol on Trade satisfactorily overall and thus fulfilled the formal requirements for establishing their FTA. The successful creation and proclamation of the SADC-FTA in August 2008 are matters of fact and indicate that no tariffs have to be paid on at least 85% of total intra-SADC trade today.[40]

4.4.2 Effectiveness

The implementation of the Protocol on Trade and the SADC-FTA shall be judged a success if the institution attains its major goals and thus provides the expected beneficial effects. According to the Trade Protocol's central provisions,[41] official documents[42] and experts,[43] the major objectives of the SADC-FTA were to increase intra-SADC trade and investment flows, to attract more FDI from outside the region, and to remove regional NTB to trade. Therefore, these central goals shall provide the benchmark to assess the performance, effectiveness and success of the SADC-FTA.

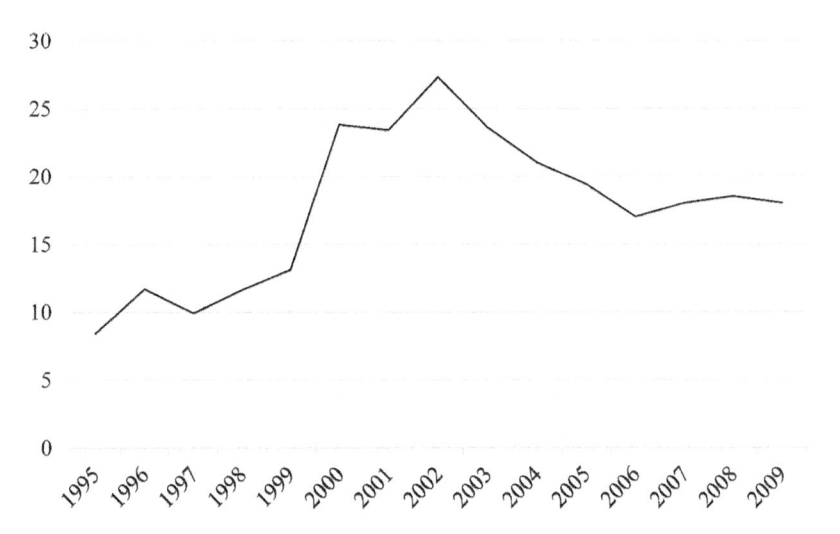

Fig. 4.2 Intra-regional trade in the SADC (as percentage of total trade) Data obtained from RIKS—Indicators and statistics of regional arrangements: http://www.cris.unu.edu/riks/web/data/show (02/05/2015) and the International Trade Centre: http://www.trademap.org/ (02/02/2015)

A convenient and important indicator to measure the success of regional economic integration in the SADC in terms of increasing intra-regional trade is to analyse the trend of intra-SADC trade flows (Tavares and Schulz 2006: 241)[44] (Fig. 4.2).

The figures show a remarkable growth of the SADC's intra-regional trade share in the year 2000—the year the Protocol on Trade came into force. This indicates that regional trade liberalisation in the course of the formation of the SADC-FTA had a causal and positive effect on intra-regional trade flows. Regional trade experts,[45] particularly SADC officials,[46] as well as a number of scientific studies and official statements corroborate this positive assessment (Behar and Edward 2011; le Pere and Tjønneland 2005: 30; Sandrey 2013).[47] Furthermore, there is consensus that the FTA's positive effect would have been even more significant if Zimbabwe's economy had not collapsed on the verge of the millennium. However, some studies argue that the SADC's intra-regional trade increased only marginally in the course of the implementation of the Trade Protocol and question whether this trend correlates positively with the formation of the SADC-FTA (Iwanow 2011;

Fig. 4.3 Intra-regional trade intensity in the SADC (in Index Points) Data obtained from RIKS—Indicators and Statistics of Regional Arrangements: http://www.cris.unu.edu/riks/web/data/show (02/05/2015)

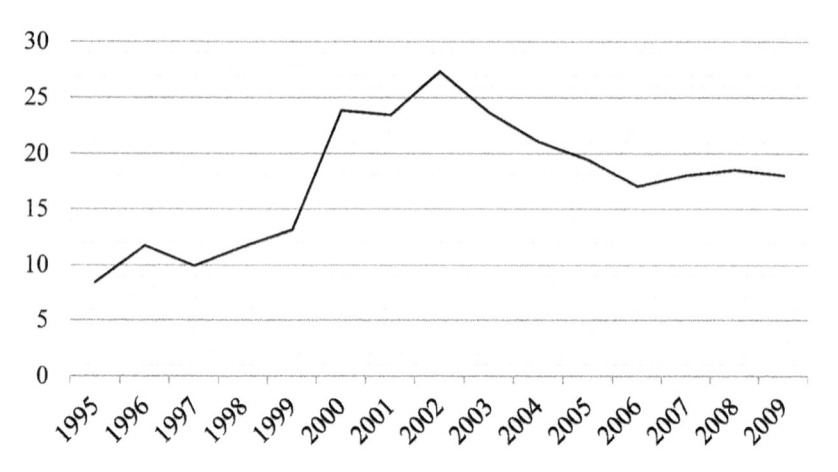

Maiketso and Sekolokwane 2007). The rather stagnant intra-regional trade shares in the SADC since the year 2000 seem to support this pessimistic view at first glance. However, the absolute value of intra-regional trade in the SADC increased significantly after the organisation's trade liberalisation measures took effect. It amounted to less than $10 billion USD in 1995 and continued to grow slowly to $12.7 billion USD by the year 2000. Thereafter, intra-regional trade increased exponentially to $20.3 billion USD in 2003 and $62.0 billion USD in 2012.

Intra-regional trade intensity is a complementary indicator for measuring the degree of regional economic integration because—in contrast to simple intra-regional trade shares—it controls additionally for a regional integration organisation's geographical expansion in terms of the number of its member states (Fig. 4.3).

The index depicts, for the SADC, a remarkable increase in intra-regional trade intensity after the Protocol coming into force: Its figure almost doubled between 1999 (13.1) and 2000 (23.8) and continued to oscillate around 20.0 index points during the period of 2000–2009 (with a peak of 27.3 in 2002 and a low of 17.0 in 2006). These figures indicate a growing importance of intra-regional trade in the SADC after the organisation started to implement its regional trade liberalisation policies. However, the index is slightly decreasing since the year 2000 and seems to stagnate since the same year as well.

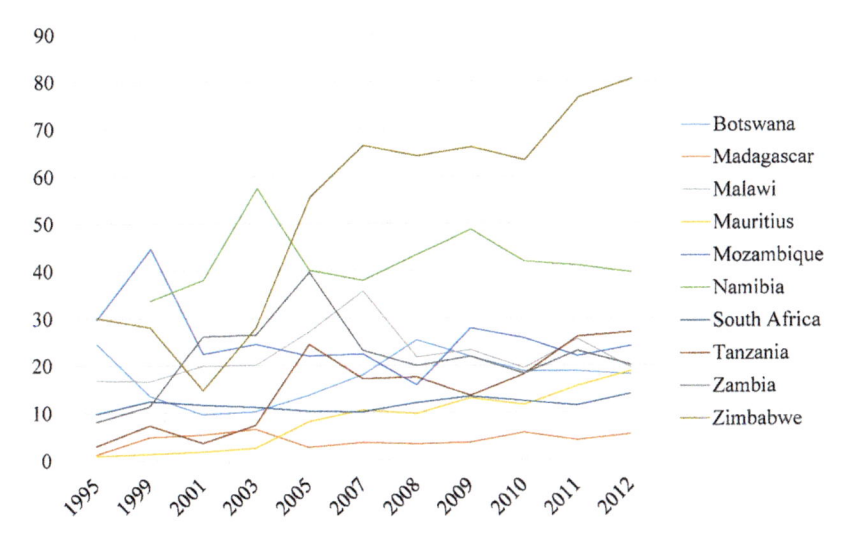

Fig. 4.4 SADC countries' intra-regional exports (as percentage of total exports) Trade data generated with the help of the WITS database: http://wits.worldbank.org/witsweb/default.aspx (06/06/2015). WITS uses combined data from the UNCTAD and the WTO. Intra-SADC trade shares of 1995 are based on averages (1991–1993) according to a database of the Industrial Development Corporation of South Africa (cf. Valentine 1998)

Aggregate trade data on SADC gives only a broad picture of recent trends in intra-regional trade flows. The following tables are more specific because they depict figures of the member countries' intra-SADC trade shares in terms of exports and imports (Fig. 4.4):

In terms of intra-regional export shares, most SADC members show very oscillating figures since the Trade Protocol came into force and depict an inconsistent trend over time. According to plain trade data, it is not entirely clear in these cases whether regional market integration actually led to an increase of their exports to other SADC members. However, this picture is obviously different with regard to Zimbabwe, Tanzania, Mauritius and even South Africa. For all of these countries, SADC became a gradually more important export destination in the course of regional trade liberalisation—particularly since the year 2000. Zimbabwe, one of the organisation's core countries, increased its intra-regional export share from 30.2% (1995) to 80.6% (2012), Tanzania from 3.1% (1995) to 27.0% (2012), the island state of Mauritius from

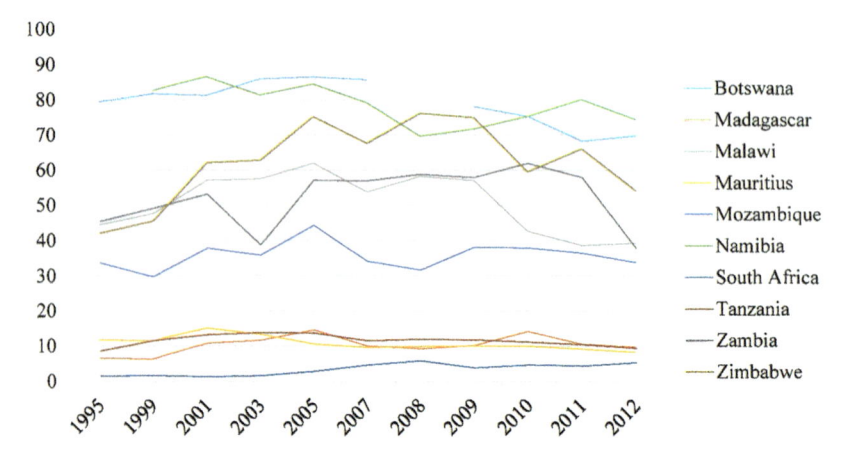

100
90
80 — Botswana
70 — Madagascar
60 — Malawi
50 — Mauritius
40 — Mozambique
30 — Namibia
20 — South Africa
10 — Tanzania
0 — Zambia
— Zimbabwe

1995 1999 2001 2003 2005 2007 2008 2009 2010 2011 2012

Fig. 4.5 SADC countries' intra-regional imports (as percentage of total imports) Trade data generated with the help of the WITS database: http://wits.worldbank.org/witsweb/default.aspx (06/06/2015). WITS uses combined data from the UNCTAD and the WTO. Intra-SADC trade shares of 1995 are based on averages (1991–1993) according to a database of the Industrial Development Corporation of South Africa (cf. Valentine 1998)

about 1% (1995) to 18.8% (2012) and South Africa from 9.8% (1995) to 24.6% (2012). These figures can clearly be associated with the implementation of the Protocol on Trade and the creation of the SADC-FTA (Fig. 4.5).

The picture looks similar with regard to most SADC member states' intra-regional import shares: volatile figures and no clear trend. It seems that some countries—like Malawi, Zambia, Zimbabwe and Mozambique—had increased their intra-SADC import share in the years following the adoption of the Protocol on Trade in the year 2000. However, this positive trend seems to have turned into a decline again after about a decade: Zimbabwe's intra-regional import share rose from 42.1% (1995) to 76.2% (2008) and decreased finally to 54.3% in 2012. Mauritius's shows a similar trend: figures grew slightly, from 11.8% to 15.0%, between 1995 and 2001 and then decreased to 8.3% in 2012. South Africa, however, is an exception: The country's intra-regional import share increased slowly but steadily from a mere 1.5% in 1995 to 6.8% of total imports in 2012. This share is certainly still small but it proves a good quadruplicating of South African imports from the SADC in less than 20 years. Pretoria's growing imports from other

SADC members are even more impressive in terms of absolute value as they increased from about $391 million USD in 1995 to about $5.4 billion USD in 2012. This positive trend is of utmost importance for the SADC because it implies that South Africa sources increasingly more commodities from its economically weaker neighbours and thus fuels their export-oriented businesses. Noteworthy in this respect are South Africa's growing regional imports of several sensitive products, notably textiles, garments and sugar (Iwanow 2011), whose trade liberalisation had been subject to special agreements.

In summary, the overall picture in the SADC is not brilliant on the whole. However, the share of intra-regional trade of some SADC states seems to have grown—despite volatile trade figures—in the course of the implementation of the Trade Protocol and in the years following the establishment of the SADC-FTA. This observation, as well as the significant growth of intra-SADC trade in absolute terms and with regard to intra-regional trade intensity, does indicate that the member countries increasingly exploit existing regional comparative advantages and intensified trading with each other. This corroborates the functionality and effectiveness of the SADC-FTA—not least because one otherwise would expect a trend of diminishing intra-regional merchandise trade in the SADC against the background of growing globalisation.

4.4.3 On FDI

Intra-SADC trade liberalisation and the establishment of the FTA seemed to have a positive effect on intra-regional investments and net FDI inflows to the entire SADC region and its member countries. One aspect, in the first instance, is the improvement of the business and investment climate in the SADC region. The SADC Business Climate Index—compiled from surveys taken from 65 international companies operating in the region—rose from 51.2 to 60.5 index points between 2006 and 2010 and indicates a correlation between regional economic integration on the one hand and improving investment climate on the other (Afrikaverein der Deutschen Wirtschaft 2012: 10). Regional trade experts from independent research institutes confirmed the latter assumption and emphasised the meaning of a good investment climate in the SADC with regard to attracting non-African FDI from overseas.[48]

Quantitative data on net FDI inflows to SADC and its member countries gives a slight but significant increase in the years following the implementation of the Trade Protocol and the establishment of the

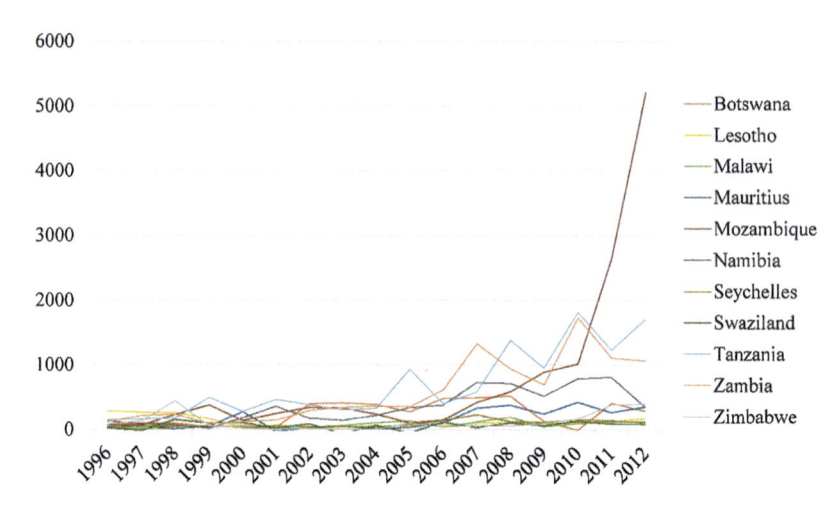

Fig. 4.6 Inward FDI flows to selected SADC countries (in millions USD at current prices and current exchange rates)

SADC-FTA. However, the country—and region-specific figures often oscillate from year to year. For this reason, any policy-related impact on FDI inflows can be diagnosed only by looking at the overall trend (Fig.4.6).

Yet the figures reveal a considerable increase of absolute net FDI inflows into a number of SADC member countries—particularly Mozambique, Tanzania and Zambia—since about the time when the Trade Protocol came into force. A similar trend can be observed with regard to the total inward FDI flows into the SADC—although these figures oscillate as well and to a strong degree represent the South African figures because Pretoria traditionally receives the lion's share of the SADC's total FDI inflows (Jenkins and Thomas 2002: 23–25) (Fig. 4.7).

Altogether, net FDI inflows to the SADC region and its member countries have significantly and continuously grown during the past years. Certainly, it is difficult to substantiate a clear causal relation between investment-friendly regional policies, such as the formation of the SADC-FTA, and FDI figures because other factors can also influence the allocation of investments. However, it is obvious that the SADC area depicts a significant increase of FDI inflows particularly since the time

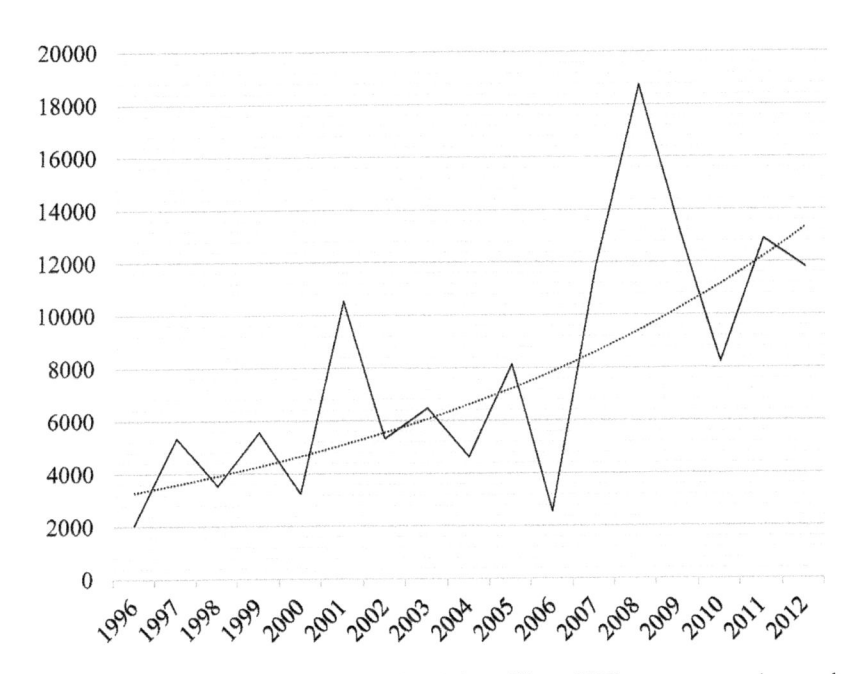

Fig. 4.7 Inward FDI flows to the SADC (in millions USD at current prices and current exchange rates)

when the member states implemented the Protocol on Trade and pushed regional trade liberalisation. This observation is corroborated by the fact that market size—according to surveys—is the major motivation of investors to locate their assets and investments in Southern Africa (Dahl 2002: 78–79; Gelb 2005: 202; Jenkins and Thomas 2002: 28). Other studies found a statistically significant positive relationship between the growth of the SADC's total trade—in particular, South African exports—and the increase of net FDI inflows to the region (Bezuidenhout and Naudé 2008).

Breaking down the FDI inflows to the SADC to the countries of origin reveals once more the key role of South Africa in the regional context. South African FDI is, for the SADC, of the utmost importance because it is not primarily resource-seeking but instead aims to penetrate regional and local markets. In contrast to FDI from overseas, intra-regional FDI materialises in a vast array of different economic sectors (e.g. retailers, telecommunication, and forwarding agencies) and therefore contributes more to socio-economic development. Therefore, its overall—and generally positive—effect on the region should not be underestimated even if its absolute volume and relative proportion are comparably low (Hartzenberg and Mathe 2005; Jenkins and Thomas 2002: 26–39).

In summary, the empirical data indicates that regional economic integration in the SADC has had a positive effect on the net inflow of FDI to the whole organisation and its member countries.

4.4.4 On NTBs

An evaluation of the Trade Protocol's impact on NTB removal in the SADC region is a challenging task because comprehensive studies on these effects have not yet been undertaken. Nevertheless, the few existing—sometimes anecdotal—case studies shall be consulted (Mthembu-Salter 2008; Pierides 2008). They draw an ambivalent but increasingly positive picture of the current situation and state that some significant regional NTBs of the past—such as pre-shipment inspections, high transport charges, price controls, foreign currency controls, state marketing, import licensing, and overly bureaucratic and arbitrary processing methods—have been abolished to considerable degrees by most SADC members in accordance with the Trade Protocol's provisions (Nyambe and Schade 2008: 15–17).

The implementation of the SADC-CD and the use of the SADC customs guarantee bond by some national customs authorities, for example, seem to have already taken positive effect and led to a reduction of transit times by about 40% in commercial vehicle traffic along the important transport route of South Africa-Zimbabwe-Mozambique-Malawi (Mthembu-Salter 2008: 16). Remarkable is also the simplification of border clearances and speedup of cross-border trade through the introduction of Africa's first one-stop border post at Chirundu (between Zambia and Zimbabwe) in December 2009.[49] The latter's success triggered demands for additional one-stop border posts in the SADC region and caused Namibia, Botswana and the DRC to consider appropriate plans in this respect.[50] Already in 2005, the SADC introduced an online monitoring mechanism for identifying, reporting and eliminating existent NTBs in the region.[51] Since then, the organisation's web-based interface—www.tradebarriers.org—received more than 300 notifications from affected or interested parties (mostly forwarding agencies or truck drivers), of which more than 200 have been resolved according to official information.[52]

Smaller technical problems—for example, the continuing use of differing software and computer systems by national customs authorities—are considered to be marginal NTBs that are likely to be resolved soon as well. However, some other NTBs in the SADC region—for example, relating to regional (transport) infrastructure—cannot be removed easily if necessary financial resources are lacking. During recent years, it was occasionally crisis-shaken Zimbabwe that put obstacles to the Trade Protocol's provisions on NTB removal by randomly applying creative methods to introduce various new ones (e.g. payment of selected import duties partly in foreign currency or redefinition of some goods into services as the latter are subject to higher taxes) in order to get access to foreign exchange. This Zimbabwean example—though exceptional and probably motivated by autocratic leadership and desperation—illustrates a typical situation where common regional institutions are weakened by a single, deviant member that follows an uncooperative strategy and thus undermines the common club good.

Table 4.4 Doing business indicator "Trading Across Borders" in the SADC

Country	2006	2007	2008	2009	2010	2011	2012	2013
Angola	14.0	20.4	23.2	16.8	24.5	27.0	34.3	38.0
Botswana	40.9	43.1	44.7	43.7	44.1	44.3	47.8	52.2
DR Congo	14.7	13.0	13.0	13.0	14.5	17.6	23.6	25.9
Lesotho	41.8	42.6	43.4	40.7	42.5	50.8	51.0	54.9
Madagascar	30.1	32.8	51.9	58.6	60.7	63.0	64.0	64.6
Malawi	13.0	15.9	22.1	23.7	27.2	28.7	30.1	32.0
Mauritius	80.7	81.0	82.6	83.2	84.9	85.5	85.4	85.9
Mozambique	51.2	52.3	53.6	54.8	57.2	57.7	58.4	59.2
Namibia	53.1	54.1	55.5	55.0	56.9	57.5	56.9	57.8
Seychelles	71.9	71.9	72.1	73.5	76.0	77.9	78.2	78.5
South Africa	56.6	57.3	58.0	54.9	55.2	56.3	58.0	69.1
Swaziland	49.5	50.0	53.0	50.0	52.3	58.7	57.6	61.9
Tanzania	40.3	49.1	49.9	50.3	51.6	52.5	58.9	56.7
Zambia	14.7	16.8	20.5	18.1	21.5	31.3	33.9	35.4
Zimbabwe	21.7	23.0	22.5	12.8	12.6	14.2	15.7	20.9

Data obtained from the doing business database: http://www.doingbusiness.org/data/distance%20to%20frontier (10/12/2015)

Despite the lack of quantifiable data on specific NTBs in the SADC, the following table gives a good overview of the situation in terms of "trading across borders"[53] in the region (Table 4.4):

For virtually all countries, the indicator displays a significant and continuous improvement in terms of merchandise trading across borders. While the situation improved notably in Angola, Madagascar, Malawi and Zambia during the past few years, it has always been quite good in the SACU member states (due to the customs union) as well as in Mauritius and the Seychelles (due to their "open door" policies) and deteriorated only in Zimbabwe (due to the economic crisis).

Altogether, the situation concerning NTB removal in the SADC is still ambivalent at the current stage. The Trade Protocol certainly sensitised member states to this problem and seems to have contributed to an improvement in the region as indicated by several measures. However, NTBs are still the most significant obstacles to trade in the region.

4.5 Résumé and Prospects

The insights on the SADC's Protocol on Trade and the institutionalisation of the SADC-FTA revealed the strong influence of the region's dominant power, South Africa, on the regional trade regime's institutional design and its inherent rules and provisions. This is not surprising because for structural reasons the Cape Republic was in a power position as it was the most important regional trading partner, (potential) export destination and source of FDI for the majority of SADC members during the mid-1990s. While all SADC member states expected economic benefits from regional trade liberalisation, South Africa expected the largest gains from regional market integration because of its economy's strength, industrial base, diversification and role as regional trade hub. Unsurprisingly, Pretoria therefore took the initiative and acted clearly as agenda-setter and "motor for integration". Smaller concessions and compromises to the advantage of the economically weaker SADC members in the course of the trade negotiations indicate that South Africa played the role of a benevolent hegemon despite asserting most of its national interests. Hence, the SADC-FTA is not an example of "open regionalism"—as could be perceived at first sight—but instead a considerably inward-orientated institution as becomes most clear in view of its complicated RoO.

Extra-regional actors neither initialised economic integration in the SADC nor caused a negative impact on the negotiation or institutionalisation of the FTA, although for structural reasons the EU was in a potential position to do so. Instead, the EU explicitly supported the SADC's market integration efforts by offering financial means through its EDF programme. Therefore, Europe rather cushioned the underlying cooperation problem in the SADC by lowering the costs for establishing the FTA project.

The institutional effects of the SADC's trade regime are still modest. According to economic data and experts, the overall impact of the Trade Protocol and the SADC-FTA is positive and a counterfactual scenario certainly indicates that, in fact, regional trade liberalisation and economic integration made a difference in the SADC: Most member states, with few exceptions, implemented the Protocol's provisions and complied to its rules. This brought the SADC-FTA not least into existence. Altogether, the SADC-FTA can be judged as an institutional success and outstanding example of regional economic integration in the Global South"with the limitation that it has not (yet) reached all of its proclaimed goals.

Notes

1. The intra-regional trade intensity index depicts the ratio between a region's intra-regional trade share and the region's share in world trade (the same applies of course for a regional block or a regional organisation as well). The index has a value of one if the weight of a region's intra-regional trade share equals the region's share in world trade. This implies "geographic neutrality" of trade flows. If the index value is higher than one, this means that the region's trade is relatively more oriented towards the region and its member countries than towards the rest of the world. Iapadre argues that "an increase of the index, revealing that the region's importance for its own trade rises more (or falls less) than its weight in world trade, can be considered as an *ex post* indication of an increase in trade integration" (Iapadre 2006: 67).
2. Because trade data on most SADC countries is under-reported and inconsistent and does not cover significant informal trade flows, the figures should not be over-interpreted, but rather regarded as a broad outline of the situation. The same applies even more with respect to quantitative data on investment flows which is rarely reported nor broken down on market- and resource-seeking investments.

3. Data obtained from RIKS—Indicators and Statistics of Regional Arrangements: http://www.cris.unu.edu/riks/web/data/show (02/05/2015).
4. In comparison, intra-regional trade intensity in the EU was remarkably lower, with an index value between 1.45 and 1.62 points during the same period. Data obtained from RIKS—Indicators and Statistics of Regional Arrangements: http://www.cris.unu.edu/riks/web/data/show (02/05/2015).
5. SADC (1994): Industry and Trade. Annual Report of the Sector Coordination Unit. Gaborone: SADC Secretariat.
   SADC (1999a): Consultative Conference on Trade and Investment. The Proceedings of the Consultative Conference held in Johannesburg, Republic of South Africa, 31 January–2 February 1996. Gaborone: SADC Secretariat. pp. 24–33.
6. SADC (1994): Industry and Trade. Annual Report of the Sector Coordination Unit. Gaborone: SADC Secretariat. pp. 11–14.
7. The comparably stronger degree of economic interdependence between the SADC countries and South Africa—and thus the better chance to exploit economic benefits from the region—was the major reason why Pretoria had chosen to join the SADC instead of the COMESA back in 1994 (Draper and Khumalo 2005: 27–29).
8. Patterns of extra-regional economic interdependence to other regions or regional economic integration schemes in Southern Africa, particularly to the COMESA, were rather marginal and of less importance during the period under observation.
9. European Commission (1995a): Communication on Supporting Regional Economic Integration in Developing Countries. COM (1995) 212 final.
   European Commission (1995b): European Community Support for Regional Economic Integration Efforts among Developing Countries. COM (95) 219 final.
10. SADC—European Community (2002): Regional Strategy Paper and Regional Indicative Programme. For the period of 2002–2007. http://aei.pitt.edu/45272/1/SACD_2002_3.pdf (08/12/2015).
11. Declaration of the EU-Southern African Ministerial Conference on 5 and 6 September 1994 in Berlin. http://europa.eu/rapid/press-release_PRES-94-194_en.htm (10/05/2016).
12. SADC (1996a): Annual Report. June 1995–July 1996. Gaborone: SADC Secretariat. p. 92.
13. SADC (2008a): SADC Free Trade Area. Growth, Development and Wealth Creation. Handbook. Gaborone: SADC Secretariat. p. 4.
14. Statement of the Chairperson of SADC and President of South Africa, Thabo Mbeki, on the occasion of the Launch of the SADC Free Trade

Area in Sandton, South Africa, on 17 August 2008. http://www.dfa.gov.za/docs/speeches/2008/mbek0818c.html (10/12/2015).
15. SADC (1996b): Decisions of the Council of Ministers. Johannesburg, South Africa, 28–29 January 1996. Gaborone: SADC Secretariat. pp. 292–293.
16. SADC (1996c): Record of the Summit. Held in Maseru, Kingdom of Lesotho, 24 August 1996. pp. 17–19.
17. SADC (2000b): Record of the Summit. Held in Windhoek, Republic of Namibia, 7th August 2000. Gaborone: SADC Secretariat. pp. 13–25.
18. SADC (2000a): Protocol on Trade. Preamble.
19. SADC (2000a): Protocol on Trade. Article 2.
20. SADC (2000a): Protocol on Trade. Article 3 (1) e.
21. SADC (2000a): Protocol on Trade. Annex II (4).
22. SADC (2000a): Protocol on Trade. Article 12 and Annex I.
23. SADC (2000a): Protocol on Trade. Article 21 (1).
24. SADC (1992): Treaty of the Southern African Development Community. Article 24.
25. Interview with Haile Taye (Senior Research Fellow Macroeconomic Forecasting and Planning) at the Botswana Institute for Development Policy Analysis (09/22/2010).
26. South Africa represented the SACU in international relations and was authorised—according to Article 5 (2) of the 1969 SACU Agreement—to conduct (trade) negotiations with third parties on behalf of the SACU as a whole. http://www.sacu.int/show.php?id=565 (10/05/2016).
27. Botswana, Lesotho, Namibia and Swaziland are often referred to as BLNS countries.
28. SADC (1996b): Decisions of the Council of Ministers. Johannesburg, South Africa, 28–29 January 1996. Gaborone: SADC Secretariat. Annex IV.
29. SADC (2000a): Protocol on Trade.
    SADC (2008b): SADC Free Trade Area. Growth, Development and Wealth Creation. Handbook. Gaborone: SADC Secretariat. pp. 7–8.
30. SADC (2000a): Protocol on Trade. Annex I (2) b.
31. SADC (2000a): Protocol on Trade. Annex I, Appendix I.
32. Interview with Peter Draper (Project Head Development through Trade Programme and Senior Trade Research Fellow) at the South African Institute of International Affairs (08/25/2010).
33. SADC (2000a): Protocol on Trade. Annex VII, Articles 4–6.
34. The so-called MMTZ countries are Malawi, Mozambique, Tanzania, and Zambia.

35. SADC (2000a): Protocol on Trade. Annex I, Appendix V.
36. SADC (2008b): SADC Free Trade Area. Growth, Development and Wealth Creation. Handbook. Gaborone: SADC Secretariat. pp. 5–8.
37. SADC (2008b): SADC Free Trade Area. Growth, Development and Wealth Creation. Handbook. Gaborone: SADC Secretariat. pp. 7–8.
38. SADC (2008b): SADC Free Trade Area. Growth, Development and Wealth Creation. Handbook. Gaborone: SADC Secretariat. pp. 8–9.
39. SADC (2008b): SADC Free Trade Area. Growth, Development and Wealth Creation. Handbook. Gaborone: SADC Secretariat. pp. 9–10.
40. SADC (2008b): SADC Free Trade Area. Growth, Development and Wealth Creation. Handbook. Gaborone: SADC Secretariat.
41. SADC (2000a): Protocol on Trade. Article 2.
42. SADC (2008b): SADC Free Trade Area. Growth, Development and Wealth Creation. Handbook. Gaborone: SADC Secretariat.
SADC (2012): Desk Assessment of the Regional Indicative Strategic Development Plan 2005–2010. p. 30.
43. Interview with Peter Draper (Project Head Development through Trade Programme and Senior Trade Research Fellow) at the South African Institute of International Affairs (08/25/2010).
Interview with Jonathan Mayuyuka Kaunda (Senior Research Fellow Public Policy) at the Botswana Institute for Development Policy Analysis (09/10/2010).
Interview with Mzukisi Qobo (Head of Emerging Powers Programme) at the South African Institute of International Affairs (08/12/2010).
44. Trade data of the SADC region must be interpreted with caution because this data is comparably weak and not very reliable—let alone completely available—because of varying methods of data collection, lack of comprehensive statistics and the high volumes of illicit and informal cross-border trade (Kalaba and Tsedu 2008: 3–4; Kennes 1999: 29).
45. Interview with Haile Taye (Senior Research Fellow Macroeconomic Forecasting and Planning) at the Botswana Institute for Development Policy Analysis (09/22/2010).
Interview with Mzukisi Qobo (Head of Emerging Powers Programme) at the South African Institute of International Affairs (08/12/2010).
46. Interview with Juma Kaniki (Senior Programme Manager Microeconomic Monitoring and Performance Surveillance) and Francis Nyathi (Programme Officer Macroeconomic Policies and Convergence) at the SADC Directorate of Trade, Industry, Finance and Investment (12/01/2008).
47. SADC (2012): Desk Assessment of the Regional Indicative Strategic Development Plan 2005–2010. p. 30.

48. Interview with Mojgan Derakhshani (Advisor SADC Finance and Investment Protocol Coordination) at the SADC Directorate of Trade, Industry, Finance and Investment (12/02/2010).
49. SADC (2012): Desk Assessment of the Regional Indicative Strategic Development Plan 2005–2010. pp. 32–33.
50. De Klerk, Eveline: Southern Africa. SADC Must Invest in One-Stop Border Post. In: New Era. 5 July 2013. http://allafrica.com/stories/201307050946.html (10/10/2016).
51. SADC home page: http://www.sadc.int/themes/economic-development/trade/non-tariff-barriers (10/10/2016).
52. SADC (2012): Desk Assessment of the Regional Indicative Strategic Development Plan 2005–2010. p. 33.
53. The indicator measures the documents (number), the time (days) and the costs (USD per container) required to export and import goods across borders. The measure is indicated on a scale from 0 to 100, where 0 represents the lowest performance (in terms of costs and time delay) and 100 the best. http://www.doingbusiness.org/methodology/trading-across-borders (10/10/2016).

REFERENCES

Adelmann, M. 2003. *Regionale Kooperation im südlichen Afrika*. Freiburg: Arnold-Bergstraesser-Institut.
Afrikaverein der Deutschen Wirtschaft. 2012. *SADC Business Climate 2010/11. Outlook 2012. A German Business Perspective. With Research provided by Rand Merchant Bank*. Hamburg: Afrikaverein der Deutschen Wirtschaft.
African Development Bank. 1993. *Prospects for Economic Integration in Southern Africa*. Oxford: Biddles.
Bauer, N.L. 2004. *African Regional Integration—The EU-SA Free Trade Agreement*. Leipzig: Universität Leipzig.
Becker, C.M. 1988. The Impact of Sanctions on South Africa and its Periphery. *African Studies Review* 31 (2): 61–88.
Behar, A., and L. Edward. 2011. *How Integrated is SADC? Trends in Intra-Regional and Extra-Regional Trade Flows Policy*. Washington: World Bank.
Bell, T. 1993. The Impact of Sanctions on South Africa. *Journal of Contemporary African Studies* 12 (1): 1–28.
Bezuidenhout, H., and W. Naudé. 2008. *Foreign Direct Investment and Trade in the Southern African Development Community*. Helsinki: UNU-WIDER.
Brenton. P., F. Flatters, and P. Kalenga. 2005. *Rules of Origin and SADC: The Case for Change in the Mid Term Review of the Trade Protocol*. Africa Region Working Paper Series (83). Washington: World Bank

Carrère, C. 2004. African Regional Agreements: Impact on Trade with or without Currency Unions. *Journal of African Economies* 13 (2): 199–239.
Chauvin, S., and G. Gaulier. 2002. Prospects for Increasing Trade Among SADC Countries. In *Monitoring Regional Integration in Southern Africa Yearbook*, vol. 2, ed. D. Hansohm, C. Peters-Berries, W. Breytenbach, T. Hartzenberg, W. Maier, and P. Meyns, 21–42. Windhoek: Gamsberg Macmillan.
Chipeta, C., and K. Schade. 2007. *Deepening Integration in SADC. Macroeconomic Policies and Social Impact. A Comparative Analysis of 10 Country Studies and Surveys of Business and Non-State Actors*. Regional Integration in Southern Africa, vol 12. Gaborone: Friedrich Ebert Stiftung.
Cleary, S. 1999. Regional Integration and the Southern African Development Community. *Journal of Public and International Affairs* 10 (1): 1–15.
COSATU. 1999. *COSATU Submission on the SADC Protocol on Trade*. Johannesburg: COSATU.
Coussy, J. 1996. Slow Institutional Progress and Capitalist Dynamics in Southern African Integration: Interpretations and Projects in South Africa and Zimbabwe. *Transformation: Critical Perspectives on Southern Africa* 29: 1–40.
Dahl, J. 2002. Regional Integration and Foreign Direct Investment: The Case of SADC. In *Monitoring Regional Integration in Southern Africa Yearbook*, vol. 2, ed. D. Hansohm, C. Peters-Berries, W. Breytenbach, T. Hartzenberg, W. Maier, and P. Meyns, 59–82. Windhoek: Gamsberg Macmillan.
Daniel, J., V. Naidoo, and S. Naidu. 2003. The South Africans have Arrived: Post-apartheid Corporate Expansion into Africa. In *State of the Nation. South Africa 2003–2004*, ed. J. Daniel, A. Habib, and Southall R, 368–390. Cape Town: HSRC Press.
Davies, R. 1996. Promoting Regional Integration in Southern Africa: An Analysis of Prospects and Problems from a South African Perspective. *African Security Review* 5 (5): 27–38.
de Lombaerde, P., and van Langenhove L. 2006. Indicators of Regional Integration: Conceptual and Methodological Aspects. In *Assessment and Measurement of Regional Integration*, ed. P. de Lombaerde, 9–41. London: Routledge.
Draper, P., P. Alves, and M. Kalaba. 2006. *South Africa's International Trade Diplomacy: Implications for Regional Integration*, Regional Integration in Southern Africa, vol 1. Gaborone: Friedrich Ebert Stiftung.
Draper, P., and N. Khumalo. 2005. Friend or Foe: South Africa and Sub-Saharan Africa in the Global Trading System. In *Reconfiguring the Compass: South Africa's African Trade Diplomacy*, ed. P. Draper, 1–37. Johannesburg: South African Institute of International Affairs.

Ebrill, L.P., and J.G. Stotsky. 1998. The Revenue Implications of Trade Liberalization. In *Trade Reform and Regional Integration in Africa*, ed. Z. Iqbal and M.S. Kahn, 66–146. Washington: International Monetary Fund.
Erasmus, H., F. Flatters, and R. Kirk. 2004. *Rules of Origin as Tools of Development? Some Lessons from SADC*. Gaborone: SADC Secretariat.
Erasmus, H., F. Flatters, and R. Kirk. 2006. Rules of Origin as Tools for Development? Some Lessons from SADC. In *The Origin of Goods. Rules of Origin in Regional Trade Agreements*, ed. O. Cadot, A. Estevadeordal, A. Suwa-Eisenmann, and T. Verdier, 259–294. Oxford: Oxford University Press.
Flatters, F. 2001. *The SADC Trade Protocol: Impacts, Issues and the Way Ahead*. Paper prepared under the USAID/RCSA SADC Trade Protocol Project. http://qed.econ.queensu.ca/faculty/flatters/writings/ff_sadc_impacts.pdf (10/10/2016).
Flatters F. 2004. SADC Rules of Origin in Textiles and Garments: Barriers to Regional Trade and Global Integration. In *The Impact of Preferential Rules of Origin in the Textile and Clothing Sector in Africa*, ed. R. Grynberg, 41–66. London: Commonwealth Secretariat.
Foroutan, F., and L. Pritchett. 1993. Intra-Sub-Saharan African Trade: Is it too Little? *Journal of African Economies* 2 (1): 74–105.
Gelb, S. 2005. South-South Investment: The Case of Africa. In *Africa in the World Economy: The National, Regional and International Challenges*, ed. J.J. Teunissen and A. Akkerman, 200–205. Rotterdam: Forum on Debt and Development.
Gibb, R. 1998. Southern Africa in Transition: Prospects and Problems Facing Regional Integration. *Journal of Modern African Studies* 36 (2): 287–306.
Goldstein, A. 2004. *Regional Integration, FDI and Competitiveness in Southern Africa*. Paris: OECD.
Grobbelaar, N. 2004. Can South African Business Drive Regional Integration on the Continent? *South African Journal of International Affairs* 11 (2): 91–106.
Haarlov, J. 1997. *Regional Cooperation and Integration within Industry and Trade in Southern Africa. The Making of Modern Africa*. Aldershot, Brookfield, and Hong Kong: Ashgate.
Hanlon, J. 1986. *Beggar Your Neighbours. Apartheid Power in Southern Africa*. London: Catholic Institute for International Relations.
Hartzenberg, T., and B. Mathe. 2005. FDI in Services in SADC: Impact on Regional Integration. In *Monitoring Regional Inegration in Southern Africa Yearbook*, vol. 5, ed. D. Hansohm, W. Breytenbach, T. Hartzenberg, and C. McCarthy, 9–24. Windhoek: Namibian Economic Policy Research Unit.
Hentz, J.J. 2005. *South Africa and the Logic of Regional Cooperation*. Bloomington and Indianapolis: Indiana University Press.

Hess, R. 2001. *Zimbabwe Case Study on Trade Negotiations*. London: Overseas Development Institute.

Holden, M. 1996. Economic and Trade Liberalization in Southern Africa. Is there a Role for South Africa? World Bank Discussion Paper, vol. 342. Washington: World Bank.

Iapadre, L. 2006. Regional Integration Agreements and the Geography of World Trade: Statistical Indicators and Empirical Evidence. In *Assessment and Measurement of Regional Integration*, ed. P. de Lombaerde, 65–85. London and New York: Routledge.

Iwanow, T. 2011. *Impact of Derogations from Implementation of the SADC FTA Obligations on Intra-SADCTrade*. Gaborone: USAID/Southern Africa.

Jenkins, C., and L. Thomas. 2001. African Regionalism and the SADC. In *European Union and New Regionalism: Regional Actors and Global Governance in A Post-Hegemonic Era*, ed. M. Telò, 153–175. Aldershot: Ashgate.

Jenkins, C., and L. Thomas. 2002. *Foreign Direct Investment in Southern Africa: Determinants, Characteristics and Implications for Economic Growth and Poverty Alleviation*. Oxford and London: CSA, CREFSA-LSE.

Jenkins, C., J. Leape, and L. Thomas. 2000. Gaining from Trade in Southern Africa. In *Gaining from Trade in Southern Africa. Complementary Policies to Underpin the SADC Free Trade Area*, ed. C. Jenkins, J. Leape, and L. Thomas, 1–23. London: Palgrave Macmillan.

Kalaba, M., and M. Tsedu. 2008. *Regional Trade Agreements, Effects and Opportunities: Southern African Development Research Network. Implementation of the SADC Trade Protocol and the Intra-SACU Trade Performance*. Pretoria: Trade and Industrial Policy Strategies.

Keet, D. 1997. Europe's Free-Trade Plans with South Africa: Strategic Responses from and Challenges to South and Southern Africa. *Development Southern Africa* 14 (2): 285–293.

Kennes, W. 1999. African Regional Economic Integration & the European Union. In *Regionalisation in Africa: Integration & Disintegration*, ed. D.C. Bach, 27–40. Oxford and Bloomington: James Currey.

Kibble, S., P. Goodison, and B. Tsie. 1995. The Uneasy Triangle—South Africa, Southern Africa and Europe in the Post-Apartheid Era. *International Relations* 12 (4): 41–61.

le Pere G, and E.N. Tjønneland. 2005. *Which Way SADC? Advancing co-operation and integration in southern Africa*, vol. 50. IGD Occasional Papers. Midrand: Institute for Global Dialogue.

Lee, M.C. 2003. *The Political Economy of Regionalism in Southern Africa*. Lansdowne and London: Lynne Rienner.

Lincoln, D. 2006. The Historical Geography of the Southern African Development Community's Sugar Protocol. *Illes i Imperis* 9: 117–130.

Lyakurwa, W. 1999. A Regional Case-Study of the SADC. In *Regional Integration and Trade Liberalization in SubSaharan Africa*, ed. A. Oyejide, I. Elbadawi, and S. Yeo, 250–280. Houndmills, London, and New York: Palgrave Macmillan.

Maiketso, J.T., and K. Sekolokwane. 2007. Countrywise Review of the Implementation of the SADC Trade Protocol. In *Proceedings of the 2006 FOPRISA Annual Conference*, ed. Kaunda J.M., 211–234. Gaborone: Lighthouse.

Makgetlaneng, S. 2005. South Africa—Southern Africa Relations in the Post-Apartheid Era: The Strategic Importance of Southern Africa to the Economic and Trade Interests of South African Companies. *Nordic Journal of African Studies* 14 (2): 235–254.

McCarthy, C. 1998. South African Trade and Industrial Policy in a Regional Context. In *Post-Apartheid Southern Africa. Economic Challenges and Policies for the Future*, ed. L. Petersson, 64–86. London and New York: Routledge.

Moran, T.E., E.M. Graham, and M. Blomström (eds.). 2005. *Does Foreign Direct Investment Promote Development?*. Washington: Institute for International Economics.

Mthembu-Salter, G. 2008. *The Cost of Non-tariff Barriers to Business along the North-South Corridor (South Africa-Zimbabwe) via Beit Bridge. A Preliminary Study*, vol. 20. Trade Policy Report. Johannesburg: South African Institute of International Affairs.

Nyambe, J., and K. Schade. 2008. *Progress Towards the SADC FTA and Remaining Challenges*. Paper presented at the FOPRISA 3rd Annual Conference, Centurion/Pretoria.

Odén, B. 2001. Regionalization in Southern Africa: The Role of the Dominant. In *Regionalization in a Globalizing World: A Comparative Perspective on Forms, Actors and Processes*, ed. M. Schulz, F. Söderbaum, and J. Öjendal, 82–99. London: ZED Books.

Oosthuizen, G.H. 2006. *The Southern African Development Community. The Organisation, its Policies and Prospects*. Midrand: Institute for Global Dialogue.

Page, S., and te Velde D.W. 2004. *Foreign Direct Investment by African Countries*. Paper presented at the InWent/UNCTAD Meeting on FDI in Africa, Addis Ababa.

Pierides C. 2008. *Non-Tariff Barriers to Trade in Southern Africa: Towards a Measurement Approach*, vol. 21. Trade Policy Report. Johannesburg: South African Institute of International Affairs.

Pietrangeli, G. 2009. Supporting Regional Integration and Cooperation Worldwide: An Overview of the European Union Approach. In *The EU and World Regionalism. The Makability of Regions in the 21st Century*, ed. P. de Lombaerde, M. Schulz, 9–43. Farnham: Ashgate.

Ricardo, D. 1977. *On the Principles of Political Economy and Taxation*, Reprint ed. Hildesheim: Olms.
Sandrey, R. 2013. *An Analysis of the SADC Free Trade Area. Tralac Trade Brief.* Stellenbosch: Trade Law Centre for Southern Africa.
Sidiropoulos, E. 2002. SADC and the EU: A Brief Overview. In *SADC-EU Relations. Looking Back and Moving Ahead*, ed. E. Sidiropoulos, D. Games, P. Fabricius, et al., 23. Copenhagen: Royal Danish Ministry of Foreign Affairs.
Sobhee, S.K., and V. Bhowon. 2007. *Deepening Integration in SADC. Mauritius—Achievements and Coming Challenges*, vol. 8. Regional Integration in Southern Africa. Gaborone: Friedrich Ebert Stiftung.
Tavares, R., and M. Schulz. 2006. Measuring the Impact of Regional Organisations on Peace Building. In *Assessment and Measurement of Regional Integration*, ed. P. de Lombaerde, 232–251. London: Routledge.
Teravaninthorn, S., and G. Raballand. 2009. *Transport Prices and Costs in Africa. A Review of the Main International Corridors.* Washington: World Bank.
Valentine, N. 1998. *The SADC's Revealed Comparative Advantage in Regional and International Trade*, vol. 15. Working Paper. Cape Town: Development Policy Research Unit.
Viner, J. 1950. *The Customs Union Issue.* New York: Carnegie Endowment for International Peace.
Vogt, J. 2007. *Die Regionale Integration des südlichen Afrikas. Unter besonderer Betrachtung der Southern African Development Community (SADC).* Baden-Baden: Nomos.
von Kirchbach, F., and H. Roelofsen. 1998. *Trade in the Southern African Development Community: What is the Potential for increasing Exports to the Republic of South Africa?* vol. 11. African Development in a Comparative Perspective. Geneva: United Nations Conference on Trade and Development (UNCTAD).
Weeks, J. 1996. Regional Cooperation and Southern African Development. *Journal of Southern African Studies* 22 (1): 99–117.
Weeks, J., and P. Mosley. 1998. Structural Adjustment and Tradables: A Comparative Study of Zambia and Zimbabwe. In *Post-Apartheid Southern Africa. Economic Challenge and Policies for the Future*, ed. L. Peterson, 171–200. London and New York: Routledge.
Weggoro, N.C. 1995. *Effects of Regional Economic Integration in Southern Africa and the Role of the Republic of South Africa: A Study of Project Coordination Approach in Industry and Trade in SADCC/SADC.* Berlin: Köster.
Zwizwai, B. 2007. *Deepening Integration in SADC. Zimbabwe—Missing SADC Macroeconomic Targets*, Regional Integration in Southern Africa, vol. 10. Gaborone: Friedrich Ebert Stiftung.

Primary Sources

European Commission. 1995a. Communication on Supporting Regional Economic Integration in Developing Countries. COM(1995) 212 final.
European Commission. 1995b. European Community Support for Regional Economic Integration Efforts Among Developing Countries. COM(95) 219 final.
SADC. 1992. Treaty of the Southern African Development Community. Gaborone: SADC Secretariat.
SADC. 1994. Industry and Trade. Annual Report of the Sector Coordination Unit. Gaborone: SADC Secretariat.
SADC. 1996a. Annual Report. June 1995–July 1996. Gaborone: SADC Secretariat.
SADC. 1996b. Decisions of the Council of Ministers. Johannesburg, South Africa, 28–29. January 1996. Gaborone: SADC Secretariat.
SADC. 1996c. Record of the Summit. Held in Maseru, Kingdom of Lesotho, 24 August 1996.
SADC. 1999a. Consultative Conference on Trade and Investment. The Proceedings of the Consultative Conference held in Johannesburg. Republic of South Africa. 31st January—2nd February 1996. Gaborone: SADC Secretariat.
SADC. 2000a. Protocol on Trade.
SADC. 2000b. Record of the Summit. Held in Windhoek, Republic of Namibia, 7th August 2000. Gaborone: SADC Secretariat.
SADC. 2008b. SADC Free Trade Area. Growth, Development and Wealth Creation. Handbook. Gaborone: SADC Secretariat.
SADC. 2012. Desk Assessment of the Regional Indicative Strategic Development Plan 2005–2010. Gaborone: SADC Secretariat.
SADC—European Community. 2002. Regional Strategy Paper and Regional Indicative Programme. For the Period 2002–2007. http://aei.pitt.edu/45272/1/SACD_2002_3.pdf. Accessed 12 August 2015.

CHAPTER 5

Exogenous Interference: The European Union's Economic Partnership Agreements and the Stalled SADC Customs Union

The creation of a customs union has been a long-desired and essential cornerstone in the SADC's agenda on regional market integration. The organisation's Regional Indicative Strategic Development Plan of 2004 provides details on this important objective. It stipulates the institutionalisation of a SADC Customs Union (SADC-CU) and sets the deadline for its formation for 2010.[1] Against this background, the envisaged SADC-CU is not only a logical consequence of the successful creation of the SADC-FTA in August 2008 but a further step towards deepening regional economic integration, a step that had been precisely predetermined. Despite the organisation's grand plan and many gestures of goodwill by a number of governments and Heads of State in the region, the SADC-CU has not yet become a reality. The following chapter shall give answers to this puzzle and explain why SADC member states did not follow their own agenda on regional market integration and failed to institutionalise the scheduled SADC customs union. In this case, it must be held that the EU as an external actor had a significant negative impact on regionalism in the SADC because it undermined one of the organisation's most important regional integration projects.

5.1 Going Beyond the Free Trade Area: Demand for a SADC Customs Union

Against the background of certain scepticism on the applicability of customs union theory on less developed countries (cf. Brown 1994; Langhammer and Hiemenz 1990), it shall be said in the first instance that the institutionalisation of a customs union is neither an irrational nor an unrealistic venture for developing countries in the Global South. The economic rationale for deeper market integration is independent of geographical location and applies also under conditions of comparably low levels of economic interdependence as long as every actor involved expects absolute benefits from participation (Viner 1950). The SACU, founded in 1910 and fully operational for more than a century, is a long-standing empirical example that supports this line of thought because it comprises mostly developing countries and certainly is part of the Global South (Draper and Khumalo 2009).

The central economic factors that fuelled the SADC member states' demand for deeper regional economic integration and for establishing a SADC-wide customs union are for structural reasons similar to those that guided their interests to demand the SADC Protocol on Trade and participate in the SADC-FTA. In parallel to the preceding chapter, the states' demand for this follow-up step of regional market integration can be deduced from structural characteristics such as patterns of economic interdependence, economies of scale and comparative cost advantages.

Despite the implementation of the Protocol on Trade and regional trade liberalisation in the course of establishing the SADC-FTA, formal intra-regional trade in the SADC remained relatively low in the run-up to the scheduled SADC-CU. Between 2000 and 2007, intra-SADC trade oscillated between 18.1% and 14.5% of total trade. More precisely, it accounted for 13–15% of total intra-regional exports and 15–21% of total intra-regional imports (Krapohl and Muntschick 2009: 19). These figures were certainly not impressive in comparison with regional integration organisations in the North but nevertheless were considerably higher than the intra-regional trade shares and absolute trade volumes in the forefront of the institutionalisation of the SADC-FTA. Again, these figures neglect the considerable informal intra-SADC trade flows which are said to add a further 30% on top of formal trade in Southern and Eastern Africa—particularly in agricultural products (above all maize, rice and beans), articles of daily use and small electronic devices (Sandrey 2012).

The importance of the regional SADC market as a trade destination for the organisation's member states *prior* to the institutionalisation of the envisaged SADC-CU is underpinned by the fact that the RTI showed—as in the forefront of the negotiations to the Trade Protocol—figures well above zero: Between 2000 and 2007, the index value varied between 27.2 (2003) as a peak and 17.0 (2007) as a low.[2] These values strengthen the meaning of intra-regional trade shares and indicate a modest level of intra-regional economic interdependence in the SADC during the period under observation.

Breaking down aggregate figures on intra-SADC trade of 2007[3] into country-specific intra-regional trade shares gives a more differentiated picture. It shows a distinct pattern of intra-regional economic interdependence for a number of SADC members that clearly resembles the economic situation in 1995 (Table 5.1).

According to these figures, the SADC market in terms of total trade was the top trading destination (in descending order) for the economies of Botswana, Lesotho, Malawi, Mozambique, Namibia, Swaziland, Zambia and Zimbabwe in 2007. Regarding exports only (in percentage of total exports), the SADC was the top or a major export market for Swaziland (78.5%), Zimbabwe (66.5%), Namibia (38.0%), Malawi (35.7%),

Table 5.1 Share of intra-regional trade of SADC countries in 2007

Country	Exports to SADC (% of total exports)	Imports from SADC (% of total imports)
Angola[a]	1.3	7.4
Botswana	18.0	85.5
DR Congo[a]	2.7	29.9
Lesotho[b]	18.1	78.3
Madagascar	3.7	10.1
Malawi	35.7	53.9
Mauritius	10.6	9.7
Mozambique	22.5	34.1
Namibia	38.0	79.3
Seychelles	0.7	9.1
South Africa	10.1	4.7
Swaziland	78.5	97.2
Tanzania	17.2	11.6
Zambia	23.2	57.1
Zimbabwe	66.5	67.5

All trade data—with the exception of Angola and the DRC—was generated with the help of the WITS database: http://wits.worldbank.org/witsweb/default.aspx (06/06/2016). The WITS uses combined data from the UNCTAD and the WTO
Trade data of Angola and the DRC were obtained by SA Trade Map of the TIPS (*Trade & Industrial Policy Strategies*) Institute: http://data.sadctrade.org/st (06/06/2016).
[a]Trade data of Angola and the DRC from 2006
[b]Trade data of Lesotho from 2004

Zambia (23.2%), Mozambique (22.5%) and to a lesser degree Tanzania (17.2%) in the same year.

For about half of the SADC member states, plain trade data implies a considerable demand for deeper regional economic integration because of their strong trade relations with partners in the region. This is because further trade liberalisation could provide more economic benefits related to economies of scale in regional terms as well as with regard to economic block-building on an international level. Moreover, many SADC countries exported a more diverse range of products to their own region than to the rest of the world in terms of the composition of their export baskets. This not only indicates a regionalisation of SADC trade but also corroborates the aforementioned assumptions on the countries' demand for deeper market integration towards a customs union (Behar and Edward 2011).

5.1.1 Comparative Cost Advantages and Political Ambition

Regional comparative cost advantages and the prospect to intensify intra-regional trade in the near future triggered additional demand for deeper regional economic integration in a number of member states and made them sympathetic to become part of a future SADC-CU. However, these aspects shall be only briefly referred to at this point because the character of comparative advantages in the SADC in 2007 was still very similar to the situation prior to the adoption of the organisation's Protocol on Trade: The developing countries continued to export, for the most part, goods from the primary sector to their SADC partners and had regional comparative advantages in agricultural products, (processed) foodstuffs and a selection of light manufactures. South Africa, in contrast, remained to have a regional comparative advantage in capital-intensive, industrial products such as (heavy and light) machineries, vehicles and transport equipment, chemical products and a variety of other (light) manufactures (Draper et al. 2006: 73–81; Rangasamy 2008).

Trade-related demand for deeper market integration was additionally fuelled by the remaining costly and trade-inhibiting NTBs in the region. The latter still affected about 20% of regional merchandise exports in 2008 and in extreme cases accounted for a tariff equivalent of up to 40% ad valorem (Gillson 2010). The SADC's mid-term review on the SADC-FTA corroborated this circumstance as it came to the conclusion that the most significant NTB-related obstacles to regional trade included timely customs clearance procedures, unsatisfactory interpretation and application of the RoO, and unharmonised standards.[4] Experts expected that the creation of a customs union would eliminate the remaining informal trade flows in the region—particularly in agricultural products—and thus contribute to the SADC's desired increase of (formal) intra-regional trade (Asche 2008: 102; Sandrey et al. 2011: 74–77).

Again and for similar reasons as in the earlier case of the SADC-FTA, the Republic of South Africa was expected to take the most profits from a SADC-wide customs union because the country had the most industrialised and diversified economy in the region. Pretoria was for this reason in the best position to exploit more regional comparative advantages and realise further gains from economies of scale by expanding its regional market. Another central argument of South Africa in favour for a future SADC-CU related to the customs union common external tariff (CET): The latter not only was expected to "lock-in" the common tariff regime for an integrated SADC market but more importantly wanted to protect South Africa's "backyard" against external competitors. The Department of Trade and Industry got to the heart of Pretoria's regional trade strategy in this respect when it demanded that the national government ensure "that the country's access to these strategic markets [i.e. the SADC market; author's note] is not overtaken by other major trading powers such as the European Union and the United States."[5]

Particularly the smaller and economically least developed non-SACU SADC members also expected economic benefits from the CET of an SADC-CU (Chauvin and Gaulier 2002: 7–8). This is because these countries expected that a future SACU-CU would match the age-old SACU and operate in the same way. The SACU not only represented a working example for a customs union in Southern Africa but had an inviting aura insofar as its common revenue pool provided its members with a lucrative financial pay-out. Since the revenue pool was contingent on the CET and thus indirectly of the massive South African trade volumes in terms of extra-regional imports, becoming a member of a customs union in which South Africa also participated was, for a number of less developed SADC countries, a very enticing project (Nyambe 2010).

Besides these rather functional considerations, further incentives for the SADC member states to demand a customs union were rooted in the observation that the Protocol on Trade and the recently established SADC-FTA proved to be quite successful institutions. They showed modest but promising effects in terms of growing intra-regional trade intensity, increasing inward FDI flows and an improving business environment already from the early 2000s onwards. This evidence suggested that the FTA apparently worked and that the members involved perceived themselves to be on the right track towards regional socio-economic development by means of regional market integration.

Against this background, the political and particularly economic benefits of a future SADC customs union had been repeatedly articulated and ostentatiously underlined by numerous different actors in virtually all political arenas—that is, on organisational, regional and national levels—for years. The most important "piece of evidence" in this respect is SADC's RISDP. This is because the regional development plan not only reflects the member states' common interests in terms of economic cooperation but also formulates the concrete objective to further regional economic block-building and market integration beyond the stage of a "simple" FTA. The RISDP sets a clear deadline for the customs union project as it stipulates the completion of negotiations and the establishment of the SADC-CU for 2010.[6]

A large number of SADC documents,[7] Council[8] and Summit records[9] as well as statements of SADC officials[10] substantiated the intention to create a customs union and gives evidence for the region-wide enthusiasm and support towards this important integration project. Several Heads of State and Government[11] of the SADC's member states frequently expressed their demand for deeper market integration and their commitment to meet their stated objective and complete the SADC customs union in due time.[12] Finally, it was the SADC Secretariat itself (in cooperation with the Committee of Ministers responsible for Trade) that presented a comprehensive draft "SADC Customs Act" with an elaborated set of rules in 2006.[13] The commission of this draft agreement by the organisation's member states not only stands for their actual demand to institutionalise a SADC-wide customs union in the near future but also speaks for the expected absolute added value of such an integration project from the regional actors' perspective.

In a nutshell, the states' demand for the SADC-CU was based not entirely on plain economic or inward-looking calculations—not least because several members of the SADC-FTA remained to have some reservations on introducing more simple RoO or a total liberalisation of trade in sensitive goods—but at least as much on political considerations and outward-oriented aspirations in the sense of community and regional (economic) block-building.

5.1.2 Interim Summary and Situation Structure

Back around 2007, virtually all SADC member states expressed an economically and particularly politically driven demand to enhance regional market integration and go beyond an FTA. Virtually all countries expected a future SADC-CU to provide absolute benefits for the entire region as well as for its individual participants—despite the (still) low level of intra-regional economic interdependence and the FTA not being fully effective yet. In this regard, the organisation's RISDP represents an aggregate of their condensed economic interests because it not only stipulated the institutionalisation of the envisaged SADC-CU in explicit terms but even set a concrete deadline for 2010. Therefore, in the eyes of the regional actors, the SADC customs union was neither a pipe dream nor an unrealistic project. This is not least because the SACU had been operating for more than a century in the very same region and therefore was often regarded as a model or nucleus for a customs union within the SADC's own institutional framework (Erasmus 2007).

Against the structural background of intra-regional economic interdependence in the SADC region and in consideration of the regional actors' clearly and repeatedly expressed demand to form a customs union, the genuine regional problematic situation prior to the negotiations on institutionalising an SADC customs union corresponded best to a prisoner's dilemma around 2007 (Fig. 5.1).

Deepening regional market integration by mutually phasing down the residual tariffs, removing the remaining NTBs and simplifying the complicated RoO could put every involved SADC state in a better position than remaining at the state of an FTA. According to this understanding, the creation of a regional club good in the form of a SADC-CU would provide better pay-offs for the participant member states than the status quo of the SADC-FTA. However, typical for a cooperation problem related to mutual trade liberalisation and market integration, every involved country has, for a plain economic *rationale*, incentives to free-ride and to consume the benefits of the aspired club good of a SADC-CU without implementing the necessary—and costly—provisions and regulations on its own. This logic explains the difficulties of achieving cooperation and the necessity of common institutions in order to "lock-in" the tariff regime.

Fig. 5.1 Genuine regional problematic situation in view of the SADC-CU

		SADC Country B	
		Customs Union	Protection
SADC Country A	Customs Union	3 / 3	1 / 4
	Protection	4 / 1	2 / 2

5.2 Caught in the Middle: The SADC Countries' Double Dependency on South Africa and the EU

The patterns of intra- and extra-regional economic interdependence of SADC countries during the mid-2000s were quite similar to those prior to the negotiations of the Trade Protocol in the mid-1990s. This is not very surprising since long-established network structures, such as trade relations, generally do not change rapidly over a period of only ten years. However, these economic ties gained a particular meaning in the run-up of the scheduled SADC-CU since SADC members were eventually to decide what trade regime to belong to.

5.2.1 Mono-Centric Economic Interdependence: South Africa as Regional Trading Hub

Fairly industrialised South Africa remained the regional economic powerhouse and crucial trade hub for the whole of Southern Africa. In 2007, South Africa's share of the total SADC GDP amounted to about 70% and the country represented more than 62% of the organisation's total merchandise trade exports and a good 50% of its combined imports (Oosthuizen 2007: 261). Pretoria's outstanding economic power position in the region became even more prominent in relative terms because the SADC's erstwhile second largest economy—Zimbabwe—fell behind as it experienced a massive economic decline, hyperinflation and currency collapse from the early 2000s onwards (Zwizwai 2007).

The following table gives a detailed picture of the country-specific intra- and extra-regional trade relations in the SADC area in 2007. It reveals that a significant number of SADC members were strongly dependent on the SADC market as a major trade destination (Table 5.2).

The trade figures show that the SADC market was the top trading destination for Botswana, Lesotho, Malawi, Mozambique, Namibia, Swaziland, Zambia and Zimbabwe in terms of total trade in 2007. This structural dependency on the regional market of a significant number of SADC members becomes even more pronounced if one takes the countries' exports shares (in percentage of total exports) additionally into account: The SADC was the top or major export destination for Swaziland, Zimbabwe, Namibia, Malawi, Zambia, Mozambique and to a lesser degree Tanzania in the same year. However, the majority of this intra-regional trade volume, in fact, was based on bilateral merchandise trade between South Africa on the one hand and the rest of the SADC countries on the other. Trading among the latter was comparably little. Therefore, the South African market was the most important destination for the large part of all intra-regional exports whereas only about 10% of the RSA's total exports were destined to the SADC region in 2007. For structural reasons, this asymmetric and mono-centric pattern of intra-SADC trade flows, which was even more distinct within the SACU region,[14] put once more South Africa in a superior regional power position at that time (Alden and Soko 2005: 368).

With regard to FDI flows, the picture of strong and asymmetric intra-regional interdependence also remained similar to the situation during the mid-1990s. The majority of the SADC member states were strongly dependent on South Africa because Pretoria provided the major share of FDI to the entire region and was the top foreign investor in seven SADC countries (Lesotho, Malawi, Swaziland, the DRC, Botswana, Mozambique and Zambia) at the turn of the millennium.[15] The reason for this regional imbalance resides in South Africa's industrialised and diversified economy: The Cape Republic is home to a variety of influential business associations, investment agencies and export-oriented companies (often parastatals) in the rank of regional or even global players. Out of the 100 top African companies (referring to annual turnovers), a mighty 74 are from South Africa (Grobbelaar 2004: 93–103; Versi 2005: 16).

Table 5.2 Pattern of trade flows of SADC members with the SADC and the EU in 2007

Country	Trade flow	Total (in 1000 US-$)	To SADC (in % of total)	To EU (in % of total)
Angola	Imports	9,544,361	7.4	37.1
	Exports	28,147,325	1.3	7.9
Botswana	Imports	3,986,915	85.8	6.0
	Exports	5,072,523	18.0	67.7
DR Congo	Imports	1,760,690	29.9	38.9
	Exports	1,453,162	2.7	54.3
Lesotho	Imports	1,399,393	78.3	2.3
	Exports	968,402	18.1	9.9
Madagascar	Imports	2,445,461	10.1	23.1
	Exports	1,339,648	3.7	62.9
Malawi	Imports	1,377,830	53.9	15.8
	Exports	868,559	35.7	39.0
Mauritius	Imports	3,898,660	9.7	27.0
	Exports	2,044,099	10.6	70.2
Mozambique	Imports	3,049,633	34.1	23.5
	Exports	2,412,075	22.5	6.1
Namibia	Imports	4,024,623	79.3	10.4
	Exports	4,040,273	38.0	44.7
Seychelles	Imports	859,172	9.1	35.8
	Exports	360,132	0.7	53.7
South Africa	Imports	79,872,556	4.7	33.7
	Exports	63,649,023	10.1	33.2
Swaziland	Imports	1,164,250	97.2	0.1
	Exports	1,082,300	78.5	14.4
Tanzania	Imports	5,919,017	11.6	17.7
	Exports	2,139,347	17.2	19.7
Zambia	Imports	3,971,132	57.1	16.8
	Exports	4,618,583	23.2	5.5
Zimbabwe	Imports	3,594,356	67.7	8.3
	Exports	3,310,184	66.5	16.5
SADC (Σ)	Imports	126,868,050	17.1	29.0
	Exports	121,505,636	12.4	27.8

All trade data—with the exception of Angola and the DRC—were obtained by the *World Integrated Trade Data Solution* (WITS): http://wits.worldbank.org/witsweb/default.aspx (06/06/2016).
Trade data of Angola and the DRC were obtained by SA Trade Map of the TIPS Institute: http://data.sadctrade.org/st (06/06/2016).
Trade data of Lesotho from the year 2004. Trade data of Angola and the DRC from 2006

The South African companies are known to do business in many different (industrial) sectors, are often engaged in joint ventures with enterprises in neighbouring SADC countries, and follow a (regional) market-seeking strategy (Taylor 2007: 154, 159, 184; Tleane 2006: 9). In recent years, South Africa therefore has been a more important investor in the rest of the SADC area than the EU, the US or Japan.

The BLNS states were in an even stronger relationship of economic dependence on South Africa in comparison with the rest of the SADC members. This is because of their membership in the SACU. The customs union distributes prorated profits from its common revenue pool to every member on an annual basis and has been economically and institutionally dominated in economical and institutional terms by Pretoria since its foundation in 1910 (Bertelsmann-Scott 2010). These SACU revenues are of the utmost importance for the economically weaker member states because they traditionally contribute a significant share to the national budget in Swaziland (63%), Lesotho (55%), Namibia (40%) and Botswana (20%). While the BLNS states therefore are strongly dependent on the SACU (and therewith not least South Africa), this is not the case for Pretoria, because the SACU contributes only less than 4% to its national budget.[16] The topic of SACU membership is highlighted at this point because the aspect of institutionalised dependency of its members on the organisation can become a decisive preference-shaping factor if the same countries had to decide whether to join a third, incompatible trade regime or not.

Against the background of this pattern of strong and asymmetric intra-SADC economic interdependence, South Africa was clearly in a relative power position in the SADC region during the mid-2000s. For this reason, Pretoria had the potential to exert the most influence on the foundation and institutional design of the scheduled SADC-CU—and thus was in a position to eventually promote the project's institutionalisation in the same way it did in the case of the SADC-FTA.[17]

5.2.2 Strong and Asymmetric North-South Relations: The EU as a Major Trading Destination

Looking beyond the region, the EU was the major extra-regional trading partner and export destination for the SADC region as a whole, for South Africa as its economic hegemon and for about half of the organisation's member states during the mid-2000s. For structural reasons, the specific character of the extra-regional economic interdependence of the SADC member states prior to the formation of the scheduled SADC-CU is of central importance. This is because a customs union not only demands the institutionalisation of a harmonised CET but also requires its constituencies to act as a unitary, single actor towards third parties in economic affairs. These inherent constraints of a customs union imply above all a strong degree of harmonised economic preferences of its members (particularly when it comes to interaction with third parties such as during inter-regional trade negotiations). Therefore, a customs union restricts per se the economic freedom of the action of its members by far more than a "simple" FTA.

According to aggregated trade flows and relative trade shares, the SADC's merchandise trade with the EU accounted for almost 28% of the organisation's total exports and 29% of its total imports in 2007. Disaggregating these figures to a country level (in percentage of total trade), Angola, the DRC, Madagascar, Mauritius, the Seychelles, South Africa and Tanzania traded comparably more with the EU than within their own regional organisation in the same year. In regard to export shares only (in percentage of total exports), the EU was the top destination not only for the region's economic great power South Africa (33.2%) but also for Mauritius (70.2%), Botswana (67.7%), Madagascar (62.9%), the DRC (54.3%), the Seychelles (53.6%), Namibia (44.7%) and Malawi (39%) in 2007 (cf. Table 5.2).

The EU was therefore the most important trading partner for about half of the SADC's member states at the time when the preparations for initialising the SADC-CU were brought on track. This asymmetric trade pattern was even to a certain degree "cemented" by institutional means through the Trade, Development and Cooperation Agreement (TDCA) trade regime. The latter governed the trade relations between South Africa (including the SACU members) and the EU since its conclusion in 1999 (Stevens 2005). Notwithstanding this, other external actors—in particular China—were also becoming increasingly important trading partners for the SADC during the first decade of the new millennium and soon may replace Europe as the organisation's most important export destination.[18]

Although many SADC countries showed a very similar structure of strong and asymmetric extra-regional interdependence to the EU in terms of trade volumes, the actual composition of each country's aggregate merchandise trade revealed significant degrees of specialisation. While raw materials and (natural) resources from the primary sector accounted in general for the lion's share of the countries' total extra-regional exports to the EU, aggregated trade data does not disclose that several SADC members in fact had quite different export baskets: some countries have specialised in the export of crude oil (Angola); fish and beef (Namibia and Botswana respectively); sugar (Swaziland and Mauritius); aluminium and copper (Mozambique) and products thereof (Zambia and the DRC); precious stones and metals (Botswana, Lesotho and Namibia); machines, manufactures and industrial products (South Africa) and other light manufactures or consumer goods and foodstuffs (Lesotho, Malawi, Mauritius, the Seychelles, South Africa, Tanzania and Zimbabwe).[19] Taking these country-specific disparities into account reveals that the character of the SADC members' dependence on the European market was not totally alike. Instead, it varied from country to country because the individual SADC states regarded different arrays of products and commodities to be essential for their export economy.

However, in contrast to the EU's central meaning for many Southern African economies, the SADC market was only a very marginal trading partner and export destination for its European counterpart: An average of only about 2–3% of the EU's total exports went to the SADC region during the first decade of the new millennium.[20] And the majority of this trade volume in fact shipped to the emerging market of South Africa—the region's trade hub and Europe's traditionally most important trade destination in Southern Africa since the colonial era (Keck and Piermartini 2008: 92–94).

This asymmetric inter-regional economic interdependence in terms of merchandise trade flows was amplified by a distinct pattern of asymmetric and rather unidirectional North-South FDI flows during the same period. The SADC as a whole received most of its absolute FDI inflows from extra-regional actors overseas—the largest part traditionally from the EU. Breaking down these external inflows to the country level shows, however, that it was again the Cape Republic, as the SADC's economic centre, that received the lion's share of these desired investments (Thomas et al. 2005). This means that the SADC as a whole was, in absolute terms, strongly dependent on extra-regional FDI inflows from the EU, although a good half of the organisation's member states depended more on FDI from South Africa. The asymmetric character of the economic relationship between both regions in terms of FDI was underpinned by the fact that the SADC region, in contrast, played virtually no role as a source of FDI for the EU (Goldstein 2004: 45–46; Sandrey 2012: 190–191).

However, the unequal relationship between the EU and the SADC in economic terms had a wider dimension than mere trade and investment flows. This is because the EU pursued a new development and cooperation strategy towards the Global South in the course of the Lisbon Process[21] since the turn of the millennium (Pietrangeli 2009: 9–43). A number of official documents and policy papers give evidence of the EU's strong intention to promote regionalism and regional economic block-building by various mechanisms and programmes in this respect,[22] not least because Europe was keen to "advertise" and spread its own model of regionalism that entailed for itself socio-economic prosperity and political stability (Börzel and Risse 2009a, b). In this context, the EU emphasised, mantra-like, that its development cooperation policies were "necessarily country or region-specific, 'tailor-made' to each partner country or region, based on the country's own needs, strategies, priorities and assets."[23]

The EU in general took a positive, encouraging and supportive position towards the SADC's agenda on deeper regional economic integration and block-building—not least against the background of the community's low level of socio-economic development and its strong trade relations with the EU. As a consequence, Europe funded the SADC's efforts on deepening regional market integration explicitly and substantially: Most of this financial support was allocated within the framework of the 10th EDF programme (2008–2013). It provided the SADC region with €116 million, of which €85 million (i.e. about 80%) were explicitly earmarked for the issue area of regional economic integration.[24] Moreover, the EU was the key contributor to the SADC's budget of which 43% had been financed by external grants in the financial year 2007/08.[25] Therefore, the EU was the SADC's major source of donor funding and its crucial financier ahead of the scheduled SADC-CU project—this was quite similar to the situation ahead of the negotiations of the SADC-FTA.

According to the empirical evidence in terms of asymmetric interdependence and relative power distribution prior to the scheduled formation of the SADC-CU, South Africa was clearly the dominant key country in the SADC region and thus the decisive actor on a regional level. Therefore, the prospect for deepening regional market integration in the SADC towards a customs union seemed generally positive at first sight—at least as long as South Africa played the role of a benevolent hegemon and supported the process. At the same time, however, South Africa itself, the SADC as an aggregate and about half of the organisation's member states showed a pattern of strong and asymmetric economic interdependence to the EU as an extra-regional actor. The remaining half of the SADC members depicted a pattern of economic relations that can be characterised as "double-asymmetric" because these states were economically dependent on the SADC market in the first place. Owing to this strong, asymmetric and unequal economic relationship between the SADC (member states) and the EU, Brussels was for structural reasons in a power position to exert external influence on genuinely regional projects in this issue area. Therefore, the institutionalisation of a SADC-CU was principally prone to extra-regional impact and interference by the EU.

In a nutshell, it therefore can be expected that regional market integration in the SADC is likely to proceed towards a SADC-CU as long as this project is supported by South Africa and not disturbed by the EU.

5.3 Compromised by an External Actor: The Interfering Impact of Europe's EPAs on the Scheduled SADC-CU

As mentioned earlier, in terms of the formation of the SADC-CU, the situation structure of the genuine regional cooperation problem at first glance resembled *ceteris paribus* a prisoner's dilemma– at least as long as patterns of extra-regional interdependence and external actors are not taken into consideration. Taking the EU as a powerful and potentially influential actor into account, one could suggest that its generous donor support to the SADC even cushioned the inherent structure of the cooperation problem. This is because the EU's support of regionalism and financial contributions could raise incentives for SADC members to engage in the establishment of the scheduled SADC-CU and thus reduce the incurring costs for its institutionalisation and maintenance.

However, the EU's external influence on the SADC's customs union project was negative. It seriously interfered with the organisation's own market integration agenda. This is because during the mid-2000s the EU was in the process of putting its trade relations with the African, Caribbean and Pacific (ACP) countries on a new contractual basis. A new policy towards the ACP states became necessary because the EU wanted to act in accordance with the WTO's set of rules after the non-reciprocal trading agreements within the Lomé-IV Convention's framework had run out in the year 2000. The Cotonou Agreement,[26] signed in June 2000, became the new statutory framework for redefining the trade relationship between the ACP countries and the EU. It demands preferential market access on the basis of reciprocity but at the same time allows for connected measures—in particular the negation of Economic Partnership Agreements (EPAs)—in order to cushion potentially negative effects of inter-regional trade liberalisation in the economically weaker partner countries in the South (Keck and Piermartini 2008: 86; Söderbaum 2007: 196–198). The EU expressed a spirit of partnership in this context and stated explicitly that "economic and trade cooperation shall build on regional integration initiatives of ACP States"[27] and emphasised that it conceptualised the EPAs as instruments for developing the ACP countries' economies.[28]

All SADC countries that did not qualify as Least Developed Countries (LDC)[29] and accordingly were not granted a status for trading under the duty- and quota-free conditions of the Everything-But-Arms (EBA) initiative were affected by this realignment of ACP-EU trade.[30] They had to sign an EPA in order to safeguard preferred access to the EU's common market. Non-agreement would have negative consequences for the "reluctant" SADC states insofar as this implied high protective tariffs and thus serious barriers to trade with the important European destination (Bilal and Stevens 2009). Similar to other regions, all ACP countries in Southern Africa, regardless of their membership in any pre-existing regional organisation, were as a result confronted with this realignment of European trade and development policy.

Acting contrary to its own ideals and policy statements,[31] the EU neither addressed its EPA offers to specific regional integration organisations consisting of ACP countries nor tailored the EPAs in a way to become compatible with those regional economic communities that were already in existence. For structural reasons, this ill-considered[32] European policy turned out to be a mess for the SADC (Maes 2012): Since the SADC—in contrast to the EU—had so far reached only the stage of an FTA and did not have a fixed CET, its members were still legally free to negotiate individual trade agreements with third parties irrespectively of their co-members' preferences and without having to agree on a regionally coordinated, unanimous and binding trade strategy.

However, in order to complete the scheduled SADC-CU, it would have been mandatory for all SADC members to agree on a common denominator when entering into EPA negotiations and accordingly submit only a single joint offer to the EU.

However, there was no SADC actorness with respect to the organisation's EPA negotiations with the EU. This was, firstly, because of the SADC Secretariat's lack of mandate and lack of capacity in terms of entering into direct EPA negotiations with the EU on behalf of the whole organisation (Oosthuizen 2006: 201) and, secondly and more importantly, because the character of the (groups of) SADC members' economic relations to the EU differed quite significantly in terms of trade volumes, trade shares and particularly the composition of national export baskets and sensitive-product groups (Bilal and Stevens 2009; Meyn 2010). This implies varying national interests with regard to the institutional design and trade-related contents of the EPAs, which shall be exemplified on the basis of the following representative SADC countries:

In addition to exporting raw materials, South Africa and the BLNS countries to a large extent exported agricultural products and processed foodstuffs (particularly beef, fruits, dairy products and sugar) to the EU as they had an inter-regional competitive advantage in these sectors. This also applied for Namibia, Mozambique and—to a lesser degree—South Africa with respect to fish and seafood. This group of SADC countries therefore exported a similar range of goods—for the most part similar agricultural products and foodstuffs—to the EU. Moreover, most of these SADC countries—particularly the BLNS states and South Africa within the frameworks of the SACU and the TDCA—were economically and institutionally closely interconnected. These economic commonalities laid the foundation for joint interests towards the EU prior to the EPA negotiations: One important common demand on the new EPA, though mainly driven by South Africa, was the exclusion of certain agricultural products, textiles, processed foodstuffs and chemical products from trade liberalisation for the purpose of protecting domestic (infant) industries (McCarthy 2008: 118–119; Saurombe 2009: 128–129). The BLNS countries also advocated—probably because of their strong economic dependence on South Africa and because the TDCA was already in place—a comparably quick but gradual opening of their national markets for more than 80% of total EU exports until 2015 (in the case of Mozambique, until 2023).[33]

Zimbabwe, in contrast, had a competitive advantage over the EU with regard to the export of tobacco, iron and steel, cotton and several meat products. The same applied for Malawi, Zambia and—to a lesser degree—Madagascar for tobacco and cotton as well. For this group of SADC countries, it was not primarily the agricultural products (with the exception of beef) that were considered to be declared as sensitive goods during EPA negations. Instead, it was, besides cotton, particularly semi-luxury products such as foodstuffs, beverages and tobacco (Meyn and Kennan 2010: 39–40). Harare additionally demanded a protective clause for its clothing and footwear industries that operated profitably on regional markets only and was not competitive on an international level (Bilal and Stevens 2009: 141–161). Zimbabwe therefore saw no advantage in negotiating an EPA in a group together with South Africa, the BLNS countries and Mozambique. This position was reinforced, on the one hand, because Zimbabwe feared to be marginalised by Pretoria if it was part of such a grouping and, on the other hand, because Harare favoured a slower pace of inter-regional trade liberalisation (i.e. a gradual market opening for 80% of total EU exports by 2022). Mauritius and the Seychelles had also pronounced national preferences in this context—notably with regard to their fishing industries as they desired a specific agreement on fisheries with the EU. Similar to Zimbabwe, they expected a better EPA deal for their issue of concern if they were not in the same group as South Africa when negotiating with Brussels.[34]

Tanzania was a different case as well. Its exports to the EU contained—besides precious metals—coffee and tea in particular but also fish and seafood, cotton and tobacco. Therefore, Tanzania's range of merchandise exports to the EU was quite similar to those of its neighbouring countries Kenya and Uganda (especially in view of the importance of coffee). The economic and institutional ties between Tanzania and both of the mentioned neighbours were also very strong because all of them were members of the East African Community (Meyn and Kennan 2010: 25–30). Despite the circumstance that owing to its status as LDC the country did not have to conclude an EPA, Tanzania favoured a very slow pace of inter-regional trade liberalisation with a gradual opening of its national market for 82% of total EU exports only by 2033. Tanzania also advocated including a sensitive-product list that contained coffee and tea, spices, fish and beef as well as a comprehensive partnership agreement on fisheries.[35] Therefore, the country's specific trade relations with the EU and its neighbours resulted in economic preferences that differed quite significantly from those of South Africa, the BLNS countries or Zimbabwe.

Given these empirical observations, it seems that a liberalisation and expected increasing of extra-regional trade with the EU in the form of EPAs were, for those SADC countries with competitive export-oriented commodities and strong export dependence on the European Single Market, an economically more promising option than a future SADC-CU with a smaller market and fiercer competitive pressure on a regional level (due to most neighbouring countries' similar export baskets).

The EPAs became even more enticing options for the ACP countries because the EU enriched the agreements—in accordance with its Aid-for-Trade[36] policy—with considerable financial means under the 9th EDF. The purpose of these "subsidies" was to compensate for potential adjustment costs associated with a bilateral EU-ACP trade liberalisation.[37] Altogether, in this context, the EU initially provided an amount of €171 million to the SADC's Regional Indicative Programme for a period of five years (2003–2007). Furthermore, the EU made an envelope of over €302.6 million available to countries of Southern and Eastern Africa (i.e. the ESA and Indian Ocean Regional Indicative Programme). In both cases, most of the money was earmarked for regional integration projects, particularly regional trade liberalisation and economic integration.[38] Against this background, it becomes clear that it was particularly the inherent development assistance that made the EPAs attractive even for those ACP countries that counted as LDC.

In regard to the theoretical framework, it seems that the underlying cooperation problem in view of the planned SADC-CU shifted towards a cooperation-averse "Rambo"-type situation if one takes into account the "shadow" of strong and asymmetric extra-regional economic interdependence to the EU and its EPA offerings (Fig. 5.2):

This is because those SADC members, which expect better payoffs from concluding extra-regional trade agreements and EPAs with the EU than from deepening regional market integration and joining a unified SADC-CU with an "institutional straitjacket" in the form of a CET (in red), become defective Rambos (in orange) on a regional level (in yellow) for the SADC as an organisation. Therefore, the provision of attractive extra-regional policy options by external actors complicated the genuine regional problematic situation—and, in this case, with very damaging effect because the different North-South free-trade regimes inherent to different EPAs were mutually exclusive with the single comprehensive South-South trade regime inherent to the envisaged SADC-CU (Muntschick 2013a).

	EU	
	Status Quo	EPA
Status Quo	2 / 2	4 / 1
EPA	1 / 4	6 / 3

SADC Country A

	EU	
	1/3	EPA
	2/4	SADC CU
EPA	SADC CU	

SADC Country A

(SADC Country B on right)

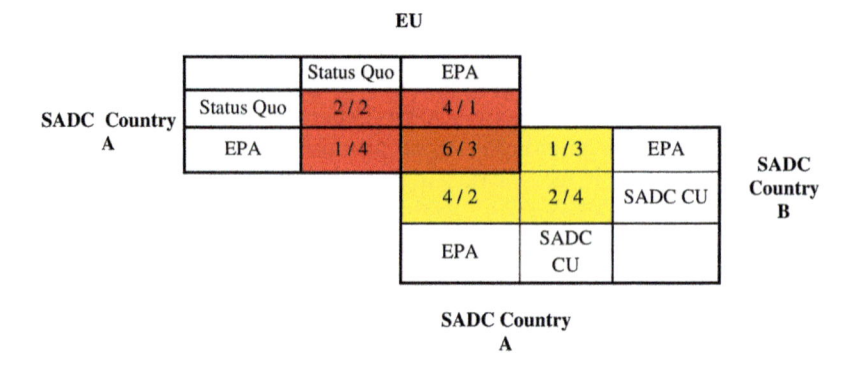

Fig. 5.2 Externally distorted problematic situation in view of the SADC-CU

5.3.1 Driven by European Incentives and Sanctions: EPA Negotiations and the Conclusion of Interim EPAs

The EU did not only interfere with the inherent structure of the regional cooperation problem. In addition, Brussels exerted significant diplomatic pressure on SADC countries to act according to its interests in the course of the EPA negotiations. Owing to the asymmetric character of SADC-EU economic relations, the EU was in a relative power position to do so and thus able to determine and alter the "rules of the game". In general, in the context of the EPA negotiations, Brussels followed a "carrot-and-stick" policy by providing incentives (i.e. development assistance inherent to the EPAs) and at the same time threatening with sanctions (i.e. market closure) if necessary (Muntschick 2013a).

The first SADC-EU negotiations meeting on EPAs took place in December 2004 (McCarthy et al. 2007: 5). In accordance with its trade strategy demanded the EU Commission the involved SADC states repeatedly and insistently to ratify the necessary measures for the reciprocal liberalisation of North-South trade within the EPAs as soon as possible—or at least initialise the process within the institutional frameworks of provisional interim EPAs (Griffith and Powell 2007: 13–25; Woolfrey 2009). Brussels issued an ultimatum for the conclusion of full EPAs for 1 January 2014[39] and signalled reluctant SADC countries to definitively exclude them from any sort of preferential access to the European market and thus impede importing from them.[40] These threats from the EU clearly underpinned its dominant (bargaining) position during the inter-regional negations but also provoked irritations and annoyance on the side of its African partners. Namibia, for example, characterised Europe's negotiating strategy as bullying, harassing and being full of colonial arrogance.[41] Windhoek regarded the EU's ultimatum as an unnecessary and unethical step since "equal partners do not give each other deadlines."[42] South Africa shared this view. It perceived the EU's negotiating tactic as uncompromising and ill-fated.[43]

The slow pace and inaction of several SADC countries in terms of initialising trade liberalisation on the conditions of the EU made the latter—rather unexpectedly—postpone its deadline several times (Lorenz-Carl 2013). However, those SADC members with strong dependence on the EU as (most) important export destination were unlikely to evade their economic constraints, the EU's diplomatic pressure and the latter's extra-regional policy alternative.[44] Hence, the situation in the SADC during the mid-2000s was not conducive to the formation of the ambitious SADC-CU at all.

The SADC was in turmoil over the EPA issue and internally divided into four fragments. This is because the organisation's members grouped themselves into the following four EPA groupings in order to negotiate, independently of each other, diverging trade regimes with the EU:

- Southern African Development Community (SADC)-EPA grouping: Angola, Botswana, Lesotho, Mozambique, Namibia, Swaziland and South Africa
- Eastern and Southern Africa (ESA)-EPA grouping: Madagascar, Malawi, Mauritius, the Seychelles, Zambia and Zimbabwe
- East African Community (EAC)-EPA grouping: Tanzania
- Economic and Monetary Community of Central Africa (CEMAC)-EPA grouping: the DRC.

If the SADC had not adhered to its plan to implement a customs union, this internal division would have been perhaps awkward but would not have jeopardised the SADC's integrity. The SADC-FTA was perfectly compatible with different extra-regional trade regimes of its members as the examples of the TDCA and the partial overlapping of the SADC-FTA with the COMESA-FTA demonstrate (Olivier 2006: 62–83). However, since the SADC classified its customs union project almost as a sine qua non for socio-economic development and as a cornerstone of its self-conception, the conflict between the SADC-CU and the EPAs was salient.

Several SADC countries of the mentioned groupings signed interim EPAs in a first step. The latter are a preliminary stage for full EPAs but guarantee continuous preferential market access to the EU on provisional conditions (Walker 2009). With regard to the SADC-EPA grouping, Botswana, Lesotho, Swaziland and Mozambique signed an interim EPA in June 2009. However, all countries—with the exception of Mozambique—stalled the relevant ratification procedures in 2010.[45] Namibia rejected the EU's offer on the grounds that regional export opportunities to the SADC and the COMESA were more important for the domestic industry than markets in the EU. Government officials gave a statement that "it will be better to utilise these opportunities [SADC and COMESA markets; author's note] than locking ourselves into a bad EPA which prevents us from utilising these markets."[46] South Africa also refrained from signing an interim EPA at that time. However, Pretoria was in a comfortable position because it enjoyed preferential market access to the EU under the decade-old TDCA. The latter was a fall-back option for South Africa (and to a lesser degree for the BLNS countries as well) if a full SADC-EPA should turn out to be less attractive—or simply not even materialise.

Of much more serious consequence for the SADC-CU project, however, was the fact that several countries of the ESA-EPA grouping (i.e. Madagascar, Mauritius, the Seychelles and Zimbabwe) signed an interim EPA in August 2009 which was different to the one signed by the members of the SADC-EPA group.[47] Tanzania did the same in a third way because the country had already chosen to sign an interim EPA on the basis of its group affiliation to the EAC-EPA grouping back in 2007.[48] The fact that several LDCs had chosen to become members of the EPA groupings as well, and initialised the ratification process by signing interim EPAs, is a clear indication of the EPAs' attractiveness in terms of financial (development) assistance. This is because there was, in fact, no danger for the LDCs to not sign an interim EPA as they could simply continue to export goods to the EU under the EBA Agreement's conditions.

The EPAs' centrifugal effect on the SADC became the moment of truth for the organisation and its agenda on regional market integration (Walker 2009: 1, 3): The signing of the interim EPAs was a clear first step towards the institutionalisation of North-South trade liberalisation between the EU and the SADC on the grounds of a number of (uncoordinated) ad hoc country groupings instead of a single joint group that represents the SADC as a whole. As a result, the EPA process undermines an encompassing SADC-CU on a territorial dimension that includes all 15 member states. This is because if full EPAs were not only ratified but also implemented, the SADC would consist of at least three groups of member states that have separate and divergent extra-regional trade regimes with the EU. The materialisation of such a Rambo situation makes a CET impossible. In June 2016, this scenario became a reality when the members of the SADC-EPA grouping signed a full EPA with the EU (Angola has the option to join the agreement in the future). The internal fragmentation of the SADC as an organisation seems now irreversible on this issue because the EAC-EPA grouping (with Tanzania as a member) finalised negotiations on a full EPA in October 2014 and the negotiations between the ESA-EPA grouping (comprising most of the remaining SADC members) and the EU are still ongoing.[49] The EU is certainly co-responsible for the internal split of the SADC because it was not keen to change its trade policies and negotiating framework towards the ACP countries. However, Brussels argues that the EPAs allow SADC countries to redefine their need on a national/regional level with respect to their relationship with the EU and moreover offer them an opportunity to realise their economic chances in the long run. All (SADC) countries, according to Brussels, are sovereign states with a freedom of choice which is why the EU keeps bilateral and varying EPA options for different groupings of SADC members open and practicable.[50]

5.4 Résumé and Prospects

This chapter has demonstrated that, to a greater or lesser extent, a number of SADC countries indeed showed a demand for the institutionalisation of a SADC customs union. This was not least because the SADC-FTA had proven to become increasingly effective in terms of removing regional barriers to trade. Moreover, the organisation's RISDP and a number of SADC officials and national leaders have repeatedly emphasised that the SADC was in need of a customs union and that such a regional project would imply absolute benefits for the entire region and its member states. Against this background, there was a clear genuine regional demand for the establishment of a SADC-CU in the member states during the mid-2000s, even if the actual benefits of such a regional club good had been a product of perceptions and high expectations.

This chapter also demonstrated that, in view of this regional project, the "shadow" of asymmetric extra-regional economic interdependence of a number of SADC countries with the EU interfered with the SADC's own market integration agenda. This happened for structural reasons in the course of the EU demanding that SADC countries conclude EPAs in order to safeguard their preferential market access to the important European common market. Against the background of their specific regional and extra-regional trade relations, several SADC members regarded the EPAs and their inherent trade regimes as compelling bilateral North-South policy alternatives to deepening South-South integration and expected them to produce better economic pay-offs than a SADC-CU could possibly provide in the near future. External influence thus transformed the structure of the genuine regional problematic situation into a cooperation-averse "Rambo"-type situation because the diverging trade regimes inherent to the different EPAs of the different EPA groupings ultimately are incompatible with the CET of the scheduled SADC-CU. Diplomatic pressure by the EU on the groups of SADC countries intensified this situation and finally made several SADC states inclined to sign interim and full EPAs.

Thus, the institutionalisation of a fully functional SADC-CU that includes all 15 member states has become highly unlikely because the EU and its EPA policies have exerted an interfering influence—be it intended or not—on the SADC's own agenda on regional market integration in this respect.

Notes

1. SADC (2004a): Regional Indicative Strategic Development Plan. Gaborone: SADC Secretariat.
2. Data obtained from RIKS—Indicators and Statistics of Regional Arrangements: http://www.cris.unu.edu/riks/web/data/show (02/05/2015).
3. The year 2007 has been chosen as a reference point to model the situation structure *prior* to the formation of the envisaged SADC customs union. This is because 2007 is in the middle between the adoption of the RISDP (in 2004) and the stated deadline for establishing the SADC-CU (in 2010).

4. SADC (2012): Desk Assessment of the Regional Indicative Strategic Development Plan 2005–2010. pp. 32–33.
5. Department for Trade and Industry (2002): South Africa's Global Trade Strategy and Agenda: A Brief Note. Pretoria: Department of Trade and Industry. p. 6.
6. SADC (2004a): Regional Indicative Strategic Development Plan. Gaborone: SADC Secretariat. pp. 66, 115.
7. SADC (2008a): Official SADC Trade, Industry and Investment Review 2007/2008. Gaborone: Southern African Marketing Co. (Pty) LTD. p. 10.
   Undisclosed Author (2009a): The Legal and Institutional Framework for Administration and Implementation of a Customs Union for the Southern African Development Community.
   Undisclosed Authors (2009b): Study on SADC Customs Union Policies. Final Report.
8. SADC (2004b): Record of the Meeting of SADC Council of Ministers held in Arusha, 12–13 March 2004. p. 303.
9. SADC (2006b): Final Communiqué of the SADC Extraordinary Summit of the Heads of State and Government to consider the Regional, Economic and Political Integration. Article 7.
10. Interview with Juma Kaniki (Senior Programme Manager Microeconomic Monitoring and Performance Surveillance) at the SADC Directorate of Trade, Industry, Finance and Investment (01/12/2008).
11. Thabo Mbeki, President of South Africa. Speech from 14 November 2006 at the SADC Parliamentary Forum. http://www.dfa.gov.za/docs/speeches/2006/mbek1114.htm (10/09/2012). Pakalitha Mosisili, Prime Minister of Lesotho. Interview with Nam News Network from 23 October 2006. http://www.namnewsnetwork.org/v3/read.php?id=MTMxODY(10/09/2012).
12. SADC (2006c): Sub-Theme on Trade, Economic Liberalization and Development. Prepared for the SADC Consultative Conference Windhoek, Namibia, 26–27 April 2006. Gaborone: SADC Secretariat. p. 7.
13. SADC (2006a): 4th Draft SADC Model Customs Act. http://www.sadc.int/files/1013/2369/4831/Final_DRAFT_SADC_Model_CUSTOMS_ACT-doc.doc (04/08/2012).
14. SACU (2009): Southern African Customs Union Annual Report 2008/09. http://www.sacu.int/publications/reports/annual/2009/part2.pdf (04/07/2016).
15. Reliable quantitative data on the SADC's intra-regional FDI flows past 2003 is not available.
16. SACU (2009): Southern African Customs Union Annual Report 2008/09. http://www.sacu.int/publications/reports/annual/2009/part2.pdf (04/07/2016).

17. SADC (2009b): Study on the Best Options for the Collection and Distribution of revenue in the SADC Customs Union. Undisclosed Document.
18. Business Report (Cape Town): "Shifting trade patterns make SA more resilient to US and EU crises". Issue of 26 August 2011.
19. Data collected with the WITS on the basis of UN COMTRADE. https://wits.worldbank.org/WITS/ (06/06/2016).
20. Data obtained from Eurostat. http://ec.europa.eu/eurostat/web/international-trade-in-goods/data/database (06/06/2016).
21. European Council. 2000. Lisbon European Council 23 and 24 March 2000. Presidency Conclusions. http://www.europarl.europa.eu/summits/lis1_en.htm (10/11/2016).
22. European Commission (2005): EU Strategy for Africa: towards a Euro-African pact to accelerate Africa's development. Annex to the Communication from the Commission to the Council, the European Parliament and European Economic and Social Committee. COM (2005) 489 final. Paragraph 3.1.2.1.
European Council (2005): The EU and Africa: Towards a strategic partnership. Conclusions by the Heads of State and Government meeting in the European Council, Brussels, 15–16 December 2005 (doc 15961/05). Paragraph 7 e.
Council of the European Union (2008): The Africa-European Union Strategic Partnership. Brussels: European Communities. pp. 27–32.
23. European Commission (2006): The European Consensus on Development. Joint statement by the Council and the representatives of the governments of the Member States meeting within the Council, the European Parliament and the Commission on European Union Development Policy: "The European Consensus" (2006/C46/01). Paragraphs 57, 72.
24. European Community—Southern African Region (2008): Regional Strategy Paper and Regional Indicative Programme 2008–2013. p. IV. http://ec.europa.eu/development/icenter/repository/scanned_r7_rsp-2007-2013_en.pdf (03/03/2015).
25. SADC (2009a): Activity Report of the SADC Secretariat. For the Period August 2007 to July 2008. Gaborone: SADC Secretariat. pp. 46–50. http://www.sadc.int/files/3813/5333/8237/SADC_Annual_Report_2007_-_2008.pdf (10/11/2016).
26. European Community: Partnership agreement between the members of the African, Caribbean and Pacific Group of States of the one part, and the European Community and its Member States, of the other part (Cotonou Agreement). http://eur-lex.europa.eu/LexUriServ/LexUriServ.do?uri=C ELEX:22000A1215%2801%29:EN:NOT (05/06/2016).
27. European Community: Cotonou Agreement. Article 35 (2).

28. European Commission (2002): Recommendation for a Council Decision authorising the commission to negotiate Economic Partnership Agreements with the ACP countries and regions. SEC (2002) 351 final. http://www.eusa.org.za/en/PDFdownload/Trade%20&%20Economic/EPA_Council_Decision_Recommendation_ACP_April_2002.pdf (10/09/2012).
29. The EU classifies Angola, the DRC, Lesotho, Madagascar and Malawi as LCDs in the SADC. Therefore, these countries enjoy duty- and quota-free access to the European market under the EBA initiative. http://trade.ec.europa.eu/doclib/docs/2013/april/tradoc_150983.pdf (05/05/2015).
30. European Union (2005): Council Regulation (EC) No. 980/2005 of 27 June 2005 applying a scheme of generalised tariff preferences (Everything-But-Arms Initiative). http://eur-lex.europa.eu/legal-content/EN/TXT/PDF/?uri=CELEX:32005R0980&from=EN (10/12/2016).
31. European Commission (2006): The European Consensus on Development. Joint statement by the Council and the representatives of the governments of the Member States meeting within the Council, the European Parliament and the Commission on European Union Development Policy: 'The European Consensus' (2006/C46/01). Paragraph 57. http://eur-lex.europa.eu/legal-content/EN/TXT/PDF/?uri=CELEX:42006X0224(01)&from=EN (05/05/2016).
32. Interview with a high-ranking official of the Delegation of the EU to the SADC and Botswana (09/24/2010). The interviewee asked to remain anonymous.
33. European Commission (2011c): Fact sheet on the Economic Partnership Agreements. SADC EPA Group. http://trade.ec.europa.eu/doclib/html/142189.htm(02/09/2016).
34. European Commission (2012c): Fact sheet on the Economic Partnership Agreements. Eastern and Southern Africa (ESA). http://trade.ec.europa.eu/doclib/docs/2012/march/tradoc_149213.pdf (10/09/2016).
35. European Commission (2012d): Fact sheet on the Economic Partnership Agreements. The Eastern African Community (EAC). http://trade.ec.europa.eu/doclib/docs/2009/january/tradoc_142194.pdf(10/09/2016).
36. Council of the European Union (2007): Conclusions of the Council and of the Representatives of the Governments of the Member States meeting within the Council: EU Strategy on Aid for Trade: Enhancing EU support for trade-related needs in developing countries. http://trade.ec.europa.eu/doclib/docs/2008/november/tradoc_141470.pdf(10/09/2016).

37. EU–ACP (2010): Second Revision of the Cotonou Agreement—Agreed Consolidated Text. pp. 19–20. http://eeas.europa.eu/archives/delegations/burkina_faso/documents/eu_burkina_faso/second_rev_cotonou_agreement_20100311_en.pdf (10/09/2016).
38. Information provided by the European Commission: http://ec.europa.eu/trade/wider-agenda/development/aid-for-trade/programmes (10/09/2016).
39. The EU Parliament pleaded in a recent resolution to extend this deadline to 1 January 2016. The EU Council has yet to approve the proposal. http://www.europarl.europa.eu/news/en/pressroom/newsletter/2012-W37/19. (18/09/2016).
40. European Commission (2011d): Proposal for a regulation of the European Parliament and of the Council amending Annex I to Council Regulation (EC) No. 1528/2007 as regards the exclusion of number of countries from the list of regions or states which have concluded negotiations. http://eur-lex.europa.eu/LexUriServ/LexUriServ.do?uri=COM:2011:0598:FIN:EN:PDF(10/09/2016).
41. Hage Geingob, Namibia's Minister for Trade and Industry. Interview in *Allgemeine Zeitung Windhoek*. Issue of 25 May 2010.
42. Hage Geingob, Namibia's Minister for Trade and Industry. Interview in *The Namibian*. Issue of 9 August 2012.
43. Robert Davies, South Africa's Minister for Trade and Industry, on regional integration, South-South cooperation and South Africa's new industrial policy. Interview at the Southern Africa Documentation and Cooperation Centre on 7 December 2009. http://www.sadocc.at/news/2009/2009-167.shtml (08/09/2016).
44. Extra-regional policy options in terms of competing South-South regional market integration projects—for example, to join a fully implemented COMESA-CU—were neither economically promising nor realistic for any SADC member state at that time (Jakobeit et al. 2005). Only Swaziland possibly had an economic interest for deepening market integration within the COMESA beyond an FTA because of its export-oriented sugar industry. However, this did not outweigh the economic benefits related to its exclusive SACU membership.
45. European Commission (2011c): Fact sheet on the Economic Partnership Agreements. SADC EPA Group. http://trade.ec.europa.eu/doclib/html/142189.htm(02/09/2016).
46. Calle Schlettwein, Namibia's Deputy Minister of Finance. Interview in: *Namibia Economist*. Issue of 31 October 2011.
47. European Commission (2012c): Fact sheet on the Economic Partnership Agreements. Eastern and Southern Africa (ESA). http://trade.ec.europa.eu/doclib/docs/2012/march/tradoc_149213.pdf (10/09/2016).

48. European Commission (2012d): Fact sheet on the Economic Partnership Agreements. The Eastern African Community (EAC). http://trade.ec.europa.eu/doclib/docs/2009/january/tradoc_142194.pdf (10/09/2016).
49. Information provided by the European Commission: http://ec.europa.eu/trade/policy/countries-andregions/regions/sadc/ (09/09/2017).
50. Interview with an official of the European Commission's Directorate General for Trade who had been involved in EPA negotiations with the SADC (04/21/2010).

REFERENCES

Alden, C., and M. Soko. 2005. South Africa's Economic Relations With Africa: Hegemony and its Discontents. *Journal of Modern African Studies* 43 (3): 367–392.
Asche, H. 2008. Preserving Africa's Economic Policy Space in Trade Negotiations. In *Negotiating Regions: Economic Partnership Agreements Between the European Union and the African Regional Economic Communities*, ed. H. Asche, and U. Engel, 79–108. Leipzig: Leipziger Universitätsverlag.
Behar, A., and L. Edward. 2011. *How Integrated is SADC? Trends in Intra-Regional and Extra-Regional Trade Flows Policy*. Washington: World Bank.
Bertelsmann-Scott, T. 2010. *SACU—One Hundred Not Out: What Future for the Customs Union*, vol. 68. Occasional Paper. Johannesburg: South African Institute of International Affairs.
Bilal, S., and C. Stevens. 2009. The Interim Economic Partnership Agreements Between the EU and African States. In *Contents, Challenges and Prospects. Policy Management Report*, vol. 17. Maastricht: European Centre for Development Policy Management (ECDPM).
Börzel, T.A., and T. Risse. 2009a. *Diffusing (Inter-)Regionalism. The EU as a Model of Regional Integration*. KFG Working Paper 7. Berlin: Otto-Suhr-Institut für Politikwissenschaft.
Börzel, T.A., and T. Risse. 2009b. *The Transformative Power of Europe: The European Union and the Diffusion of Ideas*. KFG Working Paper 1. Berlin: Otto-Suhr-Institut für Politikwissenschaft.
Brown, M.L. 1994. *Developing Countries and Regional Economic Cooperation*. Westport (Connecticut): Praeger.
Chauvin, S., and G. Gaulier. 2002. Prospects for Increasing Trade Among SADC Countries. In *Monitoring Regional Integration in Southern Africa Yearbook*, vol. 2, ed. D. Hansohm, C. Peters-Berries, W. Breytenbach, T. Hartzenberg, W. Maier, and P. Meyns, 21–42. Windhoek: Gamsberg Macmillan.
Draper, P., and N. Khumalo. 2009. The Future of the Southern African Customs Union. *Trade Negotiations Insights* 8 (6): 4–5.

Draper, P., P. Alves, and M. Kalaba. 2006. *South Africa's International Trade Diplomacy: Implications for Regional Integration*, vol. 1. Regional Integration in Southern Africa. Gaborone: Friedrich Ebert Stiftung—Botswana Office.

Erasmus, G. 2007. Is SACU Constructing an Effective Framework for Regional Integration? In *Monitoring Regional Integration in Southern Africa Yearbook*, ed. A. Bösl, W. Breytenbach, T. Hartzenberg, C. McCarthy, and K. Schade, vol 7, 228–249. Stellenbosch: Trade Law Centre of Southern Africa.

Gillson, I. 2010. *Deepening Regional Integration to Eliminate the Fragmented Goods Market in Southern Africa*. Washington: World Bank.

Goldstein, A. 2004. *Regional Integration, FDI and Competitiveness in Southern Africa*. Paris: OECD.

Griffith, M., and S. Powell. 2007. *Partnership Under Pressure. An Assessment of the European Commission's Conduct in the EPA Negotiations*. London: ActionAid, CAFOD, Christian Aid, Tearfund, Traidcraft Exchange.

Grobbelaar, N. 2004 Can South African Business Drive Regional Integration on the Continent? *South African Journal of International Affairs* 11 (2): 91–106.

Jakobeit, C., T. Hartzenberg, and N. Charalambides. 2005. *Overlapping Membership in COMESA, EAC, SACU and SADC. Trade Policy Options for the Region and for EPA Negotiations*. Eschborn: Deutsche Gesellschaft für Technische Zusammenarbeit.

Keck, A., and R. Piermartini. 2008. The Impact of Economic Partnership Agreements in Countries of the Southern African Development Community. *Journal of African Economies* 17 (1): 85–130.

Krapohl S., and J. Muntschick. 2009. Two Logics of Regionalism: The Importance of Interdependence and External Support for Regional Integration in Southern Africa. In *Proceedings of the 2008 FOPRISA Annual Conference Furthering Southern African Integration*, vol. 7 ed. J.M. Kaunda and F. Zizhou, 3–17. Gaborone: Lighthouse.

Langhammer, R.J., and U. Hiemenz. 1990. *Regional Integration Among Developing Countries. Opportunities, Obstacles and Options*. Tübingen: J. C. B. Mohr (Paul Siebeck).

Lorenz-Carl, U. 2013. When the 'Not so Weak' Bargain with the 'Not so Strong': Whose Agency Matters in the Economic Partnership Agreements? In *Mapping Agency. Comparing Regionalisms in Africa*, ed. U. Lorenz-Carl and M. Rempe, 61–76. Farnham: Ashgate.

Maes, M. 2012. 27 September 2012: 10 Years of EPA Negotiations. From Misconception and Mismanagement to Failure. *Great Insights* 1 (6): 2–3.

McCarthy, C. 2008. The SADC/SACU Interplay in EPA Negotiations—A Variation on the Old Theme of Integrating and Unequal Economies. In *Negotiating Regions: Economic Partnership Agreements between the European Union and the African Regional Economic Communities*, ed. H. Asche and U. Engel, 109–130. Leipzig: Universitätsverlag Leipzig.

McCarthy, C., P. Kruger, and J. Fourie. 2007. *Benchmarking EPA Negotiations Between EU and SADC*. Stellenbosch: Trade Law Centre for Southern Africa.

Meyn, M. 2010 Die Wirtschaftspartnerschaftsabkommen der Europäischen Union—was war, was ist und was kommen muss. In *Afrika und externe Akteure - Partner auf Augenhöhe?* ed. F. Stehnken, A. Daniel, H. Asche, and R. Öhlgeschläger, 75–89. Baden-Baden: Nomos.

Meyn, M., and J. Kennan. 2010. *Economic Partnership Agreeements: Comparative Analysis of the Agricultral Provisions*. New York: United Nations.

Muntschick, J. 2013a. Explaining the influence of extra-regional actors on regional economic integration in Southern Africa: the EU's interfering impact on SADC and SACU. In *Mapping Agency: Comparing Regionalisms in Africa*, ed. U. Lorenz-Carl, and M. Rempe, 77–95. Farnham: Ashgate.

Nyambe, J. 2010. The SADC Free Trade Area and the Way Towards a Customs Union. In *Proceedings of the 2009 FOPRISA Annual Conference, vol Report 8*, ed. C. Harvey, 153–171. Gaborone: Botswana Institute for Development Policy Analysis.

Olivier, G. 2006. *South Africa and the European Union: Self-interest, Ideology and Altruism*. Pretoria: Protea Book House.

Oosthuizen, G.H. 2006. *The Southern African Development Community: The Organisation, its Policies and Prospects*. Midrand: Institute for Global Dialogue.

Oosthuizen, G.H. 2007. The Future of the Southern African Development Community. In *South African Yearbook 2006/2007*, ed. E. Sidiropoulos, 87–98. Johannesburg: South African Institute of International Affairs.

Pietrangeli, G. 2009. Supporting Regional Integration and Cooperation Worldwide: An Overview of the European Union Approach. In *The EU and World Regionalism. The Makability of Regions in the 21st Century*, ed. P. de Lombaerde and M. Schulz, 9–43. Farnham: Ashgate.

Rangasamy, L. 2008. *Trade Liberalisation and South Africa's Manufacturing Sector. The Impact of Trade Liberalisation on the Competitiveness of the Manufacturing Sector in South Africa*. Saarbrücken: VDM Verlag Dr. Müller.

Sandrey, R. 2012. Foreign Direct Investment in South Africa. In *Monitoring Regional Integration in Southern Africa. Yearbook 2011*, ed. T. Hartzenberg, G. Erasmus, and A. du Pisani, 188–213. Stellenbosch: Trade Law Centre for Southern Africa.

Sandrey, R., H. Grinsted Jensen, N. Vink, T. Fundira, and W. Viljoen (eds.). 2011. *Cape to Cairo—An Assessment of the Tripartite Free Trade Area*. Stellenbosch: Trade Law Centre for Southern Africa.

Saurombe, A. 2009. Regional Integration Agenda for SADC "Caught in the Winds of Change". Problems and Prospects. *Journal of International Commercial Law and Technology* 4 (2): 100–106.

Söderbaum, F. 2007. African Regionalism and EU-African Interregionalism. In *European Union and New Regionalism: Regional Actors and Global*

Governance in a Post-hegemonic Era, 2nd ed., ed. M. Telò, 185–202. Aldershot, Burlington: Ashgate.

Stevens, C. 2005. The TDCA, EPAs and Southern African Regionalism. In *The TDCA: Impacts, Lessons and Perspectives for EU-South and Southern African Relations*, vol. 7, ed. T. Bertelsmann-Scott, and P. Draper, 64–86. Johannesburg: South African Institute of International Affairs.

Taylor, S.D. 2007. *Business and the State in Southern Africa: The Politics of Economic Reform*. London: Lynne Rienner.

Thomas, L., J. Leape, M. Hanouch, and Rumney R. 2005. *Foreign Direct Investment in South Africa: The Initial Impact of the Trade, Development and Cooperation Agreement between South Africa and the European Union*. London: Centre for Research into Economics & Finance in Southern Africa (CREFSA).

Tleane, C. 2006. *The Great Trek North: The Expansion of South African Media and ICT Companies into the SADC Region*. Braamfontein: Freedom of Expression Institute.

Versi, A. 2005. *The Top Companies in Africa. African Business*. London: IC Publications.

Viner, J. 1950. *The Customs Union Issue. Studies in the Administration of International Law and Organization*. New York: The Carnegie Endowment for International Peace.

Walker, A. 2009. The EC-SADC EPA: The Moment of Truth for Regional Integration. *Trade Negotiations Insights* 8 (6): 1, 3.

Woolfrey, S. 2009. *An Assessment of the Trade Measures Proposed as Part of the Department of Trade and Industry's Draft Rescue Package for the Clothing and Textile Industry*. Working Paper No. 5/2009. Stellenbosch: Trade Law Centre for Southern Africa.

Zwizwai, B. 2007. *Deepening Integration in SADC: Zimbabwe—Missing SADC Macroeconomic Targets*. Regional Integration in Southern Africa, vol. 10. Gaborone: Friedrich Ebert Stiftung—Botswana Office.

Primary Sources

Council of the European Union. 2007. Conclusions of the Council and of the Representatives of the Governments of the Member States Meeting Within the Council: EU Strategy on Aid for Trade: Enhancing EU Support for Trade-Related Needs in Developing Countries. http://trade.ec.europa.eu/doclib/docs/2008/november/tradoc_141470.pdf. Accessed 10 Sept 2016.

Council of the European Union. 2008. The Africa-European Union Strategic Partnership. Brussels: European Communities.

Department for Trade and Industry. 2002. South Africa's Global Trade Strategy and Agenda: A Brief Note. Pretoria: Department of Trade and Industry.

EU—ACP. 2010. Second Revision of the Cotonou Agreement—Agreed Consolidated Text. http://eeas.europa.eu/archives/delegations/burkina_faso/documents/eu_burkina_faso/second_rev_cotonou_agreement_20100311_en.pdf. Accessed 10 Sept 2016.

European Commission. 2002. Recommendation for a Council Decision Authorising the Commission to Negotiate Economic Partnership Agreements with the ACP Countries and Regions. SEC (2002) 351 final. http://trade.ec.europa.eu/doclib/docs/2006/september/tradoc_112023.pdf. Accessed 10 Sept 2016.

European Commission. 2005. EU Strategy for Africa: Towards a Euro-African Pact to Accelerate Africa's Development. Annex to the Communication from the Commission to the Council, the European Parliament and European Economic and Social Committee. COM(2005) 489 Final.

European Commission. 2006. The European Consensus on Development. Joint Statement by the Council and the Representatives of the Governments of the Member States Meeting Within the Council, the European Parliament and the Commission on European Union Development Policy: 'The European Consensus' (2006/C46/01). http://eur-lex.europa.eu/legal-content/EN/TXT/PDF/?uri=CELEX:42006X0224(01)&from=EN. Accessed 5 May 2016.

European Commission. 2011c. Fact Sheet on the Economic Partnership Agreements. SADC EPA Group. http://trade.ec.europa.eu/doclib/html/142189.htm. Accessed 2 Sept 2016.

European Commission. 2011d. Proposal for a Regulation of the European Parliament and of the Council Amending Annex I to Council Regulation (EC) No 1528/2007 as Regards the Exclusion of Number of Countries From the List of Regions or States Which Have Concluded Negotiations. http://eur-lex.europa.eu/LexUriServ/LexUriServ.do?uri=COM:2011:0598:FIN:EN:PDF. Accessed 10 September 2016.

European Commission. 2012c. Fact sheet on the Economic Partnership Agreements. Eastern and Southern Africa (ESA). http://trade.ec.europa.eu/doclib/docs/2012/march/tradoc_149213.pdf. Accessed 10 Sept 2016.

European Commission. 2012d. Fact sheet on the Economic Partnership Agreements. The Eastern African Community (EAC). http://trade.ec.europa.eu/doclib/docs/2009/january/tradoc_142194.pdf. Accessed 10 Sept 2016.

European Community. 2000. Partnership Agreement Between the Members of the African, Caribbean and Pacific Group of States of the One Part, and the European Community and its Member States, of the Other Part (Cotonou Agreement). http://eur-lex.europa.eu/LexUriServ/LexUriServ.do?uri=CELEX:22000A1215%2801%29:EN:NOT. Accessed 5 July 2016.

European Community—Southern African Region. 2008. Regional Strategy Paper and Regional Indicative Programme 2008–2013. http://ec.europa.eu/development/icenter/repository/Signed-RSP_PIR_ESA-2007-2013.pdf. Accessed 3 July 2015.

European Council. 2000. Lisbon European Council 23 and 24 March 2000. Presidency Conclusions. http://www.europarl.europa.eu/summits/lis1_en.htm. Accessed 10 Nov 2016.
European Council. 2005. The EU and Africa: Towards a Strategic Partnership. Conclusions by the Heads of State and Government Meeting in the European Council, Brussels, 15–16 December 2005 (doc 15961/05).
European Union. 2005. Council Regulation (EC) No. 980/2005 of 27 June 2005 Applying a Scheme of Generalised Tariff Preferences (Everything-But-Arms Initiative). http://eur-lex.europa.eu/legal-content/EN/TXT/PDF/?uri=CELEX:32005R0980&from=EN. Accessed 10 Sept 2016.
SACU. 2009. Southern African Customs Union Annual Report 2008/2009. http://www.sacu.int/publications/reports/annual/2009/part2.pdf. Accessed 4 July 2016.
SADC. 2004a. Regional Indicative Strategic Development Plan. Gaborone: SADC Secretariat.
SADC. 2004b. Record of the Meeting of SADC Council of Ministers held in Arusha.
SADC. 2006a. 4th Draft SADC Model Customs Act. http://www.sadc.int/files/1013/2369/4831/Final_DRAFT_SADC_Model_CUSTOMS_ACT-doc.doc. Accessed 4 Aug 2012.
SADC. 2006b. Final Communiqué of the SADC Extraordinary Summit of the Heads of State and Government to Consider the Regional, Economic and Political Integration.
SADC. 2006c. Sub-Theme on Trade, Economic Liberalization and Development: Prepared for the SADC Consultative Conference Windhoek, Namibia, April 26–27, 2006. Gaborone: SADC Secretariat.
SADC. 2008a. Official SADC Trade, Industry and Investment Review 2007/2008. Gaborone: Southern African Marketing Co. (Pty) LTD.
SADC. 2009a. Activity Report of the SADC Secretariat. For the Period August 2007 to July 2008, 46–50. Gabrone: SADC Secretariat. http://www.sadc.int/files/3813/5333/8237/SADC_Annual_Report_2007_-_2008.pdf. Accessed 10 Nov 2016.
SADC. 2009b. Study on the Best Options for the Collection and Distribution of Revenue in the SADC Customs Union. Undisclosed Document.
SADC. 2012. Desk Assessment of the Regional Indicative Strategic Development Plan 2005–2010. Gaborone: SADC Secretariat.
Undisclosed Author. 2009a. The Legal and Institutional Framework for Administration and Implementation of a Customs Union for the Southern African Development Community.
Undisclosed Authors. 2009b. Study on SADC Customs Union Policies. Final Report.

CHAPTER 6

Regional Security Cooperation and the SADC's Organ for Politics, Defence and Security: A Picture of Mixed Performance

Regional security cooperation has been a matter of key importance for all countries in Southern Africa for decades. After the end of colonialism, the newly independent black majority-ruled states in the SADC area soon formed a loosely institutionalised regional grouping for the purpose of mutual assistance and defence against the common threat of the remaining Apartheid government(s). The FLS and the SADCC, which both were introduced earlier in this book, were the most important and lasting examples in this respect.

The decline of the last Apartheid government in South Africa in the early 1990s also marked an end to a decade-old regional security complex in Southern Africa. However, the end of Apartheid did not mark the onset of eternal peace in the region since inter-state tensions and various (dormant) conflicts among a number of SADC countries continued to exist or broke forth again; and South Africa remained a factor of uncertainty to the region as well (Hatchard and Slinn 1995; Omari and Macaringue 2007).

Becoming aware of this changing political environment in the region, more and more SADC countries demanded a new approach to regional security cooperation. This experienced a major stimulus after South Africa joined the organisation in August 1994. Already in June 1996, the SADC Summit established the Organ for Politics, Defence and Security (OPDS) and entrusted the so-called "Organ" with the task to ensure and promote regional security cooperation.[1] Central aspects of its responsibility included military confidence-building measures as well as regional

© The Author(s) 2018
J. Muntschick, *The Southern African Development Community (SADC) and the European Union (EU)*,
https://doi.org/10.1007/978-3-319-45330-9_6

security and conflict management. The adoption of the SADC Protocol on Politics, Defence and Security Co-operation in 2001 led to a major institutional reform of the OPDS which once again demonstrates the dynamics within the SADC as an organisation (Nathan 2012; Schleicher 2006).

This chapter provides an analysis of the emergence, nature and effectiveness of institutionalised regional security cooperation in the SADC by focussing on the OPDS—the organisation's main security body—and the performance in its key areas.

6.1 THE CHANGING SECURITY COMPLEX IN SOUTHERN AFRICA: FUELLING DEMAND FOR NEW SECURITY MANAGEMENT INSTITUTIONS

Scholars of cooperation theory and rational institutionalism argue that international security problems that are based on mutual threat or external risk can be interpreted as collective action or coordination problems. This is because security problems are always situations of conflict in terms of pursuing national interests as well (Axelrod 1987; Keohane 1984). They generate demand for collective action or coordination efforts in the involved countries because mutual security cooperation bears the prospect for absolute benefits in terms of an overall improved security by means of arms limitation, transparency, confidence-building measures and so on, thus a reduction of uncertainty. All of these beneficial effects can be achieved with the help of (security management) institutions that cement cooperative behaviour (Buzan and Wæver 2003; Zürn 1992: 174–184).

6.1.1 Sources of Insecurity and Potential Conflicts as Demand-Driving Factors

In Southern Africa, the general demand for regional security cooperation can be deduced from the structural characteristics of security interdependence among the countries within the region. This makes it possible to outline the regional security complex in the SADC region at the period under observation:

Before the end of Apartheid in South Africa, the black majority-ruled states in Southern Africa faced a problematic security situation that clearly resembled an assurance game: This is because they perceived South Africa as a common enemy because of the Apartheid government's intimidations, sabotage actions and armed attacks on fellow countries. Facing Pretoria in this way as the common threat generated not only an overall demand for security cooperation in the black majority-ruled states but also a need to commit each other for taking joint action—for example, mutual logistical or military assistance and defensive measures—in case of a South African attack. Since the need to assure and coordinate (military) action was central at that time, the black majority-ruled countries institutionalised security cooperation on a regional level, initially within the FLS and later on under the umbrella of the SADCC within the ISDSC (Cawthra 1997: 208; Ngoma 2005: 96). In line with the assumptions of the situation-structural approach on problematic situations reminiscent of assurance games, both organisations—especially the FLS—were only loosely institutionalised entities with rather informal accords in the issue area of security.

The character of security interdependence in the region changed fundamentally with South Africa joining the SADC after the end of Apartheid in 1994. With the transitional Government of National Unity in place and President Nelson Mandela in office, the Cape Republic's foreign and security policy underwent a complete turn-around. Pretoria at once stopped its military assaults and destabilisation policies towards its neighbours. The major result was that the rest of the countries in the region no longer perceived South Africa as the one and only immediate threat to their national security (Alden and le Pere 2003; Omari and Macaringue 2007: 53–54). This implied that the old regional security complex in the SADC region disappeared as well.

The new regional environment, however, did not mark an end to inter-state tensions and regional conflict for the SADC region. This is because a number of minor and major regional conflicts, which had been overshadowed and suppressed by the militarised black-white antagonism through the years before, broke to the surface again. They posed a new challenge to security in the region and fuelled the SADC states' demand for a new approach on regional security cooperation. The following actual and potential conflicts in the region—which for the most part were rooted in inter-state tensions, border disputes, mutual uncertainty and political instability of governments and countries (Ressler 2007: 82–88; Williams 2001: 109)—can be identified for the period of the early and mid-1990s:

The first cluster of potential conflicts is associated with historical conflicts, in particular "left overs" from the colonial and Apartheid periods. The process of decolonisation in the SADC region, often carried out by means of violent resistance and years of armed liberation struggles, manifested not only in a proliferation of small arms in private hands throughout several countries but also in a number of fairly militarised states (Gamba 1998; Tjønneland and Vraalsen 1996: 196). This conflict-prone state of affairs became even more pronounced in the course of long-lasting "hot" conflicts. The most dangerous ones at around that time were the civil wars in Mozambique (until the early 1990s), Angola (continued despite some periods of ceasefires until 2002) and the DRC (started in 1995/96 with the Kabila rebellion) which for one reason or another always had a latent potential to spill over to neighbouring, non-involved countries (Nathan 2012; Wannenburg 2006: 263–307). These circumstances explain why SADC countries such as Angola, the DRC, Namibia, Mozambique, Zimbabwe and not least South Africa had pretty oversized armed forces at their command during the last decade of the twentieth century (Vale 1994: 154). And it was particularly this aspect of oversized, experienced and transforming armies facing each other that bore the fruit of conflict because it fuelled insecurity and caused negative security externalities for neighbouring countries in the region—occasionally even leading to military build-up (Nathan 2012: 20–22; Ohlson 1996: 12–16, 24–32).

A second cluster of potential conflicts in the region related to more or less dormant but unresolved territorial claims and border disputes among SADC members. These were not a burning issue during the time of Apartheid but came back on the table from the mid-1990s onwards—after this "external" threat had disappeared. Some of the major territorial disputes involved, for example, the Caprivi Strip (Botswana, Namibia, Zambia and Zimbabwe as claimants), the KaNgwane region (Swaziland and South Africa as claimants), the islands of the Mbamba Bay in Lake Nyasa (Malawi and Tanzania as claimants) or the Sindabezi Island on the Zambezi River (Zambia and Zimbabwe as claimants). Major regional border disputes and unresolved demarcation lines involved the Luapula Province (between the DRC and Zambia), the Orange River (between Namibia and South Africa), and along the Sedudu islands in the Chobe River (between Botswana and Namibia) (Molomo et al. 2007: 76; Ohlson 1996: 22–26; Vale 1994: 157). Although not all of these disputes were likely to cause inter-state war, they nevertheless fuelled uncertainty and tension among the antagonists involved. Therefore, they posed a threat to regional security.

A third and somewhat tragic source of potential conflict to the SADC region was the status of the new, majority-ruled South Africa and the issue of how it could be re-integrated into the region. Whether South Africa was ruled by an Apartheid or democratic government made no difference: For plain structural reasons, the country not only remained a regional giant in economic terms but also continued to be the dominant power in the region because of its sheer size (in terms of territory, population and other indictors associated with measuring power) and its strong military (Cawthra 1997: 207; Vale 1994: 155). Moreover, the disproportional distribution of resources and economic power on a regional level implied future polarisation effects and consequently a growing gap between the Cape Republic and the rest of the SADC (Tjønneland and Vraalsen 1996: 197; Vale 1996: 364–366). The result of this pattern of asymmetry was that Pretoria continued to pose a latent threat to its weaker neighbouring countries—or was at least perceived to do so. Therefore, the RSA remained the major source of insecurity to the region at the turn of the millennium.

6.1.2 Country-Specific Demand for Regional Security Cooperation

We now turn our focus from the (changing) regional environment to the country level, where it becomes clear that country-specific demand for institutionalised regional security cooperation in the SADC related in many cases to the abovementioned actual and potential regional conflicts. The following selection of SADC countries provides a comprehensive and representative overview.

Mozambique and Angola represent states that were heavily conflict-ridden at the time of the SADC's foundation in the early 1990s. By that time, both countries had experienced lasting civil wars of more than 15 years and both had become subject to the involvement of third war parties that operated on their territory. The civil war in Angola continued after the ceasefire of 1991/92—with some interludes—until 2002, but Mozambique achieved a peace settlement in 1992 (Nathan 2012: 21–22). In regard to the latter, this had two effects: Firstly, it left behind a strongly militarised country that posed a threat to its neighbours because of its oversized armed forces and the imminent proliferation of the warring factions' small arms. Secondly, it led to a reformulation of Mozambique's security conception that made Maputo an advocate for enhancing deeper regional security cooperation within the SADC's institutional architecture. Against the background of its own war experiences, Mozambique thus became devoted to the construction of regional security and conflict management institutions in order to prevent the outburst of violence or (civil) wars and promote and protect peace in the region (Lalá 2007; Wannenburg 2006: 229–235, 309–311).

Botswana, a relatively small country in terms of population and personnel strength of the military, enjoyed relative peace and stability since the time of its independence. However, the country was aware of security challenges ranging from low- to high-intensity conflicts during the mid-1990s. This is because Botswana's security has always been strongly determined by its geopolitical situation and status as a landlocked country which made it subject to the security interests and actions of its four neighbours. The government in Gaborone therefore followed a double approach to national security by maintaining a good level of military readiness and build-up on the one hand and a clear willingness to participate in a new regional security regime on the SADC level on the other hand (du Toit 1995; Molomo et al. 2007).

Namibia, Lesotho and Swaziland demanded a new regional approach towards better security cooperation in the SADC for similar reasons as Botswana on the basis of similar circumstances. Namibia, looking back on a bloody war of independence with neighbouring countries operating on its territory, stated in 1993 that "prospects for regional stability and cooperation in the 1990s are encouraging, but despite this […] defence policy must be based on the premise that Namibia may face a regional security threat in the future."[2] This resulted on the one hand in a steadily growing defence budget during the 1990s and on the other hand in a number of bilateral MoU on security issues with its neighbouring countries shortly after interdependence. Both aspects underline Windhoek's predisposition to military armament as well as its readiness for regional security cooperation (Lindeke et al. 2007: 137). Lesotho and Swaziland, both small and landlocked countries that are entirely "embraced" by South African territory, put even more emphasis on the creation of a strong regional security regime in order to control and contain Pretoria with the help of the SADC's institutions (Matlosa 2007; Mzizi 2007).

Zambia, a typical medium power in the SADC region in terms of population and territory, has faced various threats from its eight neighbouring countries throughout the years since its independence in 1964. These experiences—in particular caused by the aggressive white-minority governments in pre-independence Zimbabwe and Namibia as well as by the political instability and civil wars in Angola, Mozambique, the DRC and Zimbabwe—lastingly shaped Zambia's perception of regional (in)security. Moreover, they fuelled the country's need for a strong armed force in concert with strong regional security management institutions. From the mid-1990s onwards, when Zambia felt that regional tensions with its neighbours were fading, Lusaka therefore became one of the most dedicated proponents of the idea that regional security cooperation could be achieved only through the SADC as an organisation (Phiri 2007: 218; Sandberg and Sabel 2003).

The situation in Zimbabwe, a landlocked medium country as well, was for structural reasons somewhat similar to Zambia, besides the fact that it experienced a violent path to independence that included the involvement of neighbouring countries, particularly South Africa. From independence until the mid-1990s, Zimbabwe moreover was the lead nation in the FLS and probably the most active country in the (coordination of the) anti-Apartheid struggle against South Africa (Schoeman 2007: 156). With the regional security environment changing, Zimbabwe's security policy remained largely the same during the last decade of the twentieth century. Tensions with most of its neighbours existed over territory and for political reasons. Harare perceived them as a latent threat to national security although military attacks from neighbours were not expected. With a comparably large defence force as a back-up, Zimbabwe therefore pursued a strategy of regional security cooperation only insofar as it wanted a loosely institutionalised security cooperation body similar to the one that had existed within the old FLS. The major concern of Harare's security policy in this context was to contain South Africa within a regional security framework while maintaining its own military autarky (Adar et al. 2002; Lalá 2007: 120).

South Africa, the most powerful actor in the region, deserves special attention. While Pretoria followed a unilateral and aggressive security policy in the course of its "Total Strategy" towards most of its neighbouring countries up until the late 1980s, this changed fundamentally towards a more defensive and cooperative security approach under President Mandela from 1994 onwards (Bischoff 2006: 148–149). This implied on the one hand that Pretoria had recognised that the black majority-ruled countries in the SADC region did not pose a serious threat to its national security anymore and on the other hand that South Africa acknowledged that its own security depended to a large extent on peace and stability in the entire region. It was in particular the latter aspect that fuelled South Africa's demand for institutionalised regional security cooperation (Schoeman 2007: 166–170; Sidaway 1998: 568).

The "White Paper on National Defence for the Republic of South Africa," published in 1996, contains a whole chapter on security in a regional context and states that the country "is not confronted with by an immediate conventional military threat, and does not anticipate external military aggression in the short to medium term (± 5 years)."[3] However, it argues in this context that "a common approach to security in Southern Africa is necessary for a number of reasons"[4] and that South Africa "will encourage the development of a multi-lateral common security approach in Southern Africa. In essence, that SADC states should shape their own political, security and defence policies in cooperation with each other."[5] Being aware that South Africa was still perceived as a major factor of uncertainty for many countries in the region, the White Paper continued to mention a number of advantages of institutionalised regional security in the SADC (e.g. sharing of information, joint problem-solving, and implementing confidence- and security-building measures).[6] This proves that South Africa had a clear predisposition for a cooperative solution to the problem of regional insecurity, although the country was sensible of its power position, freedom of action and unilateral policy options (le Pere and van Nieuwkerk 2002: 197–202; Tjønneland and Vraalsen 1996).

6.1.3 *The SADC's Initiatives for Regional Security Cooperation*

Besides the abovementioned driving factors for regional security cooperation which have been deduced from the structure of the regional security complex in the SADC together with the member states' national interests, there is codified evidence that the SADC as an organisation had already addressed the issue of security cooperation from the very beginning as well. By the time of its foundation in 1992, the SADC Heads of States had already declared the common need to establish new institutional arrangements in order to ensure political stability and promote mutual security in the region.[7] This common aim also found expression in the SADC Treaty. The latter states that one of the organisation's major objectives is "the promotion of peace and security"[8] and stipulates that member states agree to "cooperate in the issue area of politics, diplomacy, international relations, peace and security"[9] by concluding a common protocol. These passages produce evidence that the SADC members put emphasis on the harmonisation of their security policies and had recognised the need to establish a new regional security regime and moreover that the loosely institutionalised security body of the old SADCC was by then outdated and unable to cope with the security challenges of the future.

However, at the time of the SADC's foundation in 1992, it was still unclear what kind of model of new regional security regime its member states aspired to adopt. There was still a clear mismatch between the SADC's vision and the organisation's codified expectations on the one hand and its obsolete, informal security body of the time of the FLS on the other hand (Nathan 2012: 26–27). Taking notice of this "institutional vacuum" within the SADC, the SADC Secretariat itself became proactive and attempted to get involved in the process of regional security cooperation from 1992 onwards. In 1993, it produced a detailed "Framework and Strategy Paper" that included a section on "politics, diplomacy, peace and security" and demanded the creation of institutional mechanisms for conflict avoidance under the SADC's umbrella.[10] A year later, the Secretariat organised a Ministerial Workshop on Democracy, Peace and Security which ended with a recommendation to the CoM that a "Protocol on Peace, Security and Cooperation be concluded and that the following structures be set up: […] a SADC committee of defence and security ministers; and a SADC sector on Conflict Resolution and Political Cooperation" (Nathan 2012: 32).

6.1.4 Interim Summary and Situation Structure

Back in the early and mid-1990s, the SADC member countries' structurally motivated demand for regional security cooperation together with the organisation's own strategy papers and the provisions of the SADC Treaty could be condensed to the following key message: Since virtually all mainland SADC states had tensions with their neighbours and perceived the latter or the regional environment (or both) as a source of insecurity, they were clearly predisposed to engage in regional security cooperation because they expected absolute benefits from a new regional security architecture. However, at the same time, all SADC countries had the fallback safety option of unilateral military armament at their disposal.

One thing needs to be made clear: There were no inter-state wars ongoing between SADC members at that time. However, there was mutual uncertainty among neighbours and a potential for violent conflicts in the region did exist. Since for these reasons all countries in the SADC region perceived varying degrees of threats to their national security and shared the common interest of state survival, improved security and socio-economic prosperity, the underlying problematic situation of the regional security complex in the SADC region clearly resembled a prisoner's dilemma—which is precisely a classic security dilemma (Fig. 6.1).

In regard to the assumptions and hypotheses of this book, the pattern of security relations in the SADC region provided countries with rational reasons to favour regional security cooperation (and thus become part of the club good of a regional security regime) over the status quo which implied mutual uncertainty and possibly an arms race. Since the demand for regional security and conflict management institutions is based on a genuine regional and actually existing cooperation problem in the SADC region, the corresponding future institutions—after being established—are unlikely to turn out to be dysfunctional or merely of symbolic nature.

Fig. 6.1 Problematic situation in view of a SADC Security Regime

		SADC Country B	
		Security Cooperation	Military Armament
SADC Country A	Security Cooperation	3 / 3	1 / 4
	Military Armament	4 / 1	2 / 2

6.2 The Long Shadow of the Table Mountain: South Africa as Regional Great Power

There exist numerous indicators that help to measure intra-regional military interdependence and illustrate the quantitative balance of military power between states in a region, especially with regard to important offensive capabilities (Nye 2008; Tjønneland and Vraalsen 1996: 199–200). This book's analysis puts its focus on the strength of the armed forces, on the military capabilities of the armed forces, and on the military expenditure of governments in absolute terms and in percentage of the GDP. This selection makes sense because these indicators are most suitable for determining the relative military power position of countries in a region and allow for comparison as well (SIPRI 2010; Meinken 2005: 5–8).

6.2.1 Intra-Regional Military Interdependence

During the early and mid-1990s, the character of security and military relations in Southern Africa clearly showed a picture of asymmetric intra-regional interdependence. With reference to the strength of the SADC members' regular armed forces as one key indicator to determine the relative (military) power distribution within the SADC area, the picture looked as follows (Table 6.1).

The table not only shows an intra-regional asymmetry in terms of military power but also indicates that there was one single country that enjoyed a marked military supremacy: Since the age of imperialism and during the time of Apartheid, it was the Republic of South Africa that had been the most powerful country in Southern Africa not only in terms of the economy but also with regard to the issue area of security. By the mid-1990s, the South African Defence Force had a personnel strength of more than 78,000 troops and thereby was the second largest armed force in the SADC region. Only the army of Angola—a country entangled in a civil war at that time—outnumbered Pretoria's military (by almost 5000 soldiers) and had a personnel strength of about 82,000 troops. Besides these two military great powers, only two of the other then–SADC members—Tanzania and Zimbabwe—commanded over sizable armed forces (approximately 50,000 soldiers each). All other countries in the region—with Zambia somehow in an intermediate position—had comparably small defence forces with a few thousand soldiers or only militias with a few hundred troops at their disposal (IISS 1994: 219–255).

Table 6.1 Strength of regular armed forces of SADC members (1994)

Country	Armed force	Tanks & armoured vehicles	Artillery	Combat aircrafts
Angola	82,000	1005	300	79
Botswana	7500	20	10	19
DR Congo	28,100	204	93	22
Lesotho	2000	18	2	0
Madagascar	21,000	30	30	12
Malawi	10,400	43	9	0
Mauritius	1300	10	2	0
Mozambique	2000	360	318	43
Namibia	8100	10	0	0
Seychelles	800	6	3	1
South Africa	78,500	4850	455	244
Swaziland[a]	3000	n/a	n/a	0
Tanzania	49,600	135	285	24
Zambia	24,000	158	142	60
Zimbabwe	46,900	261	78	64

Data obtained from IISS (1994: 249–255)
[a]Data obtained from Ressler (2007: 103)
Countries in italics were not yet members of the SADC in 1994

However, it is not only the quantitative size of an armed force that determines its strength. This is because the quality and technological level of equipment, firing power, frequency of training, and drill of personal are decisive factors for a military force's capability as well (Meinken 2005: 7–8). In regard to these qualitative aspects for the period of the early mid-1990s, South Africa and Angola—and, to a much lesser degree, Zimbabwe—were the only countries in the SADC region whose armed forces demonstrated a comparably high level of military capability.

South Africa undoubtedly had the region's most modern and technologically advanced military. Besides well-trained regular troops and special units, this included various armoured vehicles, tanks, heavy and light artilleries and aircrafts that were all fairly modern according to international standards. Several of these weapon systems, such as the Rooikat and Eland armoured cars or the G5-Impi and G6-Rhino artilleries, had been developed and produced by the country's advanced national weapon-manufacturing industry (IISS 1994: 253–254; Tjønneland and Vraalsen 1996: 197). This military manufacturing capability not only made South Africa fairly independent of weaponry imports from third actors but also contributed to Pretoria's regional power position since no other country in the SADC region had a comparable or even noteworthy arms industry. Moreover, the Cape Republic was the only country in the region with a sizable navy (including submarines) and an air force with decent airlift capacity. Both of these capabilities reinforced South Africa's regional superiority in terms of military power because they made its troops more mobile and easily deployable throughout the region—and thus extended Pretoria's sphere of (military) action (Schleicher 2006: 39; Vale 1994: 155).

Angola, admittedly, had a large armed force in terms of personnel and vehicle strength, but the country was entangled in a lasting civil at the time. This circumstance tarnished the impression of its military capabilities—not least since an allegedly large number of Angola's tanks, artilleries and combat aircrafts were fairly old or rendered inoperable because of the effects of civil war. Therefore, the quality of Luanda's armed force was at best moderate during the period under observation (Meinken 2005: 17–29; Wannenburg 2006: 233–249).

Zimbabwe had a comparably large, well-equipped and modern military at the time of its independence in 1980. At that time, the country was the military powerhouse among the black-majority ruled nations in Southern Africa which was not least the reason why Harare had become the spearhead of the FLS and SADCC (Evans 1984: 7–11; Ressler 2007: 101–106). Although Zimbabwe reduced its armed force from 130,000 to about 50,000 soldiers by the end of the 1980s, Harare continued to have one of the most modern and advanced armies in the region until the mid-1990s. Moreover, the country had a small light weapons and ammunition industry (Adar et al. 2002: 268, 275–277). In terms of quality, the Zimbabwean armed forces without a doubt were then the second best in the SADC region.

Looking at the SADC countries' annual military expenditures during the mid-1990s consolidates the earlier impression of a distinct intra-regional asymmetry in terms of military strength and capability (Table 6.2):

In regard to the figures on absolute military expenditures, which correlate with the operational capability and overall strength of a country's military (Meinken 2005: 10), South Africa was clearly in the regional lead. In 1995, the Cape Republic's defence budget amounted to almost $3.3 billion USD. Therefore, it accounted for more than 56% of total military expenditures of the entire SADC region. The fact that Pretoria's

Table 6.2 Military expenditure of SADC members (1995)

Country	Absolute Military expenditure in constant (2009) million US-$	Relative Military expenditure in % of GDP
Angola	963.0	4.6
Botswana	204.0	3.9
DR Congo[a]	98.5	1.5
Lesotho	28.7	3.7
Madagascar	46.5	0.9
Malawi	12.6	0.8
Mauritius	16.9	0.3
Mozambique	51.3	1.5
Namibia	80.8	1.9
Seychelles	10.2	2.3
South Africa	3251.0	2.1
Swaziland[a]	35.0	1.6
Tanzania	123.0	1.6
Zambia	130.0	1.6
Zimbabwe	739.0	19.1

Data collected from SIPRI (2010)
[a]Data from the year 1996
Countries in italics were not yet members of the SADC in 1994

absolute military spending was more than three times larger than that of Angola (spending $963 million USD) corroborates the impression that the latter's sizeable armed force was in a comparably bad state of maintenance. Besides Zimbabwe, whose well-equipped and advanced military consumed annual expenditures amounting to $739 million USD, virtually all other SADC countries had comparably small defence budgets during the period under observation. This evidence correlates very well to the modest strength of these countries' armed forces in terms of quantity and quality (Bischoff 2002: 293–294; Vale 1994: 155).

The data on military expenditures as a percentage of GDP complements the data on the SADC countries' absolute military spending. It is meaningful insofar as it reveals that only Zimbabwe channelled a well-above-average share of 19.1% of its GDP to its armed forces in 1995. This underscores not only the financial needs of a fairly modern army but even more the importance of a strong and advanced military for the country's government (Meinken 2005: 37–38).

Summarising the evidence for the period of the mid-1990s, the pattern of military and security interdependence in the SADC region appeared to be strongly asymmetric in character (Cawthra 2007: 235).

There was a clear regional imbalance in military capabilities with a polarisation of military power in the Republic of South Africa. It was a military great power in regional terms and the only SADC country with a noteworthy and advanced national arms industry. Both aspects not only provided South Africa a significant degree of autarky in the issue area of security but more importantly cemented the country's superiority and relative regional power position in this respect as well. Compared with the rest of the SADC region, Zimbabwe and Angola gave an impression of being regional middle powers.

6.2.2 Extra-Regional Military Interdependence

Decolonisation left the independent countries in Southern Africa with no noteworthy security relations, military linkages or (bilateral) defence agreements to former colonial powers or other extra-regional actors (Jaspert 2010: 337). This absence of any extra-regional powers' armed forces or military bases on the SADC countries' territory distinguishes the latter from some of their counterparts in West Africa where France continues to maintain bilateral military cooperation agreements—and occasionally has interfered in national affairs (Gregory 2000). However, with respect to the SADC region, it is unlikely, for structural reasons, that regional security cooperation efforts are directly affected by external influence—particularly not in a negative sense of interference—because not a single SADC country had noteworthy security or military relations—be it institutionalised or not—to extra-regional powers.

Nevertheless, the SADC—like the former SADCC—has traditionally had strong relations to extra-regional donor countries. And in this regard Europe played a major role. During the early and mid-1990s, the SADC was quite successful in attracting donor funding. First and foremost, it was the EU that channelled massive financial support to its southern counterpart via the 7th (1990–1995) and 8th (1995–2000) EDF programmes. The result was that about 80% of the SADC's entire regional integration projects were financed by extra-regional actors in 1995/96.[11] This implies a relationship of dependence.

However, this relationship did not affect the issue area of security at that time. This is because the promotion of peace and security cooperation was a focal area of neither the 7th nor the 8th EDF programme and for this reason the SADC did not receive any noteworthy EU funding for regional cooperation initiatives in these policy areas. At best, there was some vague deliberation about whether a SADC organ on security cooperation might possibly become an object of support on an ad hoc basis.[12] At the same time, it was nonetheless in the SADC member states' strong interest that their organisation under no circumstances become dependent on external funding in the very sensitive issue area of security (cooperation). The reason behind this was that this would imply a dependence on third actors—for example, in terms of funding conditions set by external donors—and possibly an exertion of influence by and accountability to the latter. The Director of the OPDS, Tanki Mothae, stressed this issue in a very focussed way by stating that "The Organ would rather suffer than accept external control!"[13] So it is not surprising that SADC members pooled the money for regional security cooperation projects from their own pockets in order to keep third actors out as much as possible.

In summary, the pattern of intra-regional security relations in the SADC area was asymmetric during the early and mid-1990s insofar as South Africa was the regional hegemon because of its outstanding military capabilities while Zimbabwe ranked second. Owing to its superior power position in this issue area, South Africa is expected to play a pivotal role with regard to the establishment, shape and effectiveness of regional security institutions. In this context, Pretoria's influence is assumed to promote cooperation since that matches with the country's national preferences. Against the background of the SADC member countries' weak extra-regional security relations, the process of regional security cooperation is not likely to be interfered with by external actors and the outside world.

6.3 THE INSTITUTIONALISATION OF THE OPDS: A POWER STRUGGLE BETWEEN SOUTH AFRICA AND ZIMBABWE

Against the background of political tensions and a state of regional insecurity, it was finally a violent coup in Lesotho in the summer of 1994 that prompted SADC countries to take action and create a new institution for regional security cooperation. The result was the hasty launch of the OPDS in 1996. Today, after the Summit, the OPDS counts as the SADC's second most important institution and is an expression of the SADC members' desire to centralise regional security cooperation in a single body under the umbrella of the SADC's organisational architecture. The OPDS has a wide range of specific objectives but its major tasks are to prevent conflicts and to promote peace, state security and political stability in the SADC region. In 2001, the SADC member states adopted the Protocol on Politics, Defence and Security Co-Operation which initialised an institutional re-launch of the Organ and made the SADC's security body work more efficiently. However, the performance of the OPDS gives a rather mixed picture over the years.

6.3.1 Negotiations and Design of the OPDS

It was not only the coup in Lesotho but particularly the recommendations of the SADC Secretariat's "Ministerial Workshop on Democracy, Peace and Security" in Windhoek and the dissolution of the FLS in July 1994 that set the stage for the negotiations on the institutionalisation of a SADC organ on security cooperation. However, inter-state bargaining on the institutional design of this body turned out to be lengthy and highly controversial because there were two different camps of SADC countries that preferred two different solutions with a substantially different institutional setting. The negotiations involved primarily two questions.

Firstly, should a new and centralised institutional body be created, or should one stick to the SADC's traditional decentralised sector-by-sector approach with Sector Coordination Units? The latter approach would have implied assigning the responsibility for the policy issue of regional security to a single member state—but to which one? This debate was not controversial and the members quickly decided in favour for the creation of a new institutional body since no SADC country wished to see a single state be in control of this very sensitive issue area (Vogt 2007: 156–157).

Secondly, should the new institution operate independently from the SADC as an organisation, or should it be embedded within the SADC's institutional architecture as a sub-body? The SADC countries were divided on this issue: Most of the former FLS countries, above all Zimbabwe, preferred the creation of an independent organisation, proposed to be called Association of Southern African States (ASA), as a new forum for regional security cooperation. Similar to the old FLS, it should be loosely institutionalised, work independently of the SADC Secretariat and "have an informal and flexible modus operandi" (Nathan 2004: 6). Other SADC countries, such as Botswana, Mozambique and most prominently South Africa, argued that a body for regional security cooperation had to be embedded within the SADC's institutional architecture since the time of the FLS and external threats had vanished.

A serious controversy and heavy bargaining on the institutional design of the future Organ arose particularly between Zimbabwe and South Africa. This is because Harare had a vital interest in preserving the existing, independent ISDSC body within a future ASA because the ISDSC had been under its influence since the creation of the FLS. Moreover, Zimbabwe regarded this institutional design as a means of avoiding South African dominance in this sensitive issue area—and in the SADC in general. Pretoria, in contrast, preferred to institutionalise regional security cooperation directly under the SADC's umbrella in order to strengthen the organisation, avoid costly institutional doubletracking and (not least) limit the influence of an ossified Zimbabwe in this important issue area (Ngoma 2005: 151–153; Söderbaum 2001: 106). Moreover, the new government under President Mandela had recognised very well that—owing to its military superiority in the SADC—South Africa was somehow co-responsible for the current situation of uncertainty in the region. This insight was one reason why Pretoria preferred the Organ to become part of the SADC because this kind of a self-imposed institutional restriction was intended to give proof of the RSA's commitment to the regional organisation and of its peaceful intentions to other member states (Ngoma 2005: 154–169; Oosthuizen 2006: 84).

The influence of external actors on regional inter-state negations on the design of the SADC's future body for regional security cooperation was virtually if not entirely negligible. This is because the donor community, above all the EU, favoured the creation of an SADC sector on regional security cooperation and signalled its willingness to financially support such a sector approach if it was embedded within the SADC's organisational framework. Accordingly, the EU's initiative aimed to support the position of the negotiating group led by South Africa. However, the EU was unsuccessful in its attempt to channel the negotiations among the SADC states to the direction it desired. In fact, Brussels's initiative was counterproductive and played into the hands of the Zimbabwe-led group because Harare stigmatised the EU's role as an imperialistic attempt to dictate the SADC's future security agenda (Nathan 2012: 32).

Against the background of this controversy and bargaining deadlock, the SADC Ministers of Foreign Affairs, Defence and Security recommended, at a meeting in January 1996, to the SADC Heads of States that an OPDS be established, which "would allow more flexibility and timely response, at the highest level, to sensitive and potentially explosive situations"[14] in the SADC region. The agreement recommended also that such an Organ become a permanent SADC mechanism that nonetheless maintains the flexible approach to regional security cooperation of the FLS (Malan 1998: 1).

In June 1996, the SADC Summit approved the creation of the OPDS and declared it to be the "appropriate institutional framework by which SADC countries would coordinate their policies and activities in the area of politics, defence and security."[15] The SADC member states agreed in consensus upon the guiding principles for the OPDS and, against this background, specified a number of central objectives.[16] Belonging to the key areas of state security, military cooperation and conflict prevention/management, these objectives stipulated the following:

- to protect the people and safeguard the development of the region against instability arising from the breakdown of law and order, inter-state conflict and external aggression
- to promote political cooperation among states [...]
- to cooperate fully in regional security and defence through conflict prevention management and resolution
- where conflict does occur, to seek to end this quickly as possible through diplomatic means. Only where such means fail would the Organ recommend that the Summit consider punitive measures.

With regard to the Organ's institutional design, the Summit agreed that the chairmanship of the Organ was to rotate on annual as well as on a Troika basis. As a compromise to satisfy the demands of Zimbabwe, the Summit elected Zimbabwe's President Robert Mugabe as the first chairman of the Organ. In order to reconcile the conflicting interests mentioned earlier, it was also decided that the ISDSC should continue to exist and become an institutional body, with a secretariat-like function, to the new Organ.[17]

However, the member states did not clearly specify whether the OPDS had in fact become a SADC body: The Summit Communiqué stated only that the Organ "shall operate at the Summit level, and shall function independently of other SADC structure."[18] Moreover, the Organ de jure did not exist since, according to the SADC Treaty, this required a specific protocol approved by the Summit that had to be ratified by two thirds of the member states (Nathan 2012: 38). By 1996, the Organ's rather unspecific and premature institutional setup therefore reflected only a sluggish compromise between the nearly deadlocking bargaining positions of Zimbabwe, the former lead nation of the FLS and the SADCC, and South Africa, the new hegemon in the SADC.

6.3.2 *The Protocol on Politics, Defence and Security Co-Operation and the Re-Launch of the OPDS*

The official launch of the Organ did not bring an end to the controversy and political tensions that had surrounded its formation process. Several SADC member states were dissatisfied with the institutional setup of the OPDS and complained that its jurisdiction and relation to the SADC remained unspecified, not least because the chairman of the OPDS, Zimbabwe's President Mugabe, put virtually no effort in establishing the envisaged institutional links between the Organ and the SADC. Instead, he allowed the ISDSC to continue operating independently and clandestinely from the organisation. Moreover, the Organ's chairmanship did not rotate since Mugabe refused to hand over the leadership position. On top of that, he pronounced several decisions of the Organ without consulting all member states. Since that time, the OPDS was sometimes referred to as "Mugabe's Organ" (Fisher and Ngoma 2005: 1; Nathan 2012: 38). All this led to a de facto suspension of the Organ from September 1997 onwards—and, in the meantime, security cooperation occurred only in an informal and ad hoc manner (Söderbaum 2001: 107).

Finally, it was again a violent coup in Lesotho and the breakout of civil war in the DRC in 1998 that revealed the institutional weakness of the Organ and put its partial dysfunctionality into the limelight. Owing to the lack of a legal framework, unclear competences and internal fragmentation,[19] the Organ was unable to adequately react to the conflict-prone crises and thus made the SADC—as an organisation—fail at large in terms of promoting peace and security in the conflict-ridden member states (Nathan 2006). Instead, it was individual SADC countries, above all South Africa and Zimbabwe, that rallied fellow members of the organisation into ad hoc coalitions in order to actively promote peace and security in regional conflicts, such as in Lesotho and the DRC respectively, in the name of the SADC as a whole (Solomon and Ngubane 2003: 3).

This unsatisfactory status quo, which had intensified disunity among member states and revealed a serious intra-SADC fragmentation, fuelled demand in SADC countries for an improvement of regional security cooperation and particularly for an institutional change of the OPDS. While all states had a common interest in reform, there remained conflicting interests on the institutional embodiment and design of such a "new" Organ. Basically, there were two polarising camps in the SADC that pursued two rather incompatible preferences.

One grouping, composed of South Africa, Botswana, Mozambique, Mauritius and Tanzania and supported by Malawi, Swaziland and Zambia, favoured that the Organ act as a governing body of a regional security regime with the task of facilitating security cooperation and conflict management by primarily political rather than military means (Nathan 2006: 610; Williams 2001: 107). This group argued again for more centralisation and an incorporation of the Organ into the SADC's institutional framework, not least in order to avoid the possibility that one single country would have too much control over this decisive body (Cawthra 1997: 209).

The other grouping, composed of Zimbabwe, Angola, Namibia and the DRC, prioritised the military nature of regional security cooperation and advocated that the Organ facilitate defence cooperation and coordinate combined military action against external aggressors (Williams 2001: 107). Just as in the mid-1990s, this group believed in an informal and flexible approach to regional security cooperation and preferred that the Organ operate independently outside and in parallel to the SADC's organisational architecture. This implied not least that it should become fairly out of reach of an alleged direct South African influence (Berman and Sams 2000: 165; Malan 1998: 2).

The discord positions again culminated in a rivalry between Pretoria and Harare: Inter-state negotiations that firstly "began as an exercise to restructure the OPDS had clearly developed into a slugging match between two combatants—South Africa and Zimbabwe" (Ngoma 2005: 153). Tensions rose until September 1997, when the issue was put to table at the SADC Summit. There, heavy bargaining between both groupings culminated in a full-blown controversy and an open dispute between the Heads of States of South Africa and Zimbabwe. The government in Harare was suspicious of a South African desire to dominate the OPDS and the SADC as a whole. It accused Pretoria of being isolated in pursuing its "quest to dominate the southern Africa region, a reflection of the fact that 'whites' still control its security establishment" (Ngoma 2005: 152). President Mandela, in view of the quasi-autonomous OPDS "hijacked" by Mugabe, remarked that the SADC Summit in 1996 had never intended "to enable such a 'Frankenstein Monster' not to be under its control" (Bischoff 2002: 296). It is said that, at the height of the debate, President Mandela threatened South Africa's exit from the SADC if Mugabe would not back down and allow the Organ to become incorporated into the organisation's institutional framework (Malan 1998: 3; Nathan 2012: 38).

With the state of affairs thus set, it took a further three years of "procrastination and behind-the-scenes wrangling" (Nathan 2004: 8) until the SADC member states agreed on the objectives, jurisdiction, institutional design and decision-making procedures of the new OPDS in clear terms in order to avoid any ambiguities and institutional paralysis for the future. The breakthrough finally occurred in August 2001 at the SADC Summit in Blantyre where SADC countries signed the Protocol on Politics, Defence and Security Co-operation in order to re-launch the Organ, formalise its institutionalisation, specify its modus operandi and confirm the SADC's common key principles on regional peace, security and defence cooperation of 1996.

The Protocol stipulated explicitly that the "general objective of the Organ shall be to promote peace and security in the Region."[20] The acting Director of the OPDS corroborated this policy stance and stressed that "our job is to coordinate all activities when it comes to peace, security and defence in the region."[21] In addition to this overall objective, the Protocol confirmed a number of specific key objectives[22] that were in fact similar to those agreed upon in 1996:

- to protect the people and safeguard the development of the region, against instability [...]
- to promote political cooperation [...]
- to develop common foreign policy approaches on issues of mutual concern
- to promote regional coordination and cooperation on matters related to security and defence.

An important novelty was a distinct regulation that stipulated that the Organ "should report to the SADC Summit and be part of SADC."[23] The OPDS thus became formally a SADC body under the SADC's organisational umbrella with the Summit becoming its supreme policy-making institution with far-reaching influence on the activities of the OPDS. The Protocol specified, in addition, that the SADC Secretariat was to become the Secretariat of the Organ with the task of "implementation of decisions of the Summit, Troika of the Summit, Organ on Politics, Defence and Security Co-operation, Troika of the Organ on Politics, Defence and Security Co-operation."[24] Finally, the member states amended the SADC Treaty in order to take these institutional changes into account.[25]

Furthermore, the Protocol specified, instead of a single chairperson, a Troika, rotating on an annual basis, to head the new OPDS. This Troika mechanism—composed of the former, the present and the incoming chairperson of the Organ—aimed to prevent a misuse of the chairmanship in terms of gaining permanent control over the Organ. This brought Zimbabwe's dominating position as "usurper" of the chair of the Organ de facto to an end. The Protocol stipulated moreover that the chairperson had to work by consultancy and coordination with the other Troika members as well as with the SADC Troika. This was the second mechanism that aimed to prevent unilateral policies or action of the Organ. The SADC countries confirmed the maintenance of the Organ's inherent structure, notably the Ministerial Committee, composed of the SADC ministers responsible for foreign affairs, defence, public security and state security, as well as the Inter-State Politics and Diplomacy Committee (ISPDC), composed of the ministers responsible for foreign affairs, and the ISDSC, composed of ministers responsible for defence, public security and state security. The two latter sub-bodies were tasked to support the Organ in matters of politics, diplomacy, defence and security (Nathan 2012: 50–53).[26]

In summary, the construction of the first Organ of 1996 was as much a hasty venture as it was an interim solution to the organisation's need for a common security institution. Its ambiguous role and unclear jurisdiction gave proof of a weak compromise which reflected the discord between South Africa's and Zimbabwe's interests (Ngoma 2005: 150–170). This changed with the adoption of the Protocol on Politics, Defence and Security Co-operation in 2001 and the member states' decision to reform their governing regional security institutions by re-launching the Organ. With the subordination of the new OPDS directly under the control of the SADC, it was South Africa that not only achieved a major diplomatic victory but also influenced the institutional design of the SADC's regional security cooperation framework most substantially (Fisher and Ngoma 2005).

6.4 Evaluation of Regional Security Cooperation Under the ODPS

Evaluating the performance and success of security cooperation in regional organisations is a difficult task because peace and security are very complex phenomena. In general, one could evaluate the organisations' stated goals and objectives in order to determine the degree of effectiveness (Nathan 2012: 13–14). According to Tavares (Tavares and Schulz 2006: 241), the best method to measure the degree of security and military integration is by focussing on the key objectives of security/military protocols and on the number and nature of common military exercises (training and operations). If one considers both with regard to the SADC, this means evaluating the performance of the OPDS on the basis of its contribution to promote peace and security in the region—with a special focus on how common military exercises and operations are conducted.

6.4.1 Implementation and Compliance

Although there were some principles, norms and objectives inherent to the 1996 agreement on the establishment of the old OPDS, there was no protocol in existence and thus no legally binding provisions for SADC members to implement—at least de jure. This—and the intra-organisational discord on the institutional design of the Organ—was the major reason why there was only partial compliance to the agreement's provisions and merely lukewarm commitment to the OPDS by most SADC countries, particularly after Zimbabwe turned out to bluntly follow a policy of non-compliance during its chairmanship of the OPDS which was characterised by, among other things, informal and clandestine decision-making, unilateral action and a break of rules with respect to the rotation of chairmanship. In a nutshell, this was a misuse of the Organ as an instrument for national policy-making (Fisher and Ngoma 2005; Malan 1998).

The adoption of the 2001 Protocol on Politics, Defence and Security Co-Operation laid the ground for the de jure institutionalisation and re-launch of the OPDS as an improved governing body of the SADC's regional security regime. In contrast to the 1996 agreement, the protocol has become a legally binding document that obliges SADC member states to implement its provisions. It was signed by virtually all SADC members (besides Madagascar and the Seychelles) in 2001 and three years later officially entered into force.[27]

Little is known about the actual stage of implementation and compliance of member states to this protocol. This is firstly because the details belong to the highly secretive issue area of security whereof SADC countries and officials are reluctant to provide satisfactory information. And this is secondly because the list of objectives and strategies is rather exhaustive if one would dare to consider every detail (van Nieuwkerk 2007: 107). One thing is clear, however: Most of the SADC countries (besides Angola, the DRC and the island states of Madagascar and the Seychelles) have ratified the protocol and initialised the implementation process on regional and national levels.[28] It is not entirely surprising that Angola and the DRC do not seem to implement the protocol since both countries belonged to the grouping of SADC countries that had never supported a re-launch of the Organ. Experts share the belief that Angola has never been very committed to regional security cooperation in the SADC at all—this is due not least to a perceived rivalry between Luanda and Pretoria as the region's strongest military powers. Moreover, the joining of the DRC to the SADC in 1997 watered down the organisation's security regime since Kinshasa is said to have more interest in gaining the SADC's support for settling its own conflicts than in contributing to the organisation's security institutions. In contrast, it is above all South Africa that is very committed to the SADC's security architecture and most compliant with the protocol's provisions and the operation of the Organ.[29, 30]

In sum, more than two thirds of SADC member states have implemented the protocol and paved the way for an improved security regime and allowing the re-launch of the OPDS. However, it is still a problem that certain member states do not fully comply with the provisions inherent to the guiding protocol for the Organ. Moreover, the Organ is chronically understaffed since only slightly more than 40 people permanently work there.[31]

6.4.2 *Effectiveness of the SADC's Military Exercises: Training and Manoeuvres*

Multinational military exercises have become a pillar of regional security cooperation in the SADC for almost two decades. Up until now, member states have undertaken a number of common manoeuvres on a considerable scale which gives proof of the countries' intention to implement confidence-building measures on a regional level, facilitate the coordination of their military and logistic capabilities, and eventually become capable of acting together in multinational peacekeeping operations. The following paragraphs give a brief illustration of the SADC's major military manoeuvres in terms of extent and achievements.

The SADC's first military exercise, called Blue Hungwe, took place in Zimbabwe in April 1997. This common operation sounded the bell for a new era of military cooperation in the region because it did not aim to prepare the participants to defend themselves against a common regional enemy. Ten SADC member states (excluding the DRC, Madagascar, Mauritius and the Seychelles) took an active part in Blue Hungwe, and the operation lasted for three weeks and involved about 1500 soldiers of the participants' defence forces (Salomon 2009: 205–206). The common exercise aimed to enhance cooperation, skills and interoperability of the armed forces, particularly by coordinating and harmonising communication procedures and tactics (de Coning 1998). In political and military respects, regional and external security experts have widely recognised Blue Hungwe as a success. Zimbabwe's President Mugabe, for example, remarked after the manoeuvre that "an exercise of this nature removes suspicion, increases transparency and builds confidence, mutual trust and understanding, among participating defence forces" (Nyambua 1998: 58). It is important to mention that the SADC states—particularly Zimbabwe—provided the greater part of the money for organising and financing of Blue Hungwe on their own. The share of external funding, donated by Great Britain, amounted to only $500,000 USD (Berman and Sams 2000: 169–170).

Operation Blue Crane was the follow-up exercise to Blue Hungwe. It took place in April 1999 in South Africa, lasted for three weeks, and was hosted by Pretoria. This time, eleven SADC member states (excluding Angola, the DRC, Madagascar and Zimbabwe) actively took part in the manoeuvre and conducted the exercise with a total of almost 5000 troops. This made Blue Crane the biggest military field exercise ever held in Africa by that time. Moreover, the manoeuvre included a land and maritime component and thus covered two branches of military services. The purpose of the operation was quite similar to that of the previous exercise but this time aimed in particular at strengthening and coordinating the SADC states' capabilities in command and control routines (Bestbier 2000: 34; de Coning 1999; Mngqibisa 2000). It was again the SADC members—particularly South Africa this time—that covered most of the expenses for Blue Crane. External support to the operation, provided by Canada and European states such as the Scandinavian countries and Germany (with a contribution of $493,000

USD), played only a minor role but was still welcome (Bestbier 2000: 7; Salomon 2009: 222).

A number of similar (albeit smaller) common military exercises—for example, Operation Tanzanite (2002 in Tanzania), Operation Blue Angel (2003 in Zambia), Operation Thokgamo (2005 in Botswana), Operation Blue Ruvuma (2006 in Tanzania), Operation Golfinho (2009 in South Africa), Operation Blue Cluster (2011 in South Africa), Operation Zambeze Azul (2013 in Zambia) and Operation Welwitchia (2013 in Namibia)—have been undertaken in the years thereafter. All of them had a similar overall purpose of military confidence-building, focussed on similar tasks, and were attended by most of the SADC's member states (Makhubelam 2009; Salomon 2009: 208–210). Since going into details on every single manoeuvre does not produce substantially new insights, it is important to take account of the fact that all of these military exercises have been generally judged as successful and vital in terms of regional defence force cooperation and confidence-building on the SADC level.

The common manoeuvres reduced mutual perceptions of threat and produced transparency. Moreover, the participant states improved the coordination of their military and logistic capabilities in the course of these exercises—not least because they took place on a regular basis in fairly short time intervals. However, the regional cooperation in military exercises provided functional benefits not only in terms of consolidating and enhancing security on a regional level but also in a rather symbolic respect because the SADC's member states and the organisation itself became increasingly visible as a (capable) regional actor (Salomon 2009: 215–225). In both of these aspects, it was the OPDS that played a key role in facilitating cooperation and achieving this success. South Africa, however, was probably the most crucial actor on which everything ultimately depended. This is because Pretoria contributed a major part in financing and organising the exercises (Mandrup 2009: 17), although extra-regional financial and logistical support, particularly from European states (Albaugh 2000: 132), additionally fostered these regional security cooperation projects and thus contributed to their success.

In summary, the SADC and the OPDS performed very well in regional security cooperation with a focus on confidence-building measures and military cooperation in terms of common exercises and training operations.

6.4.3 Effectiveness of the SADC's Military Exercises: Operations and Conflict Management

Promoting peace and security in the SADC and safeguarding the development of the region against instability have been key objectives of the organisation's security regime. In order to assess the performance of the Organ in this regard, the following section will focus on two short case studies: the crises in Lesotho (1998) and Madagascar (2009). Both represent typical examples of intra-regional conflicts and political crises that have been perceived as serious threats to peace and security in the SADC by the member states.[32] Moreover, the case of Lesotho stands as an example for conflict management under the rule of the old Organ whereas the more recent case of Madagascar provides insights on the operation of the renewed Organ.

6.4.4 The Case of Lesotho

In August 1998, the Kingdom of Lesotho was shocked by political tensions—again after 1994—when ruling King Letsie III clashed not only with the major opposition party after the parliamentary elections but also with some members of the military who staged a mutiny. Violence broke out in the capital city of Maseru. In September 1998, the elected and legitimate government under Prime Minister Mosisili finally became convinced to ask the SADC for help because the coup threatened to destabilise the whole country (Matlosa 1999; Neethling 1999). The government in Lesotho addressed its pledge for help directly to the SADC during this national crisis because the regional organisation had committed itself to promote regional security through the creation of the OPDS, among whose central objectives were to "safeguard the development of the region, against instability arising from the breakdown of law and order" and to "cooperate fully in regional security and defence through conflict prevention management and resolution."[33]

In contrast to the coup in 1994, where no Organ existed and the SADC remained apathetic (de Coning 1998), this time regional actors became involved by means of multilateral action: On 22 September 1998, the South African National Defence Force (SANDF) launched a military intervention in Lesotho with 600 troops together with a smaller army contingent of approximately 200 soldiers from Botswana in an operation called "Boleas". In the course of this operation, which lasted until 19 October 1998, the coalition was able to pacify the country and restore public order after defeating the mutinous armed forces in Lesotho's capital city of Maseru (Neethling 1999; Santo 1999).

Although the outcome of this military intervention in Lesotho was certainly effective in that law and order were restored, political chaos avoided, the legitimate government kept in place and peace secured, the question remains whether the mission was in fact really a result of the SADC's regional security cooperation mechanisms (i.e. the OPDS) or simply the result of a coalition of the willing led by South Africa (Berman and Sams 2000: 184–185; Neethling 1999: 6–7). While the governments of South Africa and Botswana, as troop providers, were undoubtedly involved into the process of planning and policy coordination prior to the intervention in Lesotho, it was only Zimbabwe and Mozambique that are said to have belonged to an inner circle of SADC states that actively took part in a decision-making process within the OPDS (Berman and Sams 2000). Apart from these countries and the members of the Troika, however, other SADC states probably became involved only by participation on a Summit level later on (Ngoma 2005: 167; van Nieuwkerk 1999: 17). Therefore, it remains unclear which legal procedure or decision-making process had finally laid the true ground for the intervention in Lesotho—and whether the SADC's OPDS explicitly authorised the decision to intervene and mandated South Africa and Botswana with the execution of the task in the name of the organisation as a whole (Malan 1998; Williams 1999).

According to official SADC diction of the Summit of 1999 in Maputo, the coup in Lesotho failed "as result of SADC military intervention in the form of Botswana and South African forces, in response to a request from the Lesotho government."[34] This statement corroborates the regional character of the "Boleas" operation and emphasises the decisive role of the SADC as an organisation with respect to restoring regional political stability and security. However, owing to the unclear role of the Organ and the likely non-involvement of a number of member states in the decision-making and authorisation process, some experts argue that the intervention in Lesotho was less a SADC initiative and more a unilateral action of South Africa in cooperation with Botswana. In any event, the intervention proved effective in terms of promoting regional peace and security in the SADC (Berman and Sams 2000: 185; Nathan 2006: 612).

6.4.5 The Case of Madagascar

Crisis in Madagascar broke out around March 2009 after political tensions between the ruling and opposition parties had finally culminated into violence. Civil protest and uprising against the acting President Ravalomanana made him flee in exile after transferring his governmental power to a military council. The armed forces, however, quickly delegated the power to Andry Rajoelina, who was the mayor of the city of Antananarivo and had become the former president's key political opponent during the past years. Designated to power by the military, Rajoelina became Madagascar's ruling president and the "legitimate" leader of the country on the basis of popular support. However, his unconstitutional seizure of power and the ousting of the legitimate government with the help of the military were internationally condemned as a coup. It caused particularly strong protest among the governments in the SADC region. With political turmoil and de facto military rule in Madagascar prevailing, the country not only became unstable on a national level but also was increasingly perceived as a threat to the entire SADC region (Cawthra 2010: 13–17; du Pisani 2011: 32–35).

In contrast to the Lesotho case of 1998, the SADC's reaction to the Madagascan crisis and the unconstitutional regime change happened instantly—and unanimously. On 19 March 2009, the Troika of the OPDS assembled for an Extraordinary Summit and stated that the SADC "condemns in the strongest terms the unconstitutional actions that have led to the illegal ousting of the democratically elected President of a SADC Member State"[35] and emphasised that it "cannot recognize Mr Rajoelina as President of Madagascar."[36] The Organ justified its position by referring to Rajoelina's violation of "the core principles and Treaty of SADC, the African Union and the United Nations Charters."[37] The Organ threatened to impose political and economic sanctions on Madagascar for the purpose of encouraging the usurpers to restore law and order in the island state. Swaziland and Angola even suggested that the Organ should consider mandating the SADC with a military intervention in order to achieve this goal (Cawthra 2010: 20).

In the end, the recommendation of the Organ turned out to be non-military but strict in a political sense. The SADC opted in the first instance for diplomatic sanctions. On 30 March 2009, an Extraordinary Summit of the SADC Heads of States met in Swaziland. It confirmed the statement of the Organ and expressed its support for a reinstatement of former President Ravalomanana. Most importantly, however, it "suspended Madagascar from all Community's institutions and organs until the return of the Country to constitutional normalcy with immediate effect"[38] and "urged SADC to stand united and firm against the illegal removal of the democratically elected Government of Madagascar by the Military and their allies."[39] With the suspension of Madagascar from the SADC, the very same regional organisation not only executed its most severe diplomatic sanction available on a member state but also proved itself as an unitary actor with functioning institutions as well as a coordinated policy and action on regional security matters (du Pisani 2011: 32–35; van Nieuwkerk 2010).

Despite the abovementioned diplomatic sanctions, the SADC became keen to take a proactive role in the settlement of the Madagascan crisis and engaged in conflict management and mediation as the lead organisation. The Extraordinary SADC Summit of June 2009 paved the way for this task and underlined the organisation's role as a provider of regional security. It appointed "Joaquim A. Chissano, former President of Mozambique, assisted by a high level team of mediators to lead and coordinate the all-party dialogue in Madagascar"[40] and emphasised its willingness to closely cooperate with the AU, the UN and the international community. At the same time, any idea of a future military intervention for the purpose of solving the crisis was dismissed (Cawthra 2010: 20).

Altogether, the SADC's—and primarily the Organ's—role in the Madagascan crisis in terms of conflict management and the promotion of peace and security proved to be fairly successful. This is not least because the Organ implemented a dual strategy of sanctioning on the one hand and constructive cooperation and conflict management on the other. The SADC became the leading actor in mediating the Madagascan crisis although the whole process later became embedded within a broader AU framework. The work of the Organ thus prevented an outbreak of chaos and civil war and helped to contain the potentially destabilising effects of the Madagascar crisis (Cawthra 2010: 21–23). In January 2014, the SADC lifted the suspension of the island state in view of free presidential elections and the restoration of law and order.[41]

6.5 Résumé and Prospects

The institutionalisation of regional security cooperation in the SADC emerged against the background of a diffuse security dilemma with a number of (latent) intra-regional conflicts that had a potential to turn into violence or inter-state wars. This unsatisfactory and costly situation of mutual uncertainty and threat in the region fuelled demand in member states to create a common security regime for the purpose of promoting regional peace and security. Hence, there in fact existed a genuine regional cooperation problem in the SADC in the mid-1990s.

South Africa and to a lesser degree Zimbabwe were the centres of gravity in the regional security complex because of their advanced military capacities. The Cape Republic, however, had the strongest and most modern military at its command and therefore was the superior regional power in this issue area. This gave South Africa room to exert significant influence on the institutionalisation and design of the SADC's security regime. Although the earlier 1996 agreement and the creation of the "old" and weakly institutionalised OPDS somehow reflect a stalemate between the rivalling powers of South Africa and Zimbabwe, it was only the adoption of the Protocol on Politics, Defence and Security Co-operation in 2001 and the redesign of the new OPDS which highlight Pretoria's final assertiveness. External actors did not get involved in this process, and the SADC's small and weaker member states, which in security matters had little to offer the organisation besides their goodwill to cooperate, did not significantly shape the institutional design of the OPDS. In fact, they can even be regarded as free-riders on the SADC's regional security regime.

In regard to performance and effectiveness, the promotion of peace and security in the SADC and safeguarding the development of the region against instability have been key objectives of the OPDS. Altogether there has not been a single inter-state war between SADC members since the foundation of the organisation—despite the number of (latent) intra-regional conflicts that were mentioned at the beginning of this chapter. In the eyes of the Organ, the "SADC region is relatively stable."[42] Whether the OPDS is ultimately (co-)responsible for this positive state of affairs is not easy to assess.

The SADC's common military exercises are clear examples of the Organ's success in terms of confidence-building because they enhanced transparency and reduced uncertainty and mistrust among SADC members under conditions of the regional security dilemma. However, the organisation's account with regard to common military operations and proactive conflict management reveals a mixed picture.

In regard to the intervention in Lesotho in 1998, it remains questionable whether the mission was deliberated and deployed by the SADC as an organisation or whether it was a coalition of the willing led by South Africa. In any case, the SADC's institutional mechanisms of regional security cooperation, particularly the performance of the old OPDS, were weak and allowed Pretoria to take unilateral action. Nevertheless, the "Boleas" operation became a success in terms of the outcomes—and the organisation always officially declared it a common SADC intervention (Ngoma 2005: 167–168). In regard to conflict management and mediation in Madagascar from 2009 onwards, the SADC managed to follow a common approach and acted as a single actor through the OPDS. The redesign of the Organ with its clear-cut jurisdiction under the umbrella of the SADC was certainly one important aspect that facilitated its success in dealing with the Madagascan crisis.

In sum, the performance of institutionalised regional security cooperation in the SADC has certainly improved after the Organ's reform in 2001 compared with the situation before when "Mugabe run amok with the mystical Organ" (Malan 1998). In particular, the organisation's confidence-building measures and common military exercises are widely recognised as major successes and give proof of the Organ's good performance (Cawthra et al. 2007: 244–249; Ngoma 2005: 228–229). However, the organisation still demonstrates a weakness when it comes to military operations and conflict management. The same is true with regard to a number of other objectives, particularly those related to human security (van Nieuwkerk 2012: 10). Taking a counter-factual perspective, however, does help to provide more clarity: The Organ is not only symbolic in nature and certainly made a positive difference on the SADC countries' regional threat perceptions and on the whole security situation in the region. However, its performance is mixed insofar as the Organ has not (yet) demonstrated a satisfactory degree of success and effectiveness in terms of attaining its own goals.

Notes

1. SADC (1996b): Extraordinary Summit of Heads of States. Communiqué. 28 June 1996. Gaborone. p. 2.
2. Republic of Namibia (1993): Statement on Defence Policy. Windhoek: Ministry of Defence. pp. 6, 11. http://www.mod.gov.na/documents/264813/280846/DEFENCE+POLICY.pdf (12/04/2016).

3. Republic of South Africa (1996): Defence in a Democracy. White Paper on National Defence for the Republic of South Africa. May 1996. Chap. 4 (3). http://www.dod.mil.za/documents/WhitePaperonDef/whitepaper%20on%20defence1996.pdf (12/04/2016).
4. Republic of South Africa (1996): Defence in a Democracy. White Paper on National Defence for the Republic of South Africa. May 1996. Chap. 4 (13). http://www.dod.mil.za/documents/WhitePaperonDef/whitepaper%20on%20defence1996.pdf (12/04/2016).
5. Republic of South Africa (1996): Defence in a Democracy. White Paper on National Defence for the Republic of South Africa. May 1996. Chap. 4 (12). http://www.dod.mil.za/documents/WhitePaperonDef/whitepaper%20on%20defence1996.pdf (12/04/2016).
6. Republic of South Africa (1996): Defence in a Democracy. White Paper on National Defence for the Republic of South Africa. May 1996. Chap. 4 (16–22). http://www.dod.mil.za/documents/WhitePaperonDef/whitepaper%20on%20defence1996.pdf (12/04/2016).
7. SADCC (1992): Towards the Southern African Development Community: A Declaration by the SADC Heads of State and Government of Southern African States. Windhoek: SADCC. pp. 9–10.
8. SADC (1992): Treaty of the Southern African Development Community. Gaborone. Article 5.
9. SADC (1992): Treaty of the Southern African Development Community. Gaborone. Article 21 (3).
10. SADC (1993): Southern Africa: A Framework and Strategy for Building the Community. Harare. pp. 24–26.
11. SADC (1996a): Annual Report. June 1995–July 1996. Gaborone: SADC Secretariat.
12. SADC—European Community (2002): Regional Strategy Paper and Regional Indicative Programme. For the period of 2002–2007. pp. 21, 35.
13. Interview with Tanki Mothae (Director of the OPDS) at the SADC Headquarters (09/29/2010).
14. SADC (1996c): Record of the Meeting of SADC Ministers Responsible for Foreign Affairs, Defence and Security, 18 January 1996. Gaborone.
15. SADC (1996b): Extraordinary Summit of Heads of States. Communiqué. 28 June 1996. Gaborone. p. 2.
16. SADC (1996b): Extraordinary Summit of Heads of States. Communiqué. 28 June 1996. Gaborone. p. 4.
17. SADC (1996b): Extraordinary Summit of Heads of States. Communiqué. 28 June 1996. Gaborone. p. 4.
18. SADC (1996b): Extraordinary Summit of Heads of States. Communiqué. 28 June 1996. Gaborone. p. 4.

19. Statement on the SADC's web page: http://www.sadc.int/documents-publications/show/809 (11/10/2016).
20. SADC (2001a): Protocol on Politics, Defence and Security Co-operation. Article 2.
21. Interview with Tanki Mothae (Director of the OPDS) at the SADC Headquarters (09/29/2010).
22. SADC (2001a): Protocol on Politics, Defence and Security Co-operation. Article 2.
23. SADC (2001a): Protocol on Politics, Defence and Security Co-operation. Article 3.1.
24. SADC (2001a): Protocol on Politics, Defence and Security Co-operation. Article 14.1 (b).
25. SADC (2001b): Treaty of the Southern African Development Community, as Amended. Articles 9.1, 9a, 10a, and 14.1 (b).
26. SADC (2001a): Protocol on Politics, Defence and Security Co-operation.
27. Information according to the SADC's web page: http://www.sadc.int/documents-publications/show/809 (11/10/2016).
28. Information on the status of SADC Protocols: http://www.tralac.org/images/Resources/SADC/Status%20of%20Protocols%20and%20Declarations%20in%20SADC%20as%20at.%20August%202012.pdf (12/10/2016).
29. Interview with Anthoni van Nieuwkerk (Associate Professor at the Centre for Defence and Security Management) at the Graduate School of Public and Development Management at the University of the Witwatersrand (08/06/2010).
30. Interview with Gilbert Khadiagala (Jan Smuts Professor and Head of the Department of International Relations) at the University of the Witwatersrand (10/07/2010).
31. Interview with Tanki Mothae (Director of the OPDS) at the SADC Headquarters (09/29/2010).
32. The SADC and the Organ have been involved in a few additional intra-regional conflicts by means of military operation (civil war in the DRC) and conflict management (mediation in Zimbabwe) during the past two decades (Tavares 2011). Since military intervention in the DRC in 1997/98 followed a similar logic as in the case of Lesotho, this work will focus on the latter case only. Conflict management in Zimbabwe started in the year 2000 and resembles the SADC's mediation efforts in the case of Madagascar. However, the SADC never declared the political instability in Zimbabwe to be a threat to the region and followed a strategy of "quiet diplomacy" in order to solve the conflict (Meyns 2002: 154–165). Hence, the case of Zimbabwe shall not serve as an example for the SADC's proactive conflict management.

33. SADC (1996b): Extraordinary Summit of Heads of States. Communiqué. 28 June 1996. Gaborone. pp. 2, 3.
34. SADC (1999b): Record of the Summit held in Maputo, Mozambique, 18 August 1999. Maputo, p. 3.
35. SADC (2009b): Extraordinary Summit of the Organ on Politics, Defence and Security Co-operation. Ezulwini, 19 March 2009. Article 10.
36. SADC (2009b): Extraordinary Summit of the Organ on Politics, Defence and Security Co-operation. Ezulwini, 19 March 2009. Article 11.
37. SADC (2009b): Extraordinary Summit of the Organ on Politics, Defence and Security Co-operation. Ezulwini, 19 March 2009. Article 11.
38. SADC (2009c): Extraordinary Summit of SADC Heads of State and Government. Communiqué. Lozitha Royal Palace, 30 March 2009. Article 16.
39. SADC (2009c): Extraordinary Summit of SADC Heads of State and Government. Communiqué. Lozitha Royal Palace, 30 March 2009. Article 22.
40. SADC (2009d): Extraordinary Summit of SADC Heads of State and Government. Communiqué. Sandton, 20 June 2009. Article 9, ii.
41. Information according to the SADC: http://www.sadc.int/news-events/news/sadc-lifts-madagascar-suspension/ (12/10/2016).
42. Interview with Colonel Gerson Marco Sangiza (Senior Officer for Defence Affairs and Planning at the OPDS) at the SADC Headquarters (09/29/2010).

REFERENCES

Adar K.G., R. Ajulu, and M.O. Onyango. 2002. Post-Cold War Zimbabwe's Foreign Policy and Foreign Policy-Making Process. In *Globalization and Emerging Trends in African States' Foreign Policy-making Process: A Comparative Perspective of Southern Africa*, vol. 1, ed. K.G. Adar and R. Ajulu, 263–280. Aldershot: Ashgate.

Albaugh, E.A. 2000. Preventing Conflict in Africa: Possibilities of Peace Enforcement. In *Peacekeeping and Peace Enforcement in Africa: Methods of Conflict Prevention*, ed. R.I. Rotberg, E.A. Albaugh, H. Bonyongwe, C. Clapham, J. Herbst, and S. Metz, 111–210. Washington: The World Peace Foundation.

Alden, C., and G. le Pere. 2003. South Africa's Post-Apartheid Foreign Policy—from Reconciliation to Revival? London: International Institute for Strategic Studies.

Axelrod, R. 1987. *Die Evolution der Kooperation*. München: R. Oldenbourg Verlag.

Berman, E.G., and K.E. Sams. 2000. *Peacekeeping in Africa: Capabilities and Culpabilities*. Geneva and Pretoria: UN Institute for Disarmament Research, Institute for Security Studies.

Bestbier, A. 2000. Military Participation in Exercise Blue Crane. In *Peacekeeping in the New Millenium: Lessons Learned From Exercise Blue Crane*, ed. C. de Coning and K. Mngqibisa, 23–34. Durban: African Centre for the Constructive Resolution of Disputes (ACCORD).

Bischoff, P.-H. 2002. How Far, Where To? Regionalism, the Southern African Development Community and Decision-Making into the Millenium. In *Globalization and Emerging Trends in African States' Foreign Policy-Making Process: A Comparative Perspective of Southern Africa*, ed. K.G. Adar and R. Ajulu, 283–306. Aldershot: Ashgate.

Bischoff, P.-H. 2006. Towards a Foreign Peacekeeping Commitment: South African Approaches to Conflict Resolution in Africa. In *South African Foreign Policy After Apartheid*, ed. W. Carlsnaes and P. Nel, 147–163. Midrand: Institut for Global Dialogue.

Buzan, B., and O. Wæver. 2003. In *Regions and Powers. The Structure of International Security*. Cambridge: Cambridge University Press.

Cawthra, G. 1997. Subregional Security: The Southern African Development Community. *Security Dialogue* 28 (2): 207–218.

Cawthra, G. 2007. Comparative Perspectives on Regional Security Co-operation Among Developing Countries. In *Security and Democracy in Southern Africa*, ed. G. Cawthra, A. du Pisani, and A. Omari, 23–44. Johannesburg: Wits University Press.

Cawthra, G. 2010. *The Role of SADC in Managing Political Crisis and Conflict: The Cases of Madagascar and Zimbabwe*. Maputo: Friedrich-Ebert-Stiftung.

Cawthra, G., K. Matlosa, and A. van Nieuwkerk. 2007. Conclusion. In *Security and Democracy in Southern Africa*, ed. G. Cawthra, A. du Pisani, and A. Omari, 233–249. Johannesburg: Wits University Press.

de Coning, C. 1998. Conditions for Intervention: DRC and Lesotho. *Conflict Trends* 1: 20–23.

de Coning, C. 1999. Exercise Blue Crane. A Unifying Moment for SADC. *Conflict Trends* 1: 19, 23.

du Pisani, A. 2011. The Security Dimension of Regional Integration in SADC. In *Monitoring Integration in Southern Africa. Yearbook 2010*, ed. A. Bösl, A. du Pisani, G. Erasmus, T. Hartzenberg, and R. Sandrey, 23–45. Stellenbosch: Trade Law Centre of Southern Africa.

du Toit, P. 1995. *State Building and Democracy in Southern Africa: Botswana, Zimbabwe and South Africa*. Washington: United States Institute of Peace Press.

Evans, M. 1984. The Front-Line States, South Africa and Southern African Security: Military Prospects and Perspectives. *Zambezia XII* 5: 1–19.

Fisher L.M., and N. Ngoma. 2005. *The SADC Organ. Challenges in the New Millenium.* vol. 114. ISS Paper. Pretoria: Institute for Security Studies.

Gamba, V. 1998. Small Arms Proliferation in Southern Africa: The Potential for Regional Control. *African Security Review* 7 (4): 57–72.

Gregory, S. 2000. The French Military in Africa: Past and Present. *African Affairs* 99: 435–448.

Hatchard, J., and P. Slinn. 1995. The Path Towards a New Order in South Africa. *International Relations* 12 (4): 1–26.

International Institute for Security Studies (IISS). 1994. *The Military Balance 1994–1995.* London: Brassey's.

Jaspert. J. 2010. *Regionalismus im südlichen Afrika. Die Handels- und Sicherheitspolitik der SADC.* Wiesbaden: VS Verlag.

Keohane, R.O. 1984. *After Hegemony Cooperation and Discord in the World Political Economy.* Princeton: Princeton University Press.

Lalá, A. 2007. Mozambique. In *Security and Democracy in Southern Africa*, ed. G. Cawthra, A. du Pisani, and A. Omari, 108–122. Johannesburg: Wits University Press.

le Pere, G., and A. van Nieuwkerk. 2002. Facing the New Millenium: South Africa's Foreign Policy in a Globalizing World. In *Globalization and Emerging Trends in African States' Foreign Policy-Making Process*, ed. K.G. Adar and R. Ajulu, 173–210. Aldershot: Ashgate.

Lindeke, B., P. Kaapama, and L. Blaauw. 2007. Namibia. In *Security and Democracy in Southern Africa*, ed. G. Cawthra, A. du Pisani, and A. Omari, 123–141. Johannesburg: Wits University Press.

Makhubelam, I. 2009. SADC Standby Force Borne Exercise Golfinho. *South African Soldier* 16 (10): 11–13.

Malan, M. 1998. *Regional Power Politics Under Cover of SADC. Running Amok with a Mythical Organ.* vol. 35. Occasional Paper. Pretoria: Institute for Security Studies.

Mandrup, T. 2009. South Africa and the SADC Stand-By Force. *Scientia Militaria, South African Journal of Military Studies* 37 (2): 1–24.

Matlosa, K. 1999. The Lesotho Conflict: Major Causes and Management. In *Crisis in Lesotho: The Challenge of Managing Conflict in Southern Africa*, ed. K. Lambrechts, 9–13. Braamfontein: Foundation for Global Dialogue.

Matlosa, K. 2007. Lesotho. In *Security and Democracy in Southern Africa*, ed. G. Cawthra, A. du Pisani, and A. Omari, 80–97. Johannesburg: Wits University Press.

Meinken, A. 2005. *Militärische Kapazitäten und Fähigkeiten afrikanischer Staaten. Ursachen und Wirkungen militärischer Ineffektivität in Sub-Sahara Afrika.* Berlin: Stiftung Wissenschaft und Politik.

Meyns, P. 2002. The Ongoing Search for a Security Structure in the SADC Region: The Re-establishment of the SADC Organ on Politics, Defence and Security. In *Monitoring Regional Integration in Southern Africa. Yearbook Volume 2*, ed. D. Hansohm, C. Peters-Berries, W. Breytenbach, T. Hartzenberg, W. Maier, and P. Meyns, 141–168. Windhoek: Gamsberg Macmillan.

Mngqibisa, K. 2000. Exercise Blue Crane. In *Peacekeeping in the New Millenium: Lessons Learned From Exercise Blue Crane*, ed. C. de Coning and K. Mngqibisa, 13–22. Durban: African Centre for the Constructive Resolution of Disputes.

Molomo, M.G., Z. Maundeni, B. Osei-Hwedie, I. Taylor, and S. Whitman. 2007. Botswana. In *Security and Democracy in Southern Africa*, ed. G. Cawthra, A. du Pisani, and A. Omari, 61–79. Johannesburg: Wits University Press.

Mzizi, J.B. 2007. Swaziland. In *Security and Democracy in Southern Africa*, ed. G. Cawthra, A. du Pisani, and A. Omari, 172–191. Johannesburg: Wits University Press.

Nathan, L. 2004. *The Absence of Common Values and Failure of Common Security in Southern Africa, 1992–2003*, vol. 50. Crisis States Programme Working papers serie. London: LSE Crisis States Research Centre.

Nathan, L. 2006. SADC's Uncommon Approach to Common Security, 1992–2003. *Journal of Southern African Studies* 32 (3): 605–622.

Nathan, L. 2012. *Community of Insecurity: SADC's Struggle for Peace and Security in Southern Africa*. Farnham: Ashgate.

Neethling, T. 1999. Military Intervention in Lesotho: Perspectives on Operation Boleas and Beyond. *The Online Journal of Peace and Conflict Resolution* 2 (2): 1–12.

Ngoma, N. 2005. *Prospects for a Security Community in Southern Africa: An Analysis of Regional Security in the Southern African Development Community*. Pretoria: Institute for Security Studies.

Nyambua, M. 1998. Zimbabwe's Role as Lead Nation for Peacekeeping Training in the SADC Region. In *Resolute Partners: Building Peacekeeping Capacity in Southern Africa*, ed. M. Malan, 56–60. Pretoria: Institute for Security Studies.

Nye, J.S. 2008. *Understanding International Conflicts: An Introduction to Theory and History*, 7th ed. London: Pearson.

Ohlson, T. 1996. Conflict and Conflict Resolution in a Southern African Context. In *Peace and Security in Southern Africa*, ed. I. Mandaza, 1–58. Harare: SAPES Books.

Omari, A., and P. Macaringue. 2007. Southern African Security in Historical Perspective. In *Security and Democracy in Southern Africa*, ed. G. Cawthra, A. du Pisani, and A. Omari, 45–60. Johannesburg: Wits University Press.

Oosthuizen, G.H. 2006. *The Southern African Development Community. The Organisation, its Policies and Prospects*. Midrand: Institute for Global Dialogue.

Phiri, B.Jube. 2007. Zambia. In *Security and Democracy in Southern Africa*, ed. G. Cawthra, A. du Pisani, and A. Omari, 206–220. Johannesburg: Wits University Press.

Ressler, V. 2007. *Die Perspektiven regionaler Integration im südlichen Afrika. Eine Analyse vor dem Hintergrund der einzelstaatlichen Interessen*. Frankfurt am Main: Peter Lang.

Salomon, K. 2009. *Konfliktmanagement durch ECOWAS und SADC. Die Rolle Nigerias und Südafrikas in subregionalen Interventionen: Ein Beitrag zum Frieden?* Saarbrücken: Südwestdeutscher Verlag für Hochschulschriften.

Sandberg, E., and N. Sabel. 2003. Cold War Regional Hangovers in Southern Africa: Zambian Development Strategies, SADC and the New Regionalism Approach. In *The New Regionalism in Africa*, ed. J.A. Grant and F. Söderbaum, 159–178. Aldershot, Burlington: Ashgate.

Santo, S. 1999. Conflict Management and Post-Conflict Peacebuilding in Lesotho. In *Crisis in Lesotho: The Challenge of Managing Conflict in Southern Africa*, ed. K. Lambrechts, 14–15. Braamfontein: Foundation for Global Dialogue.

Schleicher, H.-G. 2006. *Regionale Sicherheitskooperation im Südlichen Afrika: SADC und OPDSC*. Leipzig: Universität Leipzig.

Schoeman, M. 2007. South Africa. In *Security and Democracy in Southern Africa*, ed. G. Cawthra, A. du Pisani, and A. Omari, 155–171. Johannesburg: Wits Univeristy Press.

Sidaway, J.D. 1998. The (Geo) politics of Regional Integration: The Example of the Southern African Development Community. *Environment and Planning D: Society and Space* 16 (5): 549–576.

Söderbaum, F. 2001. The Dynamics of Security and Development Regionalism in Southern Africa. In *Security and Development in Southern Africa*, ed. N. Poku, 103–121. Westport: Praeger.

Solomon, H., and S. Ngubane. 2003. *One Step Forward, Two Steps Back: Reflections on SADC's Organ on Politics, Defence and Security Cooperation*. vol 33. SAIIA Report. Johannesburg: South African Institute of International Affairs.

Stockholm International Peace Research Institute (SIPRI). 2010. *SIPRI Yearbook 2009. Armaments, Disarmament and International Security*. Solna: Stockholm International Peace Research Institute.

Tavares, R. 2011. The Participation of SADC and ECOWAS in Military Operations: The Weight of National Interests in Decision-Making. *African Studies Review* 54 (2): 145–176.

Tjønneland, E.N., and T. Vraalsen. 1996. Towards Common Security in Southern Africa: Regional Cooperation After Apartheid. In *South Africa and Africa: Within or Apart?* ed. A. Adedeji, 193–214. Cape Town: SADRI Books.

Vale, P. 1994. Reconstructing Regional Dignity: South Africa and Southern Africa. In *South Africa. The Political Economy of Transformation*, ed. S.J. Stedman, 153–166. Boulder: Lynne Rienner.
Vale, P. 1996. Regional Security in Southern Africa. *Alternatives: Global, Local, Political* 21 (3): 363–391.
van Nieuwkerk, A. 1999. The Lesotho Crisis: Implications for South African Foreign Policy. In *Crisis in Lesotho: The Challenge of Managing Conflict in Southern Africa*, ed. K. Lambrechts, 16–19. Braamfontein: Foundation for Global Dialogue.
van Nieuwkerk, A. 2007. Organizational Dimensions of Security Cooperation in the Southern African Development Community. In *Proceedings of the 2006 FOPRISA Annual Conference*, vol. 3, ed. J.M. Kaunda, 99–127. Gaborone: Botswana Institute for Development Policy Analysis.
van Nieuwkerk, A. 2010. SADC's Common Foreign Policy. In *Proceedings of the 2009 FOPRISA Annual Conference*, ed. C. Harvey, vol. Report 8, 97–112. Gaborone: Botswana Institute for Development Policy Analysis.
van Nieuwkerk, A. 2012. *Towards Peace and Security in Southern Africa. A Critical Analysis of the Revised Strategic Indicative Plan for the Organ on Politics, Defence and Security Co-operation (SIPO) of the Southern African Development Community*. Maputo: Friedrich-Ebert-Stiftung.
Vogt, J. 2007. *Die Regionale Integration des südlichen Afrikas. Unter besonderer Betrachtung der Southern African Development Community (SADC)*. Baden-Baden: Nomos.
Wannenburg, G. 2006. *Africa's Pablos and Political Entrepreneurs. War, the State and Criminal Networks in West and Southern Africa*. Johannesburg: South African Institute of International Affairs.
Williams, R. 1999. Challenges for South and Southern Africa Towards Non-Consensual Peace Mission? In *From Peacekeeping to Complex Emergencies. Peace Support Missions in Africa*, ed. J. Cilliers and G. Mills, 153–174. Johannesburg: South African Institute of International Affairs.
Williams, R. 2001. From Collective Security to Peace-Building? The Challenges of Managing Regional Security in Southern Africa. In *Regional Integration in Southern Africa: Comparative International Perpectives*, ed. C. Clapham, G. Mills, A. Morner, and E. Sidiropoulos, 105–114. Johannesburg: South African Institute of International Affairs.
Zürn, M. 1992. *Interessen und Institutionen in der Internationalen Politik: Grundlegung und Anwendung des situationsstrukturellen Ansatz*. Opladen: Leske + Budrich.

Primary Sources

Republic of Namibia. 1993. Statement on Defence Policy. Windhoek: Ministry of Defence. http://www.mod.gov.na/documents/264813/280846/DEFENCE+POLICY.pdf (12/04/2016).
Republic of South Africa. 1996. Defence in a Democracy. White Paper on National Defence for the Republic of South Africa. May 1996. http://www.dod.mil.za/documents/WhitePaperonDef/whitepaper%20on%20defence1996.pdf (12/04/2016).
SADCC. 1992. Towards the Southern African Development Community: A Declaration by the SADC Heads of State and Government of Southern African States. Windhoek: SADCC.
SADC. 1992. Treaty of the Southern African Development Community. Gaborone: SADC Secretariat.
SADC. 1993. Southern Africa: A Framework and Strategy for Building the Community. Harare.
SADC. 1996a. Annual Report. June 1995–July 1996. Gaborone: SADC Secretariat.
SADC. 1996b. Extraordinary Summit of Heads of States. Communiqué. 28th June 1996. Gaborone.
SADC. 1996c. Record of the Meeting of SADC Ministers Responsible for Foreign Affairs, Defence and Security, 18th January 1996. Gaborone.
SADC. 1999b. Record of the Summit held in Maputo, Mozambique, 18th August 1999. Maputo.
SADC. 2001a. Protocol on Politics, Defence and Security Co-operation.
SADC. 2001b. Treaty of the Southern African Development Community, as Amended.
SADC. 2009b. Extraordinary Summit of the Organ on Politics, Defence and Security Co-operation. Ezulwini, 19th March 2009.
SADC. 2009c. Extraordinary Summit of SADC Heads of State and Government. Communiqué. Lozitha Royal Palace, 30th March 2009.
SADC. 2009d. Extraordinary Summit of SADC Heads of State and Government. Communiqué. Sandton, 20th June 2009.
SADC—European Community. 2002. Regional Strategy Paper and Regional Indicative Programme. For the Period 2002–2007.
Tavares, R., and M. Schulz. 2006. Measuring the Impact of Regional Organisations on Peace Building. In *Assessment and Measurement of Regional Integration*, ed. P. de Lombaerde, 232–251. London: Routledge.

CHAPTER 7

The SADC Standby Force and Its Regional Peacekeeping Training Centre: Uncertain Operational Readiness and Future of an Externally Fuelled Brigade

The creation of a regional standby force has been a major project and cornerstone in the SADC's agenda on regional security cooperation since the re-launch of the OPDS at the turn of the millennium. Stimulated by the AU's call for the establishment of an African Standby Force (ASF) on the basis of the continent's recognised regional economic communities, SADC members took efforts to comply with this Pan-African task and initialised a process of developing their own regional standby force. The organisation's Strategic Indicative Plan for the Organ of 2004 picked up this objective and provided, among other things, details on the build-up of a future SADC Standby Force (SSF). The SADC soon declared the latter to be a vital step towards deepening regional security integration in the SADC and improving the organisation's conflict management capacity.

In August 2007, the SADC member states agreed upon an MoU on the creation of a SADC Brigade and an associated Regional Peacekeeping Training Centre (RPTC). These remarkable dynamics in the SADC's regional security cooperation policy and activities came as quite a surprise because there had been no imminent external security threats to the organisation and its member states during the mid-2000s. However, the actual state of operational readiness of the SADC's regional standby force and the RPTC is rather unclear.

This chapter shall give answers to the abovementioned puzzles and aims to explain why the SADC countries decided to expand institutionalised regional security cooperation towards creating an SSF and an RPTC.

Both will be critically scrutinised with regard to their state of affairs and actual institutional performance. In this case, it must be held that the EU as an external actor had an ambivalent impact on regionalism in the SADC because it by turns provided and withdrew the financial support to this specific regional cooperation project.

7.1 Fuelled from Outside: Genuine (Non-)Demand in SADC Countries for a Regional Standby Force

The formation of an integrated regional armed force (e.g. an SADC standby brigade) is supposed to require either a pre-existing, elaborated regional security architecture with supranational elements as a given point of departure or an imminent extra-regional threat to the security of the region and its member states. In the first case, such a regional brigade would represent the avant-garde and actorness of a regional integration organisation in the issue area of security. Under the second scenario, it stands rather for a joint regional reaction to an external threat by means of a coordinated and institutionalised defence measure.

Since the establishment of a regional standby force bears significant institutional (opportunity) costs with respect to finance (e.g. equipment, communication with partners, and maintenance) and national security (e.g. contributing part of the own defence force, disclosure of information on defence matters, and hand-over of command if necessary) for all participant countries, it seems for them only in case of the second scenario rational to put efforts into such a costly project (Jervis 1978: 1978; Wallander and Keohane 1999). The reason is that institutionalised cooperation towards the creation of an SSF would then be happening on the grounds of an existing problematic situation (i.e. an external threat to SADC countries) with a prospect of absolute gains (security by means of common defence). However, with reference to the first case, any establishment of a regional brigade would be happening independently of an actual regional cooperation problem and therefore constitute a needless luxury product.

7.1.1 Demand for a SADC Brigade in Southern African Countries

The structural demand for deepening institutionalised regional security cooperation towards the formation of a regional standby force shall be deduced from the pattern of security interdependence among the SADC countries. The point in time shall be immediately before the adoption of the MoU on the creation of the SADC Brigade. This analytical procedure enables one to reconstruct the regional security complex of 2007 and thus helps to find evidence for an underlying regional cooperation problem.

First of all, the SADC region seemed to be in a state of relative peace during the mid-2000s. The civil war in Angola had come to an end in 2002, and the Second Congo War in the DRC ended in 2003. Hence, there were neither inter-state wars between SADC countries nor civil wars within member states ongoing during the period under observation. Moreover, no country in the region feared a concrete threat or immediate invasion by a foreign extra-regional power according to a 2004 study on the SADC countries' perceived security problems (Cawthra and van Nieuwkerk 2004: 15–16; Vale 1996: 363–366). Notwithstanding the existence of some of the latent inter-state conflicts and political tensions (as mentioned in Chap. 6), the overall security situation in the SADC was—with the re-launched OPDS in place—certainly not seriously conflict-prone but instead fairly peaceful at that time. Against this background, it is actually difficult to find concrete evidence for structurally motivated demand from within the region with the aim of deepening regional security cooperation towards the creation of a common regional standby brigade.

In regard to national preferences and security policies in the SADC countries, there is likewise little empirical evidence that an ample number of member states followed a distinct policy that aimed to integrate (part of) their armed forces or articulated concrete demand for establishing a SADC Brigade (Hendricks and Musavengana 2010; Williams 1999: 171). In fact, many countries in the region shared the view "that the creation of a standing peacekeeping force in the region is neither desirable nor practically feasible."[1] This is not surprising because most of the SADC members count as LDCs. They did not have excess financial and military capacity that could be pooled into the creation of a regional armed force or into expensive out-of-area deployments and peacekeeping missions (Oosthuizen 2006: 299–300).

However, an exception to this general SADC-wide position was South Africa. Since 1996, the Cape Republic had always declared that it was willing to take an active part in "multi-national peace support operations on the continent."[2] In this context, Pretoria repeatedly emphasised that it wanted to deepen cooperation with its SADC partners and enhance the organisation's capacity by contributing to international peacekeeping missions and thus enable the SADC to launch and take the lead in such operations over the medium term on its own. In this context, the South African government explicitly declared that the country was prepared to contribute military resources to (regional) standby arrangements under the umbrella of the AU and the SADC.[3] However, Pretoria's tangible readiness to promote the build-up of an SSF is rooted not only in its intention to simply advance regional security cooperation and foster peace and stability in Southern Africa. South Africa's motivation behind these efforts was at least as much an interest in cementing the country's position as the SADC's lead nation and thereby expand its status as a middle power on a global level. Therefore, the RSA's commitment to develop the SADC's peacekeeping and conflict management capacity was less a response to a genuine regional cooperation problem in the SADC but rather a strategy to pursue its own foreign policies and continental or global ambitions (Bischoff 2006; Williams 1999).

7.1.2 Organisational Demand

It is noteworthy, however, that the SADC as an organisation repeatedly underlined the need for deeper regional security cooperation and a regional standby brigade since the turn of the millennium. The most important document in this respect is the SADC's SIPO (van Nieuwkerk 2011: 180–181). The document reflects the member states' common interests and goals insofar as it stipulates strategies to enhance regional security cooperation and improve the performance of the Organ. According to the SIPO, a central objective in this context is to develop a peacekeeping capacity of national defence forces and coordinate the participation of countries in international and regional peacekeeping operations.[4] The most central tasks to achieve this objective include the build-up of a regional peace support operational capability based on standby arrangements (i.e. a regional standby force) and the development and maintenance of an RPTC.[5] The SIPO's agenda is, however, rather a toolbox of policy advice since its recommendations are neither mandatory nor legally binding.

The SADC Protocol on Politics, Defence and Security Co-operation of (2001) provides further orientation in this context because it contains some substantive points that later became part of the SIPO's objectives. However, only one paragraph relates to the issue of creating a regional standby force. In this respect, the protocol stipulates that the SADC countries should "develop a peacekeeping capacity of national defence forces and co-ordinate the participation of State Parties in international and regional peacekeeping operations."[6] This specification is identical with the one that is part of the SIPO. However, the provision does not contain further details on how to develop such a regional peacekeeping capacity, nor concrete policy measures or a deadline. These aspects—and the fact that the whole issue is mentioned only once—indicate that the SADC countries did not put the creation of a regional standby force high on their agenda, which gives good reasons to presume a lack of intrinsic motivation to emphatically promote and engage in this project.

Moreover, the fact that there are virtually no official SADC documents, Council and Summit records or statements of SADC officials that could substantiate a common intention to create a regional standby force underpins the impression that there was no region-wide enthusiasm and support towards this cooperation project. Only the ISDSC is said to have elaborated several recommendations on how to set up a regional peacekeeping brigade and a training centre during the years of 1998/99. However, these recommendations had been clearly framed on the ECOMOG[7] experience in West Africa. Thus, they were more likely the result of inter-regional policy diffusion than of genuine regional demand in the SADC. In the end, these recommendations did not initiate the establishment of a common SADC standby brigade anyways (Macaringue 2007: 118).

In sum, the clear majority of SADC countries' did not articulate an explicit demand for a common SSF during the mid-2000s and the decade before. There were, at best, some immature considerations on creating a regional standby force on an intra-organisational level.

7.1.3 Interim Summary and Situation Structure

In light of all of these aspects, the genuine problematic situation in the SADC region with regard to establishing a regional peacekeeping force clearly resembled a Deadlock game (with defection as the dominant strategy) during the mid-2000s. The policy option for member states to deepen institutionalised regional security cooperation by pooling (parts of) their national defence forces under the umbrella of a regional command structure did not seem to offer prospects for absolute gains for any SADC country at that time. Therefore, the policy option of keeping the status quo—that is, "defection" in terms of maintaining a full national

Fig. 7.1 Genuine regional problematic situation in view of an envisaged SADC Standby Force

		SADC Country B	
		SADC Standby Force	Status Quo
SADC Country A	SADC Standby Force	2 / 2	1 / 4
	Status Quo	4 / 1	3 / 3

security autarky by not ceding any part of (or authority over) the national defence force to a regional institution—was the most attractive option for virtually all SADC countries. This preference is not surprising, because the intra-regional security dilemma had already been alleviated by the (re-)launch of the Organ and by implementing its confidence-building measures (de Coning 1999; Macaringue 2007) (Fig. 7.1).

If there was actually no genuine regional cooperation problem but instead a situation resembling a "Deadlock" game where non-cooperation was the actors' dominant strategy as sketched above, then there were in fact no incentives for the SADC countries to leave the status quo and engage in a (potentially costly) institutionalised cooperation project. Therefore, the emergence of a (costly) regional institution—here, an SSF—seems rather unlikely from a regional point of view.

7.2 Asymmetric Intra- and Extra-Regional Interdependence: South Africa's Military Power and the EU's African Peace Facility

As in the previous chapter, patterns of intra-regional military interdependence in the SADC area shall be deduced by analysing the strength of the member states' armed forces, their equipment and capabilities, and the governments' military expenditures (in absolute figures and as a percentage of the GDP). The SADC's extra-regional military or security relations shall be worked out by focussing on (bilateral) defence agreements, military aid, and logistical and financial contributions to the issue area of security. The year 2007 will be taken as a reference year because that was when the SADC states decided on the formation of the SADC Brigade.

7.2.1 Intra-Regional Military Interdependence

During the first decade of the twenty-first century, the pattern of intra-regional security and military interdependence in Southern Africa in structural terms was by and large similar to the situation of the mid-1990s. In regard to the strength of the SADC countries' regular armed forces, the picture in 2007 looked as follows: Table 7.1

The table above shows clearly an intra-regional asymmetry in terms of military power distribution. This is because three SADC countries had significantly larger armed forces than the rest of the member states. By the mid-2000s, the DRC's armed forces had a personnel strength of almost 160,000 soldiers and therefore was in the regional lead. One should not forget, however, that the country had just experienced a lengthy civil war a few years earlier and that the demobilisation of Kinshasa's inflated army was still ongoing. The same applied for Angola where the civil war had ended only in 2002 and left behind an armed forces consisting of 107,000 soldiers—then the region's second largest. South Africa, with about 62,000 soldiers at its command, had the third largest defence force in the region.

Apart from these three, only Tanzania and Zimbabwe had comparatively sizable armies, of more than 20,000 soldiers each. All other countries in the region—with Madagascar and Zambia somehow in the middle—had only small defence forces, of a few thousand soldiers. In fact, virtually all SADC member states—despite the two that had been entangled by civil wars—had reduced the personnel strength of their armed forces compared with the time of the mid-1990s when regional security cooperation in the SADC was not yet institutionalised. This indicates an improvement in the overall security situation in the region which can be related to the OPDS being in place and operating.

Since it is not only the sheer number of soldiers that stand for an army's strength, qualitative aspects such as modernity of equipment shall additionally be taken into account in order to determine the countries'

Table 7.1 *Strength of regular armed forces of SADC members (2007)*

Country	Armed force
Angola	107,000
Botswana	9000
DR Congo	159,000
Lesotho	2000
Madagascar	14,000
Malawi	5000
Mauritius	2000
Mozambique	11,000
Namibia	9000
Seychelles	0
South Africa	62,000
Swaziland[a]	[a]3000
Tanzania	27,000
Zambia	15,000
Zimbabwe	29,000

Data collected from ISS (2009: 277–328)
[a]Data obtained from Ressler (2007: 103)

Table 7.2 *Military expenditure of SADC members (2007)*

Country	Absolute military expenditure in constant (2009) million US-$	Relative military expenditure in % of GDP
Angola	2247	3.7
Botswana	317	2.6
DR Congo[a]	94	1.7
Lesotho	40	2.4
Madagascar	82	1.1
Malawi	42	1.7
Mauritius	27	0.4
Mozambique	57	0.7
Namibia	239	2.7
Seychelles	11	1.1
South Africa	3577	1.3
Swaziland[a]	101	3.1
Tanzania	162	1.0
Zambia	200	1.7
Zimbabwe	[a]107	[a]2.1

Data collected from ISS (2009: 475–477)
[a]Data from the year 2006 (SIPRI 2010)

true military capacity. In this respect, the situation in 2007 was again quite similar to the one during the mid-1990s: South Africa and, to a quite lesser degree, Angola were the only countries in the region whose armed forces had comparatively modern military equipment at their disposal. Most experts agree, however, that the South African National Defence Force by far outclassed all the other armed forces in the SADC region in terms of quality of equipment, armament, motivation, operational readiness and overall military capacity. The armies of Angola and the DRC, in contrast, were exhausted from the recent civil wars (de Coning 2005: 102–105; Hull and Derblom 2009) Table 7.2.

If the SADC countries' annual military expenditures of 2007 are taken into account as an additional indicator in order to determine their military capacity, this picture of an intra-regional asymmetry becomes clearer—and more differentiated.

South Africa spent more than $3.5 billion USD on its defence force in 2007 and, with these figures, clearly remained the country with by far the largest absolute military expenditures in the region. Just as in the decade before, Angola was the region's second biggest spender on military, having absolute expenditures of more than $2.2 billion USD in the same year. Luanda's defence budget thus had grown to about 75% of Pretoria's absolute military expenditures by 2007. The rest of the SADC members display comparably insignificant figures on military expenditures, although virtually all of the countries' defence budgets had slightly increased during the decade before. An outstanding exception of this trend is Zimbabwe, where the politico-economic crisis had resulted in severe spending cuts during the first decade of the twenty-first century (Hentz 2004).

The figures on the SADC countries' relative military expenditures as a percentage of GDP corroborate the aforementioned evidence. In 2007, Angola had spent 3.7% of its GDP on its military and therefore was— just as during the mid-1990s—in the lead of the SADC. Moreover, these figures substantiate the country's recent military build-up motivated by Luanda's strategic ambitions to balance South Africa and become a more important player in the SADC (de Coning 2005: 102–105). All other countries, with the exception of Swaziland, spent less than 3% of their GDP on their armed forces.

The SADC member states' contributions to the organisation's annual budget illustrate the intra-regional power distribution in the issue area of security as well. This is because traditionally the SADC pays the costs for cooperation in this policy field, for the most part, on its own. In 2006/07, South Africa contributed the largest share (about 20%) to the SADC's budget, followed by Angola (about 10%) and Tanzania (about 8%). This indicates that South Africa accordingly had the most leverage on how the SADC money on regional security cooperation efforts was going to be spent.[8]

Altogether, the abovementioned figures and criteria indicate that South Africa held a relative military supremacy in the SADC region during the period under observation. The only country that to some degree challenged Pretoria's relative regional power position in the issue area of security was possibly Angola. Zimbabwe's formerly quite strong regional power position, in contrast, had virtually faded by the mid-2000s. It is for this reason that the Cape Republic is assumed to play a decisive role in any regional efforts that aim to establish a common SSF. However, since serious regional demand for such a regional armed force was virtually non-existent among SADC member states, it seems necessary that South Africa would have to act as a benevolent hegemon and sponsor of this regional club good if Pretoria wished to make it become a reality.

7.2.2 Extra-Regional Military and Security Interdependence

A decade after the end of Apartheid in Southern Africa and more than four decades after the period of decolonisation, the SADC member states did not show noteworthy patterns of military interdependence and security relations or (bilateral) defence or status of force agreements to extra-regional actors, either to former colonial powers or to present-day great powers such as the USA. That is why, in the issue area of regional security cooperation, the SADC countries were, for structural reasons, rather immune to any (interfering) exertion of influence by extra-regional actors—in contrast to several francophone countries within the framework of the ECOWAS in West Africa (Gregory 2000).

However, the SADC had traditionally strong relations with extra-regional donor countries for decades (Odén 2000: 255, 261). In the years of 2006/07, almost 60% of the SADC's organisational budget of about $46 million USD had been financed by external actors, namely the EU in concert with "Additional Voluntary Contributions" of individual EU member countries (Tjønneland 2006: 8). The remaining part was procured by the SADC members on their own while South Africa contributed the lion's share.[9] In regard to the issue area of security, however, external donor support to the SADC played only a minor role insofar as the organisation was dismissive to disclose any details of its regional security cooperation agenda and activities to outsiders (i.e. Western donors).

However, the early and mid-2000s witnessed the evolution of two new strands of extra-regional security relations and inter-regional cooperation between the SADC on the one side and external actors such as the AU and the EU on the other side. This had quite an important impact on the SADC's own regional security efforts since its policies aimed exactly at this issue area as will be outlined in the following:

Firstly, it was the AU that became increasingly interested to address security problems on the continent by means of a new peace and security approach, which was guided by the imperative "African solutions to African problems". This new AU policy was clearly part of the so-called "African Renaissance" concept but also a result of the disengagement and loss of strategic interest of the Western world in Africa after the end of the Cold War (Klingebiel 2005). Against this background, the AU agreed on the Protocol on the Establishment of the Peace and Security Council in 2002. It defined a common African Peace and Security Architecture (APSA) as a collective institutional framework for carrying out the AU's new tasks in the field of peace, security and defence.[10] One of the major objectives of the AU in this context was the development of a military capacity (about 20,000 troops) to manage conflicts and complex peacekeeping operations on the continent (Sidiropoulos and Meyn 2006: 8-9).

The APSA was without doubt a breakthrough with regard to the development of Africa's "own" peacekeeping capabilities because it set the goal to institute an ASF by 2010.[11] A special feature of the APSA in this respect was its explicit reference to the continent's regional economic communities, such as the SADC or ECOWAS. The AU had recognised their pivotal role for an effective functioning of its continental security institutions and therefore assigned them the role as building blocks for the continental security architecture. This applied of course to the Union's plans on the creation of the ASF as well. In the course of this policy of subsidiarity, the AU as a result demanded that all five of its mandated regional economic communities—including the SADC—establish regional standby brigades (3,500-5,000 troops each) by 2010. This was in order to facilitate the build-up of the ASF and provide rapid regional reaction capability to counter regional crises and conflicts (Franke 2009: 153-177; Sidiropoulos and Meyn 2006: 9). Hence, the AU put distinct normative pressure on the SADC and its member states to implement the provisions of the APSA and establish a regional standby brigade as part of a larger ASF until 2010.

Secondly, one could observe a growing pattern of extra-regional security relations between the SADC and the EU—partially via the AU as a proxy—since the mid-2000s. It was the EU that became increasingly interested in improving inter-regional security cooperation with Africa—not least as a result of the growing threat by global terrorism and civil wars in failed states (Sidiropoulos and Chevallier 2006: 15, 18–19; van Langenhove 2012). The EU's strategy included a closer cooperation with the AU as well as with the mandated regional integration organisations on the continent. It stipulated, among other things, to develop "African [peacekeeping] capabilities, such as the AU's African standby force"[12] and support future African peacekeeping operations.[13] Therefore, enabling the AU and the continent's regional integration organisations to take responsibility for their own peace and security issues was high on the EU's own security agenda.

In December 2003, the EU therefore decided to establish the African Peace Facility (APF) in reaction to a request by African state leaders at an AU Summit a few months earlier.[14] The aims of this specific development fund were to strengthen the AU's strategy on continental peace and security cooperation and to support the implementation of the APSA framework. This included support to the operationalisation of the ASF. Altogether, the EU channelled almost €440 million through the first APF (2004–2007) for peace support operations and capacity building on the regional and continental level under the provisions of the 9th EDF (including additional voluntary contributions of selected EU member states).[15] Although the greater part of this money had been allocated to support peacekeeping operations in Africa, a share of more than €26 million had been earmarked for APSA capacity building which in fact implies indirect financial support to regional organisations (including the SADC) for the very same purpose. These capacity-building activities were complemented by an additional amount of €7.7 million from South Africa's heading of the EU budget.[16]

With the aim to intensify inter-regional security cooperation and build a long-term partnership of equals between the EU and the AU, Brussels moreover offered clear prospects to prolong the APF mechanism and increase its budget from 2008 onwards. This was not least in order to demonstrate the EU's commitment to continue inter-regional cooperation. Primarily, however, it allowed for sound and more long-term planning on the AU's and the regional organisations' sides in terms of implementing the APSA and its continental and regional peace and security cooperation measures. Accordingly, the EU announced it would allocate a first envelope with a total of €300 million to its second APF under the 10th EDF for the period of 2008–2010. This included the provision of financial support for ongoing capacity-building programmes on continental and regional levels in the amount of €65 million. However, the APF contracted only €20 million for the regional communities and their capacity-building programmes for, among other things, creating the regional standby brigades.[17]

Apart from the rather new and indirect APF funding mechanism, the EU and its member states had channelled funding for the promotion of specific security cooperation projects in the SADC directly through the EDFs as well (Franke 2007). By this means, the SADC ought to receive up to €11 million for the construction and maintenance of an RPTC from Denmark under the umbrella of the 9th EDF. The United Kingdom and Germany announced they would provide up to €8.1 and €7.2 million respectively for capacity building in the issue area of security cooperation in the same context.[18] The following 10th EDF allocated for the SADC a total amount of €116 million,[19] of which, however, only €17.4 million had been earmarked to support regional political cooperation and the implementation of selected peace and security projects such as the build-up of a SADC standby brigade.[20]

Altogether, there has been a significant increase in extra-regional funding from the EU for security cooperation and peacekeeping in Africa since the creation of the APSA and the APF mechanism shortly after the turn of the millennium. However, the SADC in fact received only a marginal share of these funds.[21] Nevertheless, there were increasing prospects to receive continuous financial support for regional capacity building in the field of security and the creation of a regional peacekeeping force.

7.2.3 Interim Summary and Situation Structure

In summary, South Africa was in a regional power position but neither individual SADC countries nor the organisation as a whole exhibited noteworthy patterns of asymmetric interdependence to extra-regional actors in the issue area of security. Against this background, any process of regional security cooperation in the region—if it should ever occur—is principally more dependent on South Africa's policy preferences and actions than in danger to be interfered from outsiders for plain structural reasons.[22]

Against this background, the early and mid-2000s witnessed a stronger engagement of the AU and the EU in terms of inter-regional security cooperation: The AU demanded that the SADC create a peacekeeping capacity by normative means. With Brussels accordingly offering significant financial funding for the build-up of continental and regional peacekeeping capacities through the APF and EDF via the AU's APSA framework, an externally fuelled regional cooperation problem materialised in the SADC region. This appeared insofar as the SADC member states were required to engage in specific security cooperation projects on a regional level (e.g. the establishment of an SSF) in order to get access to financial resources from the EU's funding mechanisms (Brosig 2011).

In theory, these external financial contributions (particularly the prospect of increasing inflows) acted as a cooperation-conducive intervening context variable on the regional situation in the SADC. It had an incentive effect insofar as it transferred the genuine problematic situation (i.e. the "Deadlock" game with non-cooperation as the actors' dominant strategy) towards an externally fuelled coordination game with distributive effects (Fig. 7.2).

	EU	
	No Cooperation	SADC Standby Force
SADC Country A — No Cooperation	2 / 2	4 / 1
SADC Country A — SADC Standby Force	1 / 4	5/5

3 / 4	SADC Standby Force	SADC Country B
3 / 3	Status Quo	
SADC Standby Force	Status Quo	

SADC Country A

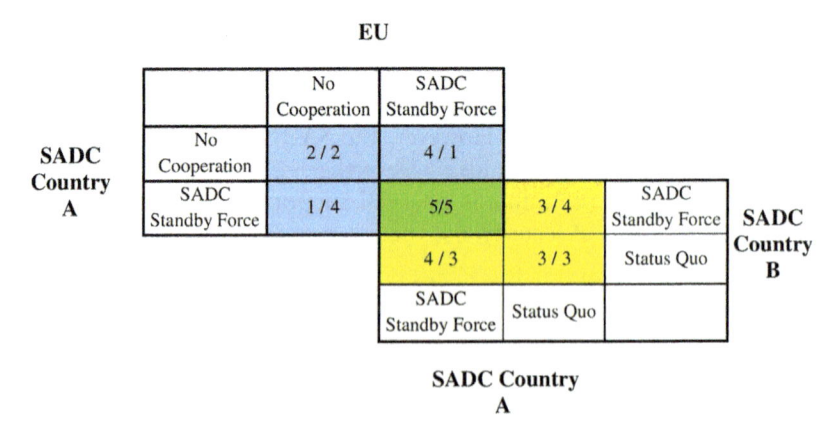

Fig. 7.2 Externally fuelled problematic situation in view of the planned SADC Standby Force

The figure above illustrates this backdrop of extra-regional relations of the SADC countries to the EU in terms of its effect on the cooperation problem on a regional level and the pay-offs for the countries' policy actions: The EU provided the SADC countries significant financial contributions (and the prospect of more) via the EDF, APF and APSA mechanisms on the condition that they choose to engage in regional security cooperation towards the build-up of an SSF. Thus, the genuine regional situation structure on the SADC level (in yellow) became affected by the SADC countries' extra-regional relations with the EU/AU (in blue) insofar as the latter increased the absolute pay-offs for a cooperative strategy on a regional level under conditions of inter-regional cooperation (in green) and thereby turned it into a more profitable policy option than the status quo. Therefore, regional cooperation in the SADC likewise implied inter-regional cooperation between the SADC and the EU/AU.

Against this background, institutionalised regional security cooperation in the SADC towards establishing a common SSF is likely to develop according to the incentives provided by influential external actors (here, the EU/AU). Moreover, it is likely to prosper and become effective only as long as the latter continue to provide external funding and support. This makes the project at the same time subject to the danger of interfering extra-regional impact since donors could stop their support for various reasons.

7.3 Regional Consensus: Negotiations and Institutionalisation of the SADC Standby Force

The SADC countries' desire to fulfil the AU's expectations and institutionalise a common regional peacekeeping force led to the signing of an MoU on the Establishment of a SADC Standby Brigade in August 2007. The document provides the participant SADC states a legal basis for the operationalisation of the standby force under the provisions of the AU's APSA as well as SADC's Protocol on Politics, Defence and Security Co-operation and the SIPO agenda. Moreover, the MoU gives information on the planned standby brigade's purpose, functions, training facilities, deployment and command structure. It is the founding document of what we know today as the SSF.

7.3.1 Negotiations and Institutional Design of the MoU

There is clear evidence that the AU's decision to set up an ASF along with the EU's initiative to launch the APF served as major stimuli for the SADC countries to engage in inter-state negotiations on the institutionalisation of their own regional peacekeeping force. SADC executive secretary Tomaz Salomao corroborated this in a statement in which he declared that the SADC Brigade "has been set up within the provisions of the African Union that require that each of its five regional economic communities need to have such standby forces with the sole aim of peace-support operations in the region."[23] EU officials, in contrast, pointed out that the SSF is a "true" SADC project despite being aware of the EU's and AU's support to the project.[24]

The first exchange of ideas on how to organise and institutionalise a future SADC brigade took place at an ISDSC meeting in 2004 (Salomon 2009: 217). There seemed to be no serious conflicts of interests among the SADC members about whether to establish a common peacekeeping force, because the Summit declared only a few months later in a public statement that it had "initiated the conceptualisation of the SADC Standby Force."[25] The SADC states' ability to make such a quick decision was remarkable against the background of notoriously lengthy decision-making procedures on other policy issues (e.g. in the forefront of the SADC-FTA).

What followed were inter-state negotiations on the details of this common project and consultations with military and defence experts on how to implement it. Both took place within the framework of an ISDSC subcommittee among the SADC countries' ministers responsible for defence during April and May 2005.[26] These inter-state negations must have been rather non-controversial in character since the participant countries shared similar preferences and because of the fact that no disputes have been made public. There was only some minor disagreement between South Africa and Zimbabwe—which both dominated the negotiations (Motsamai 2014; Nathan 2012: 35)—on particular specifications such as the character of common (military) standards and the harmonisation of operational procedures (Baker and Maeresera 2009: 107; Salomon 2009: 216–219).

It became evident, however, that Pretoria acted, above all, in a very committed and supportive way to the project. The Cape Republic offered to contribute a disproportionately larger share to the institutionalisation and maintenance costs of the planned SADC brigade as well as to its envisaged troop contingent. Though vague, this proposition corresponded not only to the country's strong ambition to become the SADC's and Africa's lead nation in peace support operations but also to the role of a benevolent regional hegemon—which South Africa could easily play because of its status as regional great power in terms of military capabilities (Mandrup 2009: 18).

After the successful conclusion of these inter-state negotiations a few months later, all SADC countries (with the exception of the Seychelles) signed the Memorandum of Understanding on the Establishment of a SADC Standby Brigade on 16 August 2007. This was the official birth of the SADC Brigade that became known as the SSF (van Nieuwkerk 2011: 186). It is noteworthy that the SADC countries agreed "only" on an MoU—which in fact is a declaration of intent—and not on a legally binding protocol. This is clearly an indicator for a rather low degree of formal institutionalisation which corresponds to the theoretical assumptions on institutionalised regional cooperation against a pattern of low intra-regional interdependence in problematic situations resembling coordination games.

Moreover, it is noteworthy that the adoption of the SADC MoU and the inauguration of the SSF happened only four months after the EU's APF mechanism contracted, for the first time, a significant amount of money ($20 million USD) for capacity-building measures under the APSA framework—and in the very same month when the first tranche of this money was actually paid ($7.4 million USD in August 2007).[27] Unfortunately, there is no concrete proof of a causal relation between both events since the donors have not made available detailed data showing the exact destination of their financial contributions. However, it seems that it was not just a coincidence that these events correlated in time.

In regard to the central contents of the MoU, the overall function of the brigade was "to participate in missions as envisaged in Article 13 of the Protocol Establishing the Peace and Security Council of the AU"[28] which includes being able to perform the following:

- observations and monitoring missions
- other types of peace support missions
- intervention in a State Party in respect to grave circumstances or at the request of that State Party—or to restore peace and security

- preventive deployment for conflict management
- peace-building.

Against the background of its core military functions, it becomes clear that the SADC Brigade had been designed in the first place as an instrument to conduct regional peacekeeping missions—and thus to serve the AU's tasks according to the APSA framework.

In regard to the rules of deployment and its command and control structure, the MoU stipulated that the standby brigade "shall only be deployed on the authority of the SADC Summit [...] on a SADC, AU or UN mandate."[29] It called moreover for the establishment of a Planning Element (PLANELM) as a separate instrument at the SADC Headquarters. The PLANELM should operate autonomously as a tool of the OPDS with the task to manage the SADC standby system on a daily basis. Article 12 emphasised that the command structure at the headquarters should be strictly representative of all contributing state parties and that the standby force's command structure should be harmonised to AU and United Nations (UN) standards in order to enable smooth interaction.[30]

Article 9 proposed the establishment of a main logistics depot for the standby brigade, whereas Article 8 called upon the participant state parties to contribute personnel as well as major and minor equipment as required and agreed to. Article 11 noted against this background that the SADC was to reimburse each contributing state party for their personnel and material expenditures.[31] However, the MoU did not specify details on the state parties' contributions at that point and thus remained rather vague on a very important issue. The likely explanation for the lack of guidelines on this aspect is the fact that the SADC states were still unsure about the AU's concrete demands on the SADC's share for the continental ASF as well as about the external financial support that would eventually materialise through the APF/APSA schemes. Article 11, however, indicates clearly that the institutionalisation of the SSF should not involve any net costs for the contributing state parties. This corroborates the initial presumption on the project's character as an externally fuelled regional club good.

Against the background of the AU's requirements on constituting the continental ASF,[32] the SADC countries only later came to an understanding that in total the SADC standby brigade should be composed of 4000–5000 troops, including a mobile headquarters, three infantry battalions, an intelligence and logistics company, naval and air force capabilities as well as a police and civil component (Mandrup 2009: 18; Salomon 2009: 215–219). Since the standby force had not been conceptualised as a standing army, the state parties to the MoU decided to contribute their specific contingents of personnel and military equipment to a common "standby pool"—depending on their military capacity. In case of deployment, the commanding staff would then assemble the brigade according to the mission-specific needs from the forces available in the pool within a short period of time (Baker and Maeresera 2009: 107; Macaringue 2007: 123–124). This had two advantages: firstly, a brigade deployment could go ahead even if one or more state parties were unable or unwilling to participate and, secondly, a strong state, like South Africa, could act as a lead nation in terms of guiding a mission or facilitating an effective brigade despite the lack of contributions from weaker member countries (Hull and Derblom 2009: 69; Mandrup 2009: 16–20).

It is noteworthy that South Africa, as a country with a superior military capability in regional terms, pledged the lion's share of personnel and equipment to the common standby pool. Pretoria offered to initially contribute, among other things, "a parachute battalion, engineering capability, sanitation (including a field hospital), harbour patrol boats, signal capacity, divers, naval support vessel and air transport" (Mandrup 2009: 19). This gives proof of the country's readiness to support the standby brigade with military equipment that other SADC states were unable to deliver. Moreover, it emphasises the importance of a regional lead nation for such advanced regional cooperation projects (Nathan 2012: 60).

A central cornerstone in SADC's efforts to operationalise its regional standby force concerned its education and professional training and, for this purpose, the establishment of an associated peacekeeping training facility. The SADC realised in this context that Zimbabwe already hosted a military training facility that had been established under the aegis of the ISDSC back in 1996. Supported by external funding from the governments of Denmark and Britain, this RPCT had become fairly active during the years of 1997–2001 and hosted, among other things, a number of workshops, training sessions, peacekeeping operations courses and occasionally supported the regional military exercises of the SADC member states. Thus, over time, it had become a recognised and truly multinational body (Adelmann 2012: 333; Berman and Sams 2003: 64).

The formerly generous European donors, however, abruptly cut down their funding to the Harare-based training centre in January 2002 as a reaction to the increasingly autocratic rule of President Mugabe and the serious political crisis in Zimbabwe (Kinzel 2007: 5). The sudden withdrawal of this significant extra-regional source of support had as a consequence that the RPTC had to quit its work. It became entirely paralysed for more than three years.[33] Against this background, the Zimbabwean government issued a formal offer to the SADC to make use of the "donor-abandoned" training facility and host it as the RPTC for the common standby brigade. The SADC CoM accepted Harare's proposal in the summer of 2004 and decided also that the training centre was to become a full SADC institution under the management of the Organ, a procedure which the SADC called "mainstreaming" of the RPTC.[34] Following the official handover in August 2005, the RPTC fell directly under the control of the SADC Secretariat and the Directorate of the Organ.[35]

With the RPTC for education and training of the SADC peacekeeping operations thus being principally available, it was a logical consequence that the SADC countries referred to this institution in their MoU on the establishment of the SADC Standby Brigade in 2007. The MoU stipulated in this context in Article 13 that the state parties' military units assigned to the common standby force were to achieve standardised training objectives and that the RPTC was to develop and impart such common training standards to the future SSF.[36]

Altogether, the institutional design of the MoU reflects, in the first place, consensus among the participating member states in terms of their willingness to cooperate towards this ambitious common project. The proposed strictly intergovernmental character of the standby force's command structure underlines this aspect of consensual decision-making. However, the MoU, at the same time, gives the impression of a slightly indifferent piece of work. This is because most provisions are rather vague in character and a concrete deadline for accomplishing the goals is missing. The reason behind this could be the rather vague external expectations for the SADC brigade, particularly on the part of the EU. Accordingly, Brussels did not exert any direct influence on the inter-state negotiations on a SADC level and the design of the document. A South African influence on the MoU prevails only insofar as, in principle, the mechanism of the "standby pool" allows the deployment of the SSF by a lead nation. Moreover, the document contains statements on regional peacekeeping (operations) that are very similar to Pretoria's national foreign policy doctrine.

7.4 Evaluation of the SADC Standby Force and Its Regional Peacekeeping Training Centre

In order to conduct an informative evaluation of the standby force and its training centre, it is noteworthy to mention that the SADC pursued the institutionalisation of the SSF and its associated RPTC somewhat in parallel to the development of the underlying MoU. This is quite an unconventional procedure in terms of chronological order. It is probably owed to the fact that external actors either put pressure on the SADC (i.e. the AU's demand to contribute to the planned ASF) or provided incentives (i.e. the EU through the EDF and APF) to speed up the institutionalisation process in a certain way. Leaving these causal relations aside, the SADC declared the SSF officially operational on the very same day when its member states had signed the corresponding MoU. As if to demonstrate this, the SADC celebrated the inauguration of the SSF with a big military parade at the gates of the conference location in Lusaka on the same occasion (Mandrup 2009: 2). Whether this official statement and symbolic gesture matched reality or whether the SSF is just a paper tiger will be elaborated upon in the following paragraphs.

7.4.1 Implementation and Compliance

Because the MoU on the establishment of the SADC Brigade is not a legally binding protocol but rather a legal guideline or framework, the signing SADC countries are obliged neither to ratify the document nor to implement the inherent provisions into national law. While all SADC members (with the exception of the Seychelles) became state parties to the MoU by their signature in August 2007 and thus put the MoU into practice, little is known about whether the states actually put effort into complying with the provisions on a national level and thus make the SSF become a reality on regional grounds. This is because the SADC, the OPDS as well as the organisation's member states generally do not release to the public any sound information on the status of the state parties' national compliance to the MoU in the issue area of security (Hull and Derblom 2009: 47).

However, a recent white paper on South Africa's foreign policy pointed out that the country "will work together with SADC and its member states to maintain the readiness of the SADC Brigade."[37] This is corroborated by the fact that Pretoria substantiated its national contributions to the "standby pool" and currently provides, among other things, eight army units (including a brigade tactical headquarters, mortar batteries, motorised infantry, parachute airborne infantry, intelligence and maintenance troops), six helicopters and one transport aircraft, six vessels and two hospital units for the SSF.[38] According to the South African government, the country is able to do so because its national defence force is a relatively powerful and disciplined force with modern equipment and some surplus capacity. In view of these troop contributions, there are reasons to wonder whether the SSF is in fact a real joint SADC project when South Africa is in reality the main provider (Mandrup 2009: 20). Other member states such as Botswana, Lesotho, Malawi, Mozambique, Tanzania and Zimbabwe have officially pledged some personnel and equipment for the "standby pool" as well. Against this background, the total strength of the SSF is said to be around 4000 troops maximum. Troop pledges thus seem complete, although details have not been fully disclosed so far (Hull and Derblom 2009: 73). It remains unclear whether or to what degree these troops are actually available, mounted and short-term deployable at demand (Aboagye 2012: 4; Lautier 2013).

An AU report on the status and readiness of the ASF and its regional brigades reviewed the SSF's stage of implementation by focussing on its constituent components. In view of its components of military relevance, it noted that the framework documents, the MoU, the PLANLEM,[39] a (training) centre of excellence, and the troop pledges from member states were functional and in place. Outstanding areas, however, are the SSF's permanent headquarters and its logistic depot, neither of which is yet in place.[40] According to very recent information, the SADC member states decided to deviate from the MoU's provisions insofar as not to establish a permanent brigade headquarters but only a provisional one in case of the SSF's deployment (Aboagye 2012). In regard to the logistic depot, the member states decided to locate it in Botswana, but no construction works have begun so far. Altogether, the AU's and other reports concluded that the SSF is not fully operational and not really deployable thus far.[41]

The shortfalls in the institutionalisation of the SSF in terms of the state parties' implementation of and compliance with some of the MoU's provisions derive from the fact that there is obviously a shortage of financial resources in most member states. This is because the EU has channelled the largest part of its funding through the APF or APSA programme to multinational peacekeeping operations in Africa or other programmes of the AU up until today. Capacity-building programmes on a continental and regional level (such as the build-up of the ASF and its regional components) have received only a minor share of the EU's financial contributions so far:

In fact, during the period of 2004–2011, the EU committed a total of only €51 million for the various continental and regional capacity-building programmes under its APF programme.[42] It is unclear how much of this money was finally channelled directly to the SADC but it was probably less than €3 or 4 million. Most of this funding seems to have been used for the implementation of the PLANEM since the EU earmarked a sufficient amount of this money to allow the SADC to pay 15 permanent staff members in this institution.[43] It is therefore not surprising that particularly the PLANELM is today functional and in place. However, the overall amount of external funding was certainly not enough to unfold a significantly supportive impact on the SADC's developing countries' implementation efforts towards creating a fully operational standby brigade on a regional level.

With regard to the EU's latest APF APSA Support Programme (2011–2014) under the 10th EDF, Brussels earmarked a total of €40 million for capacity-building measures in the AU and its regional organisations. The SADC's share, however, added up to only €4.334 million until the end of 2014.[44] About €2.2 million of this amount went to the build-up of the SSF.[45] This was probably less money than the SADC states had expected at the time when they decided to initialise the process of institutionalising their own SSF.

The impact of insufficient external funding becomes most clear in the example of the SSF's planned logistic depot. According to experts, the SADC countries face great difficulties to construct and maintain this great undertaking by regional means because they need more regional leadership and external donors' assistance (Mandrup 2009: 16–17). Moreover, most SADC members—particularly the LDC—have problems to provide adequate military equipment for such a logistic depot. This is firstly because their armed forces in general have little equipment (that is fully operational) and secondly because national governments have so far been fairly reluctant to transfer part of their (operational) equipment to the territory of a third country (i.e. to a common logistic depot) since this implies that the very same equipment would not be available at home in case of a state of defence or other emergency (Hull and Derblom 2009: 73; Lautier 2013).

The implementation process of the RPTC—the most important pillar with regard to the SSF's future peacekeeping skills and capacity—was likewise prone to external influence due to its strong dependency on extra-regional donors. It was mentioned earlier that the Harare-based training facility had been strongly donor-dependent since its foundation in the mid-1990s and that it had become inoperative after the European donors (particularly Denmark) stopped their support as a result of economic sanctions against Zimbabwe in 2002 (Kinzel 2007: 5). This institutional paralysis continued for several years because virtually all SADC countries were reluctant to contribute and fund the institution adequately on their own during that time (Chirwa and Namangale 2009: 166). However, the military training centre in Harare was not officially closed—despite diplomatic pressure from the European Parliament on several SADC countries in order to discipline Zimbabwe's autocratic President Mugabe (Adelmann 2012: 333).

However, with the RPTC becoming an official SADC institution for the purpose of training the future SSF under the provisions of the MoU, this dissatisfactory situation changed. With the inter-state negotiations on the design of the MoU still under way, the SADC member states agreed to fulfil the latter's (envisaged) provisions concerning the RPTC in advance. For this purpose, they provided just enough resources to officially re-open the training facility in August 2005 (Adelmann 2012: 334). Owing to this commitment, the (training) centre of excellence became formally implemented and thus de facto in place.[46]

7.4.2 Performance and Effectiveness

The performance and effectiveness of the SSF and its RPTC yield mixed results. The planning and formal institutionalisation of the SSF can be regarded as a success in that the participating state parties adopted the institutional framework. However, it remains an open secret that the implementation process of the MoU has not yet been completed and that the full operational capability and deployability of the SSF are still very questionable. Experts and other observers state that it is very difficult to assess the actual operational readiness of the SSF. This is because the SADC is very secretive about its current situation and does not provide detailed information on the operational readiness of those troops that have been pledged to the "standby pool" by its member countries. In any case, it is fairly unlikely that the SSF could be fully operational and deployable without a common logistic depot in place (Lautier 2013; Tavares 2010: 61–62).

From a counterfactual perspective, there has not yet been any deployment of the SSF since the SADC officially declared the standby brigade operational in August 2007, even though there had been some opportunities to engage in peacekeeping operations in Madagascar or the DRC during the past years. A recent deployment of a few SADC countries' armed forces in the DRC against so-called "M23 rebels" in Goma in early 2013 has sometimes been declared as deployment of the SSF. However, it was rather a few SADC states (South Africa, Tanzania and to a lesser degree Malawi and Zimbabwe) that individually contributed some troop contingents together with other African countries to a multinational intervention brigade in the DRC under the umbrella of the UN. Hence, this was not an employment of the SSF, although the SADC seems to have declared a readiness to "go on its own" if necessary.[47]

The RPTC, in contrast, demonstrates a much better degree of performance than the SSF on the whole. This is not least because the institution has recovered from its period of "donor-abandonment" and paralysis. Since the central mission of the RPTC is "to study the theory and practice of peace support operations and to coordinate peace support training in the SADC region"[48] in terms of qualifying the SSF for action and deployment, a good indicator for assessing its performance and operational success is the number of training contributions and courses to the preparation of peacekeeping personnel which it has organised so far. In this context, it is noteworthy that the RPTC seems to have offered only a single military training course during the years of 2002–2007 (Davies 2014: 29). This period of relative inactivity, with only one course taking place in 2006, is exactly the period in which the former external donors (particularly Denmark and the United Kingdom) provided no funding for the training centre. It is also the time when the SADC took over (in 2005) and started to maintain the RPTC all on its own.

Major improvements in the RPTC's functionality and performance can be observed from 2008 onwards. Since then, more than nine different peacekeeping and peace support operations training courses have been taken place (Davies 2014: 29). The major reason behind this success is the fact that external donors had decided to revive their financial support to the RPTC: From 2008 onwards, it was firstly the German Government that fuelled regional security cooperation with an amount of €2.2 million until 2011. From 2011 until 2014, Berlin channelled another €1.6 million directly to the RPTC via its international cooperation agency Gesellschaft für Internationale Zusammenarbeit (GIZ), particularly for the development of training curricula, the implementation of training courses and the centre's staff.[49] Brussels took more time to make up its mind whether to re-start supporting the RPTC again. However, since the (still) Harare-based training facility had become an entirely SADC institution for the purpose of training the SSF since 2005, the EU had somehow lost its rhetorical entrapment with respect to sanctioning Zimbabwe and in March 2012 decided to channel an amount of more than €1.575 million[50] of its €11.4 million support programme to all African Training Centres directly to the SADC's RPTC.[51]

Today, the RPTC is a fully functional institution that supports the build-up and training of the developing SSF according to its mission and capacities. According to the centre's commander, the RPTC's major achievement is its "contribution towards enabling SADC Member States to send well-trained personnel to peace missions through the many hundreds of peacekeepers we have trained through the years, thereby successfully carrying out our mandate."[52] Other observers corroborate the director's self-assessment and come to the conclusion that the RPTC has been very effective in providing the relevant training exercises required to improve the knowledge and effectiveness of SSF personnel (Chirwa and Namangale 2009: 27; Lautier 2013).

In a nutshell, the process of establishing the SSF seems to be advanced although the regional force seems not to be ready for operation and deployment yet. Therefore, the SSF is not able to fulfil its central objective more than nine years after its official launch by SADC leaders. However, this is less the fault of the RPTC and is not due to a lack of military training since the SSF's training centre performs fairly well (at least since 2008).

7.5 Résumé and Prospects

In summary, there is evidence that the institutionalisation of the SSF did not happen on the basis of a genuine regional cooperation problem in terms of, for example, a security dilemma inherent to the SADC region or an external actor threatening to attack the regional organisation and its member states. In fact, there was actually no need for the SADC countries to demand the establishment of a common regional brigade from a plain structural regional perspective. Only South Africa as the SADC's regional hegemon showed vague signs of interest towards strengthening its regional and global peacekeeping capacity in order to underline its position as emerging power—at best via the SADC as an organisation.

Instead, it was the AU and particularly the EU as extra-regional actors that encouraged SADC countries to engage in deepening regional security cooperation and create a regional standby force for the sake of the continent. From 2004 onwards, the EU promised the SADC significant amounts of money for the build-up of an SSF for the purpose of contributing its part to a future African peacekeeping force. The EU provided by means of its financial incentives, channelled via the APF mechanism and the AU's APSA framework, an external stimulus that transformed the genuine regional "Deadlock" in the SADC towards an actual regional problematic situation (reminding of a coordination game with distributive effect) where cooperative behaviour promised absolute benefits.

The result of these external incentives was that the SADC countries quickly agreed on an MoU on the establishment of a common SADC Brigade in 2007 and declared the common regional force to be operational immediately thereafter. Without a doubt, South Africa became prominently engaged in the institutionalisation and build-up of the standby force as the regional lead nation and most significant contributor of personnel and material. However, it was ultimately extra-regional actors such as the EU and European countries as well as the AU that have fuelled the institutionalisation and operational capability of the SSF and the RPTC to the largest part so far. By funding more than €85 million to the APSA framework under the APF programme until today, the EU has become the most important supporter of institutionalised security cooperation in terms of capacity building for regional peacekeeping brigades in the whole of Africa. Although neither the EU nor the AU took part directly in the regional inter-state negotiations on the design of the MoU, there is evidence that the document made particular reference to the demands of the AU on continental and regional peacekeeping outlined in its APSA framework. Therefore, the MoU certainly carries the AU's mark.

In regard to issues of performance and institutional effectiveness, the build-up of the SSF has made significant progress and is fairly advanced at the current stage. In particular, the RPTC has been performing well throughout recent years. According to experts, the SADC's regional standby force has the best military potential of all planned regional standby brigades in Africa. This is not least due to South Africa's outstanding military and logistical capabilities and strong commitment in terms of troop pledges. However, the institutionalisation of the SSF has not been completed so far, as its headquarters and logistic depot are not yet in place. This proves that the SSF currently lacks an operational readiness—in spite of official declarations to the contrary.

In summary, there are good reasons to believe that the SSF and the RPTC are certainly not only symbolic in nature but in fact to a significant degree the result of an external exertion of influence by the EU. Since there had been no genuine regional demand for the SSF in SADC member states, the institutionalisation process and success of the SSF are likely to proceed only insofar as the external donors continue to provide support. This makes the SSF prone to interfering external influence insofar as it is in the end the external donors—and here in fact the EU—that decide and determine what the progress and future of the SSF will be.

Notes

1. Republic of South Africa (1996): Defence in a Democracy. White Paper on National Defence for the Republic of South Africa. May 1996. Chap. 4 (24). http://www.dod.mil.za/documents/WhitePaperonDef/whitepaper%20on%20defence1996.pdf (12/04/2016).
2. Republic of South Africa (1996): Defence in a Democracy. White Paper on National Defence for the Republic of South Africa. May 1996. Chap. 4 (2). http://www.dod.mil.za/documents/WhitePaperonDef/whitepaper%20on%20defence1996.pdf (12/04/2016).
3. Republic of South Africa (1999): White Paper on South African Participation in International Peace Missions. Pretoria. pp. 18, 25, 29–30. http://www.pmg.org.za/docs/2003/appendices/030326peace.ppt (20/06/2016).
4. SADC (2004c): Strategic Indicative Plan for the Organ. Objective 6. p. 28.
5. SADC (2004d): Strategic Indicative Plan for the Organ. Objective 6. I–iii. p. 28.
6. SADC (2001a): Protocol on Politics, Defence and Security Co-operation. Article 2.2 (k).

7. The ECOWAS Monitoring Group (ECOMOG) was a multinational armed force that had been set up by the ECOWAS for the purpose of conducting peacekeeping operations in regional conflicts (Adebajo 2002).
8. SADC (2006c): Record of the Meeting of the Council of Ministers. Held in Maseru, 15–16 August 2006. p. 2.
9. South Africa is the regional paymaster and is said to contribute roughly 20% to the SADC's budget (interview with a SADC official who asked to remain anonymous at the SADC Headquarters, September 2010).
10. AU (2002): Protocol relating to the Establishment of a Peace and Security Council of the African Union. Article 13 (1–3). https://www.au.int/sites/default/files/treaties/7781-file-protocol_peace_and_security.pdf (07/22/2016).
11. AU (2002): Protocol relating to the Establishment of a Peace and Security Council of the African Union. Article 13 (1–3). https://au.int/sites/default/files/treaties/7781-file-protocol_peace_and_security.pdf (07/22/2016).
12. European Council (2005): The EU and Africa: Towards a strategic partnership. Conclusions by the Heads of State and Government meeting in the European Council, Brussels, 15–16 December 2005 (doc 15961/05). pp. 64–65.
13. European Council (2005): EU Strategy for Africa: towards a Euro-African pact to accelerate Africa's development. Annex to the Communication from the Commission to the Council, the European Parliament and European Economic and Social Committee. COM(2005) 489 final. Annex. pp. 101–102.
14. EU Council (2003): Decision No. 3/2003 of the ACP-EC Council of Ministers on the use of resources from the long-term development envelope of the ninth EDF for the creation of a Peace Facility for Africa. http://eur-lex.europa.eu/legal-content/EN/TXT/PDF/?uri=CELEX:22003D0003(01)&from=EN (03/08/2016).
15. European Commission (2010): Annual report. The African Peace Facility 2009. https://ec.europa.eu/europeaid/sites/devco/files/annual-report-2009-african-peace-facility_en.pdf (02/08/2016).
16. Council of the European Union (2011): Three-Year Action Programme for the African Peace Facility, 2011–2013 (10th EDF). Annex. 6. http://www.europarl.europa.eu/meetdocs/2009_2014/documents/sede/dv/sede291111actionprogramme_/sede291111actionprogramme_en.pdf (12/11/2016).
17. European Commission (2011a): Annual report. The African Peace Facility 2010. https://ec.europa.eu/europeaid/sites/devco/files/annual-report-2010-african-peace-facility_en.pdf (02/08/2016).

18. SADC—European Community (2002): Regional Strategy Paper and Regional Indicative Programme. For the period 2002–2007. Annex 12. p. 54.
19. European Community—Region of Eastern and Southern Africa and the Indian Ocean (2008): Regional Strategy Paper and Regional Indicative Programme 2008–2013. p. 44. https://eeas.europa.eu/sites/eeas/files/east_africa_2008_2.pdf (03/07/2016).
20. European Community—Southern African Region (2008): Regional Strategy Paper and Regional Indicative Programme 2008–2013. p. IV. http://ec.europa.eu/development/icenter/repository/scanned_r7_rsp-2007-2013_en.pdf (04/07.2016).
21. Detailed figures have not been disclosed.
22. This assumption has been corroborated by a survey of experts who confirmed that external influence on regional security cooperation issues is comparably marginal in the SADC (Jaspert 2010: 337).
23. Gaotlhobogwe, Monkagedi (2007): SADC Military Organ Set For Historic Launch in Lusaka. *Mmegi Newspaper*. Volume 24, No. 116. Issue of 6 August 2007.
24. Interview with Jens Møller (Principal Administrator Africa-EU Partnership, African Peace Facility) at the European Commission's Directorate General for Development and Cooperation (05/03/2012).
25. SADC (2004c): Record of the Summit. Grand Baie, 16–17 August. Article 5.10.1.
26. SADC (2005): Record of the 26th Session of the Inter-State Defence and Security Committee (ISDSC). Boksburg, 11–14 July 2005. pp. 81–85.
27. European Commission (2011a): Annual report. The African Peace Facility 2010. p. 13. https://ec.europa.eu/europeaid/sites/devco/files/annual-report-2010-african-peace-facility_en.pdf (02/08/2016).
28. SADC (2007a): Memorandum of Understanding amongst the Southern African Development Community Member States on the Establishment of a Southern African Development Community Standby Brigade. Article 4.
29. SADC (2007a): Memorandum of Understanding amongst the Southern African Development Community Member States on the Establishment of a Southern African Development Community Standby Brigade. Articles 7, 1 and 2.
30. SADC (2007a): Memorandum of Understanding amongst the Southern African Development Community Member States on the Establishment of a Southern African Development Community Standby Brigade. Articles 7, 12.
31. SADC (2007a): Memorandum of Understanding amongst the Southern African Development Community Member States on the Establishment of a Southern African Development Community Standby Brigade. Articles 6, 8, 9, 11.

32. AU (2002): Protocol relating to the Establishment of a Peace and Security Council of the African Union. Article 13. https://www.au.int/sites/default/files/treaties/7781-file-protocol_peace_and_security.pdf (07/22/2016).
33. SADC (2008): SADC RPTC. Vision for the Future. Final Report of an Independent Study Commissioned by the Directorate Of the SADC Organ on Politics, Defence and Security Cooperation on the Vision of the Regional Peacekeeping Training Centre. Gaborone: SADC Secretariat. pp. 6–7.
34. SADC (2004b): Record of the Meeting of the Council of Ministers. Held in Grand Baie, 16–17 August.
35. SADC (2008): SADC RPTC. Vision for the Future. Final Report of An Independent Study Commissioned by the Directorate Of the SADC Organ on Politics, Defence and Security Cooperation on the Vision of the Regional Peacekeeping Training Centre. Gaborone: SADC Secretariat. p. 7.
36. SADC (2007a): Memorandum of Understanding amongst the Southern African Development Community Member States on the Establishment of a Southern African Development Community Standby Brigade. Article 13.
37. Republic of South Africa (2011): Building a Better World: The Diplomacy of Ubuntu. White Paper on South Africa's Foreign Policy. Final Draft. p. 21. https://www.gov.za/sites/default/files/foreignpolicy_0.pdf (12/11/2016).
38. Republic of South Africa (2014): South African Defence Review 2014. Chap. 7. p 5. http://www.gov.za/sites/www.gov.za/files/defencereview_2014_ch10-13.pdf (06/08/2016).
39. The PLANLEM is composed of military and civilian staff on secondment of the SADC member states on rotation. Today, it is the only permanent structure of the SSF and operates as an instrument under the ISDSC (Hull and Derblom 2009).
40. AU (2010): African Peace and Security Structure (APSA). 2010 Assessment Study. Zanzibar 2010. p. 40. http://www.securitycouncilreport.org/atf/cf/%7B65BFCF9B-6D27-4E9C-8CD3-CF6E4FF96FF9%7D/RO%20African%20Peace%20and%20Security%20Architecture.pdf (07/07/2016).
41. AU (2010): African Peace and Security Structure (APSA). 2010 Assessment Study. Zanzibar 2010. p. 40. http://www.securitycouncilreport.org/atf/cf/%7B65BFCF9B-6D27-4E9C-8CD3-CF6E4FF96FF9%7D/RO%20African%20Peace%20and%20Security%20Architecture.pdf (07/07/2016).
42. European Commission (2012a): Annual report. The African Peace Facility 2011. p. 27. https://ec.europa.eu/europeaid/sites/devco/files/annual-report-2011-african-peace-facility_en.pdf (05/08/2016).

43. Interview with Jens Møller (Principal Administrator Africa-EU Partnership, African Peace Facility) at the European Commission's Directorate General for Development and Cooperation (05/03/2012).
44. European Commission (2011b): Commission Decision of 29.07.2011 on an action to be financed under the African Peace Facility from the 10th European Development Fund—African Peace and Security Architecture Support Programme. C(2011)5379. p. 9.
45. European Commission (2014): Annual report. The African Peace Facility 2013. p. 31. http://www.africa-eu-partnership.org/sites/default/files/documents/ar2013_apf_web_0.pdf (10/11/2016).
46. SADC (2008): SADC RPTC. Vision for the Future. Final Report of an Independent Study Commissioned by the Directorate Of the SADC Organ on Politics, Defence and Security Cooperation on the Vision of the Regional Peacekeeping Training Centre. Gaborone: SADC Secretariat. pp. 6–7.
47. Roux, A. (2013): South Africa and the UN Intervention Brigade in the DRC. ISS Today. 24 April 2013. http://www.issafrica.org/iss-today/south-africa-and-the-un-intervention-brigade-in-the-drc (12/12/2016).
48. SADC (2008c): SADC RPTC. Vision for the Future. Final Report of An Independent Study Commissioned by the Directorate Of the SADC Organ on Politics, Defence and Security Cooperation on the Vision of the Regional Peacekeeping Training Centre. Gaborone: SADC Secretariat. p. 7.
49. SADC (2014b): Joint Media Release on the Handing Over of Accommodation to SADC Regional Peacekeeping Training Centre by the Government of the Federal Republic of Germany. p. 2. http://www.sadc.int/files/7713/9505/2070/HANDING_OVER_OF_ACCOMMODATION_TO_SADC_REGIONAL_PEACEKEEPING_TRAINING_CENTRE_2.pdf (12/10/2016).
50. Annex to an undisclosed cooperation agreement between the EU and the AU on the decision to support the African Training Centres in Peace in Security. p. 9.
51. European Commission (2012b): Commission Decision of 12/03/2012 on an action to be financed under the African Peace Facility from the 10th European Development Fund—Support to the African Training Centres in Peace and Security. C(2012) 1479. http://ec.europa.eu/europeaid/documents/aap/2012/aap-spe_2012_intra-acp_p2_en.pdf (10/12/2016).
52. SADC (2014a): Interview with Brigadier General Christopher Chella. In *The Peace Trainer*. Issue 3. SADC RPTC. p. 6.

REFERENCES

Aboagye, F. 2012. *A Stich in a Time Would Have Saved Nine. Operationalising the African Standby Force*. Policy Brief (34). Pretoria: Institute for Security Studies.

Adebajo, A. 2002. *Liberia's Civil War. Nigeria, ECOMOG, and Regional Security in West Africa*. London: Lynne Rienner Publishers.

Adelmann, M. 2012. *SADC—An Actor in International Relations? The External Relations of the Southern African Development Community*. Freiburg: Arnold-Bergstraesser-Institut.

Baker, D.-P., and S. Maeresera. 2009. SADCBRIG Intervention in SADC Member States: Reasons to Doubt. *African Security Review* 18 (1): 106–110.

Berman, E.G., and K.E. Sams. 2003. The Peacekeeping Potential of African Regional Organizations. In *Dealing with Conflict in Africa: The United Nations and Regional Organizations*, ed. J. Boulden, 35–77. New York, Basingstoke: Palgrave.

Bischoff, P.-H. 2006. Towards a Foreign Peacekeeping Commitment: South African Approaches to Conflict Resolution in Africa. In *South African Foreign Policy After Apartheid*, ed. W. Carlsnaes and P. Nel, 147–163. Midrand: Institut for Global Dialogue.

Brosig, M. 2011. The EU's Role in the Emerging Peace and Security Regime in Africa. *European Foreign Affairs Review* 16 (1): 107–122.

Cawthra, G., and A. van Nieuwkerk. 2004. *Regional Renaissance? Security in a Globalized World*. Maputo/Berlin: Friedrich Ebert Stiftung.

Chirwa, M., and C. Namangale. 2009. SADC Training Needs for Peace Support Operations: The Case for a Greater Role for the Regional Peacekeeping Training Centre. In *Furthering Southern African Integration: Proceedings of the 2008 FOPRISA Annual Conference*, ed. J.M. Kaunda and F. Zizhou, 159–169. Gaborone: Lightbooks.

Davies, O.V. 2014. SADC Standby Force: Preparation of Peacekeeping Personnel. *Conflict Trends* 2: 26–29.

de Coning, C. 1999. Exercise Blue Crane. A Unifying Moment for SADC. *Conflict Trends* 1: 19, 23.

de Coning, C. 2005. A Peacekeeping Stand-By System for SADC: Implementing the African Stand-by Force Framework in Southern Africa. In *People, States and Regions. Building a Collaborative Security Regime in Southern Africa*, ed. A. Hammerstad, 83–116. Braamfontein: South African Institute of International Affairs.

Franke, B. 2007. Military Integration in Southern Africa: The Example of SADC's Standby Brigade. In *South African Yearbook of International Affairs 2006/7*, ed. E. Sidiropoulos, 183–190. Johannesburg: South African Institute of International Affairs.

Franke, B. 2009. *Security Cooperation in Africa: A Reappraisal*. Boulder: Lynne Rienner.
Gaotlhobogwe, Monkagedi. 2007. SADC Military Organ Set for Historic Launch in Lusaka. *Mmegi Newspaper* 24 (116). Issue of 6th August 2007.
Gregory, S. 2000. The French Military in Africa: Past and Present. *African Affairs* 99: 435–448.
Hendricks, C., and T. Musavengana, (eds). 2010. *The Security Sector in Southern Africa*. Pretoria: Institute for Security Studies.
Hentz, J.J. 2004. State Collapse and Regional Contagion in Sub-Sahara Africa: Lessons for Zimbabwe. *Scientia Militaria* 32 (1): 143–156.
Hull, C., and M. Derblom. 2009. *Abandoning Frontline Trenches? Capabilities for Peace and Security in the SADC Region*. Stockholm: Swedish Defence Research Agency.
Jaspert, J. 2010. *Regionalismus im südlichen Afrika. Die Handels- und Sicherheitspolitik der SADC*. Wiesbaden: VS Verlag.
Jervis, R. 1978. Cooperation Under the Security Dilemma. *World Politics* 30 (2): 167–214.
Kinzel, W. 2007. *Afrikanische Sicherheitsarchitektur—ein aktueller Überblick*. GIGA Focus Afrika 1/2007. Hamburg: GIGA.
Klingebiel, S. 2005. Regional Security in Africa and the Role of External Support. *The European Journal of Development Research* 17 (3): 437–448.
Lautier, J. 2013. The SADC Standby Force. In *Africa Conflict Monthly Monitor*, ed. J. Hall, 68–71. Johannesburg: Consultancy Africa Intelligence.
Macaringue, P. 2007. Military Dimensions of Security Cooperation in the Southern African Development Community. In *Proceedings of the 2006 FOPRISA Conference*, ed. J.M. Kaunda, 115–127. Gaborone: Lightbooks.
Mandrup, T. 2009. South Africa and the SADC Stand-by Force. *Scientia Militaria, South African Journal of Military Studies* 37 (2): 1–24.
Motsamai, D. 2014. *SADC 2014–2015: Are South Africa and Zimbabwe Shaping the Organisation?* Policy Brief 70. Pretoria: Institute for Security Studies.
Nathan, L. 2012. *Community of Insecurity. SADC's Struggle for Peace and Security in Southern Africa*. Farnham: Ashgate.
Odén, B. 2000. The Southern Africa Region and the Regional Hegemon. In *National Perspectives on the New Regionalism in the South*, vol. 3, ed. B. Hettne, A. Inotai, and O. Sunkel, 242–264. London: Macmillan Press.
Oosthuizen, G.H. 2006. *The Southern African Development Community. The Organisation, Its Policies and Prospects*. Midrand: Institute for Global Dialogue.
Ressler V. 2007. *Die Perspektiven regionaler Integration im südlichen Afrika. Eine Analyse vor dem Hintergrund der einzelstaatlichen Interessen*. Frankfurt am Main: Peter Lang.

Salomon, K. 2009. *Konfliktmanagement durch ECOWAS und SADC. Die Rolle Nigerias und Südafrikas in subregionalen Interventionen: Ein Beitrag zum Frieden?* Saarbrücken: Südwestdeutscher Verlag für Hochschulschriften.
Sidiropoulos E., and Chevallier R. 2006. *The European Union and Africa Developing Partnerships for Peace and Security.* SAIIA Report, vol. 51. Johannesburg: South African Institute of International Affairs.
Sidiropoulos, E., and M. Meyn. 2006. *Creating Incentives for Reform: The EU Accession Process.* SAIIA Report, vol. 52. Johannesburg: South African Institute of International Affairs.
Stockholm International Peace Research Institute (SIPRI). 2010. *SIPRI Yearbook 2009. Armaments, Disarmament and International Security.* Solna: Stockholm International Peace Research Institute.
Tavares, R. 2010. *Regional Security. The Capacity of International Organisations.* New York: Routledge.
Tjønneland, E.N. 2006. *SADC and Donors—Ideals and Practices. From Gaborone to Paris and Back.* Gaborone: Botswana Institute for Development Policy Analysis.
Vale, P. 1996. Regional Security in Southern Africa. *Alternatives: Global, Local, Political* 21 (3): 363–391.
van Langenhove, L. 2012. *The EU as a Global Regional Actor in Security and Peace.* Bruges: UNU-CRIS.
van Nieuwkerk, A. 2011. The Regional Roots of the African Peace and Security Architecture: Exploring Centre-Periphery Relations. *South African Journal of International Affairs* 18 (2): 169–189.
Wallander, C.A., and R.O. Keohane. 1999. Risk, Threat, and Security Institutions. In *Imperfect Unions. Security Institutions Over Time and Space*, ed. H. Haftendorn, R.O. Keohane, and C.A. Wallander, 21–47. Oxford: Oxford University Press.
Williams, R. 1999. Challenges for South and Southern Africa Towards Non-Consensual Peace Mission? In *From Peacekeeping to Complex Emergencies. Peace Support Missions in Africa*, ed. J. Cilliers, and G. Mills, 153–174. Johannesburg: South African Institute of International Affairs.

Primary Sources

AU. 2002. Protocol Relating to the Establishment of a Peace and Security Council of the African Union. https://au.int/sites/default/files/treaties/7781-file-protocol_peace_and_security.pdf. Accessed 22 July 2016.
AU. 2010. African Peace and Security Structure (APSA). 2010 Assessment Study. Zanzibar 2010. http://www.securitycouncilreport.org/atf/cf/%7B65BFCF9B-6D27-4E9C-8CD3-CF6E4FF96FF9%7D/RO%20

African%20Peace%20and%20Security%20Architecture.pdf. Accessed 7 July 2016.
Council of the European Union. 2011. Three-Year Action Programme for the African Peace Facility, 2011–2013 (10th EDF). http://www.europarl.europa.eu/meetdocs/2009_2014/documents/sede/dv/sede291111actionprogramme_/sede291111actionprogramme_en.pdf. Accessed 11 Dec 2016.
European Commission. 2010. Annual Report. The African Peace Facility 2009. https://ec.europa.eu/europeaid/sites/devco/files/annual-report-2009-african-peace-facility_en.pdf. Accessed 8 Feb 2016.
European Commission. 2011a. Annual Report. The African Peace Facility 2010. https://ec.europa.eu/europeaid/sites/devco/files/annual-report-2010-african-peace-facility_en.pdf. Accessed 8 Feb 2016.
European Commission. 2011b. Commission Decision of 29.07.2011 on an Action to be Financed under the African Peace Facility from the 10th European Development Fund—African Peace and Security Architecture Support Programme. C (2011)5379.
European Commission. 2012a. Annual Report. The African Peace Facility 2011. https://ec.europa.eu/europeaid/sites/devco/files/annual-report-2011-african-peace-facility_en.pdf. Accessed 8 Aug 2016.
European Commission. 2012b. Commission Decision of 12/03/2012 on an Action to be Financed under the African Peace Facility from the 10th European Development Fund – Support to the African Training Centres in Peace and Security. C (2012) 1479. http://ec.europa.eu/europeaid/documents/aap/2012/aap-spe_2012_intra-acp_p2_en.pdf. Accessed 12 Oct 2016.
European Commission. 2014. Annual Report. The African Peace Facility 2013. http://www.africa-eupartnership.org/sites/default/files/documents/ar2013_apf_web_0.pdf. Accessed 11 Oct 2016.
European Community—Region of Eastern and Southern Africa and the Indian Ocean. 2008. Regional Strategy Paper and Regional Indicative Programme 2008–2013. https://eeas.europa.eu/sites/eeas/files/east_africa_2008_2.pdf. Accessed 7 Mar 2016.
EU Council. 2003. Decision No. 3/2003 of the ACP-EC Council of Ministers on the Use of Resources from the Long-Term Development Envelope of the Ninth EDF for the Creation of a Peace Facility for Africa. http://eur-lex.europa.eu/legal-content/EN/TXT/PDF/?uri=CELEX:22003D0003(01)&from=EN. Accessed 8 Mar 2016.
European Council. 2005. The EU and Africa: Towards a Strategic Partnership. Conclusions by the Heads of State and Government Meeting in the European Council, Brussels, 15–16 December 2005 (doc 15961/05).
Republic of South Africa. 1996. Defence in a Democracy. White Paper on National Defence for the Republic of South Africa. May 1996. http://

www.dod.mil.za/documents/WhitePaperonDef/whitepaper%20on%20 defence1996.pdf. Accessed 4 Dec 2016.
Republic of South Africa. 1999. White Paper on South African Participation in International Peace Missions. Pretoria. http://www.pmg.org.za/docs/2003/appendices/030326peace.ppt. Accessed 20 June 2016.
Republic of South Africa. 2011. Building a Better World: The Diplomacy of Ubuntu. White Paper on South Africa's Foreign Policy. Final Draft. https://gov.za/sites/default/files/foreignpolicy_0.pdf. Accessed 11 Dec 2016.
Republic of South Africa. 2014. South African Defence Review 2014. http://www.gov.za/sites/www.gov.za/files/defencereview_2014_ch10-13.pdf. Accessed 8 June 2016.
SADC. 2001. Protocol on Politics, Defence and Security Co-operation.
SADC. 2004a. Regional Indicative Strategic Development Plan. Gaborone: SADC Secretariat.
SADC. 2004b. Record of the Meeting of the Council of Ministers. Held in Grand Baie, 16th–17th Aug.
SADC. 2004c. Record of the Summit. Grand Baie, 16th–17th Aug.
SADC. 2004d. Strategic Indicative Plan for the Organ on Politics, Defence and Security Cooperation. Gaborone: SADC Secretariat.
SADC. 2005. Record of the 26th Session of the Inter-State Defence and Security Committee (ISDSC). Boksburg, 11th–14th July 2005.
SADC. 2006. Record of the Meeting of the Council of Ministers. Held in Maseru, 15–16 August 2006.
SADC. 2007. Memorandum of Understanding Amongst the Southern African Development Community Member States on the Establishment of a Southern African Development Community Standby Brigade.
SADC. 2008. SADC RPTC. Vision for the Future. Final Report of an Independent Study Commissioned by the Directorate of the SADC Organ on Politics, Defence and Security Cooperation on the Vision of the Regional Peacekeeping Training Centre. Gaborone: SADC Secretariat.
SADC. 2014a. Interview with Brigadier General Christopher Chella. In: *The Peace Trainer*. Issue 3. SADC RPTC.
SADC. 2014b. Joint Media Release on the Handing Over of Accommodation to SADC Regional Peacekeeping Training Centre by the Government of the Federal Republic of Germany. http://www.sadc.int/files/7713/9505/2070/HANDING_OVER_OF_ACCOMMODATION_TO_SADC_REGIONAL_PEACEKEEPING_TRAINING_CENTRE_2.pdf. Accessed 10 Dec 2016.
SADC—European Community. 2002. Regional Strategy Paper and Regional Indicative Programme. For the Period 2002–2007.

CHAPTER 8

The Southern African Power Pool: An Electrifying Project with Untapped Potential

A major part of regional infrastructure cooperation in the SADC involves the energy sector and in particular the field of electricity—especially power[1] trading and transmission.[2] This issue has become very important for the regional organisation during the past two decades, although international electricity cooperation is not an entirely new phenomenon in Southern Africa. It actually dates back to the time of colonialism. Early efforts in this regard led to long-term contracts on electricity trade between individual countries. However, today these arrangements are reminiscent of bilateral cooperation rather than of institutionalised regional cooperation embedded in a broader framework of regionalism (Isaksen and Tjønneland 2001: 39; Tshombe 2008).

The end of Apartheid in South Africa implied a change in political and structural preconditions in the SADC region. This paved the way for a more comprehensive approach to the problem of regional electricity shortages on the one hand and excess supply generation on the other. Regional cooperation led to the foundation of the Southern African Power Pool (SAPP) as a SADC body in 1995. Within the framework of the SAPP, the Short-Term Energy Market (STEM) was introduced as a central electricity trading institution in April 2001. The latter was succeeded by the Day Ahead Market (DAM), a more competitive market that started to operate in 2009. Both markets constituted the vital centrepiece of the SAPP at their time of existence. Besides, the SAPP addresses other important tasks such as coordinating its members' energy policies and the construction of power generation capacities in the

© The Author(s) 2018
J. Muntschick, *The Southern African Development Community (SADC) and the European Union (EU)*,
https://doi.org/10.1007/978-3-319-45330-9_8

267

region, maintaining and extending the regional power grid, and creating common regional standards of quality and supply.[3]

This chapter aims to analyse the emergence, dynamics and effectiveness of institutionalised regional electricity cooperation in the SADC with a focus on recent developments in the SAPP and performance of the STEM and the DAM.

8.1 REGIONAL IMBALANCES AND POWER SHORTAGES: THE DEMAND FOR REGIONAL ELECTRICITY COOPERATION

Access to electricity and security of power supply are vital needs for individual households as well as for the national economies of entire states. A well-functioning power system with sufficient electricity generation capacities is of strategic importance. This is because it not only is an essential part of a country's infrastructure but also affects crucial issue areas such as the economy and security. Moreover, it is impossible to enhance socio-economic development without taking care of adequate energy and electricity supply.

8.1.1 General Logic of Demand for Institutionalised Regional Electricity Cooperation

Generally speaking, structural demand for institutionalised regional electricity cooperation in every single country ultimately stems from its net electricity balance (i.e. national power generation in relation to national power consumption) on the one hand and from the nature of its prevailing pattern of electricity interdependence with neighbouring countries on the other. Given the fact that electricity is a tradable good and that some countries are (potential) electricity importers (i.e. consumers) or exporters (i.e. suppliers), the analogy between electricity and merchandise trade becomes clear. Accordingly, a country's demand for institutionalised regional electricity cooperation—in other words, a regional electricity regime—is based on its aspired absolute benefits from such an interconnected regional power grid and integrated regional electricity market with better trading opportunities.

The specific benefits from an institutionalised regional electricity market (i.e. a regional power pool) are as follows: All participating countries can expect to profit from better electricity supply security since combined systems are less vulnerable to disturbance in transmission lines or unexpected outages of power plants. Furthermore, an integrated regional power system fosters economic efficiency with regard to electricity generation because it offers better economies of scale compared with a smaller national market. More importantly, a power pool helps its members to reduce costs to meet national peek demands in electricity consumption and to diminish losses resulting from excess production. This is because ideally the countries can simply trade surplus electricity to members with surplus demand or insufficient electricity generation capacity. For those countries that are in the position of being importers of electricity, additional benefits stem from externalising investments for new power plants or from lower costs for providing operating reserve facilities or from both. Furthermore, individual countries could reduce the risks and costs of planning and constructing new electricity generation capacities by communitising such expenses on all participants of the power pool. Electricity-exporting countries stand to benefit from lowering costs for existing spinning reserves and from revenues by selling such excess power (Lopes and Kundishora 2000: 214; Matinga 2004: 92–93).

Hence, a power pool with an institutionalised electricity market does not only provide better electricity supply security in its member states but contributes ideally to cost-effective production, an optimised use of power generation and transmitting infrastructure, and eventually lower consumer prices.

8.1.2 Demand for a Regional Electricity Regime in Southern Africa

Early demand for institutionalised regional electricity cooperation in Southern Africa occurred within the old SADCC when some black majority–ruled countries engaged in coordinating the planning, development and strengthening of power transmission lines among each other in order to avoid and reduce dependency on electricity imports from South Africa. For this purpose, the organisation's member states established a Technical and Administrative Unit (TAU) under the umbrella of the SADCC in 1980. Its major tasks were to act as coordinating agency for the energy sector and to attract donor funding in order to initiate and promote their regional projects.[4] The outcomes were quite remarkable: The SADCC was successful in raising donors' funds, particularly from Europe and the US, and acquired altogether about $155 million USD by the early 1990s. These externally provided financial means had a catalysing impact on the SADCC's regional electricity cooperation projects because they allowed the organisation to realise two important interconnection projects: a 66-kilovolt (kV) power line to connect southern Zambia with northern Botswana and a 220-kV transmission line between Zimbabwe and Botswana which allowed the latter to substitute its electricity imports from South Africa with power generated in Zambia and Zimbabwe (Raskin and Lazarus 1991: 161–165, 173).

A severe drought in the SADC region in 1992 caused extensive nation- and region-wide power shortages due to dwindling hydro-electricity generation capacities. The natural disaster boosted the states' demand for regional electricity cooperation and in this way had a decisive and catalysing effect on institution building in the SADC. This is because, in view of the drought's negative effects, many governments started to realise that there was an uneven distribution of power generation resources in the SADC region: The enormous hydro-electricity reserves and large power stations were in the north (e.g. the Kariba and Inga Dam), and the major coal deposits and most of the thermal power plants were in the south (particularly in the Gauteng province of South Africa). It became clear that these resources could be turned to good account for consumers and national energy security by pooling and improving regional interconnection (Bowen et al. 1999; Merven et al. 2010).

Although several older transnational power transmission lines had already been in place in the SADC by the mid-1990s, there was still an insufficient level of regional interconnectedness. Moreover, there was no regional institution for international short-term electricity exchange that could be used as a fall-back option in case of unexpected national energy shortages. The same applied for the long-term bilateral contracts on cross-border electricity trade that a few SADC countries had concluded before the mid-1990s. However, these bilateral contracts enabled the parties to trade electricity only on the basis of prearranged and strictly limited volumes. Therefore, these agreements were far too inflexible to provide an adequate solution to a country that experienced unexpected peaks in power demand. Moreover, they could not protect an importer against unforeseen problems occurring in their supply partner, such as station outages, system failures, power line disruptions or even insufficient generation capacity (UNECA 2004: 35–37; ECA 2009: 8, 19–23; Bowen et al. 1999: 187).

Against this background, an institutionalised regional electricity regime that facilitated short-term electricity trading as well as a better interconnection of the SADC's national power systems became high on the agenda for all SADC countries concerned (UNECA 2004: 39; Rugoyi 1998: 1998). The country-specific demand for institutionalised regional electricity cooperation in the SADC can be deduced from structural characteristics based on the ratio of electricity generation and consumption of individual member countries at the time prior to the first regional arrangement.

Several of the organisation's (mainland) members had insufficient national electricity generation capacities (measured in megawatts, MW) in relation to their levels of national consumption in the early years of the new SADC. In 1996, the countries with constant surplus demand were, in descending order, Zimbabwe (−388 MW), Botswana (−128 MW), Lesotho (−76 MW), Swaziland (−75 MW), Mozambique (−36 MW), Namibia (−14 MW) and even Tanzania (−1 MW).[5] For structural reasons, these countries had a strong demand for a regional electricity regime with enhanced trading facilities in the SADC. They faced chronic shortages of national power generation and, as net importers of electricity, were in quite a vulnerable position. For this reason, these countries had a strong preference for an institutional solution on a regional level since that not only promised individually improved energy security but also helped to avoid one-sided dependencies on a single supplier or specific power line (Bowen et al. 1999).

On the other hand, a number of SADC members had oversized national electricity generation capacities and produced considerable—even vast—amounts of surplus electricity on a regular basis for years. Back in 1996, the countries with excess production were, in descending order, South Africa (+2,160 MW), former Zaire (+1,985 MW), Zambia (+604 MW), Angola (+145 MW) and to a lesser extent Malawi (+7 MW) as well.[6] With regard to the figures, it becomes clear that, for structural reasons, these countries' demand for enhanced regional cooperation, improved interconnection and an institutionalised regional electricity market is for the most part rooted in market-seeking motives since they were (potential) net exporters of electricity. They regarded electricity as a tradable good that could be exported like any other consumer good. It provided high profits under the condition that national power generation was a comparably cheap undertaking (which it actually was because of large and easily accessible coal deposits).

Owing to its vast amount of surplus power generation during the 1990s, South Africa in particular most emphatically demanded a regional electricity regime—preferably tailored to its own national standards. Moreover, the RSA expected that an expansion of the regional power grid would serve its national export intentions by opening trading opportunities and facilitating (additional) electricity trade. Pretoria's preference does not come as a surprise given that the country's parastatal Eskom, by far the SADC region's largest power producer with an operating capacity of 22 heavily subsidised power plants,[7] was a source of comparably cheap electricity because of its enormous volumes of surplus power generation at that time (Daniel and Lutchman 2006: 497–500).[8] For similar reasons, export-oriented Zaire was keen to participate in a regional energy regime. This is because the country expected that membership in a SADC-wide power pool could provide resources for a reinforcement of its transmission lines to Southern Africa and thereby allow larger electricity exports to Zimbabwe—and eventually South Africa in the future—via Zambia.[9]

Although a few long-term bilateral contracts on electricity trade were in place, there was still an increasing and pressuring demand for additional short-term access to electricity in many (of these) SADC states during the mid-1990s. This was rooted in more frequent blackouts, operational problems of (dilapidated) power generation systems and a lack of national reserve or spinning capacities.[10] The prevailing disequilibria and imbalances of the electricity situation in the SADC region during these years were reinforced by seasonal circumstances and periodical peeks in consumer consumption (e.g. caused by, among other things, the growing use of air conditioners and electric heaters), lack of adequate power transmission lines[11] and uncoordinated national energy policies (Rugoyi 1998).

There were also long-term energy-related factors that fuelled demand for regional cooperation: A number of scientific energy and electricity consumption projections from the 1990s forecasted an exponentially increasing electricity demand for the SADC region and its member states for the next two or three decades to come. These studies expected in parallel to growing (urban) populations and national GDP an increasing energy intensity and electricity consumption in the SADC economies, particularly in the industry sector (e.g. electronic machinery and other equipment), the commercial and services sector (e.g. heating, cooling, and electronic equipment), the transport sector (e.g. rail) and not least due to growing access to electricity in the urban and rural residential sector (e.g. cooking, air conditioning, and electronic devices) (Merven et al. 2010: 18–22; Rosnes and Vennemo 2009: 3–4).

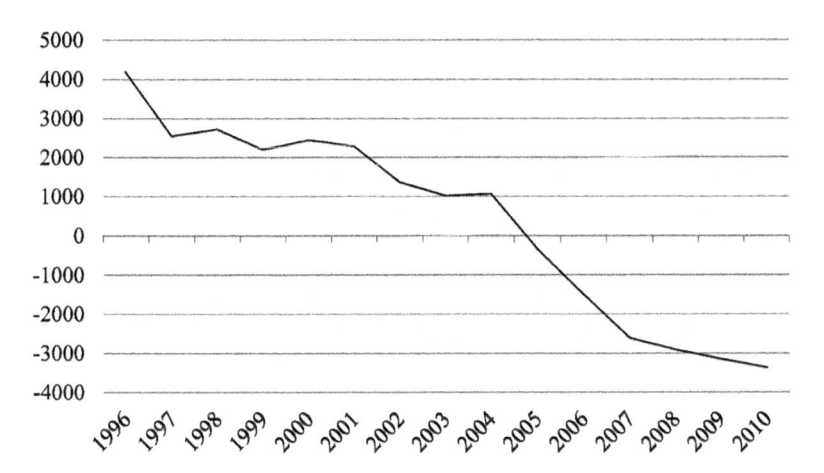

Fig. 8.1 Forecast of the SADC's internal electricity generation capacity (in MW) for 1996–2010

Against this background, the electricity demand growth rate for the SADC in total was expected to amount to an average of 2.0–5.7% per year for the period of 1996–2020, with Mozambique, Angola, Namibia and Lesotho producing the strongest growth rates with values between 3.4% and 13.1% per year (Bowen et al. 1999: 187). Later projections expected the total energy demand in the SADC to be about 2.5 times larger in 2030 than in 2005 and forecasted particularly strong increases in electricity consumption in Mozambique, Zambia and South Africa (Merven et al. 2010: 19–22). However, this growing electricity demand in the SADC and its member states stood in contrast to the forecasts on regional electricity generation capacities. Official sources expected a growing mismatch between national electricity production and consumption in the region that implied steadily decreasing internal surplus generation capacities for the SADC as a whole (Fig. 8.1).[12]

The graph illustrates that the SADC's once-large internal surplus generation capacity was expected to diminish constantly over the years—and most likely to turn into a negative internal surplus generation capacity from 2005 at the latest. Experts predicted that the SADC was to face a very critical situation by 2010 if no coordinated action took place in terms of exploiting further regional electricity trade and generation potentials (Lopes and Kundishora 2000: 213).

Furthermore, important demand-driving factors in (potential) participants of a regional electricity regime in the SADC were based on the expected financial profits. Profound scientific research and projections that focussed on the absolute financial gains related to membership in a SADC power pool provided sound calculations for the near future in this respect: Studies from the early 1990s expected the potential savings of an integrated regional approach to power sector development in the SADC to amount to about 20% for the period from 1995 to 2010 compared with the costs that were to arise if countries would individually develop their national power sectors (Bowen et al. 1999: 193–196; Matinga 2004: 92). A study conducted by a World Bank–funded think tank in the mid-1990s predicted that savings of up to $100 million USD could be realised in a centralised and competitive power pool in lieu of (existing) bilateral trading agreements. In the same years, estimates of South African economists even estimated $130 million USD in regional savings in the event that an encompassing electricity regime would materialise (Sebitosi and Okou 2010: 1450).

Some projections revealed considerable potential for intra-regional electricity trade in the SADC, especially in the north-south direction from the large hydro plants in the DRC to the mining and manufacturing industries in South Africa and Zimbabwe (Rosnes and Vennemo 2009: 46; Tshombe 2008: 61–78). A study from the late 1990s expected annual gains from regional electricity trade amounting to $0.8 million USD for Botswana, $3.3 million USD for the DRC, $10.5 million USD for Mozambique, $2.5 million USD for Namibia, $30.4 million USD for South Africa, $19 million USD for Zambia and $22.6 million USD for Zimbabwe under the condition that a regional electricity market was created (Bowen et al. 1999: 196). According to later scenarios, as much as $1.1 billion USD in annual energy costs could be saved by enhancing regional electricity integration in the SADC (Ranganathan and Foster 2011). Regional costs for infrastructure and particularly power plant construction could be reduced by $3 billion USD over a 20-year period if coordinated regional planning would prevail over countries' individual utility expansion (Sebitosi and Okou 2010: 1451).

In sum, the SADC countries' structurally motivated demand together with the projections and conclusions of a variety of official statements and scientific research studies can be condensed to a common denominator: All SADC states with electricity generation imbalances could improve their national energy security and export opportunities and generate additional socio-economic development by creating a common regional electricity market that facilitated short-term electricity trade across borders. This includes connecting their national power grids within the regional framework of an institutionalised common power pool. In political science language, the latter institution would represent a regional "club good" and provide joint gains from which only participant member states could benefit (Muntschick 2013b: 115–117).

8.1.3 Interim Summary and Situation Structure

Against this background, the genuine problematic situation in the issue area of electricity resembled an assurance game in the SADC region during the early and mid-1990s. Regional cooperation in the form of pooling national power systems with the help of regulative institutions offered prospects for absolute gains for every participant actor with a power generation imbalance—provided that other interconnected/interconnectable countries followed the same cooperative strategy as well. In contrast, a strategy of defection—that implies a national autarky-policy related to power generation and to renounce regional power trading opportunities—was significantly more costly than a coordinated regional solution. This is because separate national approaches implied, among other things, lengthy processes for power plant construction—measures that did not help in the acute situation (Fig. 8.2).

Since the problematic regional situation resembled an assurance game, there was a distinct need for common institutions in order to initialise and perpetuate cooperative behaviour of all actors involved. According to theory, one would expect that such governing institutions are unlikely to be very strong or coercive in character since the participants would not have any incentives to defect from a cooperative strategy once a mutually benefiting regional solution (here, an energy regime) was in place. Hence, states are likely to agree upon rather weak institutions that primarily serve coordinating purposes and ensure cooperation by, for example, providing information and monitoring mechanisms.

Fig. 8.2 Problematic situation in view of the SAPP

		SADC Country B	
		Autarky	Electricity Regime
SADC Country A	Autarky	1 / 1	3 / 2
	Electricity Regime	2 / 3	4 / 4

8.2 ASYMMETRIC INTRA-REGIONAL ELECTRICITY INTERDEPENDENCE IN THE SADC REGION: SOUTH AFRICA HOLDING THE PLUG

The pattern of intra- and extra-regional electricity interdependence in the SADC region and its member states can be best derived from analysing the countries' power generation capacities together with their intra- and extra-regional electricity import and export flows (de Lombaerde et al. 2008: 159). Given important factors such as donor contributions for electricity cooperation, the picture in the SADC reveals that South Africa and the EU are in key positions as regional and external actors, respectively.

8.2.1 Asymmetric Intra-Regional Electricity Interdependence

The pattern of intra-regional electricity interdependence in the SADC region was strongly asymmetric in character when the member states started their first efforts to enhance regional cooperation and establish a Southern African Power Pool. During the mid-1990s, as for many decades before, South Africa was clearly the region's powerhouse—or, literally, power plant. This was due to the country's large power generation capacity, constant surplus electricity production and key position as the most important supplier of electricity, at least for the southern part of the SADC region[13]. South

Africa's special status dates back to the time of Apartheid when the country's national power utility, Eskom, pursued a massive expansion of its power generation capacity in order to promote energy self-sufficiency and guarantee national energy security. This brought Eskom not only the title as Africa's largest energy utility but also a position among the top five electricity producers in the world (Daniel and Lutchman 2006: 497–500; Horvei 1998).

In terms of electricity generation, South Africa's Eskom surpassed all other power utilities in the SADC region with an available net installed capacity of about 32,000 MW back in 1996. This was more than ten times the installed capacity of (former) Zaire (2,480 MW), Mozambique (~ 2,000 MW) and Zambia (1,774 MW)—the three next biggest electricity producers in the region.[14] Since Eskom provided its surplus electricity at a cheap price at that time, it was for several neighbouring countries' power utilities (e.g. in Swaziland or Lesotho) not cost-effective to build (additional) power generation facilities on their own, not least because their overall national demand in general had always been very modest.[15] This contributed to intra-regional asymmetry and made several countries considerably dependent on electricity imports from Eskom and South Africa.

This distinct asymmetry in intra-SADC electricity relations also prevailed in terms of physical structures such as transnational power transmission lines and interconnections in the region. The national power utilities of nine SADC member states were, to varying degrees, physically interconnected by the mid-1990s. The strength of interconnectedness between different countries can be derived from the number of existing power transmission lines on the one hand and their operating voltage (which corresponds to the lines' electricity transfer capacity in megawatts) on the other. This leads to the conclusion that South Africa's power utility, Eskom, most obviously was in the centre of the SADC's interconnected power grid. Pretoria maintained a radial network of comparably strong power lines to all (!) of its neighbouring countries and therefore was as the "power hub" in an incomplete[16] spoke in a regional key position. After all, the remaining SADC members—with the exception of Zimbabwe—were directly connected to only one or two neighbouring countries (Hofmann 2009: 69). Given the SADC countries' net balance of electricity generation and consumption together with the specific pattern of transnational power transmission lines, it becomes clear that Lesotho, Swaziland and Namibia were, for structural reasons, in the most distinct relation of dependence since they were not only demanders of electricity but also interconnected only with South Africa (ECA 2009: 9–13; Horvei 1998).

This pattern of asymmetric intra-regional electricity interdependence based on power generation capacities and power transmission lines gives evidence to conclude that in this issue area South Africa was in a relative power position in the SADC region. The fact that South Africa's Eskom owned essential parts of the subcontinent's electricity infrastructure and the utility's prominent role as the SADC's most important producer of (surplus) electricity substantiate this evidence. Therefore, owing to its dominant power position, South Africa is not only expected to be a major driving force for regional electricity cooperation in the SADC region but also likely to assert its national preferences with respect to the institutional design of a regional electricity regime.

8.2.2 Extra-Regional Electricity Interdependence of the SADC

Extra-regional electricity relations of the SADC countries with external actors can best be described as insignificant. This is because the region and its member states were—and actually are—not dependent on electricity imports from overseas, nor did a noteworthy, interconnected external export market for potential trade in surplus electricity ever exist.[17] Because physical or trade-based extra-regional electricity relations in SADC countries have been virtually non-existent, for plain structural reasons neither external actors nor competing extra-regional policy alternatives for electricity cooperation outside the region were available. Hence, there were no extra-regional actors that were in a position to interfere with the SADC countries' initial efforts to advance institutionalised regional electricity cooperation back in the mid-1990s (Muntschick 2013b).

While the SADC and its member states have been dependent neither on extra-regional electricity imports nor on an important external market for making profits by selling excess energy, the organisation nevertheless has been strongly dependent on external funding since its foundation in 1992. This applies also for regional energy cooperation because the SADC has traditionally attracted considerable amounts of donor funding from external actors for regional projects in this issue area (Tjønneland 2006). The old SADCC received financial support from Europe and the USA for the most part, particularly for the renewal, improvement and expansion of its regional power transmission lines during the time of Apartheid (Raskin and Lazarus 1991).

The SADC experienced similar sympathy from overseas in this respect: From the late 1990s to 2006, several external actors—notably the United States Agency for International Development (USAID), the Development Bank of Southern Africa (DBSA) and the World Bank—supported regional electricity cooperation efforts in the SADC by financing feasibility studies and providing technical assistance to the nascent SAPP and its Coordination Centre (UNECA 2004: 41). At about the same time, the EU recognised this subject as well and became increasingly involved. Brussels bundled its development assistance for energy and electricity cooperation by launching its new Energy Initiative for Poverty Eradication and Sustainable Development in 2002. The latter's overall intention was to improve energy security and access to electricity in developing countries, particularly in the ACP states.[18]

However, the EU's plan started to materialise only a few years later when the European Commission proposed the establishment of an ACP-EU Energy Facility (AEF) in 2004. This first AEF had a total budget of €220 million for the period of 2006–2009 and was financed under the framework of the 9th EDF. A central objective of the European programme was to "improve governance and framework conditions in the energy sector at regional, national and local levels."[19] Part of the money was explicitly earmarked for supporting institutionalised regional energy integration within regional initiatives, such as the SAPP in Southern Africa, and for improving power lines and cross-border connections. The second AEF, financed under the 10th EDF, contained similar intentions and provisions and had been endowed with a budget of €200 million for the period of 2009–2013.[20] Although most of the AEF's money had been neither earmarked for regional electricity initiatives and related governing mechanisms (such as power pools) nor intended to be channelled entirely to ACP countries in Southern Africa, it nevertheless provided considerable financial incentives for countries to participate—and remain engaged—in a regional electricity regime like the SAPP.

In regard to the SADC, significant external support for institutionalised electricity cooperation came not only from the EU but also from several European countries, namely the Scandinavian countries. The available data[21] on the inflow of external funding to the SAPP demonstrates that extra-regional actors contributed quite significantly to the power pool's annual budgets and total assets (Fig. 8.3).

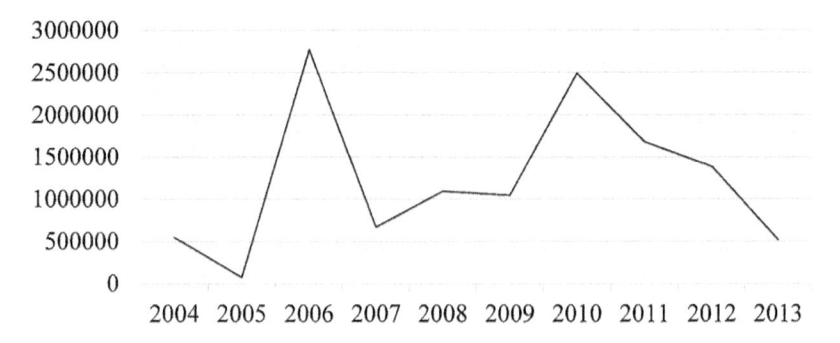

```
3000000
2500000
2000000
1500000
1000000
500000
0
     2004 2005 2006 2007 2008 2009 2010 2011 2012 2013
```

Fig. 8.3 Inflow of external funding to the SAPP (in USD)

Altogether, the inflow of external funding available to the SAPP in absolute figures amounted to sums between less than $100,000 USD and more than $2.7 million USD per year during the period under observation (cf. Fig. 8.3). In order to enhance its visibility in the donors' community and attract more external funding, the SAPP started to convene regular donor meetings since the turn of the millennium. On such occasions—taking place in 2001, 2005, 2009 and 2012—the power pool presented itself to the international donors' community in order to report on its activities and clarify its priority electricity cooperation projects. This strategy seems to have worked out: The inflow of external funds increased significantly every year after a donors' convention took place (Muntschick 2013b: 123–124).

The importance of external funding for the SAPP becomes even more apparent if one looks at how much this money has actually contributed to the power pool's total assets. The following table provides profound insights.

During the period observed, external funding contributed a minimum share of 12% and a maximum share of 46% to the SAPP's total assets. Since 2008, the share of external funding has turned to a steady level of a good 20% (cf. Fig. 8.4). These figures give good reasons to argue that external financial support has been an important pillar for institutionalised regional electricity cooperation in the SADC—at least for the past decade (Muntschick 2013b: 123).

Taking this considerable degree of external donors' funding into account, one can conclude that for structural reasons the SADC showed

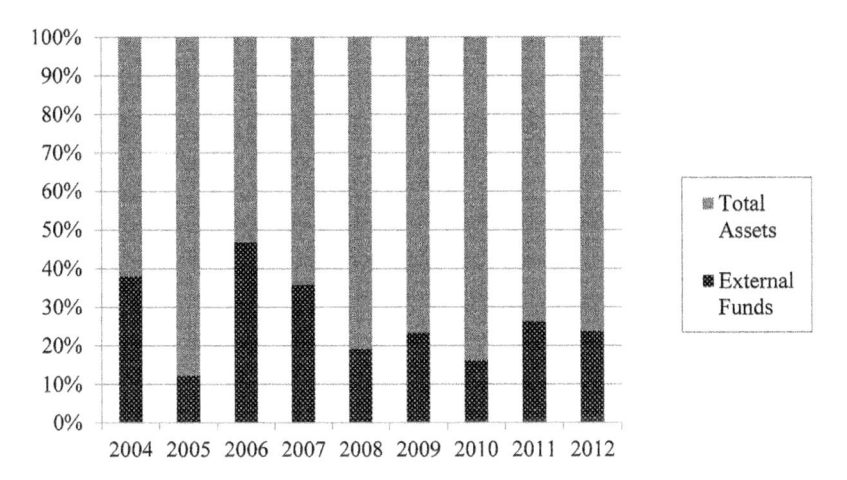

Fig. 8.4 Contribution of external funding to the SAPP's total assets

a pattern of significant asymmetric extra-regional interdependence with external actors (namely European donors) in the issue area of regional electricity cooperation. This relation was rather marginal during the mid-1990s but became increasingly important from 2006 onwards. Therefore, the EU and other European donors are in a position to exert influence on the establishment, design and effectiveness of recent and planned regional electricity cooperation projects in the SADC and the SAPP. However, this form of external impact is assumed to be positive. This is because it relates to financial contributions that facilitate institutionalised regional cooperation by lowering the costs of cooperation and institution-building (or maintenance) for the actors on a regional level (i.e. increasing the joint gains of cooperation). This altruistic type of external influence by means of support could shift the inherent structure of the genuine problematic situation towards a more cooperation-conducive type of game (i.e. a coordination game with distributive effects).

8.3 The Southern African Power Pool and Its Trading Platforms: Powered by External Funding?

The SADC countries' growing demand for institutionalised regional electricity cooperation led to the adoption of the Southern African Power Pool Inter-Utility Memorandum of Understanding

(SAPP-IMoU) by SADC's national power utilities and the subsequent Intergovernmental Memorandum of Understanding (IMoU). Both IMoUs express the need for a regional electricity regime for the purpose of improving regional energy security by facilitating intra-regional electricity trade, interconnecting the national power-grids and coordinating national energy policies. The official documents demonstrate the involved countries' commitment to regional electricity cooperation under the provisions of the SADC Treaty.[22] In a nutshell, both IMoUs call for an expansion of regional energy trading and the pooling of national power systems, ultimately leading to the birth of the SAPP in 1995.

8.3.1 Negotiations and Design of the SAPP's Institutional Framework

Against the background of the aforementioned problematic energy situation in the region, it was initially the national power utilities from SADC's mainland countries that developed the first agreement on institutionalised regional electricity cooperation: the SAPP-IMoU. Since all national power utilities were parastatals at that time, it was after all the involved countries that empowered their own power utilities to pursue their national interests during the inter-utility negotiations on the governing institutional framework for regional electricity cooperation. Since all of these power utilities recognised the future individual and joint benefits of a regional power pool in terms of reducing national costs of power generation and improving system reliability and energy security, there were no notable conflicting interests on how to specify such a framework's general provisions, principles and objectives. Because of this broad regional consensus, the national power utilities, after only a few meetings, agreed on the SAPP-IMoU's key contents and signed the agreement on 7 December 1994 (Rugoyi 1998; Tshombe 2008: 84–86).

Accordingly, the SAPP-IMoU's central objective was "to facilitate the establishment of the Southern African Power Pool (SAPP) which in turn has the objective to provide reliable and economical electric supply to the consumers of each of the SAPP Members consistent with reasonable utilisation of natural resources."[23] For this purpose, Article 1 of the IMoU set the basic principles and operating guidelines for the SAPP that aimed at (a) the coordination of and the cooperation in the planning and operation of the various systems to minimise costs while maintaining reliability and (b) the full recovery of costs and the equitable sharing of the resulting benefits.[24]

Furthermore, the SAPP-IMoU specified the envisaged power pool's operating principles and the responsibilities of its members. It stipulated its organisational structure and decision-making procedures with the SAPP Executive Committee as the central governing organ and with several subcommittees for various tasks (management, operating, planning and environment). In addition, the SAPP-IMoU called for the establishment of a SAPP Coordination Centre for the purpose of coordinating the power utilities' day-to-day operations and making the power pool work.[25]

After the SAPP-IMoU had been signed, the member states' national governments followed suit and concluded a similar agreement with virtually the same content. This second agreement, known as IMoU, was signed by seven SADC members on 28 August 1995 after it had been approved by the SADC Council and the mandated Energy Ministers a few days earlier.[26] The IMoU became operative in January 1996 and led to the establishment of the SAPP as a regional institution under the umbrella of the SADC in the same year. It therefore represents the central agreement for institutionalised regional cooperation in the issue area of electricity in the SADC.[27]

Since the SAPP-IMoU had been the blueprint for the later IMoU, there is little need to focus on its history or the details of inter-state bargaining that possibly preceded its conclusion, especially since there is in fact no evidence of any controversial negotiation process. Official documents corroborate this assumption. There is only one statement in a short paragraph that the SADC Council simply approved the IMoU by consensus.[28] Furthermore, there is no evidence that extra-regional actors from overseas became involved in the elaboration of the IMoU and the founding process of the SAPP at any time. For these reasons, the focus of analysis shall henceforth be on how the SAPP as an institution was conceptualised and how its core projects progressed.

The SAPP has been designed as a cooperative pool among equal partners. Its key vision is to develop a fully competitive electricity market in the SADC region as soon as possible. The pool points out that its major objectives in this context include the "development of a world class, robust, safe, efficient, reliable and stable interconnected electrical system in the southern African region", to "coordinate and enforce common regional standards of quality of supply" and the "measurement and monitoring of system performance." By these means, the SAPP committed itself not only to improve regional energy security in the SADC but also to "provide reliable and economical electricity supply to the consumers of each of the SAPP members" [29] as well.

The strong institutional relationship between the SAPP and the SADC is of utmost importance for the pool's functionality and has been codified in the IMoU. The latter stipulates that the SAPP was to be embedded in the SADC's organisational framework and emphasises that the agreements concerning the power pool have to be consistent with the provisions of the SADC Treaty.[30] While in practice the SAPP is managed through the SADC Secretariat, it is the energy ministers of the member states who ultimately are responsible for strategic policymaking and grand decisions on issues concerning the power pool. However, daily operating routines in the context of electricity cooperation were decided to be carried out by the members' national power utilities on their own (UNECA 2004: 40; ECA 2009: 28). With the pool's decision-making procedures being based on consensus and all operating partners having equal voting rights, the SAPP is clearly of intergovernmental character. The Coordination Centre is responsible for exchanging information, monitoring the pool operation and paying attention to the members' commitment to the agreements. It is the SAPP's only organ with a touch of supranationality but it lacks any significant competences (Muntschick 2013b: 127).[31]

The following power utilities were the founding members of the SAPP (Table 8.1).

In this context, it is noteworthy that Zaire already became a member of the SAPP in 1996 although the country obtained SADC membership only one year later. In order to understand this peculiarity, it is important to reflect on South Africa's national energy strategy. The Cape Republic wanted Zaire to become part of a regional electricity regime because Kinshasa's vast hydro-electric power generation potential could possibly supply the SADC region, and especially South Africa, with its surplus power—in particular, as soon as the regional demand of the rest of the SADC exceeded the available generation capacities.[32] Therefore, it was first and foremost Pretoria that urged for an official cooperation between SADC members and (then) Zaire in the issue area of electricity within the framework of the SAPP. The South African initiative was crowned with success because a paragraph declaring the SADC's desire for institutionalising regional electricity cooperation with Zaire found explicit expression in the IMoU and finally was approved by the SADC Council.[33]

Table 8.1 The SAPP members (1996)

Country	Name of power utility
Angola	Empresa Nacional de Electrcidade (ENE)
Botswana	Botswana Power Corporation (BPC)
DRC (Zaire)	Societe Nationale d'Electricite (SNEL)
Lesotho	Lesotho Electricity Company (LEC)
Malawi	Elcctricity Supply Commission of Malawi (ESCOM)
Mozambique	Electricidade de Mozambique (EDM)
Namibia	South West Africa Water and Electricity Corporation (SWAWEK)
South Africa	South Africa's Electricity Supply Commission (Eskom)
Swaziland	Swaziland Electricity Board (SEB)
Tanzania	Tanzania Electricity Supply Company (Tanesco)
Zambia	Zambia Electricity Supply Corporation (ZESCO)
Zimbabwe	Zimbabwe Electricity Supply Authority (ZESA)

Moreover, South Africa played a decisive role in shaping the Operating Guidelines of the SAPP. These define, among other things, the specific regulations for power plant operation, wheeling of electricity, frequency and safety standards as well as the sharing of costs. According to experts, Pretoria was able to assert itself in this regard and framed the SAPP's most important norms and standards according to its own national interests (i.e. Eskom's standards). This applied most clearly with regard to wheeling frequency[34] and metering systems (Tshombe 2008). It culminated in the institutionalisation of an "Eskom Control Area" within the SAPP where the power utilities of Botswana, Lesotho, Namibia, Mozambique and Swaziland fell under the control of Eskom's monitoring and tie-line control systems regarding transnational power flows (Rugoyi 1998: 435–436). This strong South African influence on the design of the SAPP and its Operating Guidelines does not come as a surprise, because most transmission lines, interconnectors and hubs of the SAPP's power network are on South African soil and operated by its national power utility (Hammons 2011).

8.3.2 The Institutionalisation of the Regional Electricity Market: The STEM and the DAM

The prospect of participating in a regional electricity market that facilitates short-term electricity trade was the major motivation for the SADC countries' to become members of the SAPP. However, it took more than five years before the power pool's institutional body became operative and launched the first regional electricity market. In April 2001, the SAPP announced the official opening of the STEM and declared that from now on it offered a marketplace for trading electricity that had not been covered by long-term contracts. This was a big step forward. Although daily operations started only in January 2002, the STEM soon became the most recognised project of regional energy cooperation in the SADC region—and in Africa—at that time (Muntschick 2013b: 129–130; Robinson 2009).

The STEM was designed to operate as follows: Each day before 9 a.m., the national power utilities submitted their bids and offers to the power pool's Coordination Centre, depending on whether they intended to sell or buy electricity. The Coordination Centre's task was to act as a broker and match the bids and offers on the same day, after the closure of the market in the morning. The centre provided transparent information on the respective sales offers and demand, monitored the capacity of the interconnected power transmission lines, gave logistical support and finally organised the inter-utility contracts on electricity trade and wheeling (UNECA 2004: 28–29). However, the market prices were matched only at the sellers' offers. Owing to this practice, however, the STEM turned out to be an incomplete and not fully competitive market (Hammons 2011: 406; Muntschick 2013b: 129–130).

Official documents reveal that the SAPP members accomplished the institutionalisation of the STEM—as well as the SAPP Pool Plan, the Energy Wheeling on SAPP System and the Coordination Centre—almost entirely on their own—and with their own financial resources.[35] Eskom played the most prominent role in this respect. It contributed the lion's share of funding to the SAPP and the STEM at that stage. However, in this context, it is noteworthy that particularly the USAID and the World Bank provided at least small-scale support for the STEM project by funding feasibility studies and offering technical assistance (UNECA 2004: 40–41).

The SAPP members already started to plan for a new market platform with improved trading mechanisms shortly after the STEM had been put into operation. The reasons behind this process, which started in 2003, were some shortcomings of the STEM—mainly because it was cumbersome and neither a fully integrated nor competitive market yet. These constraining circumstances fuelled the SAPP members' demand for a fully flexible and competitive regional electricity market in order to increase intra-regional trade in electricity and enhance supply security.[36]

However, the point in time for starting this initiative was surprising insofar as the electricity volumes traded via the STEM happened to decrease right at the same time because of diminishing surplus power generation capacities in the SAPP region (Muntschick 2013b: 130–131).

Given the fact that there seemed to be no pressing need for a new short-term electricity market within the SAPP from its members' plain regional perspective, it is noteworthy that the development of just this kind of market—later known as the DAM—started to take shape in 2004. The planning and institutionalisation of the DAM were clearly fuelled by extra-regional actors. This is because a January 2004 agreement between the government of Norway and the SAPP provided the power pool with a grant of 35 million Norwegian Kroner (about $7.5 million USD). Norway earmarked this funding for the establishment of a competitive regional electricity market under the SAPP's umbrella and thus sponsored the institutionalisation of the DAM substantially during its founding years of 2004/2005 (Hammons 2011: 407; Tjønneland et al. 2005: 37). The EU channelled an additional $0.7 million USD through its first ACP-EU Energy Facility to the SAPP at that time. Brussels's funding had been earmarked for capacity building in power network operations and thus contributed to the operation of the Coordination Centre and the DAM as well.[37] Sweden provided more than $0.5 million USD for the SAPP for similar purposes during the period of 2006–2008 and therefore was also a significant external supporter.[38]

Fuelled by considerable external support in terms of finance and consultancy on a regular basis, the DAM as the SAPP's new electricity trading platform finally became operational in December 2009. It operates as follows: Based on power generation and electricity transaction bids that are offered to the SAPP in advance, the DAM sets prices for electricity as of 11 a.m. the previous day (i.e. one day before the volumes can actually be physically wheeled). These DAM prices are determined on an hourly basis and communicated to all SAPP members with the Coordination Centre acting as market operator. Trade takes place if bid and sales offers match at a certain price. Thus, the DAM—and this is its most innovative feature—provides a mechanism that allows rather direct trade between the interacting partners—quite similar to an auction market.[39] In contrast to the STEM, the DAM is in principle open to other, independent power producers and distributors besides the national (parastatal) power utilities. This feature implied not least the birth of a competitive electricity market because it aims at weakening the national power utilities' tacit monopoly on power generation and supply (ECA 2009: 29–30).

External actors continued to provide financial assistance to the power pool, and particularly to its regional electricity market, even well after the birth of the DAM, as Figs. 8.3 and 8.4 indicate. While Norway remained the most important donor in the aftermath of the 2004 agreement, the EU, for example, commissioned under its second EU-ACP Energy Facility a new tranche of $1.25 million USD for a technical assistance project in support of the SAPP in 2012.[40] Between 2010 and 2011, the World Bank provided about $0.3 million USD directly to the SAPP's budget[41]—and additionally much larger amounts to the DRC for the Grand Inga project as well (Ngwawi 2012: 2–3).

Altogether, the operating costs of the SAPP are for the most part covered by the members' annual contributions (based on a formula codified in the IMoU) and the short-term market's participation fees (calculated on the basis of traded volumes). However, extra-regional actors became increasingly involved in initialising and supporting the SAPP's projects (notably the DAM) as donors from 2004 onwards.

8.4 Evaluation of the SAPP

In order to evaluate the SAPP's institutional performance, it is reasonable to firstly examine whether its members implemented the power pool's governing memoranda and complied with their inherent provisions. The effectiveness of the SAPP as a whole shall be assessed in a second step by focussing on the power pool's central objectives and projects of regional electricity cooperation in terms of goal attainment.

8.4.1 Implementation and Compliance

The adoption of the SAPP-IMoU together with the IMoU by all SADC members (except the island states) paved the way for the institutionalisation of the SAPP as the SADC's electricity regime. In accordance with similar aims codified in the SADC Treaty, the SADC's Protocol on Energy and the RISDP (Matinga 2004), the SAPP's member states acknowledged in both agreements to focus their efforts on creating a regional market for short-term electricity trade as well as on improving the regional power grid. The SAPP-IMoU and the IMoU officially

Table 8.2 The SAPP members (2016)

Country	Name of power utility	Status
Angola	Rede Nacional de Transporte de Electricidade (RNT)	Non-operating
Botswana	Botswana Power Corporation (BPC)	Operating
DRC	Societe Nationale d'Electricite (SNEL)	Operating
Lesotho	Lesotho Electricity Company (LEC)	Operating
Malawi	Electricity Supply Commission (ESCOM)	Non-operating
Mozambique	Companhia de Transmissao de Mozambique (MOTRACO)	Observer
Mozambique	Electricidade de Mozambique (EDM)	Operating
Mozambique	Hidroelectrica de Cahora Bassa (HCB)	Observer
Namibia	Namibia Power Corporation (NamPower)	Operating
South Africa	South Africa's Electricity Supply Commission (Eskom)	Operating
Swaziland	Swaziland Electricity Board (SEB)	Operating
Tanzania	Tanzania Electricity Supply Company (Tanesco)	Non-operating
Zambia	Copperbelt Energy Corporation (CEC) (independent transmission company)	Operating
Zambia	Lunsemfwa Hydro Power Company (LHPC) (independent power producer)	Operating
Zambia	Zambia Electricity Supply Corporation (ZESCO)	Operating
Zimbabwe	Zimbabwe Electricity Supply Authority (ZESA)	Operating

entered into force in August 1995 after the document had been signed and ratified by the actors involved.

Countries that ratified and implemented all documents governing the SAPP, and moreover were interconnected with at least one partner through the power pool's network, gained the status of operating members. Today, most mainland SADC member states are operating members of the SAPP (cf. Table 8.2).[42] So far, only Angola, Malawi and Tanzania remain non-operating members because they are not yet connected to the regional power grid. This is also the reason why the three countries have been incapable of implementing some of the IMoU's central provisions—notably to constitute and take an active part in the regional electricity market. Therefore, in this case, non-implementation is not a sign for defection, particularly since non-operating members are principally allowed to engage in all SAPP activities except those issues directly related to the operation of the pool. And Angola, Malawi and Tanzania do cooperate in this regard.[43]

The operating member states continued to successfully implement the central provisions of the memoranda on regional and national levels during the years following the official inauguration of the power pool. This resulted, in the first place, in the institutionalisation of the regional common electricity market with improved intra-regional trading opportunities.

Compliance of the involved states is confirmed by the fact that the STEM and DAM markets not only had been institutionalised as part of the regional electricity regime but also were fully functional and operating in practice as the volumes of intra-regional electricity trade via the SAPP indicate (cf. details in the following sections). In regard to the DAM, eleven out of the SAPP's sixteen members comply with the "DAM Book of Rules" and the "DAM Participation Document" and therefore are eligible for trading via this platform.[44] This applies also for independent power utilities, which is distinct evidence of the SAPP members' compliance with the IMoU's provisions in terms of liberalising their national electricity markets and granting independent producers access to the SAPP and to its grid.

8.4.2   Effectiveness of the SAPP's Regional Electricity Markets

The SAPP's central objectives and projects are, on the one hand, the creation of a functioning short-term regional electricity market (i.e. the STEM and the DAM) and, on the other hand, the interconnection and expansion of the regional power grid. Hence, these major goals provide benchmarks to assess the performance and success of the institution. The effectiveness of regional electricity cooperation in the SADC shall consequently be evaluated by quantifying the volumes of cross-border electricity trade through the SAPP's trading platforms and by scrutinising the recent development and upgrading of the regional power grid.

8.4.3   Effectiveness of the STEM

During its time of operation, electricity trading in the STEM market was only partially crowned with success: The STEM trade volumes covered only about 5–10% of total regional trade in electricity. A structural problem related to the fact that the market was neither fully liberalised nor competitive yet: On the one hand, demand almost always exceeded the available supply offers in the STEM; on the other hand, the sellers often did not benefit from higher prices offered by buyers, because trade was concluded at the sellers' price offers. Pricing mechanisms thus constrained trade. Moreover, the STEM mechanisms were inflexible insofar as they generally took priority in serving bilateral agreements over other, potentially more efficient dispatches of surplus supply (UNECA 2004: 46–49).

During its early time of operating in 2002, up to 120 gigawatt hours (GWh) of electricity were traded through the STEM per month. The monthly volumes oscillated between a minimum of 20 and a maximum of 60 GWh during the following months until mid-2005. Since then, however, regional electricity trade through the STEM diminished to less than 20 GWh per month (on average) until the end of 2006 (Fig. 8.5).[45]

Data on electricity trade between some of the SAPP members—notably between South Africa's Eskom on the one side and NamPower, LEC, HCB and SEC on the other—provides evidence that trading through the STEM generated wheeling charges that were about 50% lower than those related to bilateral trade agreements (Disenyana and Samuel 2009: 19). Therefore, the price for electrical energy provided by the STEM was much lower and the participant member utilities reported savings of up to $2 million USD already by July 2002 (UNECA 2004:

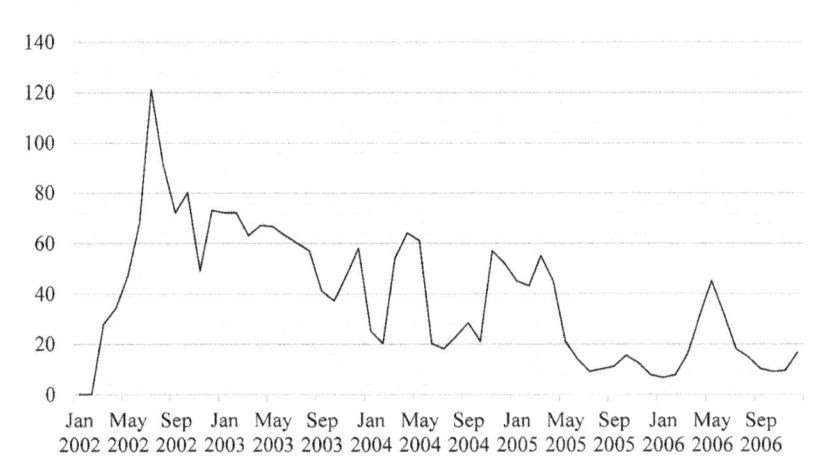

Fig. 8.5 SAPP electricity trade through the STEM in GWh (2002–2006)

70–71). This implies that electricity trading via the STEM was cost-efficient and provided absolute gains for those parties involved.

However, diminishing surplus generation power supply in the SADC region finally led to decreasing power trade via the STEM. The main reason for this decline is rooted in South Africa's national power crisis. The country's plants were not able to generate large volumes of surplus electricity anymore, because Pretoria did not keep step with exponentially increasing national electricity consumption by installing new power generation capacities.[46] Moreover, the pool's infrastructure constrained power transmission because of poor power lines, susceptible interconnectors and obsolete generation techniques. Against this background—and with the development of the DAM under way—the STEM became slowly but steadily dormant. It was finally closed down in late 2006 (ECA 2009: 29; Hofmann 2009: 29).

8.4.4 Effectiveness of the DAM

The power crisis in Southern Africa not only implied a major challenge for the implementation of a competitive regional market but also had a negative impact on the effectiveness of the newly established DAM. Despite a steady inflow of external donors' funding.[47] Therefore, the DAM-traded electricity volumes were in the beginning relatively low. The figures oscillated between a minimum of less than 1 GWh and a maximum of almost 55 GWh during the period of August 2010 and August 2014 (cf. Fig. 8.6).[48]

According to statements of SAPP officials, these low trade volumes occur on the one hand because the SAPP members have not yet fully adjusted to the new trading platform and on the other hand—and this is critical—because of unsuccessful market-cross caused by mismatches of potential buyers' and sellers' prices. This implies that a competitive regional electricity market has been successfully institutionalised—and is actually operating—even though the traded volumes are still below expectations (ECA 2009: 29).[49] So far, power trade over the DAM covers with less than 10% only a marginal part of total electricity trade among the SAPP members.[50]

However, it is noteworthy that short-term electricity trade via the DAM has increased remarkably since 2013. This is because of Zimbabwe's improved financial solvency, which allowed ZESA to import larger electricity volumes again (Kaseke 2013: 10–14), and particularly

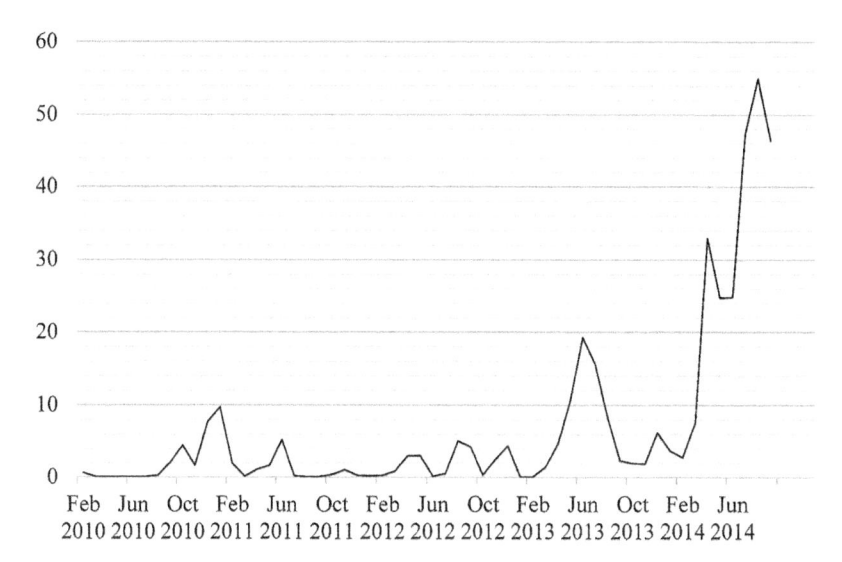

Fig. 8.6 SAPP electricity trade through the DAM in GWh (2010–2014)

because of the steady expansion of the regional power grid.[51] Moreover, the rising figures correspond to the fact that in general the electricity volumes in sales bids and buys bids had always been much larger than the volumes that were finally traded. According to the SAPP's chief market analyst, Musara Beta, "The potential to trade in the DAM is there but the current transmission capacity is not allowing member countries to fully exploit the competitive market. The problem is not with the market but with the system" (Sikuka 2013: 10). Hence, it is mainly the SAPP's poor interconnections and insufficient power line capacities that constrained a full exploitation of the still-untapped short-term trade potential in the region.

Notwithstanding these transmission constraints, DAM membership certainly provided better trading opportunities and absolute gains for the pool's operating members. According to SAPP officials, "Those (utilities) that are participating in the competitive market have realised huge financial rewards" (Sikuka 2013: 10). This is because in general the average DAM clearing price of short-term electricity has been much lower than typical bilateral prices that had been fixed on a long-term contractual basis.

8.4.5 The Infrastructure Projects

Besides establishing a regional electricity market, SAPP members made progress in terms of improving and expanding the regional power grid. Since its foundation, the power pool successfully enhanced the interconnectedness of its members by completing the following major infrastructure projects in accordance with its priority list (Hammons 2011: 402–403; Muntschick 2013b: 128):

- Building a 400-kV interconnector linking Matimba (South Africa) and Insukamini (Zimbabwe) via Botswana in 1995.
- Installing a 330-kV interconnector linking Mozambique with Zimbabwe in 1997.
- Connecting the Phokoje substation (Botswana) to the Matimba (South Africa) transmission line in 1998.
- Restoring the 533-kV power lines between Cahora Bassa (Mozambique) and the Apollo substation (South Africa) in 1998.
- Building a 400-kV power line in order to connect Camden (South Africa) via Edwaleni (Swaziland) to Maputo (Mozambique) in 2000. This project was crucially important for supplying the power-guzzling Mozal Aluminium Smelters in Maputo with much-needed electricity.
- Building a 400-kV power line in order to connect Aggeneis (South Africa) and Kookerboom (Namibia) in 2001.
- Building a 400-kV power line connecting Arnot (South Africa) and Maputo (Mozambique) in 2001.
- Installing the 220-kV Zambia-Namibia interconnector in the Caprivi Region in 2006.
- Constructing the 300-MW high-voltage connection between Zambia and Namibia in the Caprivi Region in 2010. This important project improved the interconnection of the northern and western parts of the SAPP's grid.

Moreover, a number of other infrastructure projects are currently under construction. This includes notably the Zizabona transmission project (involving Zimbabwe, Zambia, Botswana and Namibia with the aim of establishing a Western corridor in the SAPP's grid), the 400-kV interconnector project between Zambia and Tanzania (aiming to connect Tanzania to the SAPP's grid) or the DRC-Zambia 220-kV interconnector.[52] Additional projects are still under review or at various planning stages (NORAD 2007).[53] In this context, it is noteworthy that extra-regional donors (particularly the World Bank and to a lesser degree Denmark and Norway) often played an important role for the realisation of regional electricity infrastructure projects. This is because they channelled significant financial means to those SADC countries involved and thus supported regional electricity cooperation under the SAPP's umbrella—at least indirectly. The South African government-owned DBSA acted as an important financial backer in this regard as well and provided funding to, among other things, NamPower, SEB, Zesco, EDM, CEC and LHPC.[54] This highlights not least the key role of South Africa for electricity cooperation in the SADC (ECA 2009: 41–44; NORAD 2007: 18–21).

Besides expanding and improving the regional power grid, SAPP members are active in enhancing regional energy security by coordinating their national electricity policies—a strategy that has been on the SAPP's priority list since regional surplus power generation supplies diminished increasingly. Measures include first and foremost the coordinated refurbishment, de-mothballing and commissioning of (new) power plants in the region (Hammons 2011: 411; Ngwawi 2012: 4). This common approach allows SAPP members to postpone, where necessary, capital expenditure on new plants on behalf of the existence of an interconnected regional power pool, which is an important and cost-effective aspect in view of developing the economies in the SADC region.[55]

There is evidence that the SAPP's coordinated infrastructure measures have been successful in terms of promoting regional energy security in the SADC region. Official SADC sources came to the conclusion that "projects for the sharing of power among countries have progressed significantly" and that "tangible results have been recorded on the load management strategies."[56] From a contra-factual perspective, there is evidence that institutionalised electricity cooperation helped to prevent a regional scenario afflicted by severe power shortages and more frequent blackouts. One indicator that substantiates this presumption refers to the available installed electricity generation capacity of the power pool and its member states (cf. Table 8.3).

Excluding the figures from Angola, Malawi and Tanzania, the total available installed electricity generation capacity in the SAPP increased by more than 20% since the foundation of the institution. South Africa, the regional powerhouse, made the largest contribution to this overall

Table 8.3 The SAPP's available installed electricity generation capacity (in MW)

Country	Available installed capacity (1999)	Available installed capacity (2013)	Variation (in %)
Angola	326	1480	+354
Botswana	118	322	+173
DRC	n/a	1170	n/a
Lesotho	74	72	−3
Malawi	214	287	+34
Mozambique	2245	2279	+2
Namibia	384	360	−6
South Africa	34,853	41,074	+18
Swaziland	41	70	+71
Tanzania	783	1143	+46
Zambia	1774	1845	+4
Zimbabwe	1708	1600	−6
Total SAPP	42,520	51,702	+22

Data taken from (Bowen 1999 #963@188)
Data according to the SAPP: http://www.sapp.co.zw/demand.html (10/04/2014)

positive development because Pretoria followed a growth-oriented energy policy for the past years.

8.5 Résumé and Prospects

In summary, it was mainly imbalances in supply and demand of electricity in the SADC region that caused a regional cooperation problem that initialised demand for institutionalised electricity cooperation and a power pool with an integrated electricity market in its mainland member states. South Africa was in a relative regional power position in this issue area because it was in the centre of the region's power grid and its national energy giant, Eskom, provided (cheap) power to a number of neighbouring electricity-dependent states. From the beginning, Pretoria therefore was able to exert significant influence on the institutional design and inherent norms of the SAPP and its regulative framework. SAPP members successfully established the STEM as the first integrated regional electricity market in the SADC region—with extra-regional actors playing, as donors, only a minor role.

Diminishing surplus electricity generation volumes in the SADC region from the mid-2000s onwards did, for structural reasons, mitigate in parallel the genuine regional cooperation problem and the need for an integrated regional electricity market. Intra-regional trade in electricity decreased significantly against this background. This finally led to the closure of the STEM.

The institutionalisation of the DAM occurred although genuine regional demand for a platform for short-term electricity trade had already been mitigated in light of the growing power crisis in the region; establishing the DAM market was certainly not a salient solution to this specific problem. Nonetheless, monetary incentives and support from extra-regional donor countries—namely from Norway and the EU—reduced the costs associated with the institutionalisation of a regional electricity market. This made it easier for SAPP members to press ahead with the installation of the DAM. External funding thus provided major incentives for SAPP members to engage in deeper regional electricity integration (Hammons 2011: 402; Muntschick 2013b: 128).

Altogether, the SAPP as an institution is largely functional and operating at present. Many experts see the power pool as a successful and outstanding example for regional electricity cooperation among developing countries (UNECA 2004: XI; Hofmann 2009: 104–105).[57] However, its actual state of performance is certainly capable of improvement. The reason for this is that the SAPP suffers not only on an incomplete power grid with partially insufficient transmission lines and failure-prone interconnectors but also on the enduring SADC-wide power crisis that implies diminishing surplus supply in combination with rising consumer demand. Moreover, intra-regional trade through the regional electricity market is still relatively low. The result is a functioning DAM that does not perform very well in terms of traded electricity volumes. However, it is likely to continue operating as long as extra-regional monetary incentives for this institution keep on bubbling.

For the SAPP to become more effective, regional electricity infrastructure has to be enhanced by building additional and stronger power transmission lines, interconnecting all SADC countries to the power grid and tapping the DRC's vast hydro-generating potential. However, it has become clear that for structural reasons the SAPP—particularly its regional electricity market—has been increasingly exposed to external influence since the regional power crisis took effect. This may also affect its functionality and institutional performance (at least indirectly). It implies that if SAPP members do not generate strong and profit-oriented demand for institutionalised regional electricity cooperation on their own and from within the region, the SAPP—particularly the DAM—is in danger of becoming paralysed, notably in the event that extra-regional actors decide to stop their support.

Notes

1. The terms "electricity" and "power" are used synonymously in the context of energy issues.
2. Focus area according to the SADC: http://www.sadc.int/themes/infrastructure/en/ (10/12/2016).
3. Details available on the SAPP's web page: http://www.sapp.co.zw (10/12/2016).
4. SAPP (1998): SADC SAPP Annual Review Report, 28 August 1995–March 1997. Harare: Southern African Power Pool. p. 1.
5. SAPP (1998): SADC SAPP Annual Review Report, 28 August 1995–March 1997. Harare: Southern African Power Pool. p. 20.
6. SAPP (1998): SADC SAPP Annual Review Report, 28 August 1995–March 1997. Harare: Southern African Power Pool. p. 20.
7. Most of these thermal power plants had been commissioned in the course of South Africa's autarky policies during the time of Apartheid. At that time, Pretoria not only was keen to supply its national electricity demands entirely by itself but also aspired to bring some of its smaller neighbours in a relationship of dependency by providing cheap—and subsidised—electricity contingents (Horvei 1998).
8. SAPP (1998): SADC SAPP Annual Review Report, 28 August 1995–March 1997. Harare: Southern African Power Pool. p. 20.
9. Societé Nationale d'Electricité (2000): Trente ans de vie de SNEL 1970–2000. Kinshasa: Gombe.
10. SAPP (1998): SADC SAPP Annual Review Report, 28 August 1995–March 1997. Harare: Southern African Power Pool.
11. On average, between 5% and 25% of an individual SADC country's generated power is lost due to old and decayed power transmission lines (SAPP 2007: 29).
12. SAPP (1998): SADC SAPP Annual Review Report, 28 August 1995–March 1997. Harare: Southern African Power Pool. p. 20.

13. SADC (1996a): Energy. Annual Report of the Sector Coordination Unit. Johannesburg, 1–4 February 1996. p. 6.
14. SAPP (1998): SADC SAPP Annual Review Report, 28 August 1995–March 1997. Harare: Southern African Power Pool. p. 17.
15. Eskom (2010): Factsheet "Eskom and the Southern African Power Pool". http://www.eskom.co.za/content/ES_0007SAfPowPoolRev5~1.pdf (10/10/2016).
16. Incomplete insofar as Angola, Malawi, Tanzania and the island states of Mauritius and the Seychelles were not interconnected with other SADC members by any power transmission lines at all.
17. The DRC joined the SADC only in 1997. The country will not be regarded as an extra-regional actor *prior* to the institutionalisation of regional electricity cooperation in the SADC, because the DRC had been involved in the negotiations on establishing the SAPP straight from the beginning (Njiramba 2004).
18. European Union Energy Initiative: https://europa.eu/capacity4dev/euei (12/11/2016).
19. European Commission (2012): The ACP-EU Energy Facility. Improving access to energy services for the poor in rural and peri-urban areas. Brussels: European Union. p. 14.
20. European Commission (2009): The ACP-EU Energy Facility. Improving access to energy services for the poor in rural and peri-urban areas. Brussels: European Communities.
    European Commission (2012): The ACP-EU Energy Facility. Improving access to energy services for the poor in rural and peri-urban areas. Brussels: European Union.
21. Data extracted from the SAPP's annual reports. Slight inaccuracies may exist due to minor changes in the SAPP's own accounting policies on grants from 2009 onwards.
22. SADC (1992): Treaty of the Southern African Development Community. Gaborone: SADC Secretariat. Article 5, 21.
23. SAPP (1994): SAPP Inter-Utility Memorandum of Understanding. Article 1.
24. SAPP (1994): SAPP Inter-Utility Memorandum of Understanding. Article 1.
25. SAPP (1994): SAPP Inter-Utility Memorandum of Understanding.
26. SADC (1995a): Council Decisions. Johannesburg, Republic of South Africa, 25–26 August 1995. p 8.
27. SADC (1996b): Record of the SADC Council of Ministers Meeting, 28–29 January 1996. p. 11.

28. SADC (1995a): Council Decisions. Johannesburg, Republic of South Africa, 25–26 August 1995. p. 8.
29. All citations: Southern African Power Pool: http://www.sapp.co.zw (25/11/2016).
30. SAPP (1995): Intergovernmental Memorandum of Understanding.
31. Details available on the SAPP's web page: http://www.sapp.co.zw (10/12/2016).
32. Department of Minerals and Energy (1998): White Paper on the Energy Policy of the Republic of South Africa. Pretoria: Government Printer. http://www.energy.gov.za/files/policies/whitepaper_energypolicy_1998.pdf (10/08/2016).
33. SADC (1995b): Record of the Council of Ministers. Held in Maseru, Lesotho, 21–22 August 1996. p. 250.
34. In regard to frequency control, the SAPP members agreed on a common frequency band of 49.95–50.05 Hz. This aligns almost exactly with Eskom's own standard of 50 Hz. Information according to the SAPP: http://www.sardc.net/editorial/sadctoday/list.asp?pubno=v15n3 (10/12/2014).
35. SADC (2002): Energy Sector. Annual Report July 2001–June 2002. pp. 30–34 and 75–77.
36. SADC (2007): Record. Meeting of the SADC Ministers responsible for Energy on the 25 April 2007 in Harare, Zimbabwe. pp. 15–16.
37. European Commission (2009): The ACP-EU Energy Facility. Improving access to energy services for the poor in rural and peri-urban areas. Brussels: European Communities. pp. 19–20.
38. Information taken from the SAPP's annual reports of 2006–2008.
39. Information according to the SAPP: http://www.sapp.co.zw/market-overview (10/10/2016).
40. European Union (2012): ZW-Harare: EDF—technical assistance project in support to the Southern African Power Pool (SAPP). Published in the Supplement to the Official Journal of the European Union (2012/S 221-362912).
41. Information taken from the SAPP's annual reports of 2010–2011.
42. SAPP (2014): Workings of the SAPP. Presentation by Lawrence Musaba (Coordination Centre Manager). http://cdn.entelectonline.co.za/wm-418498-cmsimages/SAPPOverview_SAIEEPresidentialLecture.pdf (02/03/2016).
43. Information according to the SAPP: http://www.sapp.co.zw/about-sapp#members (10/10/2016).

44. SAPP (2013): 2012 Annual Report. Harare: Southern African Power Pool. p. 20.
45. Data on electricity trade is based on the SAPP's annual and monthly reports.
46. Madlala, O. (2006): Plans to avert Southern African energy crisis as demand outstrips supply in SADC region. In: Engineering News. Published on 6 October 2006. http://www.engineeringnews.co.za/article/plans-to-avert-southern-african-energy-crisis-as-demand-outstrips-supply-in-sadc-region-2006-10-06 (12/05/2016).
47. SAPP (2011): DAM Monthly Performance Report. November 2011. Harare: Southern African Power Pool. p. 3.
48. Data is based on the SAPP's annual and monthly reports.
49. SAPP (2011): DAM Monthly Performance Report. November 2011. Harare: Southern African Power Pool. p. 2.
50. Estimation based on data from the SAPP's annual and monthly reports of 2010–2013.
51. SAPP (2013): 2012 Annual Report. Harare: Southern African Power Pool. p. 73.
52. Solomons, I. (2014): Power transmission projects in Southern Africa. In: Engineering News. Published on 18 April 2014. http://www.engineeringnews.co.za/article/power-transmission-projects-progress-in-southern-africa-2014-04-18 (10/08/2016).
53. SAPP (2013): 2012 Annual Report. Harare: Southern African Power Pool. pp. 14–16.
54. Information based on a confidential document "Typical projects financed in SADC" provided by the DBSA.
55. Statement of the Department of Energy of the Republic of South Africa. http://www.energy.gov.za/files/esources/electricity/electricity_powerpool.html (06/09/2016).
56. SADC (2012): Desk Assessment of the Regional Indicative Strategic Development Plan 2005–2010. Gaborone: SADC Secretariat. p. 44.
57. SADC (2012): Desk Assessment of the Regional Indicative Strategic Development Plan 2005–2010. Gaborone: SADC Secretariat. pp. 43–44.

REFERENCES

Bowen, B., F.T. Sparrow, and Z. Yu. 1999. Modeling Electricity Trade Policy for Twelve Nations of the Southern African Power Pool (SAPP). *Utilities Policy* 8: 183–197.

Daniel, J., and J. Lutchman. 2006. South Africa in Africa: Scrambling for Energy. In *State of the Nation: South Africa 2005–2006*, ed. S. Buhlungu, J. Daniel, R. Southall, and J. Lutchman, 484–509. Cape Town: Lutchman.

de Lombaerde, P., E. Dorrucci, G. Genna, and F.P. Mongelli. 2008. Quantitative Monitoring and Comparison of Regional Integration Processes: Steps Toward Good Practise. In *Elements of Regional Integration. A Multidimensional Approach*, ed. A. Kösler and M. Zimmek, 149–179. Baden-Baden: Nomos.
Economic Consulting Associates (ECA). 2009. *The Potential of Regional Power Sector Integration. South African Power Pool (SAPP)—Transmission & Trading Case Study*. London: Economic Consulting Association Limited.
Hammons, T.J. 2011. *Electricity Infrastructure in the Global Marketplace*. Rijeka: InTech.
Hofmann, M.E. 2009. *Resource Diplomacy in Southern Africa. Necessity, Structures and Security Implications for the Southern African Development Community (SADC) Region*. Saarbrücken: VDM.
Horvei, T. 1998. Powering the Region: South Africa in the Southern African Power Pool. In *South Africa in Southern Africa*, ed. D. Simon, 146–163. Oxford: James Currey.
Isaksen, J., and E.N. Tjønneland. 2001. *Assessing the Restructuring of SADC—Positions, Policies and Progress*. Bergen: Chr. Michelsen Institute.
Kaseke, N. 2013. Emergence of Electricity Crisis in Zimbabwe. Reform, Response and Cost Implications. *Journal of Business and Management & Social Sciences Research* 2 (10): 10–14.
Lopes, V., and P. Kundishora. 2000. The Southern African Power Pool: Economic Dependency or Self Sufficiency? In *Environmental Security in Southern Africa*, ed. D. Tevera, and S. Moyo, 207–225. Harare: SAPES Books.
Madlala, O. 2006. Plans to Avert Southern African Energy Crisis as Demand Outstrips Supply in SADC Region. In *Engineering News*. Published on 6th October 2006. http://www.engineeringnews.co.za/article/plans-to-avert-southern-african-energy-crisis-as-demand-outstrips-supply-in-sadc-region-2006-10-06. Accessed 5 Dec 2013.
Matinga, M.N. 2004. Pooling African Power: Issues, Developments and Outlook of a Reforming and Integrating Southern African Power Sector. In *Monitoring Regional Integration in Southern Africa*, Yearbook vol. 4, ed. D. Hansohm, W. Breytenbach, T. Hartzenberg, and C. McCarthy, 91–105. Windhoek: Namibian Economic Policy Research Unit.
Merven, B., A. Hughes, and S. Davis. 2010. An Analysis of Energy Consumption for a Selection of Countries in the Southern African Development Community. *Journal of Energy in Southern Africa* 21 (1): 11–24.
Muntschick, J. 2013b. Regional Energy Cooperation in SADC: Is the Southern African Power Pool currently powered by External Funding? In *Monitoring Regional Intergration in Southern Africa. Yearbook 2012*, ed. A. du Pisani, G.

Erasmus, and T. Hartzenberg, 113–139. Stellenbosch: Trade Law Centre for Southern Africa.

Ngwawi, J. 2012. Energy Sector Plan Targets Surplus, Sets Priorities. *SADC Today* 15 (1).

Njiramba, M.M. 2004. Pooling African Power: Issues, Developments and Outlook of a Reforming and Integrating Southern African Power Sector. In *Monitoring Regional Integration in Southern Africa Yearbook*, vol. 4, ed. D. Hansohm, W. Breytenbach, T. Hartzenberg, and C. McCarthy, 91–105. Windhoek: Namibian Economic Policy Research Unit.

NORAD. 2007. *Review and Recommendations on Norway's Role as Lead ICP for Energy within SADC. Report from a Fact-finding Mission*. Oslo: Norwegian Agency for Development Cooperation (NORAD).

Ranganathan, R., and V. Foster. 2011. *The SADC's Infrastructure. A Regional Perspective*. New York: The World Bank.

Raskin, P., and M. Lazarus. 1991. Regional Energy Development in Southern Africa: Great Potential, Great Constraints. *Annual Energy Environ* 16: 145–178.

Robinson, P. 2009. *The Potential for Regional Power Sector Integration. South African Power Pool (SAPP) Transmission & Trading Case Study*. London: Economic Consulting Associates.

Rosnes, O., and H. Vennemo. 2009. *Powering Up: Costing Power Infrastructure Investment Needs in Sub-Saharan Africa*. Oslo: Econ Pöyry.

Rugoyi, E. 1998. The Interconnection of the Southern African Power Pool. *Oil and gas law and taxation review* 12: 434–439.

Sebitosi, A.B., and R. Okou. 2010. Re-thinking the Power Transmission Model for Sub-Saharan Africa. *Energy Policy* 38: 1448–1454.

Sikuka, K. 2013. Day Ahead Market—Regional Energy Trading Gains Momentum Competitive Electricity Market Allows Member States to Buy and Sell. *SADC Today* 15 (3).

Tjønneland, E.N. 2006. *SADC and Donors—Ideals and Practices. From Gaborone to Paris and Back*. Gaborone: Botswana Institute for Development Policy Analysis.

Tjønneland, E.N., J. Isaksen, and G. le Pere. 2005. *SADC's Restructuring and Emerging Policies. Options for Norwegian Support*. Bergen: Chr, Michelsen Institute.

Tshombe, J.-M.L.-M. 2008. *Evaluating Power Trading in Selected Countries of the Southern African Development Community*. Dissertation. Cape Town: Cape Peninsula University of Technology.

United Nations Economic Commission for Africa (UNECA). 2004. *Assessment of Power Pooling Arrangements in Africa Economic Commission for Africa*. Addis Ababa: UN ECA.

Primary Sources

Eskom. 2010. Factsheet "Eskom and the Southern African Power Pool". http://www.eskom.co.za/content/ES_0007SAfPowPoolRev5~1.pdf. Accessed 10 Oct 2016.
European Commission. 2009. The ACP-EU Energy Facility. Improving Access to Energy Services for the Poor in Rural and Peri-Urban Areas. Brussels: European Communities.
European Commission 2012: The ACP-EU Energy Facility. Improving access to energy services for the poor in rural and peri-urban areas. Brussels: European Union.
European Union. 2012. ZW-Harare: EDF—Technical Assistance Project in Support to the Southern African Power Pool (SAPP). Published in the Supplement to the Official Journal of the European Union (2012/S 221-362912).
SADC. 1992. Treaty of the Southern African Development Community. Gaborone: SADC Secretariat.
SADC. 1995a. Council Decisions. Johannesburg, Republic of South Africa, 25–26 August 1995.
SADC. 1995b. Record of the Council of Ministers. Held in Maseru, Lesotho, 21–22 August 1996.
SADC. 1996a. Energy. Annual Report of the Sector Coordination Unit. Johannesburg, 1–4 February 1996.
SADC. 1996b. Record of the SADC Council of Ministers Meeting 28–29 January 1996.
SADC. 2002. Energy Sector. Annual Report July 2001–June 2002.
SADC. 2007. Record. Meeting of the SADC Ministers responsible for Energy on the 25th April 2007 in Harare, Zimbabwe.
SADC. 2012. Desk Assessment of the Regional Indicative Strategic Development Plan 2005–2010. Gaborone: SADC Secretariat.
SAPP. 1994. SAPP Inter-Utility Memorandum of Understanding.
SAPP. 1995. Intergovernmental Memorandum of Understanding.
SAPP. 1998. SADC SAPP Annual Review Report 28 August 1995–March 1997. Harare: Southern African Power Pool.
SAPP. 2007. 2006 Annual Report. Southern African Power Pool. Harare: Southern African Power Pool.
SAPP. 2011. DAM Monthly Performance Report. November 2011. Harare: Southern African Power Pool.
SAPP. 2013. 2012 Annual Report. Harare: Southern African Power Pool.
SAPP. 2014. Workings of the SAPP. Presentation by Lawrence Musaba (Coordination Centre Manager). http://cdn.entelectonline.co.za/

wm-418498-cmsimages/SAPPOverview_SAIEEPresidentialLecture.pdf. Accessed 3 Feb 2014.

Societé Nationale d'Electricité. 2000. Trente ans de vie de SNEL 1970–2000. Kinshasa: Gombe.

Solomons, I. 2014. Power transmission projects in Southern Africa. In *Engineering News*. Published on 18th April 2014. http://www.engineeringnews.co.za/article/power-transmission-projects-progress-in-southern-africa-2014-04-18. Accessed 8 Oct 2014.

CHAPTER 9

Conclusion

This book provided a theory-driven analysis of the new regionalism in the Global South on the example of the SADC in Southern Africa. It had two major mutually reinforcing aims, of which one was theoretical and the other empirical in nature. The theoretical aim was to take some steps towards developing a coherent middle-range theory on regionalism that takes the influence of extra-regional actors explicitly into account whilst refraining from Euro-centric ideas and tenets. The empirical aim was to analyse and explain the emergence, institutional design and performance of regionalism in the SADC whilst focussing on the organisation's five most important integration projects. This implied making reference to the research puzzles and addressing the guiding research questions that were outlined at the beginning of this work.

The added value of this study to the scientific debate and research on regionalism in the Global South in general and on the SADC in particular is twofold. This is because the book addresses two major research gaps in the literature.

Firstly, the study provided detailed and profound empirical insights on the emergence, institutional design, dynamics and performance of regionalism in the SADC on the whole as well as with a focus on its central policy areas. In this regard, the empirical documentation and case analysis of the SADC are comprehensive and encompassing because methods of careful process tracing in combination with the qualitative analysis of an extremely large number of the most relevant primary and secondary sources have been applied in the course of this work.

Quantitative data and expert interviews complete the picture. Hence, this book contributes to the under-researched field of regionalism in the Global South insofar as it provides in-depth empirical knowledge on the case of the SADC which so far has not been the focus of systematic research from a political science perspective. Particularly the systematic evaluation of regionalism in the SADC in terms of analysing its institutional performance and effectiveness is an outstanding achievement in this respect.

Secondly, and perhaps more importantly, this work elaborated a comprehensive middle-range theory on the analysis of regionalism that takes extra-regional relations and the potential influence of external actors explicitly into consideration. The applied modified situation-structural approach is an important innovation in this respect because it is neither Euro-centric nor "south-centric" or "SADC-centric" in character and therefore provides a universal as well as useful alternative to mainstream theories on regional integration. It addresses the research gap on theory-driven and comparative research on regionalism insofar as it includes the horizontal perspective in the analysis of regionalism—i.e. extra-regional actors—but goes beyond theories on diffusion because it does not take the Euro-centric perspective for granted and focuses not "only" on the unidirectional diffusion of norms and ideas. Instead, it provides an explanation of the mechanisms and functional logic of external influence on the emergence, institutional nature and effectiveness of regionalism from a plain structural and thus fairly "neutral" perspective.

9.1 Empirical Findings on Regionalism in the SADC

The empirical case analysis provides clear evidence that regionalism in the SADC does perform fairly well in total. The SADC is not an institutional façade, and regional integration in the SACD has made a positive difference for its member countries. This is because several "grand" regional cooperation projects have been successfully institutionalised within the SADC's framework since its foundation in 1992. This deserves recognition because the organisation is still young in international terms and because its members for the most part are from developing and the least developed countries. However, one should not overlook that there are still deficiencies in view of many of these cooperation projects in place. This puts the SADC's overall success partly into perspective. The organisation and its member countries face a number of challenges and difficulties in implementing the SADC's very visionary and ambitious regional integration agenda(s). This, however, is not uncommon for most regionalisms in the South and is even typical for older and well-established regional integration organisations such as the EU.[1]

In the central issue area of the economy, the SADC has made remarkable progress in adopting a common Protocol of Trade in the year 2000 that led to the establishment of a fully functional SADC-FTA in 2008. The overall performance of the FTA is still below expectations in terms of increasing intra-regional trade flows. Nevertheless, some SADC states' share of intra-regional trade (particularly exports) seems to have grown in the course of the implementation of the Trade Protocol and in the years following the creation of the SADC-FTA. This observation, as well as the significant growth of intra-SADC trade in absolute terms and with regard to regional trade intensity, gives proof that the SADC countries intensified merchandise trade with each other as a result of regional market integration. There is also evidence that the SADC region attracted growing inflows of FDI in the course of regional trade liberalisation towards the SADC-FTA. Although the ease of merchandise trading across borders has improved in most member countries, there are still many trade-inhibiting NTBs in place that counteract the overall achievements of the FTA. Altogether, the SADC-FTA is certainly not a symbolic or dysfunctional institution—it has just not yet reached its full potential. Counterfactual scenarios corroborate this assessment.

The SADC-CU is the SADC's second major integration project in the issue area of the economy. Scheduled to be institutionalised in 2010 according to the SADC's RISDP, the SADC-CU has without a doubt been a cornerstone in the SADC's agenda on regional economic integration. However, the SADC failed to achieve this goal and will probably never achieve it in the future. The reason is that several SADC member states preferred to group together and conclude separate extra-regional trade regimes (so-called EPAs) with the EU instead of opting for a regional SADC-CU in a first step. The conclusion of various EPAs by various groups of SADC members therefore undermined the genuine regional efforts to establish a common SADC-CU. This is because these EPAs were mutually exclusive with a CET—which is the prerequisite for the institutionalisation of a functional SADC-CU. Thus, it becomes clear that the EU's EPAs had a lasting interfering impact on the SADC's scheduled customs union project and are at least co-responsible for the fact that the SADC will not achieve its second major step towards deepening regional market integration.

In the issue area of security, the SADC has made considerable progress in creating a regional security regime since the mid-1990s. The Organ for Politics, Defence and Security became its governing body and has the task of ensuring and promoting regional security cooperation. Rather informally and loosely institutionalised in 1996, the "first" OPDS not only became a bone of contention between South Africa and Zimbabwe but also turned out to be rather dysfunctional because of its unclear status and jurisdiction during its early years of existence. In 2001, however, SADC member states adopted a common Protocol on Politics, Defence and Security Co-operation which implied a major institutional reform of the OPDS and the assignment of a clear-cut jurisdiction. Central aspects of its responsibility included military confidence-building measures and regional cooperation towards improving security and conflict management. Under the guidance of the re-launched OPDS, SADC countries carried out a number of common military exercises which stand as clear examples for the organisation's success in terms of military cooperation and confidence-building. In the case of these common exercises, the SADC enhanced transparency and reduced uncertainty and mistrust among its member states. However, the community's achievements in terms of common military operations and proactive conflict management show mixed results. This is because the SADC failed to conduct a united security policy and conflict management strategy towards the security-related crises in Lesotho, the DRC and Zimbabwe. Only in the recent crisis in Madagascar did the SADC, under the aegis of the Organ, prove to be a united actor and successful conflict manager. Altogether, the performance of the SADC's regional security regime and the OPDS shows a mixed picture and is still below expectations. Taking the counter-factual perspective, however, gives evidence that the OPDS is neither dysfunctional nor only symbolic in nature, even though it had been paralysed during the late-1990s until its re-launch in 2001. Today, the existence of the OPDS as the governing body of the SADC's security regime makes a positive difference in the member countries' regional threat perceptions and has improved the whole security situation in the region, not least because there has not been a single inter-state war between SADC member countries since the foundation of the organisation in 1992.

The SADC Standby Force and the associated training centre constitute the SADC's second major integration project in the issue area of security. Guided by the AU's desire to constitute a continental standby force on the basis of the continent's five major regional integration organisations and fuelled by the prospect of gaining financial support from the EU, SADC member states adopted an MoU on the establishment of a SADC Brigade in 2007 which paved the way for the official launch of the SSF shortly afterwards. In the following years, the SADC has made noteworthy progress in the build-up of its regional standby force. Today, the PLANLEM, a regional peacekeeping training centre of excellence, and the troop pledges from member states are functional and in place. Outstanding areas, however, are the SSF's permanent headquarters and its logistic depot. It is worth pointing out that the RPTC has shown good performance in the training of SADC peacekeeping personnel in recent years even though the centre had been virtually inoperable for a few years until 2008 because of the lack of donor support. While the institutionalisation and build-up process of the SSF seem to be almost completed, it remains unclear whether the SSF is actually ready for operation. Although the SSF had been officially declared operational in 2007, there has been no deployment of the SSF so far. This fact sparks suspicion that the SSF could be a prestigious and symbolic endeavour—possibly for the purpose of pleasing the desires of the AU and attracting donor support from the EU—rather than the result of actual cooperation needs on a regional level. However, it is probably still too early to judge whether the SSF is only a shadow army since the build-up has not been completed and since there has not been an acid test in terms of an official call for a general deployment yet.

In the issue area of the infrastructure, SADC countries have engaged in energy cooperation and focussed particularly on regional electricity cooperation. The organisation has made remarkable progress in terms of establishing a regional electricity regime and launched the SAPP as a SADC body in 1995. Within the framework of the SAPP, the STEM had been introduced as a market platform for short-term electricity trading in 2001. The DAM, an enhanced and more competitive trading platform, succeeded the STEM and started to operate in 2009. Altogether, the SAPP is functional and has proven operational readiness in recent years. Its overall performance, however, is still below expectations and certainly capable of improvement. This is because the STEM- and DAM-traded electricity volumes remain comparably low (although there has been a considerable increase in short-term electricity trade via the DAM during the past two years). It is worth pointing out, however, that the SAPP itself is ultimately not responsible for its underperformance. This is because the region suffers not only from an incomplete power grid with insufficient transmission lines but also from the recent regional power crisis which entailed diminishing surplus supply and consequently decreasing electricity volumes for trade. Despite this, regional electricity cooperation in the SADC within the SAPP's framework has produced additional achievements. These include a number of coordinated infrastructure projects that expanded the regional power grid and enhanced its interconnectedness. Moreover, the SADC countries are increasingly active in coordinating their national energy polices and power plant constructions. Altogether, the total available installed electricity generation capacity in the SAPP has increased by more than 20% since the foundation of the institution in 1995. From a contra-factual perspective, there is evidence that most of the countries in the region would have been affected by more serious power shortages and frequent blackouts if the SAPP and its infrastructure projects had not been in place.

In sum, regional integration in the SADC has made remarkable progress in the three most important policy areas. With reference to this book's guiding research questions, the empirical evidence demonstrates—in a nutshell—that the SADC countries take an active part in institutionalised regional cooperation for the purpose of gaining absolute benefits from collective action, whether economy-, security- or infrastructure-related profits. To a large extent, the nature and institutional design of regionalism in the SADC reflect the preferences and demands of South Africa. Owing to its economic power and asymmetric relationships of dependency to its neighbouring countries, the Cape Republic holds the position of a regional hegemon and thus is an important key country for regionalism in the SADC. It fulfilled the expectations insofar as Pretoria acted as a "motor for integration" in most issue areas (e.g. in view of the institutionalisation of the SADC-FTA, the Organ or the SAPP). External actors, notably the EU, had an ambivalent influence on regionalism in the SADC in terms of unfolding a facilitating, as well as occasionally interfering, impact on the organisation's major integration projects, as can be seen in the case of the scheduled SADC-CU and the RPTC. Altogether, however, regionalism in the SADC performs fairly well and certainly is not just a symbolic undertaking with non-functional institutional façades.

9.2 THEORETICAL INSIGHTS ON THE LOGIC OF REGIONALISM

The theoretical framework of this work ensured the scientific quality of the analysis in order to provide profound answers to the research questions in terms of explaining the emergence, institutional design and performance of regionalism in the SADC from a political science perspective. According to George and Bennett, "case study findings can have implications both for theory development and theory testing" (George and Bennett 2005: 109). The empirical findings of this study on the SADC should be understood primarily as plausibility probes that contribute to theory development and refinement that may be more rigorously tested in future research. Although the findings produced by the five case studies provide good evidence of the functional logic of regionalism and the explanatory power of the theoretical framework, applying the latter to additional cases would certainly increase the confidence in the plausibility of the findings, particularly regarding the causal significance of the independent variable.

Given the case study's empirical evidence and insights on regional integration in the different policy areas in the SADC, it has become clear that regionalism follows different functional logics under particular conditions. There is no simple "one size fits all" explanation to regional integration in the SADC, because regionalism is neither entirely outward-oriented nor an utterly inward-oriented and regional-born project. However, what matters in every case is certainly the underlying situation structure of the cooperation problems. With reference to the five sub-cases of this book, the explanatory power of the theoretical framework, its major assumptions and hypotheses unfold as follows:

The adoption of the Protocol on Trade and the establishment of the SADC-FTA in 2008 clearly followed the internal line of the argument of the theory applied in this study. Patterns of modest intra-regional economic interdependence among SADC countries invoked a genuine regional problematic situation that resembled a prisoner's dilemma. This fuelled demand in SADC states to adapt policies of regional trade liberalisation and lock-in regional cooperation by establishing formal regional institutions. The SADC-FTA became the regional club good that all countries wanted to achieve in order to realise absolute gains by means of regional market integration. South Africa was in a regional power position since most of its fellow SADC members showed a pattern of strong and asymmetric intra-regional economic interdependence to the Cape Republic. Almost half of the SADC countries, however, showed this kind of pattern to the EU as an external actor. Nevertheless, there was little room for exerting external impact on regional market integration in the SADC since a common FTA was compatible with third trade arrangements of its members to outsiders. According to the hypotheses of the internal line of the argument, the emergence and success of regionalism in view of the SADC-FTA were likely to happen and its institutional design to be most significantly influenced by South Africa. The empirical evidence confirms the hypothesis and gives proof of the good explanatory power of the situation-structural approach in this sub-case: The Protocol on Trade and the SADC-FTA have become a reality, and South Africa has been the major driving force and most influential designer of this institutional arrangement. Extra-regional actors, like the EU, were not in a position to exert any interfering impact on regional integration in this respect. So far, the SADC-FTA has shown a modest degree of effectiveness because it has not yet reached all of its goals. However, that is exactly what one would have expected against the background of a modest level of intra-regional economic interdependence. Thus, the institution is certainly not symbolic in nature, because it has made a difference and provides institutional benefits for all members in terms of better trading opportunities and market access.

The external line of the argument explains the failure of SADC countries to proceed with regional market integration towards institutionalising the scheduled SADC-CU. This is because, as an extra-regional actor, the EU had an interfering impact on the structure of the underlying genuine regional cooperation problem. During the mid-2000s, about half of the SADC member states had strong and asymmetric trade relations with the EU that outweighed their economic relations with their neighbours—particularly in terms of merchandise exports. This put Brussels, for plain structural reasons, in a potential power position towards these SADC countries, although South Africa remained the regional hegemon because of the pattern of asymmetric intra-regional economic interdependence to the other SADC members. By the time Brussels proposed—and later demanded—that SADC countries should conclude EPAs in order to safeguard market access to the EU, it was particularly the SADC states with stronger extra-regional than intra-regional economic relations that regarded the North-South EPAs as an economically more promising policy alternative compared with deepening South-South integration towards a SADC-CU. These countries expected the bilateral EPAs to produce better economic pay-offs than a future SADC-CU could possibly ever provide, at least in the short term. The empirical evidence corroborates the hypotheses of the external line of the argument: In the course of this external influence, the structure of the genuine regional problematic situation in the SADC transformed into a cooperation-averse "Rambo"-type situation. This is because any SADC country's cooperative policy choice with the EU as an extra-regional actor in terms of concluding an EPA automatically implied defection in view of cooperating towards the scheduled SADC-CU and its CET on the regional level. But choosing the extra-regional policy option in line with their individually most promising economic prospects is exactly what happened in several SADC countries. Proving the explanatory power of the situation-structural approach, the EU as an external actor thus had an interfering and disturbing impact on regionalism in the SADC—be it intended or not. For this reason, the SADC and its member states will not be able to successfully institutionalise a fully functional customs union that includes all 15 members in the near future.

The institutionalisation of regional security cooperation in the SADC and the establishment of the OPDS followed the internal line of the argument on regionalism. The situation was that a number of various (latent) intra-regional tensions and conflicts had the potential to turn into violence or even inter-state wars during the mid-1990s. This produced a diffuse genuine regional cooperation problem in the SADC that resembled a security dilemma. The involved negative security externalities caused a "costly" situation that fuelled demand in SADC states to create a common regional security regime for the purpose of safeguarding and promoting regional peace and security. South Africa and to a lesser degree Zimbabwe were the most powerful countries and centres of gravity in this regional security complex because of their advanced military capabilities. Noteworthy relations of the SADC or individual member states with extra-regional actors did not exist in the issue area of security. According to the hypotheses of the internal line of the argument, the emergence of successful regionalism was likely because there existed a dilemma-type genuine regional problematic situation in the SADC area in the issue area of security during the mid-1990s. South Africa and to a lesser degree Zimbabwe were most likely to influence the institutional design of the SADC's common security regime while extra-regional interference was unlikely to occur. The empirical evidence confirms the theoretical expectations: The SADC countries established the OPDS as the governing structure of the regional security regime and legally enshrined their common security objectives in the Organ's area of responsibility. However, the details on its institutional design became a bone of contention between South Africa and Zimbabwe. This led to an unsatisfactory result and institutional paralysis of the "first" Organ in 1996. South Africa's growing regional power position in the issue area of security allowed the country to initialise the re-launch of the OPDS in 2001. This time, Pretoria was more self-assertive with regard to the "second" Organ's institutional design and jurisdiction as it became a genuine SADC body. In regard to the effectiveness of the SADC's security regime under the guidance of the OPDS, the second hypothesis of the internal line of the argument is corroborated as well: The institution demonstrated a mixed picture of performance because it had been virtually paralysed during the time of its contested institutional status. After streamlining and reforming the OPDS under Pretoria's aegis, there has been a noteworthy improvement of the Organ in terms of functioning, outputs and outcomes. This is evident in view of its involvement in the Madagascar mediation process and particularly regarding the SADC's regular common military exercises. The latter stand for the Organ's success in terms of confidence-building because regular manoeuvres have contributed to reducing uncertainty and mistrust among SADC members. It is not least for this reason that there has not been any danger of inter-state war in the region since then.

The adoption of the MoU on the establishment of a SADC Standby Brigade in 2007 and the subsequent creation of the SSF and its associated RPTC represent examples of the functional logic of the external line of the argument on regionalism. In the first place, the institutionalisation of the SSF was not grounded on a genuine regional cooperation problem in the issue area of security in the SADC—such as a security dilemma or an external threat to the organisation and its member states. Back then, no actual demand in SADC countries to establish an expensive regional standby force for structural reasons was rooted from within the region. South Africa, the superior regional military power, did not articulate a striking demand for a regional brigade. However, the AU and particularly the EU as extra-regional actors provided incentives for SADC countries to engage in deepening regional security cooperation towards the creation of a common standby force from the mid-2000s onwards. Brussels promised the SADC significant amounts of donor funding under its APF programme for the build-up of an SSF according to the demands of the AU. By offering these financial incentives for the SSF as a specific regional cooperation project in the SADC, the EU to a large extent sponsored the absolute cooperation gains for the regional collective good that otherwise would not have been achieved. In accordance with the theoretical assumptions of the external line of the argument, this pattern of asymmetric extra-regional interdependence between the EU and the SADC became supportive to the process of institutionalised regional cooperation in the latter organisation. This is because the provision and expectation of (more) donor funding transformed the structural pattern of the genuine non-problematic situation of a "dead-lock" game to a coordination game with distributional effect. That implies a more cooperation-conducive situation. According to the situation-structural approach, the emergence and success of regionalism (albeit with rather weak institutions) were therefore likely. With the EU being in an external power position because of the SADC's dependence on its financial resources with respect to this cooperation project, the hypotheses of the external line of the argument assume that Brussels was in a position to have an impact on the institutionalisation and design of the SSF. For the same reason, however, the project is likely to be rather unstable in its progress and performance because the crucial external EU source of support could dry up at any time for reasons beyond the region's scope. The empirical evidence of the SSF and its RPTC strengthens the explanatory power of the theoretical framework and its hypotheses: In the particularities on the deployment of the SSF, the institutional design of the MoU had been influenced by South Africa, the regional military power. Its central provisions, however, address primarily the overall objectives of the AU's and EU's programmes concerning capacity-building for the continental and regional standby forces. This confirms the assumption that regional powers are likely to shape and influence institutionalised regional cooperation projects only as long as extra-regional actors in a potential power position do not work against it. Concerning institutional effectiveness, it is noteworthy that the build-up of the SSF somehow proceeded in parallel to the external provision of financial resources for capacity-building. In this context, the correlation between the increase in external donors' funding to the RPTC and its course portfolio is remarkable, too. However, the provision of external support for institutional capacity-building seems to have been below the SADC's expectations and regional needs so far because the establishment of the SSF has not been completed yet. This gives reasons to assume that the (future) success of the SSF ultimately depends on the support and goodwill of the EU as the most important external donor. Therefore, the SSF is going to be less stable than if it were a project of entirely regional origin. It is more prone to a danger of institutional standstill since this external source of support may come to an end for various reasons. The turbulent history of the RPTC's performance and paralysis throughout the years gives a good example in this respect.

The institutionalisation of the SAPP and its market platforms for short-term electricity trade followed the internal line of the argument on regionalism. Regional imbalances in supply and demand of electricity caused a genuine regional cooperation problem in the SADC region during the mid-1990s. The latter generated demand in mainland SADC member states to engage in regional electricity cooperation and institutionalise an integrated regional electricity market for power trading in the sense of a regional club good. The structure of the problematic situation resembled an assurance game where a cooperative strategy could provide absolute gains for all countries involved if each of them opted for a cooperative strategy. South Africa was in a relative regional power position in this issue area because it was in the centre of the region's power grid and most of the (neighbouring) SADC countries were dependent on electricity imports from the Cape Republic. Extra-regional actors, notably the EU, at first played only a minor role because Brussels's donor contributions to regional electricity cooperation were marginal. According to the hypotheses of the internal line of the argument, regional cooperation in this issue area was likely and successful because the problematic situation resembled an assurance game and South Africa, as regional "electric" hegemon, strongly favoured the SAPP project. Accordingly, the institutional design and inherent norms of the SAPP and its regulative framework were likely to reflect the interests of South Africa—not least because external impact was unlikely to materialise because of rather negligible extra-regional relations of the SADC. The case study shows that the empirical evidence corroborates these hypotheses. The SAPP, particularly the STEM and the (increasingly interconnected) regional power grid, became the regional collective good that provided its participants absolute gains in terms of better and more profitable electricity trading opportunities and improving supply security. The operating guidelines of the STEM were to a large extent attuned to South Africa's parastatal power producer's needs and standards. It was finally the growing regional

9 CONCLUSION 319

power crisis that had limited the performance of the STEM. However, the new DAM was established although the SAPP countries' regional demand for this improved platform for short-term electricity trade had already been mitigated in light of the electricity shortages of the regional power crisis. In this case, the external line of the argument took effect because financial incentives and support from extra-regional actors—namely from the EU and Norway—reduced the costs of institutionalising the DAM and thus enticed the SAPP members to proceed with the implementation of this cost-involving project. External funding thus facilitated the institutionalisation and operability of the DAM at a time when, owing to a fading regional cooperation problem, SADC states would not have taken such a step. Today, the DAM slowly but steadily seems to pay off since its traded electricity volumes are on the rise.

Turning from specific cooperation projects to the SADC in general, it becomes clear that most of the organisation's regional integration efforts in the different policy areas have been driven by regional demand on the basis of genuine regional cooperation problems. The internal line of the argument on regionalism provided profound theory-driven explanations for the emergence, institutional design and performance of the SADC-FTA, the OPDS and the SAPP. In these cases, South Africa appeared as a major driving force and designer of regionalism in the SADC. This clearly demonstrates that the SADC is not a regional organisation which for the most part is outward-oriented or only donor-driven. However, external actors—notably the EU—certainly played a decisive role as well. The external argument on regionalism provided profound theory-driven explanations why the SADC failed to achieve its planned customs union and why the organisation became able to proceed with the build-up of its SSF. Even the emergence and operability of the SAPP's latest electricity market (the DAM) can be explained by the external logic.

Hence, both the internal and the external line of the argument of the situation-structural approach have proven strong explanatory power in view of the emergence, institutional design and effectiveness of regionalism in the SADC. It has become clear that this horizontal perspective is of utmost importance for understanding the success and failure of regionalism. Moreover, it has become clear that extra-regional actors had an ambivalent external impact on regionalism in the SADC since the EU likewise has proven to be a facilitator as well as an obstructer of specific regional cooperation projects.

9.3 OUTLOOK: PROSPECTS FOR FUTURE RESEARCH

This study has demonstrated that regionalism in the SADC as part of the Global South is a vibrant field of international activity and cooperation that deserves further attention by researchers and policymakers in both the SADC and the EU. Moreover, it has become clear that regionalism is a highly complex phenomenon that does not lend itself to simple explanations, because it involves both regional and extra-regional actors.

The strong explanatory power of this modified situation-structural approach to the analysis of regionalism, including its central assumptions and hypotheses, has been demonstrated in the case study of the SADC by means of five issue-specific sub-cases in the course of this book. Going beyond the SADC and applying this innovative theoretical approach to other examples of the new regionalism in the Global South—and possibly North—could be a next step towards probing the plausibility and global explanatory power of this theory. Eventually, the theory could help to explain the case of early European integration. This is because there is certainly evidence that extra-regional actors, notably the USA, could have played a cooperation-conducive role in terms of providing initial incentives for this European undertaking.

It is for this reason that the applied theoretical framework of this study has the potential to make a sound contribution to the academic debate and research on comparative regionalism. With its focus on structure and patterns of interdependence, the situation-structural approach does not have an inherent geographical bias and therefore is an ideal approach for analysing and explaining regionalism in all parts of the world, independent of whether the regional integration organisations form part of the Global North or Global South and regardless of whether the important extra-regional actors are China, the USA or the EU. Against this background, this study stands as an example and starting point for research on regionalism in comparison that includes the horizontal perspective and takes extra-regional actors and influence explicitly into account. While several conceptual studies and excellent works on comparative regionalism have been published in the recent past (Börzel and Risse 2015, 2016a; Krapohl 2016; Jetschke and Lenz 2011; Rosamond and Warleigh-Lack 2011), there still exist some weaknesses and potential for improvement in terms of moving beyond Euro-centrism (Jetschke and Lenz 2011), taking systematic account of extra-regional actors and external influence on regionalism (Börzel and

Risse 2016b), and broadening the scope by including policy areas besides the issue area of the economy (Krapohl 2016).

Moreover, this work and its theoretical framework could provide food for thought for further research on overlapping regionalism. Against the background of the latest wave of regionalism and the emergence of numerous new regional integration organisations, the topic has become high on the agenda in academic debates and research on regionalism during the past years (Panke and Stapel 2016; Yeo 2016). Although there is a small array of mostly empirical works on overlapping regionalism, often written by policy advisors or scholars working in the field of area studies (Jakobeit et al. 2005; Baldwin 2006; Sidaway and Gibb 1998), there is still a research gap and a lack of systematic and theory-driven studies from a political science perspective. This is unfortunate because understanding the phenomenon of overlapping regionalism and the reasons why states choose to obtain membership in more than one regional integration organisation would certainly contribute to research on regionalism in general, particularly with regard to its emergence and effectiveness.

Throughout this study, every effort has been made to provide a systematic and comprehensive contribution to a better understanding of regionalism in the SADC. In regard to the implications for future research on regionalism, in a nutshell, there is indeed a need for international relations scholars and political scientists to look beyond regionalism in Europe and expand theories on regional integration by taking extra-regional relations and the potential impact of external actors into consideration. Researchers on (comparative) global regionalism are called upon to think about this idea—and perhaps even consider the theoretical model of this study—in order to strengthen the relevance and charm of their own studies and of the entire field of regionalism research.

NOTE

1. European Council (2014): 26/27 June 2014 Conclusions. EUCO 79/14. http://www.consilium.europa.eu/uedocs/cms_data/docs/pressdata/en/ec/143478.pdf (12/11/2016).

References

Baldwin, R.E. 2006. Multilateralising Regionalism: Spaghetti Bowls as Building Blocs on the Path to Global Free Trade. *The World Economy* 29 (11): 1451–1518.

Börzel, T.A., and T. Risse. 2015. Zwischen Regionalstudien und Internationalen Beziehungen: Die vergleichende Regionalismusforschung als transdiszipilnäres Forschungsfeld. *Politische Vierteljahresschrift* 56 (2): 334–363.

Börzel, T.A., and T. Risse (eds.). 2016a. *The Oxford Handbook of Comparative Regionalism*. Oxford: Oxford University Press.

Börzel, T.A., and T. Risse. 2016b. Three Cheers for Comparative Regionalism. In *The Oxford Handbook of Comparative Regionalism*, ed. T.A. Börzel and T. Risse, 621–647. Oxford: Oxford University Press.

George, A.L., and A. Bennett. 2005. *Case Studies and Theory Development in the Social Sciences*. Cambridge: MIT Press.

Jakobeit, C., T. Hartzenberg., and N. Charalambides. 2005. *Overlapping Membership in COMESA, EAC, SACU and SADC. Trade Policy Options for the Region and for EPA Negotiations*. Eschborn: Deutsche Gesellschaft für Technische Zusammenarbeit.

Jetschke, A., and T. Lenz. 2011. Vergleichende Regionalismusforschung und Diffusion: Eine neue Forschungsagenda. *Politische Vierteljahresschrift* 52 (3): 448–474.

Krapohl, S. (ed.). 2016. *Regional Integration in the Global South. External Influence on Economic Cooperation in ASEAN, MERCOSUR and SADC*. Cham: Palgrave Macmillan.

Panke, D., and S. Stapel. 2016. Exploring overlapping Regionalism. *Journal of International Relations and Development*. Published online on 2 November 2016.

Rosamond, B., and A. Warleigh-Lack. 2011. Studying Regions Comparatively. In *New Regionalism and the European Union. Dialogues, Comparisons and New Research Agenda*, ed. A. Warleigh-Lack, N. Robinson, and B. Rosamond, 18–35. Abingdon: Routledge.

Sidaway, J.D., and R. Gibb. 1998. SADC, COMESA, SACU: Contradictory Formats for Regional 'Integration' in Southern Africa? In *South Africa in Southern Africa*, ed. D. Simon, 164–184. Oxford: James Currey.

Yeo, A. 2016. Overlapping Regionalism in East Asia: Determinants and Potential Effects. *International Relations of the Asia-Pacific* 0: 1–31.

Primary Sources

European Council. 2014. 26/27 June 2014 Conclusions. EUCO 79/14. http://www.consilium.europa.eu/uedocs/cms_data/docs/pressdata/en/ec/143478.pdf. Accessed 12 November 2016.

REFERENCES

Aboagye, F. 2012. *A Stich in a Time Would Have Saved Nine. Operationalising the African Standby Force.* Policy Brief (34). Pretoria: Institute for Security Studies.

Acharya, A. 2016. Regionalism beyond EU-Centrism. In *The Oxford Handbook of Comparative Regionalism*, ed. T.A. Börzel, and T. Risse, 109–130. Oxford: Oxford University Press.

Adar K.G., R. Ajulu, and M.O. Onyango. 2002. Post-Cold War Zimbabwe's Foreign Policy and Foreign Policy-Making Process. In *Globalization and Emerging Trends in African States' Foreign Policy-making Process: A Comparative Perspective of Southern Africa*, vol. 1., ed. K.G. Adar and R. Ajulu, 263–280. Aldershot: Ashgate.

Adebajo, A. 2002. *Liberia's Civil War. Nigeria, ECOMOG, and Regional Security in West Africa.* Boulder, London: Lynne Rienner Publishers.

Adelmann, M. 2003. *Regionale Kooperation im südlichen Afrika.* Freiburg: Arnold-Bergstraesser-Institut.

Adelmann, M. 2012. *SADC - an Actor in International Relations? The External Relations of the Southern African Development Community.* Freiburg: Arnold-Bergstraesser-Institut.

Afrikaverein der Deutschen Wirtschaft. 2012. *SADC Business Climate 2010/11. Outlook 2012. A German Business Perspective. With Research provided by Rand Merchant Bank.* Hamburg: Afrikaverein der Deutschen Wirtschaft.

Albaugh, E.A. 2000. Preventing Conflict in Africa: Possibilities of Peace Enforcement. In *Peacekeeping and Peace Enforcement in Africa. Methods of Conflict Prevention*, ed. R.I. Rotberg, E.A. Albaugh, H. Bonyongwe, C. Clapham, J. Herbst, and S. Metz, 111–210. Washington: The World Peace Foundation.

Alden, C., and G. le Pere. 2003. *South Africa's Post-Apartheid Foreign Policy - from Reconciliation to Revival?* London: International Institute for Strategic Studies.

Alden, C., and M. Soko. 2005. South Africa's Economic Relations with Africa: Hegemony and its Discontents. *Journal of Modern African Studies* 43 (3): 367–392.

Amin, S., D. Chitala, and I. Mandaza (eds.). 1987. *SADCC: Prospect for Disengagement and Development in Southern Africa*. London: Zed Books.

Amos, S. 2010. The role of South Africa in SADC regional integration: the making or braking of the organization. *Journal of International Commercial Law and Technology* 5 (3): 124–131.

Anglin, D.G. 1983. Economic Liberation and Regional Cooperation in Southern Africa: SADCC and PTA. *International Organization* 37 (4): 681–711.

Asche, H. 2008. Preserving Africa's economic policy space in trade negotiations. In *Negotiating Regions: Economic Partnership Agreements between the European Union and the African Regional Economic Communities*, ed. H. Asche, and U. Engel, 79–108. Leipzig: Leipziger Universitätsverlag.

Asche, H. 2009. Die SADC? Welche SADC? Afrikanische Regionalgemeinschaften im Übergang. In *Entwicklung als Beruf*, ed. T. Hanf, H.N. Weiler, and H. Dickow, 69–84. Baden-Baden: Nomos.

Axelrod, R. 1987. *Die Evolution der Kooperation*. München: R. Oldenbourg Verlag.

Axelrod, R., and R.O. Keohane. 1993. Achieving Cooperation under Anarchy: Strategies and Institutions. In *Neorealism and Neoliberalism: The Contemporary Debate*, ed. D.A. Baldwin, 85–115. New York: Columbia University Press.

Axline, W.A. 1977. Underdevelopment, dependence and integration: the politics of regionalism in the Third World. *International Organization* 31 (1): 83–105.

Axline, W.A. 1994. Comparative case studies of regional cooperation among developing countries. In *The Political Economy of Regional Cooperation. Comparative Case Studies*, ed. W.A. Axeline, 7–33. London: Pinter Publishers and Associated University Press.

Bach, D. 2003. New Regionalism as an Alias: Regionalisation through Trans-State Networks. In *New Regionalism in Africa*, ed. J.A. Grant, and F. Söderbaum, 21–30. Aldershot, Burlington: Ashgate.

Baker, D.-P., and S. Maeresera. 2009. SADCBRIG intervention in SADC member states: Reasons to doubt. *African Security Review* 18 (1): 106–110.

Balassa, B. 1961. *The Theory of Economic Integration*. London: George Allan & Unwin Ltd.

Baldwin, R.E. 2006. Multilateralising Regionalism: Spaghetti Bowls as Building Blocs on the Path to Global Free Trade. *The World Economy* 29 (11): 1451–1518.

Bank, A.D. 1993. *Prospects for Economic Integration in Southern Africa*. Oxford: Biddles.
Bates, R.H., A. Greif, M. Levi, and J.-L. Rosenthal. 1998. Introduction. In *Analytic Narratives*, ed. R.H. Bates, A. Greif, M. Levi, and J.-L. Rosenthal, 3–22. Princeton: Princeton University Press.
Bauer, N.L. 2004. *African Regional Integration – The EU-SA Free Trade Agreement*. Leipzig: Universität Leipzig.
Becker, C.M. 1988. The Impact of Sanctions on South Africa and its Periphery. *African Studies Review* 31 (2): 61–88.
Behar, A., and L. Edward. 2011. *How Integrated is SADC? Trends in Intra-Regional and Extra-Regional Trade Flows Policy*. Washington: World Bank.
Behrmann, G. 2008. *The Most Noble Adventure: The Marshall Plan and How America Helped Rebuild Europe*. London: Aurum Press.
Bell, T. 1993. The Impact of Sanctions on South Africa. *Journal of Contemporary African Studies* 12 (1): 1–28.
Berg, S.V., and J. Horall. 2008. Networks of regulatory agencies as regional public goods: Improving infrastructure performance. *Review of International Organizations* 3 (2): 179–200.
Berman, E.G., and K.E. Sams. 2000. *Peacekeeping in Africa: Capabilities and Culpabilities*. Geneva, Pretoria: UN Institute for Disarmament Research, Institute for Security Studies.
Berman, E.G., and K.E. Sams. 2003. The Peacekeeping Potential of African Regional Organizations. In *Dealing with Conflict in Africa: The United Nations and Regional Organizations*, ed. J. Boulden, 35–77. New York, Basingstoke: Palgrave.
Bertelsmann-Scott T. 2010. *SACU - One Hundred Not Out: What future for the Customs Union*, vol. 68. Occasional Paper. Johannesburg: South African Institute of International Affairs.
Bestbier, A. 2000. Military Participation in Exercise Blue Crane. In *Peacekeeping in the New Millenium: Lessons Learned from Exercise Blue Crane*, ed. C. de Coning, and K. Mngqibisa, 23–34. Durban: African Centre for the Constructive Resolution of Disputes (ACCORD).
Bezuidenhout H., and Naudé W. 2008. Foreign Direct Investment and Trade in the Southern African Development Community vol. 2008/88. UNU_WIDER, Helsinki.
Bhalla, A.S., and P. Bhalla. 1997. *Regional Blocs: Building Blocks or Stumbling Blocks?*. Houndmills, New York: Macmillan.
Bilal, S., and C. Stevens. 2009. *The Interim Economic Partnership Agreements between the EU and African States. Contents, challenges and prospects*. Policy Management Report, vol. 17. Maastricht: European Centre for Development Policy Management (ECDPM).

Bischoff, P.-H. 2002. How Far, Where To? Regionalism, the Southern African Development Community and Decision-Making into the Millenium. In *Globalization and Emerging Trends in African States' Foreign Policy-Making Process. A comparative perspective of Southern Africa*, ed. K.G. Adar, and R. Ajulu, 283–306. Aldershot: Ashgate.

Bischoff, P.-H. 2006. Towards a foreign peacekeeping commitment: South African approaches to conflict resolution in Africa. In *South African Foreign Policy after Apartheid*, ed. W. Carlsnaes, and P. Nel, 147–163. Midrand: Institut for Global Dialogue.

Blatter, J. 2001. Integrative Symbolik und regulative Normen bei der Institutionenbildung. Erkenntnisse vom Gewässerschutz am Bodensee. *Zeitschrift für Internationale Beziehungen* 8 (1): 5–40.

Bøås, M., M.H. Marchand, and T.M. Shaw. 2005. Conclusion: Possible Projections for the Political Economy of Regions and Regionalisms. In *The Political Economy of Regions and Regionalisms*, ed. M. Bøås, M.H. Marchand, and T.M. Shaw, 167–174. Basingstoke: Palgrave Macmillan.

Bogner, A., and W. Menz. 2005. Das theoriegenerierende Experteninterview. Erkenntnisinteresse, Wissensformen, Interaktion. In *Das Experteninterview: Theorie, Methode, Anwendung*, ed. A. Bogner, B. Littig, and W. Menz, 33–70. Wiesbaden: VS Verlag.

Boli, J., and G.M. Thomas. 1997. World Culture in the World Polity: A Century of International Non-Governmental Organization. *American Sociological Review* 62 (2): 171–190.

Börzel, T.A. 2010. *The Transformative Power of Europe Reloaded. The Limits of External Europeanization*. KFG Working Paper 11. Berlin: Otto-Suhr-Institut für Politikwissenschaft.

Börzel, T.A. 2011. *Comparative Regionalism. A New Research Agenda*. KFG Working Paper 28. Berlin: Otto-Suhr-Institut für Politikwissenschaft.

Börzel, T.A., and T. Risse. 2009a. *Diffusing (Inter-)Regionalism. The EU as a Model of Regional Integration*. KFG Working Paper 7. Berlin: Otto-Suhr-Institut für Politikwissenschaft.

Börzel, T.A., and T. Risse. 2009b. *The Transformative Power of Europe. The European Union and the Diffusion of Ideas*. KFG Working Paper 1. Berlin: Otto-Suhr-Institut für Politikwissenschaft.

Börzel, T.A., and T. Risse. 2015. Zwischen Regionalstudien und Internationalen Beziehungen: Die vergleichende Regionalismusforschung als transdiszipilnäres Forschungsfeld. *Politische Vierteljahresschrift* 56 (2): 334–363.

Börzel, T.A., and T. Risse (eds.). 2016. *The Oxford Handbook of Comparative Regionalism*. Oxford: Oxford University Press.

Börzel, T.A., and T. Risse. 2016. Three Cheers for Comparative Regionalism. In *The Oxford Handbook of Comparative Regionalism*, ed. T.A. Börzel, and T. Risse, 621–647. Oxford: Oxford University Press.

Börzel, T.A., and V. Van Hüllen (eds.). 2015. *Governance Transfer by Regional Organizations: Patching Together a Global Script*. Basingstoke: Palgrave Macmillan.

Bowen, B., F.T. Sparrow, and Z. Yu. 1999. Modeling electricity trade policy for twelve nations of the Southern African Power Pool (SAPP). *Utilities Policy* 8: 183–197.

Braun, D., and F. Gilardi. 2006. Taking 'Galton's Problem' Seriously: Towards a Theory of Policy Diffusion. *Journal of Theoretical Politics* 18 (3): 298–322.

Brenton P., F. Flatters, and P. Kalenga. 2005. Rules of Origin and SADC: The Case for Change in the Mid Term Review of the Trade Protocol. Africa Region Working Paper Series (83).

Breslin, S., and R. Higgot. 2000. Studying Regions: Learning from the Old, Constructing the New. *New Political Economy* 5 (3): 333–352.

Brosig, M. 2011. The EU's Role in the Emerging Peace and Security Regime in Africa. *European Foreign Affairs Review* 16 (1): 107–122.

Brown, M.L. 1994. *Developing Countries and Regional Economic Cooperation*. Westport (Connecticut), London: Praeger.

Burns, T., and W. Buckley. 1974. The Prisoners' Dilemma Game as a System of Social Dimension. *Journal of Peace Research* 11 (3): 221–228.

Buzan, B. 1992. Third World Regional Security in Structural and Historical Perspective. In *The Insecurity Dilemma. National Security of Thrid World States*, ed. B.L. Job, 167–189. Boulder, London: Lienne Rienner.

Buzan B., and Wæver O. 2003. *Regions and Powers. The Structure of International Security*. Cambridge: Cambridge University Press.

Cahnman, W.J. 1944. The Concept of Raum and the Theory of Regionalism. *American Sociological Review* 9 (5): 455–462.

Carrère, C. 2004. African Regional Agreements: Impact on Trade with or without Currency Unions. *Journal of African Economies* 13 (2): 199–239.

Cawthra, G. 1997. Subregional Security: The Southern African Development Community. *Security Dialogue* 28 (2): 207–218.

Cawthra, G. 2007. Comparative Perspectives on Regional Security Co-operation among Developing Countries. In *Security and Democracy in Southern Africa*, ed. G. Cawthra, A. du Pisani, and A. Omari, 23–44. Johannesburg: Wits University Press.

Cawthra, G. 2010. *The Role of SADC in Managing political crisis and Conflict: The Cases of Madagascar and Zimbabwe*. Maputo: Friedrich-Ebert-Stiftung.

Cawthra, G., K. Matlosa, and A. van Nieuwkerk. 2007. Conclusion. In *Security and Democracy in Southern Africa*, ed. G. Cawthra, A. du Pisani, and A. Omari, 233–249. Johannesburg: Wits University Press.

Cawthra, G., and A. van Nieuwkerk. 2004. *Regional Renaissance? Security in a Globalized World*. Maputo/Berlin: Friedrich Ebert Stiftung.

Chauvin, S., and G. Gaulier. 2002. Prospects for Increasing Trade among SADC Countries. In *Monitoring Regional Integration in Southern Africa Yearbook*, vol. 2, ed. D. Hansohm, C. Peters-Berries, W. Breytenbach, T. Hartzenberg, W. Maier, and P. Meyns, 21–42. Windhoek: Gamsberg Macmillan.
Chayes, A., and A. Handler Chayes. 1993. On Compliance. *International Organization* 47 (2): 175–205.
Chipeta, C. 1997. *Review and Rationalisation of the SADC Programme of Action. Volume 2: Main Report.* Cape Town: Council for Scientific and Industrial Research (CSIR) and Imani Development (Pvt) Ltd.
Chipeta, C., and K. Schade. 2007. *Deepening Integration in SADC. Macroeconomic Policies and Social Impact. A Comparative Analysis of 10 Country Studies and Surveys of Business and Non-State Actors.* Regional Integration in Southern Africa, vol 12. Gaborone: Friedrich Ebert Stiftung.
Chirwa, M., and C. Namangale. 2009. SADC Training Needs for Peace Support Operations: The Case for a Greater Role for the Regional Peacekeeping Training Centre. In *Furthering Southern African Integration. Proceedings of the 2008 FOPRISA Annual Conference*, ed. J.M. Kaunda, and F. Zizhou, 159–169. Gaborone: Lightbooks.
Christopher, A.J. 1994. *The Atlas of Apartheid*. London, New York: Routledge.
Christopher, A.J. 2001. *The Atlas of Changing South Africa*, 2nd ed. London, New York: Routledge.
Cleary, S. 1999. Regional Integration and the Southern African Development Community. *Journal of Public and International Affairs* 10 (1): 1–15.
COSATU. 1999. *COSATU Submission on the SADC Protocol on Trade*. Johannesburg: COSATU.
Coussy, J. 1996. Slow Institutional Progress and Capitalist Dynamics in Southern African Integration: Interpretations and Projects in South Africa and Zimbabwe. *Transformation: Critical Perspectives on Southern Africa* 29: 1–40.
Cox, K.R. 1969. On The Utility and Definition of Regions in Comparative Political Sociology. *Comparative Political Studies* 2 (69): 68–98.
Crocker, C.A. 1974. Military Dependence: the Colonial Legacy in Africa. *Journal of Modern African Studies* 12 (2): 265–286.
Dahl, J. 2002. Regional Integration and Foreign Direct Investment: The Case of SADC. In *Monitoring Regional Integration in Southern Africa Yearbook*, vol. 2, ed. D. Hansohm, C. Peters-Berries, W. Breytenbach, T. Hartzenberg, W. Maier, and P. Meyns, 59–82. Windhoek: Gamsberg Macmillan.
Daniel, J., and J. Lutchman. 2006. South Africa in Africa: scrambling for energy. In *State of the Nation: South Africa 2005–2006*, ed. S. Buhlungu, J. Daniel, R. Southall, and J. Lutchman, 484–509. Cape Town: Lutchman.
Daniel, J., V. Naidoo, and S. Naidu. 2003. The South Africans have arrived: Post-apartheid corporate expansion into Africa. In *State of the Nation. South*

Africa 2003–2004, ed. J. Daniel, A. Habib, and R. Southall, 368–390. Cape Town: HSRC Press.

Davies, O.V. 2014. SADC Standby Force: Preparation of Peacekeeping Personnel. *Conflict Trends* 2: 26–29.

Davies, R. 1996. Promoting Regional Integration in Southern Africa: An Analysis of Prospects and Problems from a South African Perspective. *African Security Review* 5 (5): 27–38.

de Coning, C. 1998. Conditions for Intervention: DRC and Lesotho. *Conflict Trends* 1: 20–23.

de Coning C. 1999. Exercise Blue Crane. A unifying moment for SADC. *Conflict Trends* 1:19, 23.

de Coning, C. 2005. A Peacekeeping Stand-By System for SADC: Implementing the African Stand-by Force Framework in Southern Africa. In *People, States and Regions. Building a Collaborative Security Regime in Southern Africa*, ed. A. Hammerstad, 83–116. Braamfontein: South African Institute of International Affairs.

de Lombaerde, P., E. Dorrucci, G. Genna, and F.P. Mongelli. 2008. Quantitative Monitoring and Comparison of Regional Integration Processes: Steps Toward Good Practise. In *Elements of Regional Integration. A Multidimensional Approach*, ed. A. Kösler and M. Zimmek, 149–179. Baden-Baden: Nomos.

de Lombaerde, P., and M. Schulz (eds.). 2009. *The EU and World Regionalism: The Makability of Regions in the 21st Century*. London: Ashgate.

de Lombaerde, P., and L. van Langenhove. 2006. Indicators of regional integration: conceptual and methodological aspects. In *Assessment and Measurement of Regional Integration. Routledge/Warwick Studies in Globalisation London*, vol. 13, ed. P. de Lombaerde, 9–41. New York: Routledge.

de Lombaerde, P., F. Söderbaum, L. van Langenhove, and F. Baert. 2010. Problems and Divides in Comparative Regionalism. In *Comparative Regional Integration. Europe and Beyond. The International Political Economy of New Regionalisms Series*, ed. F. Laursen, 21–39. Farnham: Ashgate.

DiMaggio, P.J., and W.W. Powell. 1983. The Iron Cage Revisited: Institutional Isomorphism and Collective Rationality in Organizational Fields. *American Sociological Review* 48 (2): 147–160.

Doidge, M. 2011. *The European Union and Interregionalism*. Farnham: Ashgate.

Downs, G.W. 2000. Constructing Effective Environmental Regimes. *Annual Review of Political Science* 3 (1): 25–42.

Downs, G.W., D.M. Rocke, and P.N. Barsoom. 1996. Is the Good News about Compliance Good News about Cooperation? *International Organization* 50 (3): 379–406.

Draper, P., P. Alves, and M. Kalaba. 2006. South Africa's International Trade Diplomacy: Implications for Regional Integration. *Regional Integration in Southern Africa*, vol. 1. Gaborone: Friedrich Ebert Stiftung - Botswana Office.

Draper, P., and N. Khumalo. 2005. Friend or Foe: South Africa and Sub-Saharan Africa in the Global Trading System. In *Reconfiguring the Compass: South Africa's African Trade Diplomacy*, ed. P. Draper, 1–37. Johannesburg: South African Institute of International Affairs.

Draper, P., and N. Khumalo. 2009. The Future of the Southern African Customs Union. *Trade Negotiations Insights* 8 (6): 4–5.

du Pisani, A. 2011. The Security Dimension of Regional Integration in SADC. In *Monitoring Integration in Southern Africa. Yearbook 2010*, ed. A. Bösl, A. du Pisani, G. Erasmus, T. Hartzenberg, and R. Sandrey, 23–45. Stellenbosch: Trade Law Centre of Southern Africa.

du Toit, P. 1995. *State Building and Democracy in Southern Africa. Botswana, Zimbabwe and South Africa*. Washington: United States Institute of Peace Press.

Ebrill, L.P., and J.G. Stotsky. 1998. The Revenue Implications of Trade Liberalization. In *Trade Reform and Regional Integration in Africa*, ed. Z. Iqbal, and M.S. Kahn, 66–146. Washington: International Monetary Fund.

Eckstein, H. 1975. Case Study and Theory in Political Science (Handbook of Political Science). In *Strategies of Inquiry*, vol. 7, ed. F.I. Greenstein, and N.W. Polsby, 79–138. Reading: Addison-Wesley.

Economic Consulting Associates (ECA). 2009. *The Potential of Regional Power Sector Integration. South African Power Pool (SAPP)—Transmission & Trading Case Study*. London: Economic Consulting Association Limited.

Ende, M. 2004. *Jim Knopf und Lukas der Lokomotivführer*. Stuttgart: Thienemann Verlag.

Erasmus, G. 2007. Is SACU constructing an effective framework for regional integration? In *Monitoring Regional Integration in Southern Africa Yearbook*, vol. 7, ed. A. Bösl, W. Breytenbach, T. Hartzenberg, C. McCarthy, and K. Schade, 228–249. Stellenbosch: Trade Law Centre of Southern Africa.

Erasmus, H., F. Flatters, and R. Kirk. 2004. *Rules of Origin as Tools of Development? Some Lessons from SADC*. Gaborone: SADC Secretariat.

Erasmus, H., F. Flatters, and R. Kirk. 2006. Rules of Origin as Tools for Development? Some Lessons from SADC. In *The Origin of Goods. Rules of Origin in Regional Trade Agreements*, ed. O. Cadot, A. Estevadeordal, A. Suwa-Eisenmann, and T. Verdier, 259–294. Oxford: Oxford University Press.

Evans, M. 1984. The Front-Line States, South Africa and Southern African Security: Military Prospects and Perspectives. *Zambezia XII* 5: 1–19.

Farell, M. 2007. From EU Model to External Policy? Promoting Regional Integration in the Rest of the World. In *Making History: European Integration and Institutional Change at Fifty. The State of the European*

Union, vol. 8, ed. S. Meunier and K.R. McNamara, 299–315. Oxford, Bloomington: Oxford University Press.
Fisher L.M., and N. Ngoma. 2005. *The SADC Organ. Challenges in the New Millenium*. vol. 114. ISS Paper. Pretoria: Institute for Security Studies.
Flatters, F. 2001. *The SADC Trade Protocol: Impacts, Issues and the Way Ahead*. Paper prepared under the USAID/RCSA SADC Trade Protocol Project. http://qed.econ.queensu.ca/faculty/flatters/writings/ff_sadc_impacts.pdf (10/10/2016).
Flatters F. 2004. SADC Rules of Origin in Textiles and Garments: Barriers to Regional Trade and Global Integration. In *The Impact of Preferential Rules of Origin in the Textile and Clothing Sector in Africa*, ed. R. Grynberg, 41–66. London: Commonwealth Secretariat.
Flick, U. 2007. *Qualitative Sozialforschung. Eine Einführung*. Reinbeck: Rowohlt.
Flyvbjerg, B. 2006. Five Misunderstandings About Case-Study Research. *Qualitative Inquiry* 12 (2): 219–245.
Foroutan, F., and L. Pritchett. 1993. Intra-Sub-Saharan African Trade: is it too Little? *Journal of African Economies* 2 (1): 74–105.
Franke, B. 2007. Military Integration in Southern Africa: The Example of SADC's Standby Brigade. In *South African Yearbook of International Affairs 2006/7*, ed. E. Sidiropoulos, 183–190. Johannesburg: South African Institute of International Affairs.
Franke, B. 2009. *Security Cooperation in Africa. A Reappraisal*. Boulder, London: Lynne Rienner.
Gamba, V. 1998. Small Arms Proliferation in Southern Africa: The Potential for Regional Control. *African Security Review* 7 (4): 57–72.
Gehring, T. 1994. Der Beitrag von Institutionen zur Förderung der internationalen Zusammenarbeit. Lehren aus der institutionellen Struktur der Europäischen Gemeinschaft. *Zeitschrift für Internationale Beziehungen* 1 (2): 211–242.
Gehring, T. 1995. Regieren im internationalen System. Verhandlungen, Normen und Internationale Regime. *Politische Vierteljahresschrift* 36 (2): 197–219.
Gehring, T. 1996. Integrating Integration Theory: Neo-functionalism and International Regimes. *Global Society* 10 (3): 225–253.
Gehring, T. 2002. *Die Europäische Union als komplexe internationale Organisation. Wie durch Kommunikation und Entscheidung soziale Ordnung entsteht*. Baden-Baden: Nomos.
Gehring, T., and S. Oberthür. 1997. Internationale Regime als Steuerungsinstrumente der Umweltpolitik. In *Internationale Umweltregime. Umweltschutz durch Verhandlungen und Verträge*, ed. T. Gehring and S. Oberthür, 9–26. Opladen: Leske, Budrich.
Gelb, S. 2005. South-South Investment: The Case of Africa. In *Africa in the World Economy: The National, Regional and International Challenges*, ed.

J.J. Teunissen, and A. Akkerman, 200–205. Rotterdam: Forum on Debt and Development.
George, A.L., and A. Bennett. 2005. *Case Studies and Theory Development in the Social Sciences*. Cambridge: MIT Press.
Gibb, R. 1998. Southern Africa in Transition: Prospects and Problems Facing Regional Integration. *Journal of Modern African Studies* 36 (2): 287–306.
Gilardi, F. 2008. *Delegation in the Regulatory State. Independent Regulatory Agencies in Western Europe*. Celtenham: Edward Elgar Publishing.
Gilardi, F. 2013. Transnational Diffusion: Norms, Ideas, and Policies. In *Handbook of International Relations*, ed. W. Carlsnaes, T. Risse, and B.A. Simmons, 453–477. London: SAGE.
Gillson, I. 2010. *Deepening Regional Integration to Eliminate the Fragmented Goods Market in Southern Africa*. Washington: World Bank.
Gilpin, R. 1987. *The Political Economy of International Relations*. Princeton: Princeton University Press.
Göhler, G. 1997. Der Zusammenhang von Institution, Macht und Repräsentation. In *Institution - Macht - Repräsentation: Wofür politische Institutionen stehen und wie sie wirken*, ed. Göhler Gea, 11–62. Baden-Baden: Nomos.
Goldstein, A. 2004. *Regional Integration, FDI and Competitiveness in Southern Africa*. Paris: OECD.
Grant, J.A., and F. Söderbaum. 2003. Introduction: The New Regionalism in Africa. In *The New Regionalism in Africa*, ed. F. Söderbaum, and J.A. Grant, 1–20. Aldershot, Burlington: Ashgate.
Grant, J.A., and F. Söderbaum (eds.). 2003. *The New Regionalism in Africa. The International Political Economy of New Regionalism Studies*. Aldershot, Burlington: Ashgate.
Gray, J. 2012. *Life, Death, or Zombies? The Endurance of Inefficient Regional Economic Organizations*. Unpublished Manuscript. Philadelphia: University of Pennsylvania.
Gregory, S. 2000. The French Military in Africa: Past and Present. *African Affairs* 99: 435–448.
Grieco, J.M. 1988. Anarchy and the Limits of Cooperation: A Realist Critique of the Newest Liberal Institutionalism. *International Organization* 42 (3): 485–507.
Grieco, J.M. 1993. Anarchy and the Limits of Cooperation: A Realist Critique of the Newest Liberal Institutionalism. In *Neorealism and Neoliberalism: The Contemporary Debate*, ed. D.A. Baldwin, 116–142. New York: Columbia University Press.
Grieco, J.M. 1997. Realist International Theory and the Study of World Politics. In *New Thinking in International Relations Theory*, ed. M. Doyle, and J. Ikenberry, 163–201. Boulder: Westview Press.

Griffith, M., and S. Powell. 2007. *Partnership Under Pressure. An Assessment of the European Commission's Conduct in the EPA Negotiations*. London: ActionAid, CAFOD, Christian Aid, Tearfund, Traidcraft Exchange.
Grobbelaar, N. 2004. Can South African Business Drive Regional Integration on the Continent? *South African Journal of International Affairs* 11 (2): 91–106.
Gruber, L. 2000. *Ruling the World: Power Politics and the Rise of Supranational Institutions*. Princeton: Princeton University Press.
Haarlov, J. 1997. *Regional Cooperation and Integration within Industry and Trade in Southern Africa. The Making of Modern Africa*. Aldershot, Brookfield, Hong Kong: Ashgate.
Haas, E.B. 1958. *The Uniting of Europe: Political, Social, and Economic Forces 1950–1957*. Stanford: Stanford University Press.
Haas, E.B. 1964. *Beyond the Nation State: Functionalism and International Organization*. Stanford: Stanford University Press.
Hammerstad, A. 2003. *Defending the State or Protecting the People? SADC Security Integration at a Crossroads*. Johannesburg: South African Institute of International Affairs.
Hammons, T.J. 2011. *Electricity Infrastructure in the Global Marketplace*. Rijeka: InTech.
Hanlon, J. 1986. *Beggar Your Neighbours. Apartheid Power in Southern Africa*. London: Catholic Institute for International Relations.
Hanlon, J. 1989. *SADCC in the 1990s. Development on the Front Line*. London: Economist Intelligence Unit.
Hansen, R.D. 1969. Regional Integration: Reflections on a Decade of Theoretical Efforts. *World Politics* 21 (2): 242–271.
Harbeson, J.W. 1994. Civil Society and the Study of African Politics: A Preliminary Assesment. In *Civil Society and the State in Africa*, ed. J.W. Harbeson, D. Rothchild, and N. Chazan, 285–300. Boulder, London: Lynne Rienner.
Hartzenberg, T., and B. Mathe. 2005. FDI in Services in SADC: Impact on Regional Integration. In *Monitoring Regional Inegration in Southern Africa Yearbook*, vol. 5, ed. D. Hansohm, W. Breytenbach, T. Hartzenberg, and C. McCarthy, 9–24. Windhoek: Namibian Economic Policy Research Unit.
Hasenclever, A., P. Mayer, and V. Rittberger. 1997. *Theories of International Regimes. Cambridge Studies in International Relations*, vol. 55. Cambridge: Cambridge University Press.
Hatchard, J., and P. Slinn. 1995. The Path Towards a New Order in South Africa. *International Relations* 12 (4): 1–26.
Hendricks, C., and T. Musavengana (eds.). 2010. *The security sector in Southern Africa*. Pretoria: Institute for Security Studies.
Hentz, J.J. 2004. State Collapse and Regional Contagion in Sub-sahara Africa: Lessons for Zimbabwe. *Scientia Militaria* 32 (1): 143–156.

Hentz, J.J. 2005. *South Africa and the Logic of Regional Cooperation.* Bloomington, Indianapolis: Indiana University Press.
Herbst, J. 2007. Crafting Regional Cooperation in Africa. In *Crafting Cooperation. Regional International Institutions in Comparative Perspective*, ed. A. Acharya, and A.I. Johnston, 129–144. Cambridge: Cambridge University Press.
Herz, J.H. 1950. Idealist Internationalism and Security Dilemma. *World Politics* 2 (2): 157–180.
Hess, R. 2001. *Zimbabwe Case Study on Trade Negotiations.* London: Overseas Development Institute.
Hettne, B. 1999. Globalisation and the New Regionalism: The Second Great Transformation. In *Globalism and the New Regionalism*, ed. B. Hettne, A. Inotai, and O. Sunkel, 1–24. London: Macmillan Press.
Hettne, B. 2005. Beyond the 'New' Regionalism. *New Political Economy* 10 (4): 543–571.
Hettne, B., and F. Söderbaum. 1998. The New Regionalism Approach. *Politeia: Journal for Political Science and Public Administration* 17 (3): 5–19.
Hettne, B., and F. Söderbaum. 2008. The future of Regionalism. Old divides, new frontiers. In *Regionalisation and Global Governance. The taming of globalisation?*, ed. A.F. Cooper, C.W. Hughes, and P.D. Lombaerde, 61–79. London, New York: Routledge.
Hirschmann, A.O. 1945. *National Power and the Structure of Foreign Trade.* Berkely, Los Angeles, New York: University of California Press.
Hitchcock, W.I. 2010. The Marshall Plan and the Creation of the West. In *The Cambridge History of the Cold War Volume 1: Origins*, ed. M.P. Leffler and O.A. Westad, 154–174. Cambridge: Cambridge University Press.
Hoffmann, S. 1966. Obstinate or Obsolete? The Fate of the Nation-State and the Case of Western Europe. *Dædalus Journal of the American Academy of Arts and Sciences* 95 (2): 862–915.
Hoffmann, S. 1982. Reflections on the Nation-State in Western Europe Today. *Journal of Common Market Studies* 21 (2): 21–77.
Hofmann, M.E. 2009. *Resource Diplomacy in Southern Africa. Necessity, Structures and Security Implications for the Southern African Development Community (SADC) Region.* Saarbrücken: VDM.
Holden, M. 1996. *Economic and Trade Liberalization in Southern Africa. Is there a Role for South Africa?* World Bank Discussion Paper, vol. 342. Washington: World Bank.
Horvei, T. 1998. Powering the Region: South Africa in the Southern African Power Pool. In *South Africa in Southern Africa*, ed. D. Simon, 146–163. Oxford, Athens, Cape Town: James Currey.
Howorth, J. 2007. *Security and Defence Policy in the European Union.* Houndmills: Palgrave Macmillan.

Hull, C., and M. Derblom. 2009. *Abandoning Frontline Trenches? Capabilities for Peace and Security in the SADC region*. Stockholm: Swedish Defence Research Agency.
Hurrell, A. 1995. Explaining the resurgence of regionalism in world politics. *Review of international Studies* 21 (4): 331–358.
Iapadre, L. 2006. Regional Integration Agreements and the Geography of World Trade: Statistical Indicators and Empirical Evidence. In *Assessment and Measurement of Regional Integration*, ed. P. de Lombaerde, 65–85. London and New York: Routledge.
Institute for Security Studies (ISS). 2009. *The Military Balance 2009*. London: Institute for Strategic Studies.
International Institute for Security Studies (IISS). 1994. *The Military Balance 1994–1995*. London: Brassey's.
Isaksen, J., and E.N. Tjønneland. 2001. *Assessing the Restructuring of SADC - Positions, Policies and Progress*. Bergen: Chr. Michelsen Institute.
Iwanow, T. 2011. *Impact of Derogations from Implementation of the SADC FTA Obligations on Intra-SADCTrade*. Gaborone: USAID/Southern Africa.
Jakobeit, C., T. Hartzenberg, and N. Charalambides. 2005. *Overlapping Membership in COMESA, EAC, SACU and SADC. Trade Policy Options for the Region and for EPA Negotiations*. Eschborn: Deutsche Gesellschaft für Technische Zusammenarbeit.
Jaspert, J. 2010. *Regionalismus im südlichen Afrika. Die Handels- und Sicherheitspolitik der SADC*. Wiesbaden: VS Verlag.
Jefferis, K.R. 2007. The Process of Monetary Integration in the SADC Region. *Journal of Southern African Studies* 33 (1): 83–106.
Jenkins, C., J. Leape, and L. Thomas. 2000. Gaining from Trade in Southern Africa. In *Gaining from Trade in Southern Africa. Complementary Policies to Underpin the SADC Free Trade Area*, ed. C. Jenkins, J. Leape, and L. Thomas, 1–23. London: Palgrave Macmillan.
Jenkins, C., and L. Thomas. 2001. African Regionalism and the SADC. In *European Union and New Regionalism: Regional actors and global governance in a post-hegemonic era*, ed. M. Telò, 153–175. Aldershot: Ashgate Publishing.
Jenkins, C., and L. Thomas. 2002. *Foreign Direct Investment in Southern Africa: Determinants. Characteristics and Implications for Economic Growth and Poverty Alleviation*. London: CSA, CREFSA-LSE, Oxford.
Jervis, R. 1978. Cooperation under the Security Dilemma. *World Politics* 30 (2): 167–214.
Jervis, R. 1982. Security Regimes. *International Organization* 36 (2): 357–378.
Jetschke, A., and T. Lenz. 2011. Vergleichende Regionalismusforschung und Diffusion: Eine neue Forschungsagenda. *Politische Vierteljahresschrift* 52 (3): 448–474.

Jetschke, A., and A. Liese. 1999. Die kulturelle Prägung staatlicher Interessen und Handlungen. Die kulturelle Prägung staatlicher Interessen und Handlungen. *Österreichische Zeitschrift für Politikwissenschaft* 28 (3): 285–300.

Kalaba, M., and M. Tsedu. 2008. *Regional Trade Agreements, Effects and Opportunities: Southern African Development Research Network. Implementation of the SADC Trade Protocol and the Intra-SACU Trade Performance.* Pretoria: Trade and Industrial Policy Strategies.

Kaseke, N. 2013. Emergence of Electricity Crisis in Zimbabwe. Reform, Response and Cost Implications. *Journal of Business and Management & Social Sciences Research* 2 (10): 1–16.

Kaseke, N. 2013. Emergence of Electricity Crisis in Zimbabwe. Reform, Response and Cost Implications. *Journal of Business and Management & Social Sciences Research* 2 (10): 10–14.

Keck, A., and R. Piermartini. 2008. The Impact of Economic Partnership Agreements in Countries of the Southern African Development Community. *Journal of African Economies* 17 (1): 85–130.

Keet, D. 1997. Europe's free-trade plans with South Africa: Strategic responses from and challenges to South and Southern Africa. *Development Southern Africa* 14 (2): 285–293.

Keman, H. 2008. Comparative research methods. In *Comparative Politics*, ed. D. Caramani, 63–82. Oxford: Oxford University Press.

Kennes, W. 1999. African Regional Economic Integration & the European Union. In *Regionalisation in Africa: Integration & Disintegration*, ed. D.C. Bach, 27–40. Oxford and Bloomington: James Currey.

Keohane, R.O. 1982. The Demand for International Regimes. *International Organization* 36 (2): 325–355.

Keohane, R.O. 1984. *After Hegemony. Cooperation and Discord in the World Political Economy.* Princeton: Princeton University Press.

Keohane, R.O. 1988. International Institutions: Two Approaches. *International Studies Quarterly* 32 (4): 379–396.

Keohane, R.O. 1990. The Concept of Interdependence: Current American Thinking. In *Soviet-American Dialogue in the Social Sciences. Research Workshops on Interdependence Among Nations*, ed. Education CoBaSSa, 37–41. Washington: National Academy Press.

Keohane, R.O. 1998. International Institutions: Can Interdependence Work? *Foreign Policy* 10 (1): 82–96.

Keohane, R.O., and J.S. Nye. 1977. *Power and Interdependence. World Politics in Transition.* Boston, Toronto: Little, Brown.

Keohane, R.O., and J.S. Nye. 1987. *Power and Interdependence* revisited. *International Organization* 41 (4): 725–753.

Keohane, R.O., and J.S. Nye. 2001. *Power and Interdependence.* New York, London, Boston: Longman.

Khadiagala, G.M. 2007. *Allies in Adversity. The Frontline States in Southern African Security, 1975–1993.* Lanham: University Press of America.
Kibble, S., P. Goodison, and B. Tsie. 1995. The Uneasy Triangle - South Africa, Southern Africa and Europe in the Post-Apartheid Era. *International Relations* 12 (4): 41–61.
Kindleberger, C. 1981. Dominance and Leadership in the International Economy. Exploitation, Public Goods, and Free Rides. *International Studies Quarterly* 25 (2): 242–254.
King, G., R.O. Keohane, and S. Verba. 1994. *Designing Social Inquirey: Scientific Inference in Qualitative Research.* Princeton: Princeton University Press.
Kinzel, W. 2007. *Afrikanische Sicherheitsarchitektur – ein aktueller Überblick.* GIGA Focus Afrika 1. Hamburg: GIGA.
Kirk, R., and M. Stern. 2005. The New Southern African Customs Union Agreement. *World Economy* 28 (2): 169–190.
Klingebiel, S. 2005. Regional Security in Africa and the Role of External Support. *The European Journal of Development Research* 17 (3): 437–448.
Kohler-Koch, B. 1989. Regime in den Internationalen Beziehungen. In *Regime in den Internationalen Beziehungen,* ed. B. Kohler-Koch, 17–85. Baden-Baden: Nomos.
Kösler, A. 2010. *Die Entwicklung der Southern African Development Community (SADC) als Building Block der panafrikanischen Einheit. Die Herausforderungen der doppelten Integration und wichtige Einflussfaktoren.* Hamburg: Verlag Dr. Kovač.
Krapohl, S. (ed.). 2016. *Regional Integration in the Global South. External Influence on Economic Cooperation in ASEAN, MERCOSUR and SADC.* Cham: Palgrave Macmillan.
Krapohl, S., and S. Fink. 2013. Different Paths of Regional Integration: Trade Networks and Regional Institution-Building in Europe, Southeast Asia and Southern Africa. *Journal of Common Market Studies* 51 (3): 472–488.
Krapohl, S., and J. Muntschick. 2009. Two Logics of Regionalism: The Importance of Interdependence and External Support for Regional Integration in Southern Africa. In *Furthering Southern African Integration. Proceedings of the 2008 FOPRISA Annual Conference,* ed. J.M. Kaunda, and F. Zizhou, 3–17. Gaborone: Lightbooks.
Krasner, S.D. 1976. World Politics and the Structure of International Trade. *World Politics* 28 (3): 317–347.
Krasner, S.D. 1982. Structural Causes and Regime Consequences: Regimes as Intervening Variables. *International Organization* 36 (2): 185–205.
Krasner, S.D. 1991. Global Communications and National Power: Life on the Pareto Frontier. *World Politics* 43 (3): 336–366.

Lalá, A. 2007. Mozambique. In *Security and Democracy in Southern Africa*, ed. G. Cawthra, A. du Pisani, and A. Omari, 108–122. Johannesburg: Wits University Press.

Langhammer, R.J., and U. Hiemenz. 1990. *Regional Integration among Developing Countries. Opportunities, Obstacles and Options*, vol. 232. Kieler Studien. Tübingen: J. C. B. Mohr (Paul Siebeck).

Laursen, F. 2010. Regional Integration: Some Introductory Reflections. In *Comparative Regional Integration. Europe and Beyond*, ed. F. Laursen, 3–20. Farnham: Ashgate.

Lautier, J. 2013. The SADC Standby Force. In *Africa Conflict Monthly Monitor*, ed. J. Hall, 68–71. Johannesburg: Consultancy Africa Intelligence.

le Pere, G., and A. van Nieuwkerk. 2002. Facing the New Millenium: South Africa's Foreign Policy in a Globalizing World. In *Globalization and Emerging Trends in African States' Foreign Policy-Making Process*, ed. K.G. Adar, and R. Ajulu, 173–210. Aldershot: Ashgate.

le Pere, G., and E.N. Tjønneland. 2005. *Which Way SADC? Advancing co-operation and integration in southern Africa*, vol. 50. IGD Occasional Papers. Midrand: Institute for Global Dialogue.

Lee, M.C. 2003. *The Political Economy of Regionalism in Southern Africa*. Lansdowne, London: Lynne Rienner.

Levy, J.S. 2008. Case Studies: Types, Designs, and Logics of Inference. *Conflict Management and Peace Science* 25 (1): 1–18.

Lincoln, D. 2006. The Historical Geography of the Southern African Development Community's Sugar Protocol. *Illes i Imperis* 9: 117–130.

Lindberg, L.N., and S.A. Scheingold. 1971. *Regional Integration: Theory and Research*. Cambridge, MA: Harvard University Press.

Lindeke, B., P. Kaapama, and L. Blaauw. 2007. Namibia. In *Security and Democracy in Southern Africa*, ed. G. Cawthra, A. du Pisani, and A. Omari, 123–141. Johannesburg: Wits University Press.

Lopes, V., and P. Kundishora. 2000. The Southern African Power Pool: Economic Dependency or Self Sufficiency? In *Environmental Security in Southern Africa*, ed. D. Tevera, and S. Moyo, 207–225. Harare: SAPES Books.

Lorenz-Carl, U. 2013. When the 'Not so Weak' Bargain with the 'Not so Strong': Whose Agency Matters in the Economic Partnership Agreements? In *Mapping Agency. Comparing Regionalisms in Africa*, ed. U. Lorenz-Carl and M. Rempe, 61–76. Farnham: Ashgate.

Lyakurwa, W. 1999. A Regional Case-Study of the SADC. In *Regional Integration and Trade Liberalization in SubSaharan Africa*, ed. A. Oyejide, I. Elbadawi, and S. Yeo, 250–280. Houndmills, London, and New York: Palgrave Macmillan.

Macaringue, P. 2007. Military Dimensions of Security Cooperation in the Southern African Development Community. In *Proceedings of the 2006 FOPRISA Conference*, ed. J.M. Kaunda, 115–127. Gaborone: Lightbooks.

Madlala, O. 2006. Plans to avert Southern African energy crisis as demand outstrips supply in SADC region. Engineering News. Published on 6th October 2006. http://www.engineeringnews.co.za/article/plans-to-avert-southern-african-energy-crisis-as-demand-outstrips-supply-in-sadc-region-2006-10-06. Accessed 12 May 2016.

Maes, M. 2012. 27 September 2012: 10 Years of EPA Negotiations. From Misconception and Mismanagement to Failure. *Great Insights* 1 (6): 2–3.

Maiketso, J.T., and K. Sekolokwane. 2007. Countrywise Review of the Implementation of the SADC Trade Protocol. In *Proceedings of the 2006 FOPRISA Annual Conference*, vol. 3, ed. J.M. Kaunda, 211–234. Gaborone: Botswana Institute for Development Policy Analysis.

Mair, S., and C. Peters-Berries. 2001. *Regionale Integration und Kooperation in Afrika südlich der Sahara. EAC, ECOWAS und SADC im Vergleich*. Forschungsbericht des Bundesministeriums für wirtschaftliche Zusammenarbeit und Entwicklung (BMZ), vol. 127. Bonn and München: Weltforum Verlag.

Makgetlaneng, S. 2005. South Africa - Southern Africa Relations in the Post-Apartheid Era: The Strategic Importance of Southern Africa to the Economic and Trade Interests of South African Companies. *Nordic Journal of African Studies* 14 (2): 235–254.

Makhubelam, I. 2009. SADC Standby Force borne Exercise Golfinho. *South African Soldier* 16 (10): 11–13.

Malan, M. 1998. *Regional Power Politics Under Cover of SADC. Running Amok with a Mythical Organ*. vol. 35. Occasional Paper. Pretoria: Institute for Security Studies.

Mandrup, T. 2009. South Africa and the SADC Stand-By Force. *Scientia Militaria, South African Journal of Military Studies* 37 (2): 1–24.

Mansfield, E.D., and H.V. Milner. 1999. The New Wave of Regionalism. *International Organization* 53 (3): 589–627.

Martin, L.L. 1992. Interests, power, and multilateralism. *International Organization* 46 (4): 765–792.

Martin, L.L., and B.A. Simmons. 1998. Theories and Empirical Studies of International Institutions. *International Organization* 52 (4): 729–757.

Matinga, M.N. 2004. Pooling African Power: Issues, Developments and Outlook of a Reforming and Integrating Southern African Power Sector. In *Monitoring Regional Integration in Southern Africa. Yearbook Vol. 4*, ed. D. Hansohm, W. Breytenbach, T. Hartzenberg, and C. McCarthy, 91–105. Windhoek: Namibian Economic Policy Research Unit.

Matlosa, K. 1999. *The Lesotho Conflict: Major Causes and Management*. In *Crisis in Lesotho: The Challenge of Managing Conflict in Southern Africa*, ed. K. Lambrechts, 9–13. Braamfontein: Foundation for Global Dialogue.
Matlosa, K. 2007. Lesotho. In *Security and Democracy in Southern Africa*, ed. G. Cawthra, A. du Pisani, and A. Omari, 80–97. Johannesburg: Wits University Press.
Mattli, W. 1999. *The Logic of Regional Integration: Europe and Beyond*. Cambridge: Cambridge University Press.
Mayer, P., V. Rittberger, and M. Zürn. 1993. Regime Theory: State of the Art and Perspectives. In *Regime Theory and International Relations*, ed. V. Rittberger, and P. Mayer, 391–430. Oxford: Clarendon Press.
McCarthy, C. 1998. South African trade and industrial policy in a regional context. In *Post-Apartheid Southern Africa. Economic challenges and policies for the future*, ed. L. Petersson, 64–86. London, New York: Routledge.
McCarthy, C. 1999. SACU & the Rand Zone. In *Regionalisation in Africa: Integration & Disintegration*, ed. D.C. Bach, 159–168. Oxford and Bloomington: James Currey.
McCarthy, C. 2003. The Southern African Customs Union in Transition. *African Affairs* 102 (409): 605–630.
McCarthy, C. 2008. The SADC/SACU interplay in EPA negotiations - A variation on the old theme of integrating and unequal economies. In *Negotiating Regions: Economic Partnership Agreements between the European Union and the African Regional Economic Communities*, ed. U. Engel, and H. Asche, 109–130. Leipzig: Leipzig Universitätsverlag.
McCarthy, C., P. Kruger, and J. Fourie. 2007. *Benchmarking EPA negotiations between EU and SADC*. Stellenbosch: Trade Law Centre for Southern Africa.
McCarthy, D.M.P. 2006. *International Economic Integration in Historical Perspective*. London: Routledge.
Meinken, A. 2005. *Militärische Kapazitäten und Fähigkeiten afrikanischer Staaten. Ursachen und Wirkungen militärischer Ineffektivität in Sub-Sahara Afrika*. Berlin: Stiftung Wissenschaft und Politik.
Merven, B., A. Hughes, and S. Davis. 2010. An analysis of energy consumption for a selection of countries in the Southern African Development Community. *Journal of Energy in Southern Africa* 21 (1): 11–24.
Meyer, J.W., J. Boli, G.M. Thomas, and F.O. Ramirez. 1997. World Society and Nation State. *The American Journal of Sociology* 103 (1): 144–181.
Meyer, J.W., and B. Rowan. 1977. Institutionalized Organizations: Formal Structure as Myth and Ceremony. *The American Journal of Sociology* 83 (2): 340–363.
Meyn, M. 2010. Die Wirtschaftspartnerschaftsabkommen der Europäischen Union - was war, was ist und was kommen muss. In *Afrika und externe*

Akteure - Partner auf Augenhöhe? ed. F. Stehnken, A. Daniel, H. Asche, and R. Öhlgeschläger, 75–89. Baden-Baden: Nomos.
Meyn, M., and J. Kennan. 2010. *Economic Partnership Agreeements: Comparative Analysis of the Agricultral Provisions*. New York: United Nations.
Meyns, P. 1984. The Southern African Development Coordination Conference (SADCC) and regional cooperation in southern Africa. In *African Regional Organizations*, ed. D. Mazzeo, 198–224. Cambridge: Cambridge University Press.
Meyns, P. 1997. From Co-ordination to Integration. Institutional Aspects of the Development of SADC. In *The Regionalization of the World Economy and Consequences for Southern Africa*, ed. H. Dieter, 163–184. Marburg: Metropolis-Verlag.
Meyns, P. 2000. *Konflikt und Entwicklung im Südlichen Afrika*. Opladen: Leske, Budrich.
Meyns, P. 2002. The Ongoing Search for a Security Structure in the SADC Region: The Re-establishment of the SADC Organ on Politics, Defence and Security. In *Monitoring Regional Integration in Southern Africa. Yearbook Vol. 2*, ed. D. Hansohm, C. Peters-Berries, W. Breytenbach, T. Hartzenberg, W. Maier, and P. Meyns, 141–168. Windhoek: Gamsberg Macmillan.
Mitrany, D. 1943. *A Working Peace System*. Chicago: Quadrangle Books.
Mngqibisa, K. 2000. Exercise Blue Crane. In *Peacekeeping in the New Millenium: Lessons Learned from Exercise Blue Crane*, ed. C. de Coning, and K. Mngqibisa, 13–22. Durban: African Centre for the Constructive Resolution of Disputes.
Molomo, M.G., Z. Maundeni, B. Osei-Hwedie, I. Taylor, and S. Whitman. 2007. Botswana. In *Security and Democracy in Southern Africa*, ed. G. Cawthra, A. du Pisani, and A. Omari, 61–79. Johannesburg: Wits University Press.
Moran, T.E., E.M. Graham, and M. Blomström (eds.). 2005. *Does Foreign Direct Investment Promote Development?* Washington, DC: Institute for International Economics.
Moravcsik, A. 1993. Preferences and Power in the European Community: A Liberal Intergovernmentalist Approach. *Journal of Common Market Studies* 31 (4): 473–524.
Moravcsik, A. 1997. Taking Preferences Seriously: A Liberal Theory of International Politics. *International Organization* 51 (4): 513–553.
Moravcsik, A. 1998. *The Choice for Europe: Social Purpose and State Power from Messina to Maastricht*. Ithaca: Cornell University Press.
Moravcsik, A., and K. Nicolaïdis. 1999. Explaining the Treaty of Amsterdam: Interests, Influence, Institutions. *Journal of Common Market Studies* 37 (1): 59–85.

Morgan, P.M. 1997. Regional Security Complexes and Regional Orders. In *Regional Orders. Building Security in a New World*, ed. D.A. Lake, and P.M. Morgan, 20–42. Pennsylvania: Pennsylvania State University Press.
Morgenthau, H. 1948. *Politics Among Nations. The Struggle for Power and Peace*. New York: Alfred A. Knopf.
Motsamai, D. 2014. *SADC 2014–2015: Are South Africa and Zimbabwe Shaping the Organisation?* Policy Brief 70. Pretoria: Institute for Security Studies.
Mthembu-Salter, G. 2008. *The Cost of Non-tariff Barriers to Business along the North-South Corridor (South Africa-Zimbabwe) via Beit Bridge. A Preliminary Study*, vol. 20. Trade Policy Report. Johannesburg: South African Institute of International Affairs.
Mufune, P. 1993. The Future of Southern African Development Coordination Conference (SADCC). *Pula: Botswana Journal of African Studies* 7 (1): 14–34.
Müller, H. 1993. *Die Chance der Kooperation. Regime in den internationalen Beziehungen*. Darmstadt: Wissenschaftliche Buchgesellschaft.
Münch, R. 2008. *Die Konstruktion der europäischen Gesellschaft. Zur Dialektik von transnationaler Integration und nationaler Desintegration*. Frankfurt, New York: Campus Verlag.
Muntschick, J. 2012. *Theorising Regionalism and External Influence: A Situation-Structural Approach*. Mainz Papers on International and European Politics 2012/2. Mainz: Chair of International Relations, Johannes Gutenberg University.
Muntschick, J. 2013a. Explaining the influence of extra-regional actors on regional economic integration in Southern Africa: the EU's interfering impact on SADC and SACU. In *Mapping Agency: Comparing Regionalisms in Africa*, ed. U. Lorenz-Carl, and M. Rempe, 77–95. Farnham: Ashgate.
Muntschick, J. 2013b. Regional Energy Cooperation in SADC: Is the Southern African Power Pool currently powered by External Funding? In *Monitoring Regional Intergation in Southern Africa. Yearbook 2012*, ed. A. du Pisani, G. Erasmus, and T. Hartzenberg, 113–139. Stellenbosch: Trade Law Centre for Southern Africa.
Muntschick, J. 2013c. Regionalismus und Externer Einfluss: Stört die Europäische Union die Regionale Marktintegration im südlichen Afrika? *Politische Vierteljahresschrift* 54 (4): 686–713.
Mzizi, J.B. 2007. Swaziland. In *Security and Democracy in Southern Africa*, ed. G. Cawthra, A. du Pisani, and A. Omari, 172–191. Johannesburg: Wits University Press.
Nathan, L. 2004. *The Absence of Common Values and Failure of Common Security in Southern Africa, 1992–2003*, vol. 50. Crisis States Programme Working papers serie. London: LSE Crisis States Research Centre.

Nathan, L. 2006. SADC's Uncommon Approach to Common Security, 1992–2003. *Journal of Southern African Studies* 32 (3): 605–622.
Nathan, L. 2012. *Community of Insecurity. SADC's Struggle for Peace and Security in Southern Africa*. Farnham: Ashgate.
Ndlovu, P.N. 2011. Campbell v Republic of Zimbabwe: A moment of truth for the SADC Tribunal. *SADC Law Journal* 1: 63–79.
Neethling, T. 1999. Military Intervention in Lesotho: Perspectives on Operation Boleas and Beyond. *The Online Journal of Peace and Conflict Resolution* 2 (2): 1–12.
Ngoma, N. 2005. *Prospects for a Security Community in Southern Africa. An Analysis of Regional Security in the Southern African Development Community*. Pretoria: Institute for Security Studies.
Ngwawi, J. 2012. Energy Sector Plan targets surplus, sets priorities. *SADC Today* 15 (1): 1–4.
Ngwawi, J. 2012. Energy Sector Plan targets surplus, sets priorities. *SADC Today* 15 (1): 2-3.
Njiramba, M.M. 2004. Pooling African Power: Issues, Developments and Outlook of a Reforming and Integrating Southern African Power Sector. In *Monitoring Regional Integration in Southern Africa Yearbook*, vol. 4, ed. D. Hansohm, W. Breytenbach, T. Hartzenberg, and C. McCarthy, 91–105. Windhoek: Namibian Economic Policy Research Unit.
NORAD. 2007. *Review and Recommendations on Norway's Role as Lead ICP for Energy within SADC. Report from a Fact-finding Mission*. Oslo: Norwegian Agency for Development Cooperation (NORAD).
Nyambe, J. 2010. The SADC Free Trade Area and the Way towards a Customs Union. In *Proceedings of the 2009 FOPRISA Annual Conference, vol. Report 8*, ed. C. Harvey, 153–171. Gaborone: Botswana Institute for Development Policy Analysis.
Nyambe, J., and K. Schade. 2008. *Progresss Towards the SADC FTA and Remaining Challenges*. Paper presented at the FOPRISA 3rd Annual Conference, Centurion/Pretoria.
Nyambua, M. 1998. Zimbabwe's Role as Lead Nation for Peacekeeping Training in the SADC Region. In *Resolute Partners: Building Peacekeeping Capacity in Southern Africa*, ed. M. Malan, 56–60. Pretoria: Institute for Security Studies.
Nye, J.S. 1965. Patterns and Catalysts in Regional Integration. *International Organization* 19 (4): 870–884.
Nye, J.S. 1968a. Central American Regional Integration. In *International Regionalism: Readings*, ed. J.S. Nye, 377–420. Boston: Little, Brown and Company.
Nye, J.S. 1968b. Introduction. In *International Regionalism: Readings*, ed. J.S. Nye, V–XVI. Boston: Little, Brown and Company.

Nye, J.S. 2008. *Understanding International Conflicts: An Introduction to Theory and History*, 7th ed. London: Pearson.
Odell, J.S. 2001. Case Study Methods in International Political Economy. *International Studies Perspective* 2: 161–176.
Odén, B. 2000. The Southern Africa Region and the Regional Hegemon. In *National Perspectives on the New Regionalism in the South. International Political Economy Series*, vol. 3, ed. B. Hettne, A. Inotai, and O. Sunkel, 242–264. London, Houndmills: Macmillan Press.
Odén, B. 2001. Regionalization in Southern Africa: The Role of the Dominant. In *Regionalization in a Globalizing World: A Comparative Perspective on Forms, Actors and Processes*, ed. M. Schulz, F. Söderbaum, and J. Öjendal, 82–99. London: ZED Books.
Ohlson, T. 1996. Conflict and Conflict Resolution in a Southern African Context. In *Peace and Security in Southern Africa*, ed. I. Mandaza, 1–58. Harare: SAPES Books.
Olivier, G. 2006. *South Africa and the European Union: Self-Interest, Ideology and Altruism*. Pretoria: Protea Book House.
Omari, A., and P. Macaringue. 2007. Southern African Security in Historical Perspective. In *Security and Democracy in Southern Africa*, ed. G. Cawthra, A. du Pisani, and A. Omari, 45–60. Johannesburg: Wits University Press.
Oosthuizen, G.H. 2006. *The Southern African Development Community. The Organisation, its Policies and Prospects*. Midrand: Institute for Global Dialogue.
Oosthuizen, G.H. 2007. The Future of the Southern African Development Community. In *South African Yearbook 2006/7*, ed. E. Sidiropoulos, 87–98. Johannesburg: South African Institute of International Affairs.
Oye, K.A. 1985. Explaining Cooperation under Anarchy: Hypotheses and Strategies. *World Politics* 38 (1): 1–24.
Page, S., and te Velde D.W. 2004. *Foreign Direct Investment by African Countries*. Paper presented at the InWent/UNCTAD Meeting on FDI in Africa, Addis Ababa.
Panke, D., and S. Stapel. 2016. *Exploring overlapping Regionalism. Journal of International Relations and Development*. Published online: 2 November 2016.
Jube, Phiri B. 2007. Zambia. In *Security and Democracy in Southern Africa*, ed. G. Cawthra, A. du Pisani, and A. Omari, 206–220. Johannesburg: Wits University Press.
Pierides, C. 2008. *Non-Tariff Barriers to Trade in Southern Africa: Towards a Measurement Approach*, vol. 21. Trade Policy Report. Johannesburg: South African Institute of International Affairs.
Pietrangeli, G. 2009. Supporting Regional Integration and Cooperation Worldwide: An Overview of the European Union Approach. In *The EU and*

World Regionalism. The Makability of Regions in the 21st Century, ed. P. de Lombaerde, M. Schulz, 9–43. Farnham: Ashgate.
Proff, H.W. 2000. *SADC—Another Institutional Papertiger in Sub-Saharan Africa or a Chance for Joint Industrial Development?* Darmstadt Discussion Papers in Economics 101. Darmstadt: TU Darmstadt.
Przeworski, A., and H. Teune. 1982. *The Logic of Comparative Social Inquiry*. Malabar: Krieger.
Ranganathan, R., and V. Foster. 2011. *The SADC's Infrastructure. A Regional Perspective*. New York: The World Bank.
Rangasamy, L. 2008. *Trade Liberalisation and South Africa's Manufacturing Sector. The impact of trade liberalisation on the competitiveness of the manufacturing sector in South Africa*. Saarbrücken: VDM Verlag Dr. Müller.
Raskin, P., and M. Lazarus. 1991. Regional Energy Development in Southern Africa: Great Potential, great Constraints. *Annual Energy Environ* 16: 145–178.
Raustiala, K. 2000. Compliance & Effectiveness in International Regulatory Cooperation. *Case Western Reserve Journal of International Law* 32 (2): 387–440.
Ravenhill, J. 2008. Regionalism. In *Global Political Economy*, 2nd ed, ed. J. Ravenhill, 172–210. Oxford, New York: Oxford University Press.
Ressler, V. 2007. *Die Perspektiven regionaler Integration im südlichen Afrika. Eine Analyse vor dem Hintergrund der einzelstaatlichen Interessen*. Frankfurt am Main: Peter Lang.
Ricardo, D. 1977. *On the Principles of Political Economy and Taxation*, Reprint ed. Hildesheim: Olms.
Rittberger, V. 1990. International Regimes in the CSCE Region - From Anarchy to Governance and Stable Peace. *Österreichische Zeitschrift für Politikwissenschaft* 19 (4): 349–364.
Rittberger, V. 1993. Research on International Regimes in Germany: the Adaptive Internalization of an American Social Science Concept. In *Regime Theory and International Relations*, ed. V. Rittberger, and P. Mayer, 3–22. Oxford: Clarendon Press.
Rittberger, V., and M. Zürn. 1990. Towards regulated anarchy in East-West relations: causes and consequences of East-West regimes. In *International Regimes in East-West Relations*, ed. V. Rittberger, 9–63. London, New York: Pinter Publishers.
Rittberger, V., and M. Zürn. 1991. Regime Theory: Findings from the Study of "East-West Regimes". *Cooperation and Conflict* 26 (4): 165–183.
Robinson, P. 2009. *The Potential for Regional Power Sector Integration. South African Power Pool (SAPP) Transmission & Trading Case Study*. London: Economic Consulting Associates.

Robson, P. 1993. The New Regionalism and Developing Countries. *Journal of Common Market Studies* 31 (3): 329–348.
Rosamond, B., and A. Warleigh-Lack. 2011. Studying regions comparatively. In *New Regionalism and the European Union. Dialogues, comparisons and new research agenda*, ed. A. Warleigh-Lack, N. Robinson, and B. Rosamond, 18–35. Abingdon: Routledge.
Rosnes, O., and H. Vennemo. 2009. *Powering Up: Costing Power Infrastructure Investment Needs in Sub-Saharan Africa*. Oslo: Econ Pöyry.
Ruggie, J.G. 1998. What Makes the World Hang Together? Neo-Utilitarianism and the Social Constructivist Challenge. *International Organization* 52 (4): 855–885.
Rugoyi, E. 1998. The Interconnection of the Southern African Power Pool. *Oil and gas law and taxation review* 12: 434–439.
Salomon, K. 2009. *Konfliktmanagement durch ECOWAS und SADC. Die Rolle Nigerias und Südafrikas in subregionalen Interventionen: Ein Beitrag zum Frieden?* Saarbrücken: Südwestdeutscher Verlag für Hochschulschriften.
Sandberg, E., and N. Sabel. 2003. Cold War Regional Hangovers in Southern Africa: Zambian Development Strategies, SADC and the New Regionalism Approach. In *The New Regionalism in Africa*, ed. J.A. Grant, and F. Söderbaum, 159–178. Aldershot, Burlington: Ashgate.
Sandrey, R. 2012. Foreign Direct Investment in South Africa. In *Monitoring Regional Integration in Southern Africa. Yearbook 2011*, ed. T. Hartzenberg, G. Erasmus, and A. du Pisani, 188–213. Stellenbosch: Trade Law Centre for Southern Africa.
Sandrey, R. 2013. *An Analysis of the SADC Free Trade Area*. Stellenbosch: Trade Law Centre for Southern Africa.
Sandrey, R., H. Grinsted Jensen, N. Vink, T. Fundira, and W. Viljoen (eds.). 2011. *Cape to Cairo - An Assessment of the Tripartite Free Trade Area*. Stellenbosch: Trade Law Centre for Southern Africa.
Santo, S. 1999. Conflict Management and Post-Conflict Peacebuilding in Lesotho. In *Crisis in Lesotho. The Challenge of Managing Conflict in Southern Africa*, ed. K. Lambrechts, 14–15. Braamfontein: Foundation for Global Dialogue.
Saurombe, A. 2009. Regional Integration Agenda for SADC "Caught in the winds of change". Problems and Prospects. *Journal of International Commercial Law and Technology* 4 (2): 100–106.
Scharpf, F.W. 2000. *Interaktionsformen. Akteurzentrierter Institutionalismus in der Politikforschung*. Opladen: Leske + Budrich.
Schimmelfennig, F. 2001. The Community Trap: Liberal Norms, Rhetorical Action, and the Eastern Enlargement of the European Union. *International Organization* 55 (1): 47–80.

Schirm, S.A. 2002. *Globalization and the New Regionalism: Global Markets. Domestic Politics and Regional Cooperation*. Malden: Blackwell Publishers.
Schleicher, H.-G. 2006. *Regionale Sicherheitskooperation im Südlichen Afrika: SADC und OPDSC.* Leipzig: Universität Leipzig.
Schoeman, M. 2007. South Africa. In *Security and Democracy in Southern Africa*, ed. G. Cawthra, A. du Pisani, and A. Omari, 155–171. Johannesburg: Wits Univeristy Press.
Scott, R.W. 1995. *Institutions and Organizations*. Thousand Oaks, London: Sage.
Sebenius, J.K. 1983. Negotiation arithmetic: adding and subtracting issues and parties. *International Organization* 37 (2): 281–316.
Sebitosi, A.B., and R. Okou. 2010. Re-thinking the power transmission model for sub-Saharan Africa. *Energy Policy* 38: 1448–1454.
Sidaway, J.D. 1998. The (Geo) Politics of Regional Integration: the Example of the Southern African Development Community. *Environment and Palnning D: Society and Space* 16 (5): 549–576.
Sidaway, J.D., and R. Gibb. 1998. SADC, COMESA, SACU: Contradictory Formats for Regional 'Integration' in Southern Africa? In *South Africa in Southern Africa*, ed. D. Simon, 164–184. Oxford, Athens, Cape Town: James Currey.
Sidiropoulos, E. 2002. SADC and the EU: A Brief Overview. In *SADC-EU Relations. Looking Back and Moving Ahead*, ed. E. Sidiropoulos, D. Games, P. Fabricius, et al., 23. Copenhagen: Royal Danish Ministry of Foreign Affairs.
Sidiropoulos, E., and E. Chevallier. 2006. *The European Union and Africa Developing Partnerships for Peace and Security*, vol. 51. SAIIA Report Johannesburg: South African Institute of International Affairs.
Sidiropoulos, E., and M. Meyn. 2006. *Creating Incentives for Reform: The EU accesssion process*, vol. 52., SAIIA Report. Johannesburg: South African Institute of International Affairs.
Sikuka, K. 2013. Day Ahead Market – Regional energy trading gains momentum Competitive electricity market allows member states to buy and sell. *SADC Today* 15 (3): 10.
Sikuka, K. 2013. Day Ahead Market – Regional energy trading gains momentum. Competitive electricity market allows member states to buy and sell. In: *SADC Today* 15 (3).
Simmons, B.A., F. Dobbin, and G. Garrett. 2006. Introduction: The International Diffusion of Liberalism. *International Organization* 60 (4): 781–810.
Stockholm International Peace Research Institute (SIPRI). 2010. *SIPRI Yearbook 2009. Armaments, Disarmament and International Security*. Solna: Stockholm International Peace Research Institute.

Snidal, D. 1985. Coordination versus Prisoners' Dilemma: Implications for International Coopertion and Regimes The. *American Political Science Review* 79 (4): 923–942.
Sobhee, S.K., and V. Bhowon. 2007. *Deepening Integration in SADC. Mauritius - Achievements and Coming Challenges*, vol. 8. Regional Integration in Southern Africa. Gaborone: Friedrich Ebert Stiftung.
Söderbaum, F. 2001. The Dynamics of Security and Development Regionalism in Southern Africa. In *Security and Development in Southern Africa*, ed. N. Poku, 103–121. Westport: Praeger.
Söderbaum, F. 2002. *The Political Economy of Regionalism in Southern Africa*. Dissertation. Gothenburg: University of Gothenburg.
Söderbaum, F. 2007. African Regionalism and EU-African Interregionalism. In *European Union and New Regionalism. Regional Actors and Global Governance in a Post-hegemonic Era*, 2nd ed, ed. M. Telò, 185–202. Aldershot, Burlington: Ashgate.
Söderbaum, F., and T.M. Shaw (eds.). 2003. *Theories of New Regionalism. A Palgrave Reader*. Basingstoke: Palgrave Macmillan.
Solomon, H., and S. Ngubane. 2003. *One Step Forward, Two Steps Back: Reflections on SADC's Organ on Politics, Defence and Security Cooperation*, vol. 33. SAIIA Report. Johannesburg: South African Institute of International Affairs.
Spindler, M. 2005. *Regionalismus im Wandel. Die neue Logik der Region in einer globalen Ökonomie*. Wiesbaden: VS Verlag für Sozialwissenschaften.
Stein, A. 1993. Coordination and Collaboration: Regimes in an Anarchic World. In *Neorealism and Neoliberalism: The Contemporary Debate*, ed. D.A. Baldwin, 29–59. New York: Columbia University Press.
Stein, A.A. 1982. Coordination and Collaboration: Regimes in an Anarchic World. *International Organization* 36 (2): 300–324.
Stevens, C. 2005. The TDCA, EPAs and Southern African Regionalism. In *The TDCA: Impacts, Lessons and Perspectives for EU-South and Southern African Relations*, vol. 7, ed. T. Bertelsmann-Scott, and P. Draper, 64–86. Johannesburg: South African Institute of International Affairs.
Tavares, R. 2010. *Regional Security. The Capacity of International Organisations*. New York: Routledge.
Tavares, R. 2011. The Participation of SADC and ECOWAS in Military Operations: The Weight of National Interests in Decision-Making. *African Studies Review* 54 (2): 145–176.
Tavares, R., and M. Schulz. 2006. Measuring the Impact of Regional Organisations on Peace Building. In *Assessment and Measurement of Regional Integration*, ed. P. de Lombaerde, 232–251. London: Routledge.

Tavlas, G.S. 2009. The Benefits and Costs of Monetary Union in Southern Africa: A critical Survey of the Literature. *Journal of Economic Surveys* 23 (1): 1–43.

Taylor, M. 1987. *The Possibility of Cooperation. Studies in Rationality and Social Change.* Cambridge: Cambridge University Press.

Taylor, S.D. 2007. *Business and the State in Southern Africa. The Politics of Economic Reform.* Boulder, London: Lynne Rienner.

Telò, M. (ed.). 2007. *European Union and New Regionalism. Regional Actors and Global Governance in a Post-Hegemonic Era. The International Political Economy of New Regionalism Series,* 2nd ed. Burlington: Ashgate.

Teravaninthorn, S., and G. Raballand. 2009. *Transport Prices and Costs in Africa. A Review of the Main International Corridors.* Washington: The Worldbank.

Terlinden, U. 2004. *IGAD - Papiertiger vor Mammutaufgaben.* Bonn: Friedrich-Ebert-Stiftung.

Thomas, L., J. Leape, M. Hanouch, and R. Rumney. 2005. *Foreign Direct Investment in South Africa: The initial impact of the Trade, Development and Cooperation Agreement between South Africa and the European Union.* London: Centre for Research into Economics & Finance in Southern Africa (CREFSA).

Thompson, L. 1992. Southern Africa. Regional Institutions and Dynamics. In *Southern Africa at the Crossroads? Prospects for Stability and Development in the 1990s,* ed. L. Benjamin, and C. Gregory, 227–254. Rivonia: Justified Press.

Tjønneland, E.N. 2005. Making SADC Work? Revisiting institutional Reform. In *Monitoring Regional Integration in Southern Africa Yearbook,* vol. 5, ed. D. Hansohm, W. Breytenbach, T. Hartzenberg, and C. McCarthy, 166–185. Windhoek: Namibian Economic Research Unit.

Tjønneland, E.N. 2006. *SADC and Donors - Ideals and Practices. From Gaborone to Paris and Back.* Gaborone: Botswana Institute for Development Policy Analysis.

Tjønneland, E.N., and T. Vraalsen. 1996. Towards Common Security in Southern Africa: Regional Cooperation after Apartheid. In *South Africa and Africa: Within or Apart?* ed. A. Adedeji, 193–214. Cape Town: SADRI Books.

Tjønneland, E.N., J. Isaksen, and G. le Pere. 2005. *SADC's Restructuring and Emerging Policies. Options for Norwegian Support,* vol. 7. CMI Reports. Bergen: Chr. Michelsen Institute.

Tleane, C. 2006. *The Great Trek North. The Expansion of South African Media and ICT Companies into the SADC Region.* Braamfontein: Freedom of Expression Institute.

Tshombe, J.-M.L.-M. 2008. *Evaluating power trading in selected countries of the Southern African Development Community.* Dissertation. Cape Town: Cape Peninsula University of Technology.
Tsie, B. 1993. The Place and Role of Imperialism in the Conflict between CONSAS and SADCC. *Pula: Botswana Journal of African Studies* 7 (1): 138–155.
Underdal, A. 1992. The Concept of Regime 'Effectiveness'. *Cooperation and Conflict* 27 (3): 227–240.
Underdal, A. 1998. Explaining Compliance and Defection: Three Models. *European Journal of International Relations* 4 (5): 5–30.
United Nations. Economic Commission for Africa (UNECA). 2004. *Assessment of Power Pooling Arrangements in Africa Economic Commission for Africa.* Addis Ababa: UN ECA.
Vale, P. 1994. Reconstructing Regional Dignity: South Africa and Southern Africa. In *South Africa. The Political Economy of Transformation*, ed. S.J. Stedman, 153–166. Boulder: Lynne Rienner.
Vale, P. 1996. Regional Security in Southern Africa. *Alternatives, Global, Local, Political* 21 (3): 363–391.
Valentine, N. 1998. *The SADC's Revealed Comparative Advantage in Regional and International Trade*, vol. 15. Working Paper. Cape Town: Development Policy Research Unit.
van Langenhove, L. 2012. *The EU as a global Regional Actor in Security and Peace.* Bruges: UNU-CRIS.
van Nieuwkerk, A. 1999. The Lesotho Crisis: Implications for South African Foreign Policy. In *Crisis in Lesotho: The Challenge of Managing Conflict in Southern Africa*, ed. K. Lambrechts, 16–19. Braamfontein: Foundation for Global Dialogue.
van Nieuwkerk, A. 2007. Organizational Dimensions of Security Cooperation in the Southern African Development Community. In *Proceedings of the 2006 FOPRISA Annual Conference*, vol. 3, ed. J.M. Kaunda, 99–127. Gaborone: Lightbooks.
van Nieuwkerk, A. 2010. SADC's Common Foreign Policy. In *Proceedings of the 2009 FOPRISA Annual Conference*, vol. 8, ed. C. Harvey, 97–112. Gaborone: Lightbooks.
van Nieuwkerk, A. 2011. The regional roots of the African peace and security architecture: exploring centre-periphery relations. *South African Journal of International Affairs* 18 (2): 169–189.
van Nieuwkerk, A. 2012. *Towards Peace and Security in Southern Africa. A critical analysis of the revised Strategic Indicative Plan for the Organ on Politics, Defence and Security Co-operation (SIPO) of the Southern African Development Community.* Maputo: Friedrich-Ebert-Stiftung.

Versi, A. 2005. *The Top Companies in Africa. African Business.* London, Paris: IC Publications.
Viner, J. 1950. *The Customs Union Issue.* New York: Carnegie Endowment for International Peace.
Vogt, J. 2007. *Die Regionale Integration des südlichen Afrikas. Unter besonderer Betrachtung der Southern African Development Community (SADC).* Baden-Baden: Nomos.
von Kirchbach, F., and H. Roelofsen. 1998. *Trade in the Southern African Development Community: What is the Potential for increasing Exports to the Republic of South Africa?* vol. 11. African Development in a Comparative Perspective. Geneva: United Nations Conference on Trade and Development (UNCTAD).
Wagner, R.H. 1983. The Theory of Games and the Problem of International Cooperation. *The American Political Science Review* 77 (2): 330–346.
Walker, A. 2009. The EC-SADC EPA: The Moment of Truth for Regional Integration. *Trade Negotiations Insights* 8 (6): 1–3.
Wallander, C.A., and R.O. Keohane. 1999. Risk, Threat, and Security Institutions. In *Imperfect Unions. Security Institutions over Time and Space*, ed. H. Haftendorn, R.O. Keohane, and C.A. Wallander, 21–47. Oxford, New York: Oxford University Press.
Wallander, C.A., H. Haftendorn, and R.O. Keohane. 1999. Introduction. In *Imperfect Unions. Security institutions over Time and Space*, ed. H. Haftendorn, R.O. Keohane, and C.A. Wallander, 2–18. Oxford, New York: Oxford University Press.
Waltz, K. 1979. *Theory of International Politics.* Reading, MA: Addison-Wesley.
Wannenburg, G. 2006. *Africa's Pablos and Political Entrepreneurs. War, the State and Criminal Networks in West and Southern Africa.* Johannesburg: South African Institute of International Affairs.
Warleigh-Lack, A. 2008. Studying regionalisation comparatively. A conceptual framework. In *Regionalisation and Global Governance. The taming of Globalisation?* ed. A.F. Cooper, C.W. Hughes, and P. de Lombaerde, 43–60. London, New York: Routledge.
Warleigh-Lack, A., and B. Rosamond. 2011. Introduction. In *Regionalism and the European Union. Dialogues, comparisons and new research directions*, ed. A. Warleigh-Lack, N. Robinson, and B. Rosamond, 3–17. Abingdon: Routledge.
Warleigh-Lack, A., and L. van Langenhove. 2010. Rethinking EU Studies: The Contribution of Comparative Regionalism. *Journal of European Integration* 32 (6): 541–562.
Weeks, J. 1996. Regional Cooperation and Southern African Development. *Journal of Southern African Studies* 22 (1): 99–117.

Weeks, J., and P. Mosley. 1998. Structural adjustment and tradables: a comparative study of Zambia and Zimbabwe. In *Post-Apartheid Southern Africa. Economic Challenge and policies for the future*, ed. L. Peterson, 171–200. London, New York: Routledge.

Weggoro, N.C. 1995. *Effects of Regional Economic Integration in Southern Africa and the Role of the Republic of South Africa: A Study of Project Coordination Approach in Industry and Trade in SADCC/SADC*. Berlin: Köster.

Wendt, A. 1992. Anarchy is what States Make of it: The Social Construction of Power Politics. *International Organization* 46 (2): 391–425.

Williams, R. 1999. Challenges for South and Southern Africa Towards Non-Consensual Peace Mission? In *From Peacekeeping to Complex Emergencies. Peace Support Missions in Africa*, ed. J. Cilliers, and G. Mills, 153–174. Johannesburg: South African Institute of International Affairs.

Williams, R. 2001. From Collective Security to Peace-Building? The Challenges of Managing Regional Security in Southern Africa. In *Regional Integration in Southern Africa: Comparative International Perpectives*, ed. C. Clapham, G. Mills, A. Morner, and E. Sidiropoulos, 105–114. Johannesburg: South African Institute of International Affairs.

Winters, L.A. 1999. Regionalism vs. Multilateralism. In *Market Integration, Regionalism and the Global Economy*, ed. R. Baldwin, D. Cohen, A. Sapir, and A. Venables, 7–48. Cambridge, New York, Melbourne: Cambridge University Press.

Woolfrey, S. 2009. *An Assessment of the Trade Measures Proposed as Part of the Department of Trade and Industry's Draft Rescue Package for the Clothing and Textile Industry*. Working Paper No. 5/2009. Stellenbosch: Trade Law Centre for Southern Africa.

Yang, Y., and S. Gupta. 2005. *Regional Trade Arrangements in Africa: Past Performance and the Way Forward*. IMF Working Papers, vol WP/05/36. Washington: International Monetary Fund.

Yeo, A. 2016. Overlapping regionalism in East Asia: determinants and potential effects. *International Relations of the Asia-Pacific* 0: 1–31.

Yin, R.K. 2003. *Case Study Research. Design and Methods*, 3rd ed. Thousand Oaks: Sage.

Young, C. 1994. In Search of Civil Society. In *Civil Society and the State in Africa*, ed. J.W. Harbeson, D. Rothchild, and N. Chazan, 33–50. Boulder, London: Lynne Rienner.

Young, O.R. 1969. Interdependencies in World Politics. *International Journal* 24 (4): 726–750.

Young, O.R. 1982. Regime Dynamics: The Rise and Fall of International Regimes. *International Organization* 36 (2): 277–297.

Young, O.R. 1992. The Effectiveness of International Institutions: Hard Cases and Critical Variables. In *Governance Without Government: Order and Change in World Politics*, ed. J.N. Rosenau and E-O. Czempiel, 160–194. Cambridge: Cambridge University Press.

Zangl, B. 1994. Politik auf zwei Ebenen. Hypothesen zur Bildung internationaler Regime. *Zeitschrift für Internationale Beziehungen* 1 (2): 279–312.

Zimmerling, R. 1991. *Externe Einflüsse auf die Integration von Staaten. Zur politikwissenschaftlichen Theorie regionaler Zusammenschlüsse.* Freiburg: Verlag Karl Alber.

Zürn, M. 1987. *Gerechte internationale Regime. Bedingungen und Restriktionen der Entstehung nicht-hegemonialer internationaler Regime untersucht am Beispiel der Weltkommunikationsordnung.* Frankurt am Main: Haag Herchen.

Zürn, M. 1992. *Interessen und Institutionen in der Internationalen Politik: Grundlegung und Anwendung des situationsstrukturellen Ansatz.* Opladen: Leske + Budrich.

Zürn, M. 1993. Problematic Social Situations and International Institutions: On the Use of Game Theory in International Politics. In *International Relations and Pan-Europe: Theoretical Approaches and Empirical Findings*, ed. F. Pfetsch, 63–84. Münster: Lit-Verlag.

Zürn, M. 1997. 'Positives Regieren' jenseits des Nationalstaates. Zur Implementation internationaler Umweltregime. *Zeitschrift für Internationale Beziehungen* 4 (1): 41–68.

Zwizwai, B. 2007. *Deepening Integration in SADC. Zimbabwe—Missing SADC Macroeconomic Targets*, Regional Integration in Southern Africa, vol. 10. Gaborone: Friedrich Ebert Stiftung.

Primary Sources

AU. 2002. Protocol Relating to the Establishment of a Peace and Security Council of the African Union. https://au.int/sites/default/files/treaties/7781-file-protocol_peace_and_security.pdf. Accessed 22 July 2016.

AU. 2010. African Peace and Security Structure (APSA). 2010 Assessment Study. Zanzibar 2010. http://www.securitycouncilreport.org/atf/cf/%7B65BFCF9B-6D27-4E9C-8CD3-CF6E4FF96FF9%7D/RO%20African%20Peace%20and%20Security%20Architecture.pdf. Accessed 7 July 2016.

Council of the European Union. 2007. Conclusions of the Council and of the Representatives of the Governments of the Member States Meeting Within the Council: EU Strategy on Aid for Trade: Enhancing EU Support for Trade-Related Needs in Developing Countries. http://trade.ec.europa.eu/doclib/docs/2008/november/tradoc_141470.pdf. Accessed 10 Sept 2016.

Council of the European Union. 2008. The Africa-European Union Strategic Partnership. Brussels: European Communities.

Council of the European Union. 2011. Three-Year Action Programme for the African Peace Facility, 2011–2013 (10th EDF). http://www.europarl.europa.eu/meetdocs/2009_2014/documents/sede/dv/sede291111actionprogramme_/sede291111actionprogramme_en.pdf. Accessed 11 Dec 2016.

Department for Trade and Industry. 2002. South Africa's Global Trade Strategy and Agenda: A Brief Note. Pretoria: Department of Trade and Industry.

Eskom. 2010. Factsheet "Eskom and the Southern African Power Pool". http://www.eskom.co.za/content/ES_0007SAfPowPoolRev5~1.pdf. Accessed 10 Oct 2016.

EU—ACP. 2010. Second Revision of the Cotonou Agreement—Agreed Consolidated Text. http://eeas.europa.eu/archives/delegations/burkina_faso/documents/eu_burkina_faso/second_rev_cotonou_agreement_20100311_en.pdf. Accessed 10 Sept 2016.

EU Council. 2003. Decision No. 3/2003 of the ACP-EC Council of Ministers on the use of resources from the long-term development envelope of the ninth EDF for the creation of a Peace Facility for Africa. http://eur-lex.europa.eu/legal-content/EN/TXT/PDF/?uri=CELEX:22003D0003(01)&from=EN. Accessed 3 Aug 2013.

European Commission. 1995a. Communication on Supporting Regional Economic Integration in Developing Countries. COM(1995) 212 final.

European Commission. 1995b. European Community Support for Regional Economic Integration Efforts among Developing Countries. COM(95) 219 final.

European Commission. 2002. Recommendation for a Council Decision authorising the commission to negotiate Economic Partnership Agreements with the ACP countries and regions. SEC (2002) 351 final. http://trade.ec.europa.eu/doclib/docs/2006/september/tradoc_112023.pdf. Accessed 10 Sept 2016.

European Commission. 2005. EU Strategy for Africa: towards a Euro-African pact to accelerate Africa's development. Annex to the Communication from the Commission to the Council, the European Parliament and European Economic and Social Committee. COM(2005) 489 final.

European Commission. 2006. The European Consensus on Development. Joint Statement by the Council and the Representatives of the Governments of the Member States Meeting Within the Council, the European Parliament and the Commission on European Union Development Policy: 'The European Consensus' (2006/C46/01). http://eur-lex.europa.eu/legal-content/EN/TXT/PDF/?uri=CELEX:42006X0224(01)&from=EN. Accessed 5 May 2016.

European Commission. 2009. The ACP-EU Energy Facility. Improving access to energy services for the poor in rural and peri-urban areas. Brussels: European Communities.

European Commission. 2010. Annual Report. The African Peace Facility 2009. https://ec.europa.eu/europeaid/sites/devco/files/annual-report-2009-african-peace-facility_en.pdf. Accessed 8 Feb 2016.

European Commission. 2011a. Annual Report. The African Peace Facility 2010. https://ec.europa.eu/europeaid/sites/devco/files/annual-report-2010-african-peace-facility_en.pdf. Accessed 8 Feb 2016.

European Commission. 2011b. Commission Decision of 29.07.2011 on an action to be financed under the African Peace Facility from the 10th European Development Fund – African Peace and Security Architecture Support Programme. C(2011)5379.

European Commission. 2011c. Fact Sheet on the Economic Partnership Agreements. SADC EPA Group. http://trade.ec.europa.eu/doclib/html/142189.htm. Accessed 2 Sept 2016.

European Commission. 2011d. Proposal for a Regulation of the European Parliament and of the Council Amending Annex I to Council Regulation (EC) No 1528/2007 as Regards the Exclusion of Number of Countries From the List of Regions or States Which Have Concluded Negotiations. http://eur-lex.europa.eu/LexUriServ/LexUriServ.do?uri=COM:2011:0598:FIN:EN:PDF. Accessed 10 Sept 2016.

European Commission. 2012a. Annual Report. The African Peace Facility 2011. https://ec.europa.eu/europeaid/sites/devco/files/annual-report-2011-african-peace-facility_en.pdf. Accessed 8 Aug 2016.

European Commission. 2012b. Commission Decision of 12/03/2012 on an Action to be Financed under the African Peace Facility from the 10th European Development Fund – Support to the African Training Centres in Peace and Security. C (2012) 1479. http://ec.europa.eu/europeaid/documents/aap/2012/aap-spe_2012_intra-acp_p2_en.pdf. Accessed 12 Oct 2016.

European Commission. 2012c. Fact sheet on the Economic Partnership Agreements. Eastern and Southern Africa (ESA). http://trade.ec.europa.eu/doclib/docs/2012/march/tradoc_149213.pdf. Accessed 10 Sept 2016.

European Commission. 2012d. Fact sheet on the Economic Partnership Agreements. The Eastern African Community (EAC). http://trade.ec.europa.eu/doclib/docs/2009/january/tradoc_142194.pdf. Accessed 10 Sept 2016.

European Commission. 2012e. The ACP-EU Energy Facility. Improving access to energy services for the poor in rural and peri-urban areas. Brussels: European Union.

European Commission. 2014. Annual Report. The African Peace Facility 2013. http://www.africa-eu-partnership.org/sites/default/files/documents/ar2013_apf_web_0.pdf. Accessed 11 Oct 2016.

European Community—Region of Eastern and Southern Africa and the Indian Ocean. 2008. Regional Strategy Paper and Regional Indicative Programme 2008–2013. https://eeas.europa.eu/sites/eeas/files/east_africa_2008_2.pdf. Accessed 7 Mar 2016.

European Community—Southern African Region. 2008. Regional Strategy Paper and Regional Indicative Programme 2008–2013. http://ec.europa.eu/development/icenter/repository/Signed-RSP_PIR_ESA-2007-2013.pdf. Accessed 3 July 2015.

European Community. 2000. Partnership Agreement Between the Members of the African, Caribbean and Pacific Group of States of the One Part, and the European Community and its Member States, of the Other Part (Cotonou Agreement). http://eur-lex.europa.eu/LexUriServ/LexUriServ.do?uri=CELEX:22000A1215%2801%29:EN:NOT. Accessed 5 July 2016.

European Council. 2000. Lisbon European Council 23 and 24 March 2000. Presidency Conclusions. http://www.europarl.europa.eu/summits/lis1_en.htm. Accessed 10 Nov 2016.

European Council. 2005. The EU and Africa: Towards a strategic partnership. Conclusions by the Heads of State and Government meeting in the European Council, Brussels, 15–16 December 2005 (doc 15961/05).

European Council. 2014. 26/27 June 2014 Conclusions. EUCO 79/14. http://www.consilium.europa.eu/uedocs/cms_data/docs/pressdata/en/ec/143478.pdf. Accessed 12 Nov 2014.

European Union. 2005. Council Regulation (EC) No. 980/2005 of 27 June 2005 Applying a Scheme of Generalised Tariff Preferences (Everything-But-Arms Initiative). http://eur-lex.europa.eu/legal-content/EN/TXT/PDF/?uri=CELEX:32005R0980&from=EN. Accessed 10 Sept 2016.

European Union. 2012. ZW-Harare: EDF — technical assistance project in support to the Southern African Power Pool (SAPP). Published in the Supplement to the Official Journal of the European Union (2012/S 221-362912).

Gaotlhobogwe, Monkagedi. 2007. SADC Military Organ Set For Historic Launch in Lusaka. *Mmegi Newspaper*. Issue of the 6th August 2007.

Hage Geingob, Namibia's Minister for Trade and Industry. Interview in: *Allgemeine Zeitung Windhoek*. Issue of the 25th May 2010.

Hage Geingob, Namibia's Minister for Trade and Industry. Interview in: *The Namibian*. Issue of the 9th August 2012.

Republic of Namibia. 1993. Statement on Defence Policy. Windhoek: Ministry of Defence. http://www.mod.gov.na/documents/264813/280846/DEFENCE+POLICY.pdf. Accessed 12 Apr 2016.

Republic of South Africa. 1996. Defence in a Democracy. White Paper on National Defence for the Republic of South Africa. May 1996. http://www.dod.mil.za/documents/WhitePaperonDef/whitepaper%20on%20defence1996.pdf. Accessed 12 Apr 2016.
Republic of South Africa. 2011. Building a Better World: The Diplomacy of Ubuntu. White Paper on South Africa's Foreign Policy. Final Draft. https://gov.za/sites/default/files/foreignpolicy_0.pdf. Accessed 11 Dec 2016.
Republic of South Africa. 2014. South African Defence Review 2014. http://www.gov.za/sites/www.gov.za/files/defencereview_2014_ch10-13.pdf. Accessed 8 June 2016
SACU. 2009. Southern African Customs Union Annual Report 2008/2009. http://www.sacu.int/publications/reports/annual/2009/part2.pdf. Accessed 4 July 2016.
SADC – European Community. 2002. Regional Strategy Paper and Regional Indicative Programme. For the period 2002–2007. http://aei.pitt.edu/45272/1/SACD_2002_3.pdf. Accessed 12 August 2015.
SADC. 1992. Treaty of the Southern African Development Community. Gaborone: SADC Secretariat.
SADC. 1993. Southern Africa: A Framework and Strategy for Building the Community. Harare.
SADC. 1994. Industry and Trade. Annual Report of the Sector Coordination Unit. Gaborone: SADC Secretariat.
SADC. 1995a. Council Decisions. Johannesburg, Republic of South Africa, 25–26 August 1995.
SADC. 1995b. Record of the Council of Ministers. Held in Maseru, Lesotho, 21–22 August 1996.
SADC. 1996a. Annual Report. June 1995–July 1996. Gaborone: SADC Secretariat.
SADC. 1996b. Decisions of the Council of Ministers. Johannesburg, South Africa, 28–29. January 1996. Gaborone: SADC Secretariat.
SADC. 1996c. Energy. Annual Report of the Sector Coordination Unit. Johannesburg, 1–4 February 1996.
SADC. 1996d. Extraordinary Summit of Heads of States. Communiqué. 28th June 1996. Gaborone.
SADC. 1996e. Record of the Meeting of SADC Ministers Responsible for Foreign Affairs, Defence and Security, 18th January 1996. Gaborone.
SADC. 1996f. Record of the SADC Council of Ministers Meeting 28–29 January 1996.
SADC. 1996g. Record of the Summit. Held in Maseru, Kingdom of Lesotho, 24 August 1996.
SADC. 1999a. Consultative Conference on Trade and Investment. The Proceedings of the Consultative Conference held in Johannesburg. Republic

of South Africa. 31st January–2nd February 1996. Gaborone: SADC Secretariat.
SADC. 1999b. Record of the Summit held in Maputo, Mozambique, 18th August 1999. Maputo.
SADC. 1999c. Record of the 7th Meeting of the SADC Trade Negotiating Forum (TNF), 25th–29th January 1999, Harare. Gaborone: SADC Secretariat.
SADC. 2000a. Protocol on Trade.
SADC. 2000b. Record of the Summit. Held in Windhoek, Republic of Namibia, 7th August 2000. Gaborone: SADC Secretariat.
SADC. 2001a. Protocol on Politics, Defence and Security Co-operation.
SADC. 2001b. Treaty of the Southern African Development Community, as Amended.
SADC. 2002. Energy Sector. Annual Report July 2001–June 2002.
SADC. 2003. Record of the Summit. Held in Dar Es Salaam, United Republic of Tanzania, 25–26 August 2003.
SADC. 2004a. Regional Indicative Strategic Development Plan. Gaborone: SADC Secretariat.
SADC. 2004b. Record of the Meeting of the Council of Ministers. Held in Grand Baie, 16th–17th August.
SADC. 2004c. Record of the Meeting of SADC Council of Ministers held in Arusha 12–13 March 2004.
SADC. 2004d. Record of the Summit. Grand Baie, 16th–17th August.
SADC. 2004e. Strategic Indicative Plan for the Organ on Politics, Defence and Security Cooperation. Gaborone: SADC Secretariat.
SADC. 2005a. Record of the 26th Session of the Inter-State Defence and Security Committee (ISDSC). Boksburg, 11th–14th July 2005.
SADC. 2005b. Record of the Summit. Held in Gaborone, Republic of Botswana, 17–18 August 2005. SADC/SM/1/2005/1-A. 27.
SADC. 2006a. 4th Draft SADC Model Customs Act. http://www.sadc.int/files/1013/2369/4831/Final_DRAFT_SADC_Model_CUSTOMS_ACT-doc.doc. Accessed 4 Aug 2012.
SADC. 2006b. Final Communiqué of the SADC Extraordinary Summit of the Heads of State and Government to consider the Regional, Economic and Political Integration.
SADC. 2006c. Record of the Meeting of the Council of Ministers. Held in Maseru, 15–16 August 2006.
SADC. 2006d. Sub-Theme on Trade, Economic Liberalization and Development. Prepared for the SADC Consultative Conference Windhoek, Namibia, April 26–27, 2006. Gaborone: SADC Secretariat.

SADC. 2007a. Memorandum of Understanding amongst the Southern African Development Community Member States on the Establishment of a Southern African Development Community Standby Brigade.
SADC. 2007b. Record. Meeting of the SADC Ministers responsible for Energy on the 25th April 2007 in Harare, Zimbabwe.
SADC. 2008a. Official SADC Trade, Industry and Investment Review 2007/2008. Gaborone: Southern African Marketing Co. (Pty) LTD.
SADC. 2008b. SADC Free Trade Area. Growth, Development and Wealth Creation. Handbook. Gaborone: SADC Secretariat.
SADC. 2008c. SADC RPTC. Vision for the Future. Final Report of an Independent Study Commissioned by the Directorate of the SADC Organ on Politics, Defence and Security Cooperation on the Vision of the Regional Peacekeeping Training Centre. Gaborone: SADC Secretariat.
SADC. 2009a. Activity Report of the SADC Secretariat. For the Period August 2007 to July 2008, 46–50. Gabrone: SADC Secretariat. http://www.sadc. int/files/3813/5333/8237/SADC_Annual_Report_2007_-_2008.pdf. Accessed 10 Nov 2016.
SADC. 2009b. Extraordinary Summit of the Organ on Politics, Defence and Security Co-operation. Ezulwini, 19th March 2009.
SADC. 2009c. Extraordinary Summit of SADC Heads of State and Government. Communiqué. Lozitha Royal Palace, 30th March 2009.
SADC. 2009d. Extraordinary Summit of SADC Heads of State and Government. Communiqué. Sandton, 20th June 2009.
SADC. 2009e. Study on the Best Options for the Collection and Distribution of revenue in the SADC Customs Union. Undisclosed Document.
SADC. 2010. Revised Edition. Harmonised Strategic Indicative Plan for the Organ on Politics, Defence and Security Cooperation. Maputo.
SADC. 2012. Desk Assessment of the Regional Indicative Strategic Development Plan 2005–2010. Gaborone: SADC Secretariat.
SADC. 2014a. Interview with Brigadier General Christopher Chella. *The Peace Trainer*. Issue 3. SADC RPTC.
SADC. 2014b. Joint Media Release on the Handing Over of Accommodation to SADC Regional Peacekeeping Training Centre by the Government of the Federal Republic of Germany. http://www.sadc.int/ files/7713/9505/2070/HANDING_OVER_OF_ACCOMMODATION_ TO_SADC_REGIONAL_PEACEKEEPING_TRAINING_CENTRE_2.pdf. Accessed 10 Dec 2016.
SADCC. 1980. Record of the Southern African Development Coordination Summit Conference. Held at Mulungushi Conference Centre, Lusaka, on the 1st April 1980.

SADCC. 1992a. Towards the Southern African Development Community: A Declaration by the SADC Heads of State and Government of Southern African States. Windhoek: SADCC.
SADCC. 1992b. Towards Economic Integration – Policy Document prepared for the 1992 Annual Conference. Belville: Centre for Southern African Studies.
SAPP. 1994. SAPP Inter-Utility Memorandum of Understanding.
SAPP. 1995. Intergovernmental Memorandum of Understanding.
SAPP. 1998. SADC SAPP Annual Review Report 28 August 1995–March 1997. Harare: Southern African Power Pool.
SAPP. 2007. 2006 Annual Report. Harare: Southern African Power Pool.
SAPP. 2010. 2009 Annual Report. Harare: Southern African Power Pool.
SAPP. 2011. DAM Monthly Performance Report. November 2011. Harare: Southern African Power Pool.
SAPP. 2013. 2012 Annual Report. Harare: Southern African Power Pool.
SAPP. 2014. Workings of the SAPP. Presentation by Lawrence Musaba (Coordination Centre Manager). http://cdn.entelectonline.co.za/wm-418498-cmsimages/SAPPOverview_SAIEEPresidentialLecture.pdf. Accessed 2 Mar 2016.
Societé Nationale d'Electricité. 2000. Trente ans de vie de SNEL 1970–2000. Kinshasa: Gombe.
Söderbaum, F., and P. Stålgren. 2010. The EU and the Global South. In *The European Union and the Global South*, ed. F. Söderbaum and P. Stålgren, 1–11. Boulder: Lynne Rienner.
Solomons, I. 2014. Power transmission projects in Southern Africa. In: Engineering News. Published on 18th April 2014. http://www.engineeringnews.co.za/article/power-transmission-projects-progress-in-southern-africa-2014-04-18. Accessed 10 Aug 2014.
Undisclosed Author. 2009. The Legal and Institutional Framework for Administration and Implementation of a Customs Union for the Southern African Development Community.
Undisclosed Authors. 2009. Study on SADC Customs Union Policies. Final Report.

Interviews

Anthoni van Nieuwkerk (Associate Professor at the Centre for Defence and Security Management) at the Graduate School of Public and Development Management at the University of the Witwatersrand (08/06/2010).
Colonel Gerson Marco Sangiza (Senior Officer for Defence Affairs and Planning at the OPDS) at the SADC Headquarters (09/29/2010).

Francis Nyathi (Programme Officer Macroeconomic Policies and Convergence) at the SADC Directorate of Trade, Industry, Finance and Investment (12/01/2008).

Gilbert Khadiagala (Jan Smuts Professor and Head of the Department of International Relations) at the University of the Witwatersrand (10/07/2010).

Haile Taye (Senior Research Fellow Macroeconomic Forecasting and Planning) at the Botswana Institute for Development Policy Analysis (09/22/2010).

Jens Møller (Principal Administrator Africa-EU Partnership, African Peace Facility) at the European Commission's Directorate General for Development and Cooperation (05/03/2012).

Jonathan Mayuyuka Kaunda (Senior Research Fellow Public Policy) at the Botswana Institute for Development Policy Analysis (09/10/2010).

Juma Kaniki (Senior Programme Manager Microeconomic Monitoring and Performance Surveillance) at the SADC Directorate of Trade, Industry, Finance and Investment (12/01/2008).

Mike Humphrey (EPA Support Facility Programme Manager) at SADC (09/27/2010).

Mojgan Derakhshani (Advisor SADC Finance and Investment Protocol Coordination) at the SADC Directorate of Trade, Industry, Finance and Investment (09/10/2010).

Mzukisi Qobo (Head of Emerging Powers Programme) at the South African Institute of International Affairs (08/12/2010).

Peter Draper (Project Head Development through Trade Programme and Senior Trade Research Fellow) at the South African Institute of International Affairs (08/25/2010).

Tanki Mothae (Director of the OPDS) at the SADC Headquarters (09/29/2010).

Index

A
ACP-EU Energy Facility (AEF), 279, 287, 299, 300
African, Caribbean and Pacific Countries (ACP), 167, 168, 171, 175, 279
African Peace and Security Architecture (APSA), 239–243, 245, 246, 251, 255, 259, 260
African Peace Facility (APF), 240–246, 249, 251, 255, 257–260, 316
African Union (AU), 30, 216, 217, 229, 232, 239–246, 249–251, 255, 257, 259, 260, 310, 311, 316, 317
Angola, 86, 87, 89, 91, 110, 113, 117, 129, 140, 155, 162, 164, 165, 173, 179, 190, 191, 193, 197–201, 207, 211, 212, 216, 231, 235, 237, 238, 271, 273, 289, 295, 299
Apartheid, 83, 86–88, 110, 112, 197, 277
Armed Force, 193, 197–200, 230, 231, 238, 257
Asymmetry
  extra-regional, 15, 50–55, 57–59, 117, 118, 164, 171, 176, 281, 317
  intra-regional, 116, 197, 199, 235, 237, 276
  power relation, 45, 49, 51, 54

B
BLNS Countries, 169, 170
Botswana, 69, 84–86, 89, 90, 96, 99, 108–111, 115–117, 138, 143, 144, 155, 161, 163–165, 173, 174, 179, 190, 192, 203, 207, 213–215, 250, 270, 271, 274, 285, 294

C
Capacity, 3, 6, 28, 39, 44, 57, 58, 63, 70, 83, 87, 98, 119, 169, 199, 229, 231–233, 237, 239–242, 245, 247, 251, 252, 255, 269, 270, 272, 273, 276, 277, 286, 287, 293, 295, 296, 312, 317
Classic Integration Theories, 8, 14

Club Good, 196
Common External Tariff (CET), 157, 164, 168, 171, 175, 176, 309, 315
Common Market for Eastern and Southern Africa (COMESA), 112, 125, 142, 173, 174, 180
Common Monetary Area (CMA), 85
Comparative cost advantage, 10, 106, 109, 111, 113, 154, 156
Compliance, 35, 37, 47, 48, 53, 210, 211, 249, 250, 290
Confidence-building, 3, 95, 187, 188, 211, 213, 218, 219, 234, 310, 316
Constructivism, 11, 13, 14
Cooperation Problem
  Assurance Game, 34, 42, 43, 189, 275, 318
  Battle of the Sexes, 41, 42
  Prisoner's Dilemma, 34, 35, 49, 313
  Rambo Game, 49
Cooperation Theory, 30, 31, 38, 41, 60, 63, 188
Cotonou Agreement, 168, 178, 180
Customs Union, 3, 10, 17, 66, 85, 93, 140, 153, 154, 156–159, 163, 164, 167, 173, 175–178, 309, 315, 319

D
Day Ahead Market (DAM), 267, 268, 287, 288, 290, 292, 293, 297, 298, 301, 311, 319
Demand for Regional Integration, 12
Democratic Republic of the Congo (DRC), 89, 91, 113, 129, 138, 165, 190, 193, 206, 207, 211, 212, 221, 231, 237, 253, 260, 274, 288, 294, 297, 299, 310

Dependence, 4, 8, 31, 45, 61, 86, 90, 91, 116, 117, 119, 163, 165, 169, 171, 173, 201, 202, 277, 317
Developing country, 1, 3, 4, 8, 15, 16, 34, 51, 53, 57, 63, 98, 119, 125, 154, 156, 251, 279, 297
Development Aid, 118
Diffusion, 14, 60–64, 72, 233, 308
Doing Business Indicator, 139
Donor, 16, 53, 119, 166, 167, 201, 204, 238, 239, 248, 252, 253, 269, 276, 278, 280, 288, 297, 311, 316–319

E
East African Community (EAC), 170, 173, 174, 179
Eastern and Southern Africa (ESA), 171, 173, 174, 179, 180, 258
Economic Community of West African States (ECOWAS), 1, 238, 239, 257
Economic Partnership Agreement (EPA)
  groupings, 173, 174, 176, 207
  negotiations, 169, 172, 181
Economies of Scale, 10, 106, 114, 154, 156, 157, 269
Economy
  asymmetry, 118, 120, 167
  capacity, 44
  development, 10, 66, 89–94, 106, 113, 117, 122, 125, 138, 158, 166, 174, 268, 275
  integration, 10–12, 18, 19, 88, 92, 99, 106, 108, 109, 112, 113, 119, 120, 128, 131, 132, 135, 138, 141, 142, 153, 154, 156, 166, 171, 309

INDEX   365

interdependence, 10, 32, 34, 71,
    90, 91, 106–108, 112, 114,
    115, 117, 118, 120, 142, 154,
    155, 159, 160, 163–165, 167,
    171, 176, 313, 314
structure, 117
Effectiveness, 5, 7, 13, 14, 25, 30, 39,
    40, 46–48, 50–52, 56–60, 62–64,
    68–70, 87, 115, 128, 130, 135,
    188, 202, 210, 218, 219, 252,
    254, 256, 268, 281, 288, 290,
    292, 308, 314, 316, 317, 319,
    321
Electricity
    generation, 19, 268–271, 273, 275,
        277, 295, 297, 312
    interdependence, 268, 276, 278
    trade, 267, 270, 272–274, 282,
        285, 286, 288, 290–292, 297,
        311, 318, 319
Eskom, 272, 277, 278, 285, 286, 291,
    296, 299, 300
Euro-Centrism, 14, 320
Europe, 1, 8, 10–13, 46, 50, 54, 64,
    65, 70, 91, 117–119, 141, 164–
    166, 173, 201, 269, 278, 321
European Development Fund (EDF),
    6, 119, 141, 166, 171, 201,
    240–243, 249, 251, 257, 260,
    279, 300
European Union (EU)
    impact, 2, 167, 230, 239, 243, 315
    influence, 16, 17, 167, 176, 248,
        256
    power, 157, 315
    regional integration, 2, 7, 8, 16, 29,
        64, 65, 90, 240, 309, 311
Everything-But-Arms (EBA), 168,
    174, 179
Export, 11, 27, 108–112, 114,
    115, 117, 124, 133, 135, 140,
    145, 155, 156, 161, 163–165,

169–171, 173, 174, 180, 272,
    275, 276, 278
External
    actors, 4, 5, 14, 15, 18, 50, 52–58,
        91, 94, 164, 167, 171, 202,
        204, 218, 238, 239, 243, 249,
        276, 278, 279, 281, 288, 308,
        312, 319, 321
    funding, 14, 120, 202, 212, 243,
        247, 251, 278–281, 297, 319
    impact, 17, 52, 54–56, 59, 281,
        314, 318, 319
    influence, 5, 7, 14, 17, 39, 52,
        54–59, 120, 167, 176, 201,
        252, 256, 258, 281, 298, 308,
        315, 320
Extra-regional
    actors, 2, 5–7, 15, 16, 18, 19, 25,
        26, 51, 54–56, 58, 59, 70, 88,
        90, 117, 119, 120, 141, 165,
        167, 201, 238, 241, 255, 278,
        279, 283, 287, 288, 296, 298,
        307, 308, 314–320
    cooperation, 57
    funding, 241
    impact, 167, 243
    influence, 14, 15, 68, 84
    interdependence, 52, 56, 67, 70,
        120, 167, 234
    investment flows, 118
    trade, 91, 117, 161, 171, 173, 175,
        176, 309

F
Façade Institution, 64
Foreign Direct Investment (FDI),
    106, 116, 118, 130, 135–138,
    140, 158, 161, 165, 166, 177,
    309
Free Trade Area (FTA), 3, 16, 66,
    105, 106, 113–115, 119–122,

128–131, 134–136, 140–144, 153, 154, 156–159, 163, 164, 166, 168, 173, 175, 180, 244, 309, 312–314, 319
Front Line States (FLS), 85, 86, 98, 187, 189, 193, 195, 199, 203–206

G
Game Theory, 33, 38, 39, 68
Global South, 2, 4–8, 11, 13–16, 27, 50, 64, 141, 154, 166, 307, 308, 320
Gross Domestic Product (GDP), 115, 160, 197, 200, 235, 237, 272

H
Hegemon, 16, 98, 117, 140, 163, 167, 202, 206, 238, 245, 255, 312, 314, 318
Hub and Spoke, 117
Human Development Index (HDI), 66, 97
Hypothesis, 64, 65, 314, 316

I
Implementation, 2, 47, 53, 93, 94, 96, 97, 113, 120, 123, 129–131, 134, 135, 138, 154, 177, 209, 211, 240, 241, 250–252, 254, 289, 292, 309, 319
Import, 8, 27, 89, 94, 109, 112, 134, 138, 139, 145, 276, 292
Informal Trade, 107, 113, 141, 157
Institutionalised Cooperation, 35, 43, 48, 49, 99, 230, 234
Institutions, 3–5, 9, 12, 16, 26–30, 33–39, 41, 42, 44–49, 53, 56–63, 71, 83, 87, 88, 90, 91, 94, 96, 98, 100, 106, 115, 123, 130, 139, 157, 159, 188, 192, 193, 196, 202, 209, 211, 217, 239, 275, 313, 317
Integration Theory
  Global Market Approach, 12, 89, 110, 111
  institutionalism, 31, 36, 38, 39, 60, 67, 188
  Liberal Intergovernmentalism, 9
  Neo-Functionalism, 9
  Neo-Realism, 8, 31, 38
  New Regionalism Approach, 12–14, 18
  political economy, 10, 11, 13, 14, 37
  Regime Theory, 36
Interdependence, 1, 9, 10, 16, 26, 27, 31–35, 41, 44, 45, 48–54, 56–59, 67, 69–72, 87, 90, 91, 106–108, 112, 114–118, 120, 142, 154, 155, 159–161, 163–167, 171, 176, 188, 189, 192, 197, 200, 230, 234, 235, 238, 241, 245, 268, 276, 278, 281, 313, 314, 317, 320
Inter-regionalism, 63, 91, 94, 119, 164, 165, 168–170, 173, 233, 239, 240, 242, 243
Inter-State Defence and Security Committee (ISDSC), 95, 189, 204–206, 209, 233, 244, 247, 258, 259
Inter-State Negotiations, 46, 54, 55, 70, 207, 244, 245, 248, 252, 255
Inter-State Politics and Diplomacy Committee (ISPDC), 95, 209
Intra-regional
  asymmetry, 116, 161, 197, 276, 278, 314
  economic interdependence, 34, 106, 108, 112, 114, 115, 117, 120, 155, 159, 313, 314
  investment flows, 135
  security interdependence, 32, 51, 188

trade, 27, 106–108, 113–115, 121, 129, 131–133, 135, 141, 142, 154–157, 161, 286, 297, 309
Investment
　extra-regional, 118
　flow, 51, 106, 107, 130, 141, 166
　intra-regional, 135
Isomorphism, 16, 60–64, 70

L

Least Developed Country (LDC), 168, 170, 171, 251
Lesotho, 84–86, 89, 108, 110, 115, 116, 143, 155, 161–163, 165, 173, 174, 177, 179, 192, 202, 203, 206, 214–216, 219, 221, 250, 271, 273, 277, 285, 300, 310
Logic of Regional Integration, 8, 15, 16, 26, 40, 88

M

Madagascar, 89, 117, 140, 164, 170, 173, 174, 179, 210–212, 214, 216, 217, 219, 221, 235, 253, 310, 316
Mandela, Nelson, 189, 193, 204, 207
Manoeuvres, 211–213, 316
Market Integration, 10, 13, 30, 89, 92, 94, 105, 106, 108, 110–113, 117, 119–123, 125, 133, 140, 141, 153, 154, 156, 158, 159, 166, 167, 171, 174, 176, 180, 309, 313, 314
Matrix, 39
Mauritius, 89, 90, 110, 112, 113, 117, 125–129, 133, 134, 140, 164, 165, 170, 173, 174, 207, 212, 299

Member State, 87, 97, 109, 114, 118, 180, 203, 216, 217
Methodology, 18
Military
　capacity, 231, 237, 239, 247
　expenditure, 197, 199, 200, 234, 237
　interdependence, 51, 197, 201, 234, 235, 238
　strength, 199
Mozambique, 85, 86, 89, 91, 108, 110, 115, 116, 125, 128, 129, 134, 136, 138, 143, 155, 161, 165, 169, 170, 173, 174, 190–193, 203, 207, 215, 217, 222, 250, 271, 273, 274, 277, 285, 294
Mugabe, Robert, 96, 205–207, 212, 219, 248, 252
Multilateral Monetary Agreement (MMA), 85, 98

N

Namibia, 69, 84, 85, 88, 89, 91, 108, 110, 113, 115, 138, 143, 155, 161, 163–165, 169, 173, 174, 177, 180, 190, 192, 193, 207, 213, 219, 271, 273, 274, 277, 285, 294
Negotiations, 45, 52, 58, 70, 71, 84, 106–108, 119, 121, 123–127, 140, 143, 154, 158–160, 164, 166, 169, 172, 180, 181, 203, 204, 244, 282, 299
New Regionalism, 1, 2, 4, 11–14, 16, 25, 28, 60, 64, 83, 88, 94, 98, 307, 320
Non-Tariff Barriers to Trade (NTB), 108, 130, 138–140, 156
North-South relations, 314

O

Official Development Assistance (ODA), 91
Organ, 3, 16, 66, 93–95, 187, 202–211, 214–219, 221, 222, 232, 234, 248, 258–260, 283, 284, 310, 312, 316
Organ for Politics, Defence and Security (OPDS), 95, 187, 188, 202–210, 213–216, 218, 219, 229, 231, 235, 246, 249, 310, 315, 316, 319
Overlapping Regionalism, 321

P

Peacekeeping, 93, 95, 211, 229, 231–233, 239–244, 246–249, 251–253, 255, 257, 311
Performance, 1, 2, 5–7, 13–16, 37, 47, 48, 50, 56, 57, 68, 70, 84, 123, 130, 144, 145, 177, 188, 203, 210, 214, 218, 219, 230, 232, 252, 253, 256, 268, 283, 290, 297, 298, 301, 307–311, 313, 316–319
Periphery, 117
Power
grid, 19, 268, 272, 275, 277, 288–290, 293–297, 312, 318
line, 270, 271, 277, 279, 292–294
positon, 43–46, 50, 54, 55, 58, 59, 70, 120, 140, 160, 161, 163, 167, 172, 194, 197, 199, 201, 202, 238, 241, 278, 296, 313, 314, 316–318
relation, 51
shortage, 268, 270, 295, 312
supply, 268, 292
utility, 277, 285
Problematic Situation, 41–43, 48–50, 52, 54, 58, 59, 63, 68, 70, 71, 106, 114, 120, 159, 160, 171, 172, 176, 196, 230, 233, 234, 242, 255, 275, 276, 281, 313, 315, 317, 318
Process Tracing, 68, 307
Protocol
Protocol on Energy, 288
Protocol on Politics, Defence and Security Cooperation, 66, 93
Protocol on Trade, 3, 18, 66, 105–108, 110, 120, 121, 123, 127–131, 134, 137, 140, 143, 144, 154, 156, 157, 313, 314

R

Rational Choice, 68
Region, 4, 12, 15, 20, 25, 26, 29, 34, 35, 53, 55, 56, 58, 59, 69, 71, 83, 84, 86, 88–91, 93–95, 98, 106, 107, 109–113, 115–117, 119, 122, 130, 135–142, 144, 153, 156–161, 163–166, 175, 178, 187–194, 196–201, 203–205, 207, 208, 210–212, 214, 216, 218, 219, 221, 230, 231, 233, 235, 237, 238, 242, 244, 253, 255, 258, 267, 268, 270, 272, 273, 275–278, 282–284, 286, 287, 292–298, 301, 309, 310, 312, 316–318
Regional
conflict, 189, 191, 206, 214, 218, 221, 257
cooperation, 3–5, 8, 9, 12, 13, 15, 17, 18, 25, 26, 28–31, 36, 39–42, 44, 46, 47, 49, 50, 52–60, 63, 64, 66, 70, 83, 84, 86–88, 93, 99, 115, 119, 167, 172, 201, 213, 218, 230, 232, 234, 242, 243, 245, 247, 254, 267, 271, 272, 275, 276, 281, 283, 296, 297, 308, 310, 312–319

defection, 52, 233, 275
electricity market, 19, 268, 271, 274, 275, 285–290, 292, 294, 296, 297, 318
hegemon, 16, 98, 202, 245, 255, 312, 314
institution, 3–5, 26, 29, 39, 43, 44, 46–48, 53, 54, 56–59, 68, 72, 83, 88, 98, 115, 139, 234, 270, 283, 313
integration; economic, 18, 106, 108, 109, 114, 119, 128, 131, 132, 135, 138, 141, 142, 153, 154, 156, 166, 309; electricity, 274, 297; infrastructure, 3, 16, 17, 66, 92, 267; market, 18, 30, 105, 106, 110, 112, 113, 117, 119–121, 123, 125, 133, 140, 153, 154, 158, 159, 166, 167, 171, 174, 176, 180, 309, 313, 314; military, 19; security, 229
member state, 3, 6–8, 16, 18, 29, 53, 56, 66, 83–86, 89, 105, 120–123, 158, 233, 272, 278, 288
norms, 17, 37, 64, 296, 308, 318
organisation, 5, 6, 13, 50, 61, 86, 92, 107, 112, 117, 141, 164, 168, 204, 210, 214, 217, 240, 241, 251, 255, 267, 319
power, 7, 19, 43, 46, 49, 50, 54, 120, 161, 199, 201, 218, 231, 237, 238, 241, 268, 272, 278, 282, 288–290, 293–296, 298, 312, 313, 316–319
security, 19, 30, 53, 85, 89, 187–189, 191–196, 201–207, 209–211, 213–215, 217–219, 229–233, 235, 238–240, 243, 254, 255, 310, 315, 316

situation structure, 39–42, 44, 49, 52, 59, 113, 159, 167, 176, 195, 233, 241, 243, 275, 313
threat, 53, 85, 219, 230, 310
trade, 11, 27, 91, 92, 106–108, 110–115, 120–123, 126, 127, 129, 131–133, 135, 137, 140–142, 156, 157, 171, 290, 309, 313
Regional Indicative Strategic Development Plan (RISDP), 92, 93, 96, 99, 100, 144, 145, 153, 158, 159, 175–177, 288, 301, 309
Regionalism
 comparative, 2, 14, 320
 definition, 10, 18
 dysfunctional, 7, 60, 62, 63, 196, 309, 310
 new, 1, 2, 4, 11–14, 16, 18, 28, 59, 60, 63, 64, 83, 88, 94, 98, 307, 320
 old, 7, 11, 13, 27, 83, 84, 88, 98
 open, 27, 89, 93, 111, 113, 140
 symbolic, 63
Regional Peacekeeping Training Centre (RPTC), 3, 95, 229, 248, 249, 252–256, 259, 260, 311, 312, 316–318
Republic of South Africa (RSA), 84, 90, 114–117, 124, 142, 157, 161, 191, 194, 197, 201, 204, 220, 232, 256, 259, 272, 299, 300
Research
 design, 18, 64, 67
 method, 40, 64, 68
Rivalry, 51, 207, 211
Rules of Origin (RoO), 121–123, 125, 126, 128, 140, 157–159

S

Security
  cooperation, 16, 19, 66, 71, 85, 86, 93, 94, 96, 100, 187–189, 191–195, 201–204, 206, 207, 209, 210, 213, 232, 235, 238, 240–242, 255, 258–260, 310, 315
  institutions, 38, 53, 202, 209, 211, 239
  interdependence, 189, 200, 230, 238
  management, 38, 188, 193
Seychelles, 89, 117, 129, 140, 164, 165, 170, 173, 174, 210–212, 245, 249, 299
Short-Term Energy Market (STEM), 267, 268, 286, 287, 290–292, 296, 297, 311, 318, 319
Situation-Structural Approach, 52
Situation Structure, 39–41, 49, 52, 59, 167, 176, 243, 313
South Africa, 16, 17, 69, 84–86, 88–91, 98, 109–118, 120, 123–129, 133–135, 137, 138, 140, 142, 143, 156, 157, 160, 161, 163–167, 169, 170, 173, 174, 177, 180, 187–191, 193, 194, 198, 199, 201–204, 206–209, 211–213, 215, 218, 219, 231, 232, 235, 237, 238, 240–242, 244, 245, 247, 250, 253, 255–257, 259, 260, 267, 270–274, 276–278, 284, 285, 291, 292, 294–296, 298, 310, 312–319
South African National Defence Force (SANDF), 214, 237
Southern African Customs Union (SADC-CU), 84, 153, 154, 156–160, 163, 164, 166, 167, 169, 171–177, 309, 315

Southern African Development Community (SADC)
  agenda, 18, 67, 83, 89, 92, 94, 153, 166, 167, 176, 204, 229, 271, 309
  brigade, 19, 229–231, 233, 235, 241, 243–246, 248–250, 253, 255, 256, 258, 259, 311, 316
  budget, 166, 200, 237, 238
  Customs Union (SADC-CU), 3, 17, 19, 66, 84, 93, 153, 154, 156–160, 163, 164, 166, 167, 169, 171, 173–178, 309, 314, 315
  Free Trade Area (SADC-FTA), 3, 10, 16, 18, 66, 105, 106, 113–115, 119–122, 128–131, 134–136, 140–142, 144, 153, 154, 156–159, 163, 166, 173, 175, 244, 309, 312–314, 319
  Key Policy Area, 92
  member state, 3, 16, 18, 29, 83, 89, 91–94, 97, 105, 107–109, 114, 118, 120, 121, 125, 127–129, 134, 140, 141, 153, 154, 156, 158, 159, 161, 164, 167, 175, 180, 194, 202, 203, 205, 206, 208–214, 216, 218, 229, 231, 234, 235, 237, 238, 240, 242, 247, 250, 252, 254, 256, 259, 273, 276–278, 289, 309–311, 314, 315, 318
  Organ, 3, 19, 95, 187, 202, 203, 205–211, 217, 218, 221, 248, 259, 260, 316
  protocol, 3, 66, 93, 95, 99, 120, 123, 132, 188, 203, 205, 208, 210, 211, 232, 243, 288
  Standby Force (SSF), 3, 16, 19, 66, 95, 229, 233, 243, 244, 247, 316

Southern African Development Coordination Conference (SADCC), 86–88, 92, 94, 98, 99, 187, 189, 195, 199, 201, 206, 220, 269, 270, 278
Southern African Power Pool (SAPP)
  Day Ahead Market (DAM), 267, 287, 288, 290, 292, 293, 297, 298, 319
  electricity generation capacity, 295, 296, 312
  electricity interdependence, 276
  electricity market, 17, 283, 285–287, 289, 290, 292, 294, 296, 297, 319
  electricity trade, 267, 282, 285, 288, 290, 291, 293, 318, 319
  institutional framework, 282
  interconnected utilities, 282, 283, 289, 295
  Intergovernmental Memorandum of Understanding (IMoU), 282–284, 288–290
  Inter-Utility Memorandum of Understanding (SAPP-IMoU), 281–283, 288
  Short-Term Energy Market (STEM), 267, 286, 287, 296, 311, 318
Standby Force (SSF), 3, 16, 66, 95, 229, 233, 234, 238, 242, 244, 245, 248–256, 259, 310, 311, 316–319
Strategic Indicative Plan for the Organ (SIPO), 92, 93, 99, 100, 229, 232, 233, 243, 256
Swaziland, 84–86, 89, 108, 110, 115, 116, 127, 143, 155, 161, 163, 165, 173, 174, 180, 190, 192, 207, 216, 237, 271, 277, 285, 294
Symbolism, 5, 16, 60, 63, 64, 67, 70

T
Tanzania, 85–87, 89, 100, 110, 116, 117, 127, 129, 133, 136, 143, 156, 161, 164, 165, 170, 173, 174, 190, 197, 207, 213, 235, 238, 250, 253, 271, 289, 294, 295, 299
Tariff, 106, 111, 112, 114, 115, 120, 122, 124, 127–129, 156, 157, 159, 179
Trade
  agreement, 122, 168, 274, 291
  data, 107, 109, 118, 133, 134, 162, 165
  extra-regional, 91, 118, 161, 163, 171, 173, 175, 176, 309
  flow, 51, 106–108, 117, 120, 130, 131, 133, 154, 157, 161, 164–166, 309
  intensity, 107, 108, 132, 135, 158, 309
  intra-regional, 27, 106–108, 113–115, 121, 122, 129, 131–133, 135, 154–157, 161, 286, 297, 309
  negotiation, 84, 119, 121, 126, 140, 164
  pattern, 161, 162, 164
  potential, 107, 109, 113, 278, 293
  restriction, 108
  share, 107, 109, 117, 131–134, 154, 155, 164, 169
Trade, Development and Cooperation Agreement (TDCA), 164, 169, 173, 174
Troika, 95, 205, 209, 215, 216

U
Unilateral Action, 210, 215, 219
United Nations (UN), 109, 178, 216, 217, 246, 253, 260
United States of America (USA), 53, 238, 278, 320

V
Variable
  dependent, 42, 65
  independent, 41, 68, 313
  intervening, 42–44, 52, 58, 242

W
World Trade Organisation (WTO), 109, 118, 129, 133, 134, 155, 168

Z
Zaire, 271, 272, 277, 284
Zambia, 85–87, 89, 91, 108, 110, 111, 113, 115, 116, 125, 127–129, 134, 136, 138, 140, 143, 155, 161, 165, 170, 173, 190, 192, 193, 197, 207, 213, 235, 270–274, 277, 294
Zimbabwe, 86, 87, 89–91, 96, 108, 110–113, 115, 117, 125–131, 133, 134, 138–140, 155, 161, 165, 170, 173, 174, 190, 193, 197–207, 209, 210, 212, 215, 218, 221, 235, 237, 238, 244, 247, 248, 250, 252–254, 270–272, 274, 277, 292, 294, 300, 310, 315, 316

Printed by Printforce, the Netherlands